ALAN WEISS
ON CONSULTING

A guided journey with

"The Rock Star of Consulting"

Other Works by Alan Weiss

Alan Weiss on Consulting (interviewed by Chad Barr, Linda Henman, Aviv Shahar)
Best Laid Plans (originally Making It Work)
Getting Started in Consulting (also in Chinese)
Good Enough Isn't Enough (also in Spanish)
Great Consulting Challenges
How to Acquire Clients
How to Establish A Unique Brand in the Consulting Profession
How to Market, Brand, and Sell Professional Services
How to Sell New Business and Expand Existing Business
How to Write A Proposal That's Accepted Every Time
Life Balance
Managing for Peak Performance (also in German)
Million Dollar Business
Million Dollar Coaching (also in Portuguese)
Million Dollar Consulting (also in Portuguese, Russian, Polish, Chinese, Korean, Arabic)
Million Dollar Consulting Proposals
Million Dollar Consulting® Toolkit
Million Dollar Referrals
Million Dollar Speaking (also in Chinese, Portuguese)
Million Dollar Web Presence (with Chad Barr)
Money Talks (also in Chinese)
Organizational Consulting
Our Emperors Have No Clothes
Process Consulting
The Consulting Bible
The Global Consultant (with Omar Kahn)
The Great Big Book of Process Visuals
The Innovation Formula (with Mike Robert) (also in German, Italian)
The Son of the Great Big Book of Process Visuals
The Talent Advantage (with Nancy MacKay)
The Ultimate Consultant
The Unofficial Guide to Power Management
The Power of Strategic Commitment (with Josh Leibner and Gershon Mader)
Thrive!
Value Based Fees
Who's Got Your Back? (with Omar Kahn)

ALAN WEISS
ON CONSULTING

A guided journey with

"The Rock Star of Consulting"

SUMMIT CONSULTING GROUP, INC.
East Greenwich, Rhode Island
2013

ISBN: 978-1-938394-05-8
Library of Congress Control Number: 2013944065
First Edition

This publication contains the opinions and ideas of its author and is designed to provide useful advice and formats to the reader on the subject matter covered. Any references to products or services in that pursuit do not constitute or imply an endorsement or recommendation. The publisher and author specifically disclaim any responsibility for any liability, loss, or risk (financial, personal, or otherwise) which may be claimed or incurred as a consequence, directly or indirectly, of the use and/ or application of any of the contents of this publication.
The publisher does not attest to the validity, accuracy, or completeness of this information. Use of a term in this book should not be regarded as affecting validity of any trademark or service mark.

Additional copies of this book are available from:

Summit Consulting Group, Inc.
Box 1009
East Greenwich, RI 02818-0964
www.summitconsulting.com

For general information about Alan Weiss's products, speaking, and consulting services please call (800) 766-7935 or (401) 884-2778. Our fax number is (401) 884-5068, and our email is info@summitconsulting.com. There are hundreds of free, indexed articles to download at www.summitconsulting.com. You may also subscribe at that site to our free, electronic newsletter: Balancing Act: Blending Life, Work, and Relationship® and Alan Weiss's Monday Morning Memo.SM Visit our blog with text, audio, and video postings daily at: www.contrarianconsulting.com

Published by Great Life Press LLC
Rye, New Hampshire 03870
www.greatlifepress.com

To Koufax, the White German Shepherd

Contents

Preface

Alan Weiss began his consulting career in 1972 working with Fortune 500 clients such as IBM, Chase, Merck, Hewlett-Packard, Ford, and scores of others. He has published over 50 books (more on consulting than any other author) in 11 languages and garnered awards and accolades around the globe.

Three highly successful consultants have interviewed Alan over the course of a year to distill his worldview, advice, and insights into the profession and our lives as professionals. This work, with over 40 hours of audio, was distilled down from source material double its current size.

We hope you'll feel as if you're chatting with Alan personally over one of his signature Jean Marc XO martinis (very dry, very cold, with a twist).

Introduction

We are thrilled to embark on this special opportunity—to engage with you in the creation of *Alan Weiss on Consulting*—a new book and audio book of unrehearsed, live conversations. Joining me will be Chad Barr, the technology guru for Solopreneurs, Linda Henman, the CEO Coach and a leadership performance expert, and international consultant, Aviv Shahar. I can't think of three better people to do this, given the diversity and the commonality of their backgrounds, their philosophies, and involvement in my community. The question on everyone's mind is, "Where did the idea come from and what will *Alan on Consulting* be about?"

Alan on Consulting came about when I realized that I had written more books on consulting than any other author and asked myself, "What is it that I need to do, if anything, beyond here?" I decided that it might be unique and rather fascinating to be interviewed by people who know the profession well and to be spontaneous. None of it is rehearsed; none of the questions was given to me beforehand. This wouldn't be a book that I read into a microphone; it would be a book that will be recorded as we talked. The transcription, with some careful editing, would provide a very different kind of textbook—a comprehensive overview of my approaches to consulting. Then I found three people who were either bold enough—or crazy enough—to join me, and here we are.

Q. What will a beginner consultant find here? How will an experienced consultant benefit by this book?

Alan: Well, what better place to be contrarian than in an introduction? I decided that I'm going to discard terms like "newcomer" and "veteran" and "master." They don't serve a purpose, because the fact is that we are all on a journey. I'd like this book to create a *commonality* of experience to make people feel that they are all members of the same profession. We're at different degrees; we're in different places. Some people do some things in consulting far better than I do. When you talk about "master consultant," it certainly doesn't mean a master of all things. What I'd like people to look at is how to improve themselves no matter where they are in the journey.

Q. How do you compare the consulting opportunities of today to the 70s, the 80s, the 90s, and even to the early 2000s?

Alan: Sometimes I think that we're all a part of *A Tale of Two Cities*, stuck on that famous first page: "It was the best of times; it was the worst of times." Dickens had a nice opening, but it's become a bit trite, because *all* times are the best of times and the worst of times. Consulting today compared to the 70s, and the 80s in particular, is considerably different. Back then it was expert-based. It was almost like hiring an expert witness for a trial: You were looking for people who knew a better way to manufacture steel, or create an insurance product, or to hire people for the chemical industry.

From the 80s to the 90s, things became more sophisticated. The internet age was just opening up, leading to a much greater emphasis on processes, on speed, and on pragmatism. In the early part of the 21st Century, things changed again. The "big eight" consultants were finding a stronger and stronger niche, because residual talent in companies had disappeared.

The downsizings, the "lean and mean movement," which really took place over two or three decades, has reduced the residual expertise in companies to the point where hiring a consultant is a very economical alternative to improve performance and productivity.

Q. Is there a practice or a mindset that you want to recommend to help make the most from the engagement for us and the reader and the listener?

Alan: Move three things forward a mile, not a hundred things forward an inch. The idea here is to make your value accessible to people of different needs, capacities, and abilities, and to invest and to profit from it. And I don't mean profit in the monetary sense; I mean to gain from it personally. I would implore readers not to dog-ear every page, put a post-it note on every paragraph, or underline every sentence. I would urge them to read something that knocks their socks off, and that's what they want to move forward first.

Now, let's engage in shaking things up.

Alan Weiss
East Greenwich, RI
June 2013

Acknowledgments

I want to thank Chad Barr, Linda Henman, and Aviv Shahar for their collegiality and friendship through these long hours and discussions. Great questions create interesting responses. Thanks also to my chief editor, Linda Popky, and editors Patty Lauterjung and Shannon Vargo.

About Alan Weiss

Alan Weiss is one of those rare people who can say he is a consultant, speaker, and author and mean it. His consulting firm, Summit Consulting Group, Inc. has attracted clients such as Merck, Hewlett-Packard, GE, Mercedes-Benz, State Street Corporation, Times Mirror Group, The Federal Reserve, The New York Times Corporation, and over 500 other leading organizations. He has served on the boards of directors of the Trinity Repertory Company, a Tony-Award-winning New England regional theater, Festival Ballet, and chaired the Newport International Film Festival.

His speaking typically includes 30 keynotes a year at major conferences, and he has been a visiting faculty member or lecturer at MIT, Harvard, Case Western Reserve University, Boston College, Tufts, St. John's, the University of Illinois, the Institute of Management Studies, and the University of Georgia Graduate School of Business. He has held an appointment as adjunct professor in the Graduate School of Business at the University of Rhode Island where he taught courses on advanced management and consulting skills. He once held the record for selling out the highest priced workshop (on entrepreneurialism) in the then-21-year history of New York City's Learning Annex. His Ph.D. is in psychology. He has served on the Board of Governors of Harvard University's Center for Mental Health and the Media.

He is an inductee into the Professional Speaking Hall of Fame® and the concurrent recipient of the National Speakers Association Council of Peers Award of Excellence, representing the top 1% of professional speakers in the world. He has been named a Fellow of the Institute of Management Consultants, one of only two people in history holding both those designations.

His prolific publishing includes over 500 articles and 50 books, including his best-seller, *Million Dollar Consulting* (from McGraw-Hill). His books have been on the curricula at Villanova, Temple University, NYU, Florida University, and the Wharton School of Business, and have been translated into German, Italian, Arabic, Spanish, Russian, Korean, Portuguese, Polish, Japanese, and Chinese.

He is interviewed and quoted frequently in the media. His career has taken him to 60 countries and 49 states. (He is afraid to go to North Dakota.) *Success Magazine* cited him in an editorial devoted to his work as "a worldwide expert in executive education." The *New York Post* called him "one of the most highly regarded independent consultants in America." He is the winner of the prestigious Axiem Award for Excellence in Audio Presentation.

He is the recipient of the Lifetime Achievement Award of the American Press Institute, the first-ever for a non-journalist, and one of only seven awarded in the 65-year history of the association.

He has coached the former Miss Rhode Island USA and Miss America candidates in interviewing skills. He once appeared on the popular American TV game show *Jeopardy*, where he lost badly in the first round to a dancing waiter from Iowa.

About the Interviewers

Dr. Linda Henman, the author of *Landing in the Executive Chair*, works with executives and boards in Fortune 500 Companies and small businesses that want to think strategically, grow dramatically, promote intelligently, and compete successfully today and tomorrow. She was one of eight succession planning experts who worked directly with John Tyson after his company's acquisition of International Beef Products. Some of her other clients include Emerson Electric, Avon, Kraft Foods, Edward Jones, and Boeing. She can be reached in St. Louis at www.henmanperformancegroup.com.

Aviv Shahar is the president of Aviv Consulting, a strategic innovation consultancy. Fortune 500 companies hire him to help their senior teams create purpose-inspired visions and innovative strategies that drive growth. Aviv believes that preparing for the future presents you with a stark choice. You can either try catching up with change that's happening around you, or you can create and lead the change. His fighter pilot experience made him realize that opportunities have expiration dates, and the cost of missed opportunity may be enormous. Aviv's work is inspired by the idea that miracles can be real. They occur when everyone in the organization shares a picture of the future they believe in, and converse from that future picture.

Chad Barr was born and raised in Israel. Chad came to the United States at age 22 determined to capture the American dream, which became a reality in 1991 when he started his own firm. His company, The Chad Barr Group, is recognized as one of the leading Internet development organization in the world and has attracted organizations that span the globe and include clients in Italy, Germany, UK, Australia, New Zealand, Canada and the United States. Chad is an Internet and business strategist, and a mentor, who successfully guides and helps his clients leverage the web to transform their businesses and create some of the finest professional communities around the globe. He has published over 100 articles, is the co-author of the book, *Million Dollar Web Presence*, with Alan Weiss.

What Does It Mean to Be a Consultant?

Genesis: The Start of a Journey

Consulting isn't something that we do for the client. It's something that the client and consultant accomplish together, one party unable to achieve the level of performance without the partnership of the other. That applies to strategy formulation, leadership development, succession planning, and virtually any other consulting specialty. The purpose of this chapter is to define clearly what consulting is, and what it isn't; to discuss the qualities and skills successful consultants need to have; and to outline some of the things you can expect to encounter as you travel the always bumpy road to consulting success.

What Is Consulting?

Q: How are consulting, coaching, counseling, and mentoring different?

Alan: A consultant is someone who uses his or her talent, expertise, behavior, and experience to improve the client's condition, primarily through providing counsel.

Coaching has traditionally been a function performed by consultants. I have done a massive amount of organization development throughout my consulting career, starting in 1972, working with thousands of major companies all over the globe. Right from the outset, I've coached the people I've consulted with because coaching helps them understand the need for change, lead the change, implement the change, anticipate obstacles, and overcome objections. Only in the last decade or so has coaching been parsed out in an attempt to make it a separate pursuit, but it's not a separate chapter; it's more of a subchapter.

Typically, a coach is someone who deals with an individual one-on-one, hired either by an individual or an organization. The coach might work with a team of people. The best coaches have an awareness of organizational change dynamics, communication practices, compensation practices, feedback, and a host of other things. Any good consultant can be a good coach.

When you coach, you are proactive, whereas a mentor, on the other hand, is someone who is reactive. As a coach, you set behavioral goals with either the client or the buyer. You set a thirty-day, sixty-day, or some other time limit because there is a reasonable expectation of change within a certain timeframe. A mentor is someone who is approached and approachable. Mentors are reactive to you.

I've been a mentor for years, and I started the Private Roster Master Mentor program. Individual entrepreneurs come to me for help. They put me on retainer for a given amount of time, which can be renewed, but *they* approach *me* for help.

Another category you didn't even mention is a subcontractor who often calls himself or herself a consultant but is really just a pair of hands. The first differentiator is that a consultant is a source of information, not a pair of hands. If you are being called into a company or project to take directions, write code, put bricks in a wall, or interview clients, you're doing all those jobs because labor is needed, not expertise.

Q: Are these definitions important for the consultant and the client to be aware of?

Alan: It is very important, for example, to know the difference between coaching and mentoring because if you aren't aware of what your responsibility is as a coach, you may sit back and say, "Well, I'm going to wait for them to come to me," which is not your charter. As a coach, your charter is to go after them and help them to change. You can't take "no" for an answer or "I haven't gotten to it" as an answer. On the other hand, if you are acting as a mentor but constantly pursuing your protégé, you're making a big mistake. That's not your role. Your role is to be there when they need you.

I tell consultants who also speak, "Call yourself a consultant who happens to be a speaker. Don't call yourself a speaker who is also consulting." Otherwise, people will feel that you're just stringing speeches or workshops together, but that's not what consulting is all about. Throughout my career, when people have asked me what I do, I have always told them I'm a consultant.

Q: Are there other misconceptions about what consultants are not?

Alan: The fact is that the motivation and the expectations of legitimate buyers—people who can write a check for your value—vary based on their motives as well as on misinformation. Some buyers think a consultant is someone who performs, at their direction, to validate a position they want to take.

Anyone who has been in this profession for more than a few months has met the buyer who says, "I want to do this, this, and that, and I want you to come in and justify it." Believing that's the role of a consultant is a pretty bad misconception. The consultant needs to first of all assess the viability of the plan, and tell the buyer whether it's a realistic course of action. Often, a request for proposal (RFP) is an arbitrary alternative that has been drawn up usually by low-level people who expect the consultant to implement it, and by definition, to support it.

Expectations of what a consultant is vary. The good news is that there is no barrier to entry into this profession, and the bad news is that there is no barrier to entry into this profession.

Q: Why is consulting more important now than in the past?

Alan: There are a few reasons. One reason is that companies no longer have the expertise in-house. Back in the 60s and 70s, it wasn't uncommon for companies to have internal departments of highly qualified consultants overseeing the organizational development of the company. But in times of recession, these departments were among the first to get cut.

Consultants are needed today because there is no longer staff within organizations responsible for implementing the strategies to help businesses grow. Too many companies become successful, and then simply breathe their own exhaust.

The best of the best realize they need objective, third-party opinions to tell them, "Yes, you did well last year; you outsmarted your competition, but you could have done much better," or "You're making great speed right now, but instead of New York, you're going to end up in Montevideo." They need people who can speak fearlessly—whose retirement plan and personal goals are not vested in that company.

Some companies are simply looking for a consultant to come in to validate plans or goals because every company—with the best of intentions, the best practices, and the best systems—decided to go a certain course. And they still need this validation.

Perhaps the overarching reason consulting is needed today more than ever is the need for best practices in an ever-changing, rapidly moving business environment. The world has become so complex, so fast, and so volatile, and that volatility is the new normal. That's not going to change. Best practices transcend industry, geography, and hierarchy. Only someone who has encountered them in varied settings—such as an independent consultant—can bring the best knowledge to any given client. No matter how open a company may be, they are still enclosed within their four walls, whether these walls are bricks and mortar, or metaphorical; they still have a difficult time looking outside their organization for ideas.

Q: When you mentor people who are convinced that they are using best practices, how do you get them to consider other possibilities, versus being in love with their own methodology?

Alan: Best practices have to be reaffirmed in the workplace. You might have a seven-step selling process that you think is the best thing since cold beer, but you must ask where it's worked, to what extent it's worked, and what the results were. Most things people are in love with are either highly theoretical or have worked only once or twice. People rarely acknowledge if something hasn't worked six or seven times if they got lucky once or twice. If it's truly a best practice, it will be borne out in the environment.

Q: You talk about consulting being about process. What do you mean by that?

Alan: There is a vast difference between process and content. *Content* is what you're involved with—automobile engines, flooring, or making bank deposit slips. The *process* is how you do it. Processes are things like conflict resolution, priority setting, decision making, problem solving, and strategy formulation. They can be superimposed over the operations of virtually any organization. I can't superimpose the creation of specialized rubber on an organization that's trying to produce a new financial investment vehicle. It won't work. But I can superimpose on both those organizations a decision-making process which takes into account objectives to be met, alternatives to be considered, or risks to be avoided.

Q: What does the future hold for consultants and consulting?

Alan: I suspect that, ironically, rather than seeing a trend toward the licensing and certification which has been attempted in coaching—with universities, diplomas, and all that nonsense—you'll see an increasingly ambiguous field that will need the kind of definition and best practices that will be found in this book.

Another development we're going to see is increased remote consulting. As technology gets more sophisticated and we have virtual office meetings and holographic images, we'll see much more virtual consulting which will address decreasing labor intensity, while enabling people to be much more global in their pursuit of consultants and in consultants' ability to respond to that.

The final thing we're going to see is an increasing need for consultants to differentiate themselves. This means clearly defining and communicating their business focus, their thought leadership, and their brands. They're going to have to show leadership in a specific niche, a wide area, and in a process. That leadership is going to be important because there will be a lot of ways to differentiate in the marketplace.

What Qualifies a Person to Be a Consultant?

Q: What would you say makes a good consultant?

Alan: In no particular order, good consultants are able to frame issues quickly so that they can identify what is in front of them. They can oversee various tasks. They can move the conversation forward without getting lost in a morass of words, discussion, and circuitous reasoning. Finally, they're able to really find the heart of the matter quickly. I call that *framing*.

Next is a masterful use of language. Language controls discussion, discussion controls relationships, and relationships control business. Consequently, you need to have tremendous command of the language in which you deal. You're not going to do very well with a project if, when you get in, you can't articulate clearly and communicate effectively.

You need a sense of humor. Humor gives you perspective. It helps you to accept rejection, be resilient, and understand that what you do, positive or negative, is probably not going to affect the course of humanity. With that kind of perspective, you can have the relief that you're working on a tiny scale in the universe, and that gives you a comfort.

Also necessary to being effective is being assertive. You have to be confident in your abilities and willing to sing your own praises. As Dizzy Dean said, "If you can do it, it ain't bragging." You also have to agree on what to do next, set a definitive date and time, and follow up diligently.

Q: What are the traits of successful consultants?

Alan: First, you must have a desire to help people. It's not enough to have the intellect. You have to have a heart to help, not just a brain that understands what is going on. Empathy, as opposed to sympathy; that is, not feeling what I feel but *understanding* what I feel, which is a key difference.

You must have the passion and desire to help people along with a commitment to the lifelong development of skills needed to help people. You must have the adaptability to help people at varying economic, social, and technological levels.

Finally, you need to have the confidence, personal esteem, and sense of self worth to be able to charge accordingly—to enter into an equitable agreement where the client benefits tremendously, but so do you. That's what partnerships are.

Q: How does a person become a consultant?

Alan: First, you need a certain experiential base. You don't wake up one morning at 20 years of age and decide to be a consultant. To acquire experience, you can become an apprentice to a consultant or work for a consulting firm. An experiential base teaches you what makes companies tick—how they operate and react internally. It helps you understand the relationship between sales and marketing; of R&D and time to market; and other relationships within an organization that impact performance.

Once you have this experiential base which takes years of learning, depending on how fast you learn and how involved your work with companies, you'll need to determine what your value proposition is. How exactly will you improve your clients' condition? I don't mean by what means; I mean to what degree? What improvements will you bring to your client? How is the client better off once you walk away?

A lot of consultants make the mistake of beginning with their methodologies, which are deliverables. They talk about the "how" rather than the "what." They should say, "Here's what you'll be able to do better once I'm gone." The value proposition would be the point on the arrow that gives someone entering this field some aerodynamics so they don't have a flying barn.

Q: Is there a particular education path to be successful as a consultant?

Alan: Consulting is a *relationship* business as opposed to a *commodity* business. Consulting requires intellectual firepower. You should be able to communicate effectively to influential people about a variety of interests, whether business or personal. Language controls discussion, discussion controls relationships, relationships control businesses.

Consultants should have a four-year college education to start. I don't care what your degree is in. Getting an MBA isn't the royal road. I tell most people not to bother. I have a Ph.D.; I have four degrees, 19 initials after my name. It hasn't helped me at all, except for my own edification.

One of the things that I've found is that, with rare exception, virtually nobody who becomes a consultant has ever been trained in marketing—and this is the marketing business. You're not going to be able to consult unless you acquire clients, so being able to market yourself is key.

Q: How do I deliver the ultimate outcome or results to the client?

Alan: In several ways. First, you reach a conceptual agreement with the client as to what the goals and outcomes of your work together are. Second, you ask yourself what you don't have to create that will deliver these results in the least amount of time, with the least amount of effort, and the least amount of cost. That's not, by any means, an unfair, illegal, immoral, or unethical thing to ask because the client is best served by a rapid resolution to the issue—which is why hourly billing is basically unethical. The client is best served with speed. The less labor you put in, the higher your margin, and that's also ideal for the client who needs fast results.

Once you have reached an agreement with the client, you organize yourself to deliver the results in the most efficient, efficacious manner possible. Then you discipline yourself to get that done—which means scheduling, which means hitting deadlines.

Q: What can we do to significantly increase our intellectual firepower?

Alan: You can't be afraid to fail. One aspect of intellectual firepower is self-esteem. Somebody asked me years ago, "How is it you're so unflappable?" I said, "It's because I'm not afraid to fail. If I fail, I fail. I don't care. It's not the end of the world; it's not the end of me; it's not the end of my family or my loved ones." If I keep failing, then I need to get in a different business. If you're not failing, you're not trying.

You have to read and write voraciously. You have to be able to read with comprehension, write with expression, speak with influence, and listen with discernment. If you can do those four things extraordinarily well, you'll be ahead of the competition. You'll be at the front of the pack every time, if not absolutely in the lead.

Q: What are some of the warning signs that we need to watch for to prevent the success trap?

Alan: Why does a knife get dull? A knife gets dull if you don't use it, if you use it on the wrong things, if you use it too much without maintaining it, or if it's not made of proper materials. Consultants can get dull in exactly the same way.

If you take on a subject matter, a client, a challenge for which you don't have the competency, you're going to get blunt. You alluded to the success trap. If you merely keep doing what you currently are proficient at doing, you'll be on a plateau. Consulting isn't a destination, it's a journey. Because society changes, economies change, and cultures, mores, and finances change, consultants continuously have to evolve.

It doesn't have to be revolutionary, but it is *evolutionary.* While you can say with some accuracy that there is nothing new under the sun, all of us in consulting are responsible for recombining its elements all the time to reflect the current world in which we live and to make it as appropriate, relevant, and effective as possible.

The Consulting Arena

Q: Why do people enter the field of consulting?

Alan: Many enter consulting because of the emotional and psychological components of the work consultants do. They want to have some freedom; they don't want someone else to call the shots or take command over their destiny. They may be frustrated by turbulent times and feel they need more latitude of action. They may be unhappy with their rate of progress and want to accelerate it.

When I wrote *Million Dollar Coaching*, I asked readers to think about people they've helped in their lives, whether they were working with them as a coach or not. How did they help them? What method did they use? What were the results? I wanted to point out that, in some way, everybody has been a coach at some point in their lives. Arbitrarily calling yourself one because you have a piece of paper or a vague certifier saying you're "approved" is ridiculous.

Q: How do people make their first break or the first success?

Alan: The most common route is to leave a company with good grace, good relationships, and all bridges intact. Then use that company as your first client.

Q: How does consulting with for-profit companies, government agencies, and non-profit entities compare?

Alan: First, some similarities. This is a relationship business. No matter who your client, you must first have a relationship with a *buyer*—not with the purchasing department, low-level people, human resources, training people, or the people sending out the requests for proposals—but with the decision-maker.

Second, everybody has money. Some people are good at giving you the impression that they don't, yet the lights are on; the parking lot is paved; there is a security person at the door; and people are getting their pay every week. Everybody has money.

Third, all of these people have goals they need to reach and could use some help getting there. A non-profit organization has to do exactly what a for-profit one does: they can't spend more than they bring in, and they have to have enough left over to reinvest in the organization so they can plan for years ahead. Consequently, all these organizations have budgets, growth expectations, and quality considerations to be met.

The dissimilarities include the following. In the small business market, the buyer is always going to be the owner, his son or daughter, or some-one connected with the founding of the company. Therefore, the emotional aspects of decision making are going to be more intense.

In the government marketplace, they often go through a request for proposal process, the RFP. But even there you can arrange to meet a buyer and become a sole source if you have a book, unique intellectual property, or unique experiences. Also, in 2009 the U.S. government passed a bill called the Federal Acquisition Regulation (FAR) Act, one of the provisions of which stated that individuals who evaluate RFP responses no longer have to award contracts solely based on lowest bid price. Instead, they can make their decisions based on highest value.

In working with charities, you should suggest that they find a sponsor to help subsidize the cost of your services. When I would speak at a health association meeting which couldn't afford my $25,000 speaking fee, Merck would underwrite it in return for having their logo on the program and a mention in the program saying, "Alan Weiss's appearance today is sponsored by Merck Pharmaceuticals." Which is win, win, win, win.

The same applies to educational institutions. They may seem highly unionized, highly regulated, and unwilling to spend money, but there are donors, people on the board—especially in private schools—and there are fundraisers.

If you try to make your money solely in small business or solely in education, you had better have a huge, huge brand. But if you are diversifying and can take those as they come along, they could be valuable additions to your revenue stream.

Q: What are the differences and the similarities in consulting with large and small start-up or family-owned businesses?

Alan: Buyers in very large companies are more numerous, and the job title doesn't always tell you who the real buyer is.

With small firms, you're dealing with an owner, there is more emotion in the decision-making process, less patience for the process, and usually family is involved. You may think you have conceptual agreement and are ready to go ahead, and suddenly the buyer may say, "I talked to my spouse and there is a problem." The spouse is almost always a buyer whether they work within the company or not, whether they have a title or not, and you need to talk to both of them. Small business is a very tough market segment to specialize in. They are most often the hardest hit during times of economic downturns.

Q: You recommend being a generalist, but in your mentoring community, you have people who focus on a niche and those who focus on functions—such as marketing and IT. How should we think of this range of opportunities?

Alan: If somebody asks, "What do you recommend is best?" I always say, "Be a generalist." But even as a generalist, I never took on financial projects, and I never took on technology or IT projects because I had no passion for them, and I had no competence in them.

You have to have market need, competence, and passion. Depending on where those three exist, depending upon their confluence, that's where your markets are. That's "markets" plural. It's best to develop expertise and try to serve more than one industry. The more you limit the industries you serve, the more difficult it will be to get business.

Q: What were some of the key factors in your success?

Alan: There are three. You must have absolute confidence in the service you provide and the self-esteem to execute it. You have to believe you can do almost anything within reason. You must be fearless—you can't be timid. My response to any inquiry about whether or not I would undertake something is, "Of course." "Alan, do you think you could…?" "Of course I can." "Would you consider doing…?" "Of course." I can always say no later, but if I say no to begin with, I can't reverse it. You need this high sense of self worth—you need to be fearless.

The last goes back to the concept of intellectual firepower. You have to recognize that you must constantly learn and develop new skills—new assets—as people ask you to do things and as you pursue additional markets. If you can't afford to invest time and energy in your own development, how can you grow your business?

Q: Let's explore one final distinction consultants make—having a local, regional, national, or global consulting practice. What are some of the differences in terms of opportunities and requirements?

Alan: I don't think anybody should set out to establish any of these. What you should do is measure your true value against the greatest market needs and determine who your buyers are. If you decide, for example, that you want to be an international consultant, but your value is that you help people only in English, that's going to limit your work to English-speaking countries.

Circumstances will help carve out, color, and shape what your practice looks like. Clearly identify your buyers, and then based on your circumstances and aspirations, make other decisions as they come along.

Q: Aren't all of us in business and consulting better off embracing the mind-set that we operate in a global marketplace?

Alan: A few things need to be recognized within your construct. First, you need to think strategically and globally, but you need to act locally. Second, "global" is not some wonderfully consistent and evenly paved road. It's a torturous, winding path of boulders, rocks, and hard-to-negotiate alleys because globally there are great inconsistencies and inequities.

There are some markets you just shouldn't pursue. When you consider consulting opportunities, it's as critical to decide both what you want to go after as well as the opportunities that are the right match for you.

Q: You said earlier that the essence of consulting is pursuing your passion using your intellectual firepower, and genuinely helping others. Isn't money, or the desire to increase it dramatically, a powerful motivator?

Alan: I don't think the desire to have more money is an effective motivator. The absence of money is actually a demotivator. The creation of discretionary time is a motivator. We all need a certain amount of money to sustain ourselves and to improve our lot.

Those who are obsessed about money are the very ones who get the most nervous when they're in front of a buyer, who compromise the most on the proposal, and who are afraid to say to a gatekeeper, "How do I get to see the person making the decision?" They are so scared by the prospect of not being able to get the new client that it actually compromises their ability to be successful.

People who say, "I'm going to do the best I can. If this works out, it will be a nice project, and I'll charge a fee commensurate with my value." These are the ones who do the best.

Consulting Challenges

Q: Assuming, even after reading all of this, someone still wants to be a consultant. Could you tell us about the challenges that you've faced in your own consulting and some of the most frequent challenges you see among those you mentor?

Alan: When I started, I faced an obstacle that still challenges people starting in the profession—to be heard, to rise above the noise. There were few really efficacious ways to do that because people didn't have websites, blogs, or even email in 1985. Today, of course, you can be known quite quickly, but the problem now is that there is so much noise, it's hard to stand out in a crowd.

When I started, there weren't enough ways to make noise; today there are too many. The way you overcome that challenge is by differentiating yourself. You don't have to be doing something that nobody else in the world is doing. Being good, being different, being provocative, being an object of interest—all those things help you stand out.

Another challenge is getting your message out there and doing it in ways that draw attention to you. Then there is the challenge of raising capital. Then, as now, you need enough money to see yourself through. If you're starting out in the business, you should have at least six months of expenses saved. That six months of savings should cover the cost of the things that will sustain you at your current standard of living—not extravagantly beyond it—just your current standard of living. You don't want to have to sell the house and the car to keep your business afloat in those first months.

In a year, you should expect to be sustaining yourself at your prior standard of living so that a year after you begin, if you're not sustaining yourself, never mind improving it. Then you must assess your effectiveness and/or relevance to the market.

Next is the great challenge of developing strong self-esteem, of believing you're good enough. Many consultants have strong needs for affiliation with a community, which is one reason I started my online community. You may want to consider working with a coach, mentor, or mastermind group—someone from whom you can get some perspective; another consultant who is doing better than you but who was where you were two years ago—to act as a sounding board and to offer counsel. Don't try to be a lone wolf in regard to your own development. You need to have people around you who can provide reference points so you can get a feel for what you're doing well so you can speed your way along the road. Being visible, raising economic capital, and developing self-esteem—all these challenges were there when I started, they're there today, and they'll be there in another ten years.

Q: You mention the challenge of rising above the noise. What are some ways to overcome this challenge to establish ourselves as experts or thought leaders?

Alan: First, you can't get lost in the mainstream. Consequently, no one calls their company Mediocre Consulting, Inc. You have to be willing to stand out from the mainstream; otherwise, you'll just be one of the crowd. Second, you have to be original. You must recombine and reinvent yourself based on the current needs of society, technology, mores, and conditions in businesses.

You also need to take advantage of the media that exists to promote your business. If you don't, there's no music. Even on a platform as huge as Twitter, every morning I post intellectual property, and I post thought leadership. I follow no one, I have about 6,000 followers right now, and that's just one way I increase my brand. I don't expect to get clients from Twitter; it's really not my market, but I do expect it to improve my brand. I have 5,000 or more postings on there, and I cross-reference people on Twitter to my blog, where I have more extensive intellectual property. You must have the discipline and dedicate the time to do that sort of thing on a regular basis.

Q: What do you still see as a recurring challenge that just doesn't seem to go away?

Alan: Beyond the struggle to develop self-esteem because that's a challenge that's constantly with us, from what I can see, a recurring challenge consultants face is what you might call *rebooting*. In computer terms, it's sort of like hitting restart. That's because of volatility, which has increased and will continue to increase because such is the nature of the modern, sophisticated, complex, co-dependent world. You must constantly reassess even the things you're good at and adjust them based on the changing needs brought about by changes in society, fluctuations in the economy, and advancements in technology.

That challenge will never go away, but I don't think that's bad. I think it's what refreshes the profession, is what keeps all of us vibrant and alive, and it gives vibrancy to our work.

Q: Earlier you mentioned markets being part of the challenge equation. What is your advice about the advantages and disadvantages of being a generalist versus working in a niche market?

Alan: The advantages of a generalist are the advantages of trolling with a huge net that goes out for ten miles versus trying to catch fish with a single rod and reel standing hip deep in the water. You have many more chances to capture buyers. When you capture fish that you're not looking for in a wide net, you let them go; you release them. You do the same for clients. Fortunately, in consulting you don't kill them. The wider your net as a generalist, the more chances you have of meeting buyers appropriate for your business; the tinier your hook, the less chance.

That doesn't mean you can't focus on a particular niche. Let's say you're in the niche of small business. You don't have to confine yourself only to small businesses that deal with selling products. You can work with small businesses that sell products and with businesses that provide services; you can define small business as up to $200 million or up to $20 million. You can expand and contract your niches as you see fit. No one is the perfect generalist; no one is all things to all people. There are things even lawyers won't do, or at least so I'm told.

Q: What are the risks of engaging with a highly political organization?

Alan: All organizations are political to some degree, so there is no risk. It's like asking what happens when you deal with an organization that has more than one person in it. I'm a political science major. Politics is that interaction that occurs when you have more than one person present, and you have an interesting confluence of individual and organizational objectives.

One of my professors once told the class that war is simply the least subtle form of communication. I never forgot that, and I guess at the extreme it's true. People sometimes find that their self-interests are similar to those of the organization. Sometimes they don't. It's the reconciliation and amelioration of those kinds of self-interests that make for politics, and politics are seldom fatal. Fortunately, we usually stop before the extreme in organizational work. I wouldn't worry about politics.

Q: You advise us to assume the client isn't damaged. What if we see evidence to the contrary? What do we do to face that challenge?

Alan: When you say the "client," of course you have to define whether the client is your buyer. If your buyer is damaged, then you have to have a conversation similar to the one I had with one owner of a small business.

> Owner: "What did you find?"
> Alan: "Well, I have good news and bad news."
> Owner: "What's the good news?"

Alan: "I found the cause of your problem."

Owner: "What's the bad news?"

Alan: "I don't have to leave your office to try and fix it."

You have to be confrontational, and you have to be candid and honest. Sometimes it's not the buyer who is damaged but some of the buyer's people—their subordinates, peers, or colleagues. You have to understand that, help the buyer understand it, and help fix the damage. The key here is to look for the evidentiary proof. There has to be evidence in the environment or observed behavior that tells you someone is damaged.

Q: What should we do if we encounter something that's just beyond our scope? For example, if we're coaching somebody and we suspect that they might have clinical problems, depression, or something like that, what then?

Alan: There are three conditions here. One is a skills/competence kind of problem, and you help that through training. Another is an attitude or behavioral problem, and you address that through coaching. But let's face it, not all problems can be fixed, and not all behaviors can be modified. That can include the conditions you asked about, which are therapeutic problems such as borderline behavioral disorders, clinical depression, or bipolar disorder.

It's always good for a consultant to have at least enough education or training in psychology to recognize the symptoms of depression or bipolar disease so that you can recognize them and realize you shouldn't mess with them. It's not your competency, it's not your place, and even if you're trained in psychology, you still don't take these on. You are there for *business* purposes, and never the twain shall meet. Suggest an employee assistance program or an outside therapist—whatever resources are available—but you can't handle something that requires a therapeutic intervention if you're there as a consultant or coach.

Q: If the person isn't willing to go with a clinical referral and take care of whatever problem I've identified, is it still okay to coach on business issues, or should I just stop the engagement?

Alan: It depends on the degree of clinical health needed. If somebody is depressed, that has to be addressed before you can deal with any kind of coaching for the simple reason that depression, as you know, masks talent and doesn't allow talent to surface. Thus, coaching someone when their talent is effectively subordinated isn't going to be very effective.

Q: What happens if you feel you've done your best, but the client doesn't implement your advice?

Alan: You say, "Have a nice day. Nice working with you. Let me know when I can be of further help. By the way, I'd like some references." It's as simple as that.

My goal in life is to make things simple. Unfortunately, I work with too many people who want to make things complex. If the client has paid you for your advice and is happy but decides not to implement, there are several possibilities here. One is that the client isn't ready to and wants to wait a little longer. Two, the client disagrees with you. Three, the client does agree with you but is intimidated to implement. Four, the client is completely distracted by something else. But who cares? You're not being paid to make sure that the client moves from point A to point B. You're only there to point the best route from point A to point B.

As long as your client isn't damaged, he or she is an adult capable of making his or her own adult decisions. You've done what you've been paid to do. They're not like a dog that needs to be petted each time you come home.

If you have completed your project in accordance with the proposal, you move on. Your agreement is never, ever to guarantee a certain result; your agreement is to provide the advice, recommendations, insights, and techniques that will help get a client to a certain result. There's nothing in your agreement that says, "I will hold a gun to your head until you do this."

Q: You recommended that we become generalists. How do you avoid the possible trap of being known as the person who is providing all things to all people?

Alan: There's really nothing wrong with that if that's how you're known because that's a rubric. You can be seen as a jack-of-all-trades. When that phrase first came into existence, it was a very positive descriptor. You had someone who could do a lot of things for you. It was valuable to know somebody like that who could do all those things.

This is a relationship business. If you have a solid relationship with a real buyer, that buyer makes you part of the decision-making process and says to you, "We need to do this over here; is this something you can handle for us?" The buyer trusts you to say, "Yes, I can," or "No, that's not my strong suit. Would you like me to find you someone who can do it?" Consequently, it's not a question of being a specialist or a jack-of-all-trades; it's a question of having a great relationship with your buyer, who trusts you to help with the buying decision.

Q: The concept of "incoming" or bombs coming at us, and relating it to challenges: How do we change our mindset when there are just too many incomings?

Alan: What you think is what you believe, and what you believe is how you act. You have to change the way you speak. If you see interest, questions, and attention coming your way as "incoming," as shells being lobbed at you, you're probably going to duck. If you see them as opportunity, you're going to run around with a bushel basket saying, "I need to catch this. I need to respond. Give me another six phones." It depends on how you react to the term incoming.

If you've been in the military and someone yells, "Incoming," you dive for cover. But in consulting, if you hear "Incoming," you should be saying, "Where? Where? Get out of my way! I've got to go grab some of that." Opportunity is all around us. Our problem is that we're so busy, or we're hiding so frequently, we don't hear it knocking.

Q: What are some of the most frequent misperceptions consultants have about their business? How do you advise mentorees overcome these?

Alan: The one that immediately comes to mind is should I be delivering or marketing? People have this faulty belief that if I'm delivering, I can't be marketing, and if I'm marketing, I can't be delivering.

Of course that's a completely inaccurate but common perception. Adopting this artificial either/or mentality results in very bad binary decisions where one activity is chosen at the expense of the other. "Should I go to the seashore or should I go to the mountains for vacation?" The real question here should provide more alternatives.

Practice what I call raising the level of the decision making. Whenever you see yourself or a client making a binary decision—choosing between either/or, up/down, right/left, yes/no—ask, "Why are you making this decision?" What is the answer? Continuing the example above, it is, "Because I need to choose a vacation site." That's your decision statement.

Similarly, you can ask clients, "Why are you deciding whether to market or deliver?" "Because I have to grow my business." That's the nature of your decision.

"Why are you deciding whether to return this call or not?" "Because I have to deal with a difficult issue." That's your decision statement.

The point you raise in questioning what the real choices are is a critical one, and you'll find that very few people are actually facing yes or no decisions. When a surgeon says, "Should I operate or not?" the real decision that must be made is "How do I best save the patient's life?"

This is the universal catholic consulting truism: If you find motive, and motive is embraced by the "why?" question, then you can help sort out objectives and alternatives. If you don't know what the client's motive is, you can't do that. You'll find that the motive is often inappropriately detoured into a very narrow kind of decision when it should be much broader.

Q: Are there key challenges you face, or do you see them all as opportunities?

Alan: I tend to look at life as one big opportunity. The challenges I face, if you want to put it in that category, are organizing myself so that I can address both the commitments that I have and the high priority opportunities that I want to take advantage of, while still having time to take prudent risk opportunities that by no means have the same guarantee of success but which I'm passionate about and I want to do. Then I work that into my life balance, personal accountabilities, writing, speaking, and so forth. Those are challenges for me, but they're very pleasant ones.

One quick closing thought that I want to share: The best way to sort through challenges, and one of the best traits you can have, is to be able to live with and deal with high degrees of ambiguity. If you need concrete answers rapidly, black and white, right or left, in or out, you're going to have a hard time being a successful person in any discipline.

You're Your Own CEO

Q: If you never worked for yourself before, the first discovery is that you're now your own boss; you're now your own CEO. How do you advise consultants to adjust their mindset to the challenge of running their own business if this is the first time they're doing that?

Alan: First, be prepared that you're going to have a pretty lousy boss! Resign yourself to that, and decide to manage up to improve your boss's behavior.

If you're a refugee from the corporate world and organizational life, understand that you won't have the resources you used to have. You're going to have to do more of the day-to-day tasks yourself, which means you're going to have to "routinize" your input. I believe that you customize your outputs but routinize your inputs.

If you need to get supplies, go to the post office, and upgrade things on your computer, you must create a systematic way of completing tasks efficiently so that you're not spending undue amounts of time on them. You're going to have to tend to the little things efficiently, or you won't have time to tackle the bigger things.

You also need to start acting like your own boss. If you are the president of your own company, you'll need to act as a peer of the buyer, not like someone who is desperately trying to make a living on their own.

Q: What are some other tips for successfully tending to the various departments, roles, and responsibilities that you'll be responsible for as you run your own business?

Alan: Learn from those who walked that path before. Finding the best instructors with the best training is the best way to proceed. Talk to people who have been there and done that. It's silly to reinvent the wheel. Talk to people who have gone out on their own. You can also read books by people who have done it.

Talk face to face with consultants who have done it. Most will sit down with you over a cup of coffee, talk on the phone, or you can hear them speak at trade association meetings. Educate yourself about what it takes to be successful. Then when you take the plunge, you still may have a 15 percent surprise rate, but that's a lot better than a 95 percent surprise rate.

Q: Are there some other classic traps, such as people neglecting certain aspects of running their own business?

Alan: One of the primary ones is that they don't manage their time well because now their time is completely their own. We all have the same amount of time—we all have 24 hours in a day—it's a construct that's entirely egalitarian. But people don't manage their time well no matter which end of the continuum they're on.

On the one hand, they get overwhelmed in trivia and low-priority stuff. On the other end of the spectrum, they don't provide enough leeway for themselves—slush time, private time, discretionary time, etc. They feel that *doing* a lot is equivalent to *accomplishing* a lot, and of course that's nonsense. They have nothing to do with each other.

Another trap is avoiding interaction or confrontation. The ability to place oneself assertively in harm's way, if you will, is essential to being successful. One of my new mentorees is showing a very disturbing pattern. He is far too tentative with buyers. He sends emails instead of picking up the phone. You have to be assertive with buyers, and act as their peer.

You have to march out there into harm's way. I love military analogies. The worst thing that will happen is you get turned down or ignored. Like any good Roman solider, you live to fight another day. This isn't a Greek world where you die for the honor of Greece on the battlefield. You're a Roman in consulting—you retreat, and you fight another day.

Q: What about personal style and personality type? How do you know how assertive to be?

Alan: That's a very good question, and the answer isn't going to please a lot of the people. There are varying types; as we all know, people are different. The standard take is that everybody can be successful, and everybody can be a failure. It depends on how flexible you are, how well you can adapt to others, etc.

If you want to succeed as a solo consultant upon whose shoulders fall the marketing responsibility and the sales responsibility, you have to be highly assertive, and that's not something you can fake. If you're moderately high assertive, you can certainly move it up to very high assertive for X hours a week while you're meeting with clients. But if you're low assertive, not highly persuasive, or highly enthusiastic, you're not going to be very effective as a marketer or consultant.

If you're hiring people, hire eager, passionate people. You can teach them your content, but you can't teach them enthusiasm. Hire enthusiastic, self-motivated people; they can learn your business. But if you hire experts in your business who aren't motivated or enthusiastic, you have a problem. Enthusiasm is contagious. Certain behaviors are more conducive to consulting success in terms of marketing and delivery, and that's just a fact of life.

Q: What's the biggest misconception about consulting?

Alan: The biggest misconception about consulting is that it provides clients with new ideas, breakthrough ideas, and completely different paths of action. In fact, as I look back over my career, 90 percent of the time I told clients what they already knew but haven't sufficiently exploited, needed validation for, or didn't put high enough priorities on. Only 10 percent of the time have I really delivered new paths, innovation, a sharp right turn, and so forth to clients. What clients often need is validation or a different light shined on what is already there.

Most of the time you can even call it simply a renewed or different appreciation. When I say to a client, "Your existing client base is a tremendous off-balance-sheet asset that you're not exploiting," the client says, "Tell me more. We're very good to our clients." And I say, "Yes, but they're not good to you, you're not getting the referral business, and you're not getting the testimonials. They're sitting there like money in the bank that's not gaining interest." Suddenly, I become extraordinarily valuable because the client is thinking, "With no capital investment, we can leverage and exponentially improve our business by leveraging something we already have."

Q: Which part of consulting is an art, and which is a science?

Alan: The diagnostic part is an art, and the prescriptive part is a science. Consultants often get them confused. You ought to be diagnostic in your marketing and prescriptive in your delivery. There are some exceptions, but when a doctor is diagnosing a patient and asking, "Does it hurt here? Does it hurt there? How long has it been doing this? When do you feel it? When don't you?" that's an art form they teach in medical school, just as I can teach consultants questions to ask.

Combining the data to form useful information, combining the information into a knowledge base, and having the wisdom to get the right prescription—that's the art form at the start of the process. After that, when you know what the issues are, the composition of the medicine—that's pure science.

Conclusion

If you're someone who still wonders if you want to be a consultant, this is how you can decide. Ask yourself if you're passionate about helping other people, and then ask yourself a second question: Am I confident that I can do this on my own, present myself well, market myself, and deliver without the help of a larger organization? If the answers to those questions are "yes," then you'll probably find consulting a very rewarding profession. This is the marketing business, and you can't consult unless someone hires you, so you must be adept at marketing in order to practice being a great consultant. It's as simple as that.

2 | Can You See the Goal Line or Just Hear the Roar of the Crowd?

Socrates once said, "If you don't know your port of call, no wind is a good wind." How do you set your direction and prioritize your objectives? How do you focus on your goals while still staying open to the opportunities that present themselves along the way?

Establishing Goals

Q: What is your definition of a goal? Should I separate business from personal ones, and are they critical to success?

Alan: The definition of a goal? A lot of people call them objectives, results, or outcomes, but essentially a goal is anything that you want to achieve. It's rarely an endpoint but rather a stop along the way. Goals are important to have because they give you some kind of direction and that port of call mentioned earlier. Goals can be varied but I think should be integrated.

In the professional services industries, such as consulting, your personal goals and professional goals are usually inseparable. You have one cohesive life, not a business life and a separate personal life. Some goals relate exclusively to your business and some exclusively to your personal life, but most will overlap in some way, and I think that allows you to make faster progress toward achieving them.

Q: Do you find having goals is critical to success?

Alan: A goal is also a metric. If you don't set goals, you really don't know if you're succeeding. If you don't know where you're going, then you won't know if you're getting there. Your goals don't have to be ironclad. Those life lists, bucket lists, and I-am-going-to-do-these-things-before-I-die lists are excessively doctrinaire and rarely take into account the fact that we are organic. We are fungible. We change.

It's important to know how you want your business to look in the short term or the medium term. Those goals are legitimate and valuable; they let you know what kind of progress you're making.

Q: You often talk about the importance of developing a sound business strategy for one's success. You talk about strategy being the "what" and tactics being the "how." How do I determine what my strategy should be? How do I develop effective tactics to support it? What role do my goals play?

Alan: If you read a dozen books on strategy, you're going to have two dozen definitions of what these things all mean. Here is my opinion—as opposed to all the other things I have discussed, which are completely objective and factual! You need a strategy, not a business plan. Unlike a plan, which extrapolates from the present, a strategy is a picture you paint of the future. Your strategy says, "This is what I want my life to look like, sound like, be like, and so on. This is my picture of the future, and I'm going to create it unfettered and on my terms."

Business plans create restrictions. With a business plan, you're likely to meet but not exceed your goals. But a picture of the future can be revised and adjusted. It should reflect some idealized point where you want to be, but whether you reach it precisely or not doesn't matter because it's a moving target, and you're going to change it as conditions warrant.

Having a strategy provides a framework within which you make decisions that influence your direction and the nature of what you do. For example, that framework might include traveling internationally for business or for personal pleasure. It might include developing a small infrastructure within your business where you have employees or subcontractors to help you free up your time. But it's only through knowing where you want to go—by having that picture of the future—that you can make decisions within some rational, comprehensive framework that will set the nature and direction of your life and your business.

The tactics you use comprise the execution or implementation of your strategy. A lot of people see tactics as steps along a linear path to an end goal. My own criteria for determining which tactics to use include asking key questions: "What is the fastest way to do it? What is the least labor-intensive way to do it? What is the most rewarding way to do it?" As you consider all these answers and integrate them, the resulting tactics should be the most effective and efficient course to get you where you want to go. That often means abandoning existing behaviors, adopting new behaviors, or just doing what you are doing more often and better.

You can have strategic goals that say, "In reaching that picture of the future, we want to achieve this." You can have tactical goals that answer the question, "How are we making progress?" In that context, goals are actually metrics stops, milestones, or mileposts. They tell you how far you have come and what kind of progress you have made.

Q: How do mission, vision, and goals affect each other?

Alan: Reaching your goals means you're getting closer to achieving your vision and how well you're implementing your mission. It's as simple as that. If you think of it in terms of a journey, just as a station stop is a stop along the way and a terminal is the final stop, a goal is a point in your journey—or mission—that gets you closer to your vision.

When they first put in the Union Pacific rail line, the easternmost terminal was St. Louis and the westernmost terminal was San Francisco. Those were the ending points, but along the way, there were scores of stations. In terms of our business and our lives, we really don't want to focus on the terminal; we want to get to the stations. The stations will change as our mission and our visions evolve, but as long as you keep reaching the next station, you'll get ever closer to where you want to be.

Q: You have said you're not a huge fan of instituting a vision or mission. Should I create them?

Alan: I really don't believe in these for individuals. I barely believe in them for organizations. In the larger sense, a mission statement is a raison d'être, the reason that you exist. As Peter Drucker pointed out in his writing, an organization is not like a tree or an animal, merely existing to perpetuate the species. An organization is created and sustained because of the contribution that it will be making to the environment.

The raison d'être, for example, for Merck Pharmaceuticals when it was "America's Most Admired Company" in the annual *Fortune* poll was to bring the greatest in scientific research to the greatest in human health care suffering. Similarly, FedEx's was to get packages delivered responsibly and unfailingly the next day. These kinds of statements create a focal point for you and for your clients, a means by which both you and your client hold you accountable.

We're all here to improve a client condition. The degree to which we do that will determine how successful we are. But establishing a mission statement to attract customers to you is borderline ridiculous. I don't think the client cares.

I do think you should share common values with your clients. If you don't believe in downsizing work—and your client wants to do downsizing work—you don't do it; you walk away. If you don't believe in multilevel marketing, don't coach people who do it. Ensuring your work, principles, and passions are aligned is important, but *mission statements for a solo practitioner is the tail wagging the dog.*

Q: If you work at or run a firm where you have employees, or what I call the corporate model of consulting, should you establish a mission statement?

Alan: Yes and no. I've seen it work and not work. Normally, as a prelude to strategy, you establish three things: values, vision, and mission. The values are what you believe in; the vision is where you want to be in the future; the mission is why you exist. When crafting your vision and your mission, here are some questions to ask: Can employees apply their company's vision and mission on the job to guide and improve their performance? Can a customer or prospect use this information to make an intelligent decision about their relationship with you? If you answered yes to both of those questions, then it makes sense for your business.

That's why FedEx said, "Guaranteed to absolutely, positively get there the next day." That's why Kodak said, "We provide memories." Kodak couldn't outsell Fuji on film, and they couldn't undercut Fuji's price, but they could use their branding to emphasize that you don't want your daughter getting married and risk not having the pictures. How effective your mission and values will be depends on how well your employees can use them to keep them focused and to keep your customers loyal to you. That's the test. If you find it works, fine; if it sits in some three-ring binder that's cross-indexed, on a dusty shelf, and no one implements it, there is no reason to have it.

Q: Are values universal, or do I establish unique ones for my business?

Alan: There are two kinds of values. Core values are the values that represent what the business and its ownership believe in. These values have a great deal to do with determining how the company invests, how it looks, how it reacts to calamity, how it seizes opportunity. You might believe that people are your greatest assets, and machinery are the expenses. In a lot of organizations, it's the reverse. The machines are the assets, and the people are treated as expenses.

The second kind of value is operating value, which is how people behave every day. If I'm at my desk and my phone rings five minutes before the day is over, I'm not going to touch it because getting out the door at 5:00 is more of a priority than providing good customer service. On the other hand, if I'm vested in my career and my company, I'm going to pick that phone up at 4:55 because it's my responsibility to the company and to that customer or prospect to do so. Those are examples of operating values.

The operating values of an organization have to be consistent and aligned with its core values. Unless you have middle managers who are exemplars to the front line employees, who conduct themselves in ways that reflect the company's core values, the operating values of the company will be inconsistent.

If you walk into a bank and the signage throughout the bank reads, "Our customers are our most important asset. If you have a suggestion, don't hesitate. We are here to serve you," the bank is communicating its core values. But if the teller who helps you doesn't say please or thank you, and when you ask for a receipt, the teller says, "You don't get a receipt with this transaction; we just don't do that," there is significant cognitive dissidence within the organization. The operating value of that teller is "Customers are a nuisance," yet the stated core value of the company is that customers are the most important asset.

The greatest influence on corporate culture, small business behavior, and individual behavior is the exemplar, the leaders of the organization. People who are in positions of authority—hierarchical leaders and influence leaders—have to model consistently the behavior that they want others to adapt. Employees notice who gets promoted, who gets recognized, and who receives the formal and informal accolades. They observe which people within the organization are rewarded and respected, and they will emulate the behavior of those individuals.

I was working with a big insurance company in Minneapolis, and I found that members of the sales force were forging applicant signatures on insurance applications. They were doing it to receive the credit for the premiums to reach their quotas in that quarter. The potential insured, who intended to buy the insurance, was on vacation, tied up, or not accessible, and it was approaching the end of the quarter. So, agents were simply forging signatures rather than have the true insured sign the forms later.

It was endemic to the culture. I asked the vice president of sales to discuss the procedure. He told me that he approved it. He had done it himself, and it was a great way to get money rolling and get ahead of plan. So, at a corporate strategy retreat with the top thirty-five officers of the company—including the CEO, who was my buyer—I included an ethical component to the program. I asked the participants, "What do you think about this practice?" Everybody there who was not in sales—in other words, all the executives—said, "Oh my God, that's abhorrent. We would never do that."

I said, "I have news for you. You're doing it."

The CEO asked, "Who is doing it?"

Jack, the vice president, said, "For God's sake Chris, you know everybody does this."

The group pointed out that this type of behavior could get the insurance commissioner involved, and it would be detrimental to the reputation of the company. Although they had core values of integrity, financial security, and trust, their operating values completely undermined those core values.

Q: What is the difference between those who achieve successes and those who don't? Does goal setting have anything to do with this result and success?

Alan: Perhaps the key differentiator is discipline. If you want to achieve goals, you need to have the discipline to get there. That discipline involves maintaining focus on your goals. Goals are useful in that sense, and identifying what specific actions you have to take to reach those goals and having the discipline to execute them. Success is about discipline, and it's not a very common commodity.

Q: Can I achieve a goal without a deadline?

Alan: A deadline is like a bookmark in time. It's important to have deadlines so you can identify when you are ready to go to the next step. A deadline is a way of imposing yourself upon the inexorable march of time. If you don't have a deadline, time keeps marching by, and you haven't gotten anywhere.

Goals, by definition, should have some time frame involved. Most goals have at the very least an implicit deadline: Do you want to do it before you die? Do you want to do it while you are still physically able to do it?

People who say, "Someday I want to see Europe" are less likely to see Europe. But those people who say, "I'm going to book my flight this week and pick a few places to visit" would probably have a much greater chance of seeing Europe. That's why deadlines are important on the steps in between as well.

Q: What is the importance of discipline, and how do I dramatically improve it?

Alan: We all have 24 hours in a day; what turns those hours into progress towards goals is how you use them. I don't suggest you allocate, document, or structure all 24 hours or even eight of them. But when hoping to reach a goal, you should outline the things you want to accomplish each day.

Some discipline is forced on us. If we don't get to work on time and we work for an organization, we get whacked. If we don't get a check in the mail in time to pay a bill, we get late fees.

It's self-discipline that makes the difference. During the course of a day, a week, a month, or a year, we need to create discipline and deadlines. How many times have you decided to do something and then realized a year has passed since you first decided or committed to do it? It happens to all of us all the time. It may be booking that trip to Europe. It may be finding the time to visit a relative who has since passed away. It may be painting the garage, and meanwhile now the garage not only needs a coat of paint, it's falling apart. Perhaps you had planned to put yourself in front of a certain prospect, and now it's too late because the prospect has hired someone else. We have all faced situations where we can't believe how much time has passed. Discipline is essential to making sure we keep track of that time and those goals, and self-discipline, by definition, has to be applied by ourselves.

To improve your discipline to achieve a goal, write it down in a calendar or somewhere visible to you every day. You can only cross it off when you do it.

If you need help, ask someone close to you to share in the accountability. Ask your spouse, your business partner, your significant other, or your colleague. The agreement may be that by this time on Friday, you will find a trainer, you will call three past clients for referrals, or you will apologize for the error made at the meeting you attended. You can use others to help hold you accountable, but you can also use things around you to remind you of that accountability.

Q: How can technology be leveraged effectively to manage such goals?

Alan: Technology is a tool. As long as you don't let it be your master, it can be extremely helpful. You can use technology to help you keep track of tasks and goals. Put them on your desktop screen. Put them in your cell phone. You can use that ridiculous technology that I absolutely hate but that pops up on your computer screen and says, "You have a meeting in 2 days, you have a meeting in 2 hours, you have a meeting in 14 minutes, oops you are overdue for your meeting" as a way of enforcing discipline. You should develop the ability to do that without an automated reminder, but sometimes you need that kind of help.

The reason I hate that little gizmo I just talked about is that I have the discipline to pick up a phone and call—just like I did for this call today—when I'm supposed to. I have the discipline to be available on a free line when someone is supposed to call me. I don't need an electronic reminder, so for me it's annoying when someone else imposes it on me because it's gratuitous. But you can certainly use that sort of technological help. Technology can play a role but will never replace the need for human accountability. When you aren't disciplined, when you don't meet deadlines, when you ignore reminders, when you're oblivious to deadlines, and so on, your life is falling apart because that behavior is never restricted to one part of your life. It permeates everything we do.

Incidentally, today we have a variation on Naisbitt's "high tech/ high touch." We have high tech *enabling* high touch. They have become complementary.

Q: Have your goals changed through the years?

Alan: When I first started in consulting, my goals were focused on putting bread on the table; toward establishing a viable and sustainable business; toward surviving. I had been fired. I had very little money in the bank. Many people tell me, "Gee, you don't know what it's like to start out in this business." But I do know what it's like under much worse conditions. If you look at Maslow's hierarchy, I was on a survival and physical safety scale when I first started in consulting.

Today my goals are different. My goals are to contribute to the communities I have founded and of which I'm a part. My goals are to enjoy my grandchildren and create a legacy for my family. I don't mean a financial legacy, which is simple. I mean a legacy of values that's enduring. My goals today are to continue to develop and acquire new talent so I can continue to explore who I am and what I can do. I may include a much more spiritual aspect as well. These kinds of goals, these kinds of important priorities in your life should change as your conditions change.

Q: What are some of the most common problems your mentorees have when setting goals?

Alan: Some set goals that are way too ambitious. Excessively optimistic goals and unreasonable goals are one problem. One guy who wanted to join the mentor program said, "I want to be a billionaire in five years." I said, "That's nice, but I'm not the right mentor for you. First of all, that's not going to happen. Second, that goal is completely unreasonable. Third, I don't want to help you do that."

Some people believe that if they have some sort of personal mantra they repeat all the time, it will happen. All that really happens with a mantra is that you just keep repeating yourself. Some people set goals based on those around them rather than looking at their own values, their own personality, their own talent, and what is important to them in life. They say things like, "This person has done that so I need to do that. She has accomplished this so I need to accomplish this." Those are misplaced goals. They are based on what others do instead of what you do.

Then you have goals that are simply trivial. They are tasks. The fact that you decided what the title of your book should be; the fact that you decided which seven prospects you are going to call; the fact that you made a decision about a database piece of software—those are trivialities. They lack action. A lot of people fool themselves by having goals that they can easily meet which don't require any work, effort, or challenge, and there is no possibility of failure. All of those are problems that people have to various degrees.

Q: How do I balance the goals of those close to me—like a spouse or partner—with my own goals?

Alan: Anyone who has a significant other, a spouse, or partner knows how difficult it can be to balance their goals with the goals of those close to them. There are things that we each individually want to do that the other might not want to do or might not want to do to the same degree. Then there are things that we both enjoy doing and want to do. My advice, having been married for 44 years and counting, is that you have to make room and time for both. There will be things that you do together that you enjoy and things you do apart that you enjoy.

As you become more successful in your occupation, you'll have more discretionary time. Some of that you'll spend together, and some of that you'll spend apart. Amazingly, that combination will enrich both of your lives.

Q: How do you distinguish between a consultant's mission and a value proposition?

Alan: That's a good question. I had a fight with an editor for my book *Million Dollar Speaking,* which came out at the end of 2010.

The development editor on the book said, "You are talking about value propositions here. You should include mission statements."

I said, "I'm not going to do that. They're not relevant."

He said, "I really think you should do that."

I went to the editor of trade books and said, "Get this guy off my book. He is supposed to be looking at what I write and improving the understanding. He is not supposed to be dabbling in my content since he doesn't understand my content." He was removed.

Because of the nature of the work we do, value proposition is all a consultant, speaker, coach, or facilitator needs. It defines how you improve a client, not who you are. Better defining how the other person is improved rather than who you are is what prospective clients will be interested in. I would tell every single person reading this to eschew mission statements—don't even bother with them—and focus on creating a value proposition that is compelling, fascinating, and as broad as you can comfortably make it.

Q: Should those value propositions change with my audience? In other words, should I customize it depending on who asked the question?

Alan: No. You should have a value proposition that attracts as many people as possible. If you work in radically different fields, which is unusual, but let's just say for the sake of our argument that you work with aspiring artists because you were an artist once yourself, and you also work in corporations implementing team building. In that case, you would have two different value propositions.

You don't want to create a different value proposition for each prospect because that's not how you help people. How you help people is by bringing your talents, experiences, education, values, and so forth into an organization. Those remain relatively constant and only change when you're working in very different communities.

I have two main value propositions. In the corporate world, I help to improve individual and organizational performance—a very broad value proposition—for corporate, primarily Fortune 1000, companies. However, that's the wholesale business. On the retail side, I create tremendous learning communities where professional services providers and entrepreneurs can learn, grow, and build their business like no place else on earth. Those are two different value statements for two different audiences.

Q: Is there any correlation between "to do" lists to goals in general?

Alan: You break down goals into smaller tasks so that you achieve a little bit at a time. Your "to do" list just breaks things down into "chunks." There are two kinds of tasks on a "to do" list. One is repetitive tasks. You may go to the post office every day. You may pay your bills twice a month. The second are tasks that, when combined, get you closer to achieving your goal.

You don't just say, "I'm going to paint the garage." What you probably say is, "First, I have to clean out the garage" or "First, I have to prime it" or "First, I'm going to do a certain wall or certain shelves."

Similarly, if you want to write a book, you're first going to write a book proposal. That means writing an outline first. That means coming up with your chapter headings and so forth. Once you do the table of contents, you don't have to do that again; then you move on to a sample chapter. A "to do" list just keeps you focused on the here and now. Whether it's short-term, medium-term, or long-term in terms of a goal, you still have to start it today.

Short- Versus Long-Term Goals: Responding to Opportunities

Q: You proposed earlier that your central goal is to improve your life and that it's wise to approach this with the idea that we really have just one life—one integrated life—rather than a separate life of professional and personal. With this in mind, are there categories or aspects of goals that you use under this broader umbrella of improving your life?

Alan: I wrote about this in my book *The Consulting Bible*. If you look at your life as integrated, many of your goals will satisfy various aspects of your life. I don't really categorize, codify, or segregate my goals. I create them as I need to. There are long-term goals which might include losing weight, staying in shape, or visiting a certain place, but I don't really put them in categories—personal, professional, and so on. A lot of goals are all encompassing. You know, that's wonderful.

A short-term goal might be to clear your email off your system every day so that you don't have email piling up. You respond quickly, and file or delete all emails. Consequently, you make sure that two or three times a day—whatever is good for your particular work style—you access your email, you deal with it, and then you move on. People without these types of short-term goals, wherein the computer is constantly telling them they have email—they're constantly diverted from whatever work they're doing to answer it—there is no rhyme or reason to their system, and at the end of each day they might still have 25 on there from two days ago.

A medium-term goal might be to create a client intervention or a workshop that needs to be in place next month. Let's say you're creating a workshop. You would probably break that larger task into smaller tasks of drafting an outline, designing the visuals, creating the handouts, and preparing the examples you want to use. You would probably also have to deal with the logistics of the facility or the site where you'll hold the workshop. If it were a client intervention, and you were planning to run focus groups, you would need to prepare your questions, decide how you want to structure the group, whether participants will be taking notes by hand or by computer, how you're going to arrange for the client to have refreshments, how you will merge this into your overall focus group feedback, and so forth.

Longer term, if you're writing a book and looking at this as a book proposal, to begin with you need to create your market platform. You need to create your outline. You need to determine your audiences. You need do a competitive analysis.

If we're sitting here on day one, what I'm saying is, "I need to check my email at 9:00 to see what came in overnight, and I'm going to check it at noon just before I have lunch, and I'm going to check it at 4:00 before I knock off." If it's the focus group, you might be saying, "Okay, I think since this is day one, today I'm going to work on the questions that I need for this focus group, and I'm going to call the client and ask for an administrative person to work with me on the logistics and support." For the book proposal, I might say, "I think today I'll work on the title, the subtitle, the audience, and the secondary audience." If you look at those three aspects of those three different sets, short, medium, and long, all of those could be completed probably well within 60 or 90 minutes.

Q: How important is it that your short-term and medium-term goals and daily tasks in some form align with a bigger direction or purpose?

Alan: It's important to have a sense of continuity, momentum, and positive inertia to your life. If you think about whatever you're doing as being a creative process, for example, compare it to writing a piece of fiction or creating a movie, there is something called the story arc. The story arc is the overall umbrella parameter kind of dynamic within which the action takes place. It sets this framework for what will take place. If your life has a framework, and your business has a framework, then you can be assured that what you're doing makes sort of collective sense. Your framework might be large or small. Your story arc might be vast or rather confined, but that's up to you. It's kind of strange to me to go through life without a story arc for your life.

You paint the picture of the future. That picture is changeable. It's a moving picture, not a snapshot, but nonetheless you're creating that picture of the future, and that's what you're aspiring to achieve. As you mature, grow, learn, and gain new experiences, that picture tends to change both in terms of form and substance. It might change from black and white to color. It might change from a normal screen to 3D. It also might enlarge. It might grow to encompass more things. Your story arc must be aimed at that vision of the future that you have. It's created by the strategy. Then you move to do what is necessary to get there.

Q: What advice do you give people who tell you, "I have my goal, but I don't seem to be able to take action?"

Alan: In terms of etiology, you have to find the cause before you can tell people how to remediate the problem. The causes here could be multifaceted. One is procrastination. People are forever making lists. But it's really a form of procrastination not to do anything. "I made the list." We talked about this not too long ago when we talked about simply doing the task part, the input part, but not the part that results in output.

We have all been in meetings where the management team or the executive committee has an easel with an agenda and items for action, and at the end of 1½ hours, that list is on another easel. It's the same list moved to another easel, and people say, "We made a lot of progress." The progress they made is the easel list is now four feet across the room.

A second cause may be that the tasks that you create are unreasonable. You can't paint the garage if you don't understand how to prime it and how to buy the right kind of paint. Should it be enamel, flat, oil based, water based? The same holds true when you want to achieve something in business. You can't achieve visibility by speaking publicly unless you have something to say, unless you know how to create a speech, unless you know how to get in front of an audience.

A third may be having an unreasonable expectation. Another is poor time management. The person has the best intentions, and the goals are reasonable, but they do so much and are so easily distracted that they can't get to them. Comedian Stephen Wright, who is a wonderfully wry, witty, dry comic says, "You know, I would love to daydream, but I keep getting distracted." That's what happens to a lot of people.

Q: How do you coach people to remedy procrastination?

Alan: Like anything else, you first need to confront them. You need to hit them right between the eyes. It's like when people say, "I can't write, I have writer's block." I say, "No you don't. That's an empty phrase. It doesn't mean anything. Sit down and start typing. Sit down and start writing." It's as simple as that. Nobody is asking you to write *War and Peace* or *The Godfather*. We are just asking you to put words on a page. You are capable of doing that.

If you have a list of things you want to do, pick one thing off the list and put it into action. Put it into work. Pick anything but start moving on it, and that will quickly surface why the person isn't handling it.

Having mentored and coached thousands of people, I've observed that some people are as afraid of success as they are of failure. If that's the case, almost inevitably there is little, short of therapy, that can get them to take action.

The internal stuff is volition. It's enthusiasm. It's motivation. It's self-worth. It's the intent to want to help others. All of that's the internal stuff.

The external stuff is simply the mechanical. On the one hand, you have the cognitive aspects. How you are talking to yourself. How you are thinking. You know, your thoughts and the words you use about yourself inform your behavior. On the external side, you have the mechanical aspect. Do you have the right tools?

If you opened the hood of my car today—or as they say, the bonnet—all you'll find is this massive engine, and you won't know what part is what. When the service people today service my car, they plug a laptop into a special port under the steering wheel, and the first thing they do is this electronic analysis of it. My father-in-law used to open the hood and say, "You know, the carburetor is off, the timing is off, and this has to be changed." He said to me once, "If you have the right tools, you can do anything." The matter of the environment, the matter of the external that you're talking about is really a question of having the right tools at your disposal.

Q: Sometimes the best things that happen to us are not planned. How can we better learn to respond to opportunities in the context of this conversation about goals?

Alan: Serendipity is a wonderful thing, and some of my greatest advances and achievements have been the result of serendipity because I was sensitive to the opportunity around me. Steve Jobs at Apple once said, "We simply jump on the next big thing." While that's a modest assessment of why Apple is so successful, he made a good point. In terms of growth, in terms of moving ahead, we don't do that remedially. We don't do that by correcting weakness.

Too many books, too many self-help books, too many gurus are simply telling you that you're damaged, you have to correct the weakness, and be like I am. I don't believe in that. I do believe, however, we have to constantly grow. We can't stay where we are, or somebody will pass us by. And one thing that might pass us by is life itself, by the way. Consequently, the way you seek opportunity is by focusing on continuous growth. When you constantly grow, you meet new opportunities.

If you look at any video games, we have a lot to learn from video games and other recreation. If you look at video games, as you achieve higher levels, you get more powers, or you get more instruments to use. They weren't available to you originally. The opportunity wasn't there until you got to that level. One reason for growth, one reason to constantly stretch ourselves is there are more and new opportunities at these increasing levels that we can boost ourselves up to.

Consider what you want to achieve in your business. Look at how they interact. In my business, I picture myself on a huge playing field. The playing field for me is so large that I can't see the horizon. I just give myself license to drive around in there, run around in there, jump, and play, and work at will.

The problem is some people's playing field is the size of a baseball stadium, which sounds very large, but it's really not. The fence is 400 feet from home plate. It seats 40,000 people. But that's it. Some people's playing field is no larger than a 20 by 20 office. Those are the prisoners of their organizations. Some people's playing field is no bigger than a postage stamp because that's the total breadth, width, and depth of which they allow themselves to enforce themselves on the environment.

If you accept the fact that serendipity happens beyond your control, but you have to recognize it's there, then the only way to increase it is to be involved in a lot of things. You have to have extensive business interests. You have to have extensive hobbies. You have to have extensive civic involvement. You have to have extensive social networks. You have to have an extensive education, and so forth and so on. I can go on and on. But the fact is, the more diverse the friends you have, the more diverse the interests you are involved in, the more diverse the initiatives you are trying to implement, the more serendipity will occur.

I have a few thousand books in my library, the great preponderance of which are fiction. I can't tell you how many times I've learned something from one aspect of my life that easily carries over to another. That's what creates serendipity, and that's what translates serendipity into very useful pragmatism.

Q: How do you develop a capacity to embrace ambiguity?

Alan: It's very easy to deal with ambiguity if you look at it in a certain manner. I'm always looking for examples. When my kids were young, we used to take them to Wildwood, NJ which has about a two-mile boardwalk. As you would imagine, they have every kind of attraction, including haunted houses. My son would never go in the haunted house. I finally said to him one day, "Jason, for goodness sakes, don't be afraid of the dark." He said, "I'm not afraid of the dark. I'm afraid of what might be in the dark." I have always thought that was wise way beyond his years.

To deal with ambiguity you have to assure people that there are things in the dark, but don't worry about it. You can deal with it. I can shine a light to you. You can create your own light. If something bumps you in the dark, it's virtually never fatal. You just have to learn to deal with it. To embrace ambiguity is to stop being afraid of what you can't see or don't know. If you stop fearing, you can deal with ambiguity.

What we should be thinking about is how we thrive. The way we thrive is by taking advantage of opportunity, which we have been talking about. Consequently, when you see a dark room, instead of hesitantly stepping into it and saying, "I hope nothing happens to me," you should go charging in, look for the light switch, carry a flashlight, light a match, whatever, and say, "I bet you there is something good in here."

Q: What has helped you develop the instincts that guide your adaptive and thriving capabilities?

Alan: I don't know what has helped me adopt the instincts. I'm driven by laziness. I've always wanted to get as much done with as least investment as I can make. For example, I can always make another dollar, but I can't make another minute. I've never learned how to do that, except by saving time somewhere else. We have talked quite a few times now that there are 24 hours in everyone's day. Consequently, my instincts have probably tended to getting as much done with as little as possible.

If you think about this in a corporate sense, great decision making is based on gaining maximum results with minimal investment of resources. That's what dramatically increases ROI. The more results you can get with the least input, the better off you are. The same thing is true for an internal combustion engine, a rocket ship, or just about anything. Even a singer. The lead in an opera doesn't always want to expend all of the energy on every note. They have to save it for the high note or for the performance that evening.

There is always this input versus output kind of dynamic. I've developed a very, very keen and sophisticated mechanism which I use to do that. My therapist told me once that I had created a set of pipes, which were incredibly intricate, which no one else could play, but I played them like a virtuoso.

How to Set Priorities

Q: We talked about goals, strategies, short-term objectives, long-term objectives. We get excited about all of this conversation, and we want it all to happen at once. We do this and our clients do this. What can you tell us about the importance of setting priorities?

Alan: Somebody once said that time is only God's way of making sure everything doesn't happen at once. But if everything is a priority, nothing is a priority. Consequently, you need to take a look at what constitutes your basis for forming priorities. This can vary, but if you look at factors such as seriousness, urgency, and growth, how *serious* is something? How much is it impacting you positively or negatively? What is the *urgency*? Is there a limited window of opportunity? Must something be fixed immediately or you can't proceed? And then *growth*. Is this thing getting worse? It is getting better? Or is it stable? If you look at just three factors like that—and it's important to take the emotionalism out—you can begin to objectively assess priorities and determine what indeed you should do first, then second, and then third.

Q: What if goals conflict? For example, say I want to be very fast in my delivery, but I also want to offer the highest quality.

Alan: This is a very, very important point you just raised for this entire undertaking, this entire book, and to everyone and anyone who reads it. That's not a conflict at all. I'll use reversal here—which is one of those pipes that I play—but the fact is the real question to ask is: If I want to be high quality in my delivery, how can I use speed to augment that quality? What often seems like a conflict, or an oxymoron, should instead be transposed, inverted, reversed so that they augment and help each other.

In this case of the example you mentioned, quality and speed are not mutually exclusive. The real question here is: How can I use speed to enhance quality, or conversely, how can I use quality to enhance speed? That's how you would set these up as dualities. Priorities you can achieve together.

Some priorities will be in conflict. For example, if you have a priority to take a vacation, but you also have some elderly ailing parents and your priority is to take care of them, then you have to make decisions between the two. If you use seriousness, urgency, and growth, you can say, "I'm going to forsake my vacation and take care of my parents. It's the right thing to do." Or you can say, "I'm going to take my family on vacation, and I'm going to fly back once a week over the course of the month to take care of my parents and get them a home healthcare worker because I think that will take care of the problem." Or you could say, "My parents have some health problems, but they can travel. I'm going to take them on vacation."

Your solution might differ from someone else's solution, but that's how you tend to deal with priorities that are in conflict. You either compromise, you merge them, or you ultimately pick one or the other.

Q: How do you take the emotion out of priority setting?

Alan: Ironically, you take the emotion out by being selfish. What you have to ask yourself is, "What will enable me to make the best contribution? What will enable me to live life the way I want to live it? What will enable me to contribute to my family the best and the most?" It's like the oxygen mask rule in airplanes: If you don't take care of yourself, you really can't take care of others. How good will your care for your elderly parents be if you're sitting there stewing that this was your only chance to have a vacation, it had been planned for two years, it was a big deal, and you can't go on it?

I can make a case that this is your speed and quality thing. I can make a case that your care will improve if you are able to also merge your vacation with it somehow. You could take a vacation that's within a shorter distance from your parents.

I think the issue that underlies your question is guilt. You can't let guilt haunt your decision making because guilt is like depression. It masks talent. It exaggerates nervousness. It can completely destroy your ability to achieve whatever you want to achieve.

Q: When you find people who are not addressing their priorities, what do you find they are doing instead?

Alan: They are procrastinating. People will rationalize and say, "It's much more important that I upgrade the software on my computer right now because I might need this advanced drawing system that allows me to draw in colors remotely using a wireless keyboard, rather than try to create the outline for my book."

Q: You help your mentorees cut away all of the extraneous and really focus on what they need to do. Could you give us a sense of how you do that?

Alan: It's sort of a *tabula rasa* principle. I start with a blank slate, which they can't do because they are so immersed in their lives, which is quite understandable. The interesting thing is that almost everybody who goes through Total Immersion—which is two full days more or less on two separate occasions—most people by 2:30 are begging me to stop because it's too much. But 95 percent of them will tell you that after 45 minutes, everything they paid was worth it, and if for some reason we had to end right there, they would be perfectly happy.

Most of the *tabula rasa* stuff occurs right at the beginning because I question basic premises, and I question basic principals. I say, "But you really are doing this, or you are not doing that, or this is cognitive dissidence, or you are not consistent here," but basically I ask the question "Why?" Why are you doing that, or why aren't you doing that?

I think the reason the Total Immersion program has grown so dramatically within my mentor program is the same reason that the mentor program itself is drawing more and more sophisticated people. The world around us, the stimuli, the choices, and the volatility has almost forced people to reach intellectual puberty earlier. By that I mean people are being forced to face the need for greater sophistication, greater introspection, greater combinations of their talents and abilities because they have no choice, or they aren't going to be competitive. Total Immersion has turned out to be the kind of interactive personalized response that best suits that.

It's very difficult to do this for yourself. I've mastered some ways to do that, but my mentor has always been my wife. She has seen my act about 400,000 times. If I can make my wife laugh, I know it's really funny. On the other hand, when she gives me a certain look, I know that I'm dead in the water.

It's important to have interaction with others whom you respect—people who can give you solicited feedback, not unsolicited feedback. One of the reasons my communities are doing so well is that people find kindred spirits there. People find people who are very successful. They also find people who are moderately successful, who are in a place similar to where they see their next step being. They find people who are where they were just a year ago. And they find some people who aren't quite as well off as they are in most cases. These communities create a low-risk, highly beneficial alternative to get the kind of feedback that helps you understand what you need to do in the complex world I described a few minutes ago.

Q: Can you walk us through some techniques for getting the most out of our day to plan our work, and then work our plan, so that we can come close to getting the amazing results that you've been able to get?

Alan: My suggestion would be this. Assuming you're not traveling, you're home, and you're in your office. I recommend getting up relatively early. I'm usually up at 6:30, but I would certainly not get up later than 7:30. Get yourself up and then get into a regimen. If you work out, work out. If you have a healthy breakfast, have a healthy breakfast. If you walk the dogs, walk the dogs. If you read the newspaper in the morning, do that. But get yourself into a regimen so you start your day the same way. The regimen might be different each day, but it repeats itself. Before your office officially opens, before people start calling and emails start rolling in, you should get your writing done.

The early morning hours are the ideal time to write your blog posts, schedule your tweets on Twitter, or work on an article or part of a book. If you have to get a newsletter out, do that early while you're fresh. Then check your daily calendar and see what is on your "to do" list for that day. What calls you have, what calls you're expecting. What tasks you're supposed to accomplish, what results you're accountable for, and map those out if you haven't already done so. There might be a 10:00 phone call scheduled. You might need to get your car checked, but you don't have a scheduled time to do that, so make sure you tend to that at some point. Handle all of the email that has come in overnight.

Check your online communities to see if there is anything going on you should know about. You don't have to stay and post, but just give a quick perusal to see what is going on. By 9:00 you should unforward your phone, and get to work on the major things you have to work on that day. Keep what you're working on varied. I never write for more than about 40 minutes at a time any more, at least on the same topic. Get yourself out of the office. Get an errand done. Have lunch somewhere. Then plan to quit sometime in mid to late afternoon. Sometimes I'm at the pool at 2:00, in the winter I'm playing with the dogs, building a model, or reading, but certainly by 4:00 you should be wrapping up.

Then you can adjust the next part of your regimen. You might have a drink before dinner. You might read the paper at that point. You might check on your email one last time. You might take the dogs for a walk. So, that should be your day, unless there is something extraordinary planned like you have a client meeting in the afternoon.

Your regimen and routine might change as you go forward. That's fine. I'm not saying be inflexible. But I am saying you need a basic regimen and routine. A baseball player always has the same fielder's glove. It's contoured to his fingers and his hand. He has leathered it, polished it, oiled it, whatever he does to it so it's supple the way he likes it. You don't change gloves. It's a big thing. They use the same bat. Just as your equipment should be the same, so should your regimen.

I tell speakers this all the time. Go out on that stage before you speak, walk around, and get a feel for it. See where the audience is going to sit. See if it creaks. If it's a big AV production, see what the limits of your movements are back and forth. If you can't do that because of another event happening there, then go to the wings, take a look from the side, and see what it looks like.

The more you familiarize yourself with something before you do it, the more comfortable you are. The less tension you have. The less stress you have. And that can apply to your daily life as well. You need to get into a regimen that keeps you operating at maximum efficiency.

Q: You have always been an advocate of finishing your work early in the day. Does that contradict the way many of us have been raised that the harder you work and the longer you work, the better results you'll get?

Alan: It contradicts it because that's crap. That's just one of the most fallacious statements I could possibly think of, and to labor under that is like trying to run a 100-yard dash with a 50-pound pack on your back. The harder you work the more fatigued you get. The longer you work the more fatigued you get. That's why Frederick Winslow Taylor, one of the first management consultants, went out of vogue so quickly. When he did his time and motion studies, he fudged the fatigue factor. He had no idea how to account for people getting tired. And that occurs mentally as well as physically, of course.

You can't possibly tell me that a lawyer is going to be as mentally acute and able to recall all of the precedents and case studies at 8:00 at night as he is at 8:00 in the morning. It's just not going to happen that way.

I'm much more creative in the morning. Can I write in the evening if I have to? Yes, but I prefer not to, and I try to never ever do that unless I have a great idea I want to write down. If you do things early, perforce, by definition very few things can happen to interfere with it. If you plan something for 4:00, you have a whole day's worth of potential interference awaiting you. Also, I don't care what your biorhythms are, you can't convince me that you're not going to be fresher and more creative in the morning than you're going to be later in the day.

Q: We have defined our strategy and set our goals. We have prioritized. We have set up the routine and addressed the priorities early. We're doing all of those things, and we're sticking to it, and yet we face a setback and just have a hard time getting over that. How do you encourage those in your mentor program to persevere when they encounter something that's just really difficult?

Alan: I tell people first of all, if you're not failing, you're not trying. And some failure is experienced more internally. You do something that just isn't good enough. Or you can't handle something. That happens to all of us; join the club. Some failure is imposed upon us externally. Somebody changes the rules. Something happens that we can't control. But you have to understand that. You know, Churchill was right. Things that we do in life, things that we try to accomplish—success is rarely final, and failure is seldom fatal. It's courage that counts.

Go back to the self-confidence and self-esteem that I mentioned earlier. If your self-esteem is consistent and it's consistently high—not narcissistic and not unreasonably high, but consistently high—then you take setbacks as a normal occurrence in life, and you bounce back. I'll give you the secret for resilience. I'll give you the biggest secret for overcoming any kind of setback, whether it be physical or emotional, and it's this.

If you consider your locus of learning to be internal, that is, you've garnered, obtained, acquired everything you know, when you face a setback or a failure, you've shot your bolt. You have nothing left to give. You've given it your best shot. You already know everything. You have nothing left. People like that take serious jolts when they have failed and often become clinically depressed.

If you define your locus of learning as external, that is, you learn from other people, you learn from being coached or mentored, you learn from experiences which you create and it's an ongoing process, when you face a setback or defeat, you say to yourself, "I need to go out and learn more. I need to talk to my coach. I need to get a new experience. I need to read another book." And in that case, you bounce back. The most resilient people are those who identify their locus of learning as external to themselves.

It's reasonable to be scared at times. It's reasonable to be upset at times over a failure. All of that's fine. But the question here is duration. To feel those emotions briefly is fine, but the key is what you do about it. You know the old rubric is true: It's not what happens to you in life; it's what you do about it. It's the speed with which you recover. Sometimes we can't control what happens to us, but we can always control what we do about it.

Q: What makes a person confident enough to respond in the moment?

Alan: Intellectual firepower. How do people best learn when you're confronted with a question? You give examples. The whole nature of this interview process that we're doing for this book, I've seen none of these questions in advance, which makes it exciting for me but makes the output customizable really for the people who are reading this and listening to it. This isn't just a compilation of other books that I've done. You have to have the wherewithal to provide examples, provide procedures, provide practices, give people contingencies, and so forth, that they can adapt things and use them in a way that makes sense for them.

Q: Itzhak Perlman, the violin player, said, "Practicing as much as you can isn't the optimum aspect to performance because if you practice something wrong, you create the wrong kind of muscle memory and the wrong kind of musical memory." Do you agree?

Alan: What Perlman is talking about is right. He may be the finest violinist in history. Some people may argue with me, but certainly if he is an example of what he believes in, it's hard to argue with it. The Perlman observation is absolutely on target, and it actually trumps what Malcolm Gladwell wrote in *Outliers*. Gladwell said that people practice 10,000 hours, whether it's Bill Gates programming something or Michael Jordan shooting jump shots, and that's what builds the memory. But the problem with his theory is that he has only taken extraordinary successful people and tried to work backwards. His analysis does work because he didn't include all the people who can't do it well because a lot of those people practice 10,000 hours too.

There is a qualitative aspect to this—you can practice the wrong habits—and you see it every day. You see speakers who use the wrong approach on stage. You see consultants use the wrong words with a client.

You see athletes who never mastered the proper functions they should go through. One of the reasons that Sandy Koufax was the greatest pitcher of all time is that he mastered the hydraulics, the mechanical aspects of pitching. Once he saw what worked best for him, he ingrained them into the same motions every single time and wound up over six years to have a record that for my money no one else has ever equaled.

A part of growing muscle is resistance. That's why dynamic tension exercises and some exercises that don't involve great weights can build muscle tone. The resistance is stretching yourself, is forcing yourself to deal with tough situations. Not pushovers. Going back to the same client who loves you and selling them new things is nice, but it doesn't really help you grow. Dealing with a tough buyer who needs proof and doesn't suffer fools gladly, that will build your intellectual muscle tone. The path of least resistance is always downhill, and we should want to climb.

Conclusion

Only a gifted few can wing it, with the operative word being "few." Even people who seemingly wing it have internal practices that guide them. I have an internal gyroscope and compass that virtually never let me down. Sometimes I don't achieve the speed I want. Sometimes I'm a couple degrees off course, and I have to correct, but I'm never just stationary. I'm never adrift.

Without a regimen, how on earth are you going to make and track your progress? Even if you do make progress, it might be in just one direction and not the other three directions you need to augment it. It all comes back to setting your directions and prioritizing your use of time.

Setting Up Infrastructure

We Build Our Houses, and Then They Build Us

3

Anyone just starting out in consulting will face some complicated and sometimes daunting decisions about how to set up the company's infrastructure, but often veteran consultants need help too. What is the ideal setup for your practice? Should you have a home office or have office space outside your home? Will the solo practitioner model work for you? If you need help, where should you find it? This chapter will help you find answers to these questions.

The Physical Location of the Office

Q: What are the benefits to working from home versus working away from home?

Alan: There are a lot of benefits to working from home. In no special order, the first is that it's much less expensive. There are significant costs associated with having an office whether you're renting or owning the space, but let's just consider renting. Aside from the cost of the monthly rent, there are utilities, insurance, perhaps a part-time person to staff it, and property taxes—and these costs mount up quickly.

My kids went to private schools from kindergarten through to graduate school, a total of about 21 years, and the cost was about $450,000. I estimated that over the course of the same 21 years, an office would have cost me about $450,000. In my case, the tuition payments were made by not having an office.

Another advantage of not having an office is that you have all the comforts of home—quite literally. If you have a pool, you can use it. If you have a yard, you can walk in it. If you live in an apartment and there are some key stores, neighbors, or whatever you want to visit, you can do that.

You have all the conveniences of home, and you don't have to get dressed. I won't go too far with this visualization, but the fact is you don't have to take a shower if you don't wish to; you don't have to shave; you don't have to put on makeup. You can be very comfortable.

Another advantage is you can work flexible hours more easily. If you have to get in the car and drive someplace, it's not as easy. You might choose to work from 7:00 to 11:00 in the morning when you're fresh, take a few hours off to be with your kids or go watch them do something, and then go back to work and perhaps do something from 6:00 to 7:00 in the evening. You have those kinds of advantages.

Some people say they have an office because they need to get out of the house. Perhaps their house is cramped, they don't have a private space, or they live in a small apartment and there isn't an area conducive to work. You do need some privacy, and you do need to be behind a closed door. If that's the case, an office may work better for you.

If your practice frequently requires you have conference facilities or sophisticated projection and electronic equipment, it may make sense to have an office where those amenities are available to you. But even then, I would say you can have access to those things—you can rent them on an as-needed basis. Don't fall into that trap of having an office because you think you need it for your ego, and you want to tell people you have an office. Clients come to my house all the time.

Q: When a business model justifies hiring staff, can we still work from home, or do we have to get an office outside the home?

Alan: I'm not a fan of having a company with employees. If your particular situation requires employees, that's different. I've known some consultants who actually have used their homes as offices, and their employees have worked in their home. They arrive in the morning and have a separate place to work. To me, that's awful. I would consider it an invasion of privacy and would discourage it. You can have a physical office where you house your employees, and you show up there as convenience dictates, but you might not need to go there very often.

Q: What are the alternatives for meeting people if you operate from home?

Alan: You can do several things. You can rent space in a conference facility. In most places, you can rent them by the hour, the half-day, or the full day. I worked with a large pharmaceutical consulting firm in New York, and for the first year I worked with them, they were in that kind of a space. They shared a conference room and copier with dozens of other companies. Years later, they moved to an office building on Wall Street and shortly after were sold for a gabillion dollars to a larger company.

You can also rent a room in a restaurant. Restaurants have private rooms and are very effective for meetings. Some of them are on higher floors; they might have a wine room; they might have a room completely separate from the dining room; and they might even provide it for you off hours because they're making some money when nobody is there.

You can belong to a private club. Virtually all of them have meeting rooms that they'll rent to you. Some will give them to you for free if you're a member. I've actually conducted programs, shot videos, and held board meetings for non-profits, that didn't have their own facility, in a private club I belong to.

The final thing I would recommend is that you go to your accountant, attorney, or other professional who might be providing you with services and ask them if you can use one of their empty offices. You'll find most decent-sized law firms and accountants either have conference rooms or empty offices, and they'll usually graciously allow you to use them. You can tell your client, "I have a great relationship with my attorney, and my attorney provides me with these offices to use, which is wonderful on his part, and I provide him in return with some consulting services."

Q: You mentioned using private clubs that allow you to just rent space and other options. Can we just meet clients at a coffee shop like Starbucks?

Alan: Never use a public place. It's okay to meet for coffee there, but you never want to take someone to a public place to conduct business, even informally. I hate having business over lunch or dinner. I don't mind having a casual lunch or dinner, as long as both parties understand we're not going to talk business there. Maybe we are building the relationship. Some of the many problems with public places are that you get interrupted, the restroom could be filthy, somebody spills something on important documents, or somebody overhears you. They're just completely inappropriate places for business, and the newer the prospect or client the more inappropriate they are.

Q: Could you talk a little bit about the ego involved in making the decision to establish an office outside your home?

Alan: I'll tell you a quick story first just to tell you how personal this is. When I was fired from my job in 1985, I went out on my own.

My wife said, "Okay, fair enough. Forget about the mortgage. Let's make this work, but what are you going to do first?" I said I was going to get an office, and she asked, "Why are you going to get an office?"

I said, "I'm on my own; and I need an office."

She asked again, "Why are you going to get an office?"

I said, "You know, I'm a consultant."

She asked a third time, "Why are going to get an office?"

I said, "Okay, obviously you have a point to make here. What is it?"

She said, "You're a consultant. You go to people, people don't come to you."

That's the first thing she said to which I had to say, "That's true."

Then she asked, "If you need an office, if it turns out that the evidence is such that you need an office, you can always go get one; but why start with one you might not need?"

I said, "Yeah, that's true too."

Here I am 28 years later, and I still don't have an office outside the home. By the way, offices within the home are completely tax deductible within the United States. I don't know about other countries. In the U.S., home offices are tax deductible as long as they're used strictly and primarily for business.

Now let me address your ego question. Many people tend to let their egos influence these types of decisions. Consultants who suffer from low self-esteem tend to try to compensate for it through artificial means. What would be the largest manifestation of that? An office. An office to them is this huge representation of respectability and legitimacy, believing that they must have a formal office with a formal shingle hung. This is the kind of ego nonsense that gets in the way, and it might sate the ego for a while, but it has really no manifestation whatsoever, no effect whatsoever, on prospects; and it has a pretty deleterious effect on the bottom line.

Q: What are some recommendations and best practices for designing your home office and organizing the space?

Alan: First of all, you need a private room with a door. I chose the smallest bedroom in the house when we bought this house. It's a six-bedroom house. There is not even a closet in here.

Then I had a designer come in, and I said to this designer, "Here is what I am going to use this office for. Here is the kind of equipment I expect to have. Here is what my business is like." I let her get to know me and how I deal with people, she spent some time talking to me, and she designed some built-in storage. I have built-in bookcases, a built-in credenza in an L-shape with a desk. I've changed the desk two or three times in 25 years, but it's amazing the built-in units that she created 25 years ago are still perfect for me.

The third thing is invest as much money as you're able on the equipment you need. In other words, buy a high-end laser printer if you're going to be doing a lot of printing. Get a high-end color printer if you'll be providing color materials or a high-end scanner if you'll be sending documents. I do a lot of audio recordings, so I have a very expensive, high-quality microphone sitting next to my computer. I have the biggest, most powerful Mac they make. My laptop, which I put in my briefcase when I go out, is over my right-hand shoulder. I have an iPad on my right. My iPhone is in front of me, and my big, main Mac computer is in front of me. All of them are the most expensive, best you can get because I use them a lot. I don't use 100 percent of their capacity, but the 20 percent of their capacity I do use I use to 100 percent effectiveness.

You should never scrimp on good equipment. Have the highest-quality equipment you can to run your business, and then put everything within reach. I can spin around in the chair I'm sitting in right now, and I can reach credit card machines, multiline phones, postage meters, labelers, and all the accoutrements without getting out of my chair. That helps productivity tremendously.

Put things in your office that please you. I have a lot of books in my office. I have the ability to play music a lot of different ways. I have mementos, photographs, and paintings all over the walls. It's a comfortable place to work. It's a salubrious place to work. It's nice being in here, sometimes I'm in here for very intense periods, and so it's a pleasant place to be.

I have a huge window overlooking my back yard, and I can see a line of evergreen trees, which even in the winter give great color. I can see gardens.

I can see the dogs when they're out there playing. I can see the bird feeders. We have a butterfly bush. I can watch hummingbirds. I can watch the dogs chase squirrels.

It doesn't feel as though I work in here. I mean, I realize I work, but it's a wonderful environment, and it's in my control. Why shouldn't it be? So whatever your means, you should create the kind of pleasant and productive atmosphere you would advise a client to do.

Churchill said, "We build our houses, and then they build us." He was talking about Parliament. But he was right in this context too. We create these structures, and if we're not careful, we can become prisoners to them, and the structures are incapable of changing themselves.

Q: What recommendations do you have for backing up the important documents we need for our business and making sure we don't lose everything if a fire or other disaster were to happen?

Alan: My recommendations are these. I have an external hard drive here in the office. Then all my files are also stored in the cloud. I use Mac products, so I have what is called Time Capsule, which allows me to automatically back up and retrieve documents. I have this wonderful software called Drop Box, which provides online storage and replicates/duplicates everything I do on all of my devices. When I was writing my book *The Consulting Bible*, every time I left my office, the files on my laptop would be updated to the very last sentence I wrote on my desktop. In fact, it already is. Whether it is my iPhone, my iPad, my desktop, or my laptop, all of these things are automatically updated.

I take a copy of all of my work every year—that is, the things I publish, my client files, and my financials—and I put them on a CD. I put these in a bank vault in a safety deposit box. By the time this is being read, I'm sure there will be even better alternatives.

The bank people kid me because I don't use the safety deposit box very much. I also have a big safe here at home. On January 2nd or 3rd of every year, for 25 years, I've deposited theses CDs in the safety deposit box. The bank manager says I'm like clockwork. However, CDs erode. Even electronic media tend to erode, but I do that to have a physical copy of the files, and I keep duplicate copies here next to my computer. I'm confident I can regain my files and get back in business if there were a catastrophe. God forbid it ever happens.

But I'll tell you this, more important than these kinds of things are the other documents in your life, your insurance policies, and things that need to be protected and safeguarded. Today with state of the art computers, it's easy to duplicate and replicate files and keep them in separate places.

Solopreneur Versus Having Staff

Q: How do people decide whether to remain a solo consultant or to partner with someone?

Alan: There are only two models in this business. They are both viable. First, you must ask yourself if you would rather be a solo practitioner, on your own, using subcontractors and others as needed, on an hourly or a time-based basis, and take all the money that you earn. And after "X" amount of time, when you stop working, there will be nothing to sell. You're not going to leave it to your kids; you're not going to sell it to a larger company; but in the meantime, you'll take all of your money out and lead a great life. (You can always sell your intellectual property, however.)

The other model is to create a company that has infrastructure or what I call a corporate model. You have staff. You have assets. You have good will. You can't take all the profit out every year. You must reinvest some of it back in the business, so you have to be more modest in what you take for yourself. You also have to invest in and care for your people to grow the business. At some point in the future, you may be able to sell the business you've grown for millions of dollars, and that will take care of the rest of your life, but you have to ask yourself whether you want to manage people.

These are the two choices you have. You have to decide which of these models works for you. Here are some things to consider for each. If you have high affiliation needs, that first model isn't going to fill them. So, either you need to get your affiliation needs met elsewhere—through professional associations, with friends, or belonging to civic groups—or you'll be both unhappy and unsuccessful. I mentor people who want to pursue either of these models, as long as they are aware of the pros and cons of each.

Another question is whether you can do without significant support functions. A lot of people come from large organizations and are used to people doing their typing, making their calls, making their appointments, or getting them lunch. Can you take back those responsibilities? Are you self-sufficient?

You also asked about a partnership, which is a little bit different than either of these two models. Even if you create a business with infrastructure and people, I advise against partnerships. Business partnerships can be worse than a bad marriage. They can cause so much stress, malaise, and financial entanglement—as well as confusion among clients and prospects—that you'll wonder what you were drinking when you got into them.

Q: What is your opinion about forming alliances to help grow your business?

Alan: I think they are fine. Alliances are wonderful because they needn't be legal; they needn't involve your companies in a contractual way. There are two conditions necessary to have successful alliances. The first is that your alliance partner has to be someone with whom you would trust your wallet. There can't be any equivocation about this. You have to be absolutely certain and convinced, without an iota or scintilla of doubt, that this alliance partner is the right person for you. You trust him or her; you can compromise; you can listen to his or her criticism. For this to be effective, you can't be in conflict with someone; you can't be distrustful. You can't be paranoid about your alliance.

The second condition is that you and your alliance partner have to bring an exponential improvement to the client and to yourselves. If each of you could do $100,000 of business with a client and together you do $250,000, that's not worth it. It's a fairly small increase, which will be eaten away by the need to manage this and coordinate. I would suggest that 1 + 1 has to equal more than two—more like 85. If one of you can do $100,000 of business, but working together you can create $300,000 worth of business, this makes sense. When you can improve the client's condition by working together to create synergy, then that makes sense.

I'm reminded of that great movie *Jerry Maguire* in which Cuba Gooding keeps shouting, "Show me the money." As long as the money is on the table, the two of you can form an alliance that's not conceptual, that's very real, and is based on business at hand.

Unfortunately, the majority of alliances are foolish. They're futile because they're conceptual. They're based on "Here is what we would do, if." People put these elaborate conceptual, hypothetical, theoretical models together without any pragmatics, without any real business at hand. You're much better off at putting together an alliance when you have real business in front of you that you deal with that's a practical reality.

Q: How do I know when I should hire or use subcontractors?

Alan: It depends on what your goals are. If you want to go the solo consultant route, you should subcontract. You can use subcontractors on a periodic basis and rely on the same group over time. According to the IRS regulations, as long as you're not providing more than 80 percent of a subcontractor's income, as long as you're not providing them with an office, and as long as they don't work expressly at your direction, they won't be considered an employee. You don't want these people considered employees, or both you and they will face a significantly higher tax liability. (You can find criteria on the IRS website.)

If your goal is to build a company and to build infrastructure, as you get large assignments, it gives you the wherewithal to start bringing on people and investing in people who will take over the implementation and some of the rainmaking. There are two things to avoid. One is over-hiring. You should hire people only when business justifies it, and always leave a little bit lacking. In other words, if you're getting some great business in, and you think you can probably hire three people, only hire two. Otherwise, you're going to have some dead time and empty offices.

The second thing is that when you hire these employees, you can't hire exclusively implementation people. You must find a rainmaker or two. For me the ratio is about 1:5 or 1:6. As one of the people in my Million Dollar Club said, "I've got all these chicks, their mouths are always open peeping, and I have to feed them." You don't want all these chicks peeping at you. You need to intersperse the delivery people with true rainmakers. Sometimes to attract and keep a rainmaker you have to give them a small portion of the business.

Q: If a consultant decides to hire staff, who should these people be?

Alan: The first principle for any support functions you need is to outsource that work to subcontractors. So, for bookkeeping, graphic design, or event planning, it makes more business sense to use temps or vendors. You don't hire full-time employees for that because you don't need those functions full time.

Secondly, the first people you contract ought to be "delivery" people. These people will either be delivering for you or delivering for the client. "Delivery" people are individuals who will either be executing tasks—such as teaching, coaching, consulting, or observing at the client location—or doing something for you such as improving technical approaches, providing administration, or doing research. Once you have a sufficient number of "delivery" people you can contract as needed and your business is growing, you should look for your first rainmaker.

I look for subcontractors who have several attributes. One is I know them for some reason: either I've known them in a professional capacity, they're part of my online community, or we have some other connection. Next, I need to see demonstrated skills: they've written a book; they have a successful track record with clients; they have intellectual property. Third is the chemistry must be right.

Q: What do you feel justifies termination of a business relationship, and what are some tips you can give us as the best way to do that?

Alan: When somebody isn't performing, you're doing them a disservice by allowing them to operate in an incompetent manner. Not only are you hurting your own business and hurting your own family, but you're hurting them. The belief that you're making concessions to help someone is a misconception because in essence, you're instead failing to council them on how to perform better. When you make concessions to anyone because you feel they're just not up to the standard that others are exhibiting, then you're categorizing them as inferior, and that's discriminatory and inappropriate.

The steps that I advise are these: Confront the underperforming individuals with evidence. Explain what the expectation was, make clear the level that they're performing at, and ask if they understand the discrepancy. If they don't, then discuss specific observed behavior and see if your perception is wrong or if they are in fact not performing.

If you conclude the issue is their performance, point out to them where they've fallen short, and provide evidence of this. Once they agree the performance isn't where it should be, then you say, "Here is how we can resolve this." Assign them a coach or agree to coach them yourself, or suggest a course or training they should attend, book they should read, and a timeline for improving. If they haven't improved by the end of that time period, then you have to remove them. You're not like Boeing, IBM, or JPMorgan. These companies can simply transfer underperformers to less-demanding positions. You can't. Poor performance will kill a small business.

If they're able to improve, then you had a skills problem, and you fixed it. If they're not able to improve, you either have a skills problem you can't fix or you have an attitude problem that can't be fixed. But, you have to get rid of them. The way to do that is by starting with an employment contract where you outline the terms of termination, guidelines for what happens when one is terminated, and what the severance will be. It's as simple as that.

When you hire a new employee, make sure to document both the details of the employee's performance as well as your interactions. If you have an informal chat with an employee in the halls, you need to go back and document it because if you are ever sued for unfair labor practices or wrongful termination, the more of a paper trail you have the more protected you'll be.

When you employ people, bad things can happen. Someone once asked Woody Hayes, the Ohio State football coach, at one point many years ago, "Why don't you ever pass the ball? Why do you always run?" He said, "Because when you pass the ball, three things can happen, and two of them are bad. Why would I do that?" When you employ people, the fact of the matter is, while they can help grow your business and give you affiliation support, they can also steal your intellectual property; they can steal customers; they can cost you customers; they can cause you grief by distracting you with personal matters; they can be absent; they can go on disability; and they can do all kinds of other things that can raise your insurance rates and decrease your productivity, costing you time and money.

I don't mean be cynical, but when you take on employees, there are risks you take on as well. The more employees you take on, the more opportunity you have for permutation of risks.

Q: How do we manage the relationship when somebody approaches us about being a subcontractor?

Alan: Unless a subcontractor approaches me with something that knocks me off my feet, I decline the offer. In other words, if they have references from people I respect hugely, or they have a piece of intellectual property that they're known for, I may consider working with them. If they say to me, "Look Alan, I'm a great delivery person. If you can ever use a technologist or a methodology approach in your business, I would be happy to subcontract," I would probably keep their name on file. Unless they have some exceptional offering, my response is typically the same, "I really am flattered that you asked. I choose the subcontractors I work with very carefully, and generally they're people I've known for a long time and in my community." I don't justify it any more than that. At that point, they have the option of joining my community. If they want to do that, learn in the process, and maybe someday subcontract, they would have more of a chance of working with me in the future.

The Starter Kit

Q: Let's start with the most basic questions: How do I determine a name for my company? What are some schools of thought about this, and which do you subscribe to?

Alan: I think if you want to name your company and really charge out of the box, you should call it McKinsey and Company. Next question?

When I was starting my company, my attorney who was setting up the corporation left a message and asked, "What do you want to call the company?" I wandered outside and said, "I just haven't thought of that." I lived in Summit, NJ, so I called the company Summit Consulting Group. People have said, "Oh that was brilliant. You know, it implies the summit, the apotheosis, the long climb." I simply lived there. I mean, if I had lived in Mediocre, NJ, I would have named it the Mediocre Consulting Group.

There is nothing wrong with naming your company after yourself. If you plan to solo consult, then it makes complete sense to use your name as your brand. There is nothing wrong with calling your company Jane Smith, Ltd. or Michael Thomas and Associates. These days nobody cares whether you have a cast of thousands, hundreds, or even if you're just working alone. It's about value. I wouldn't worry that your company name communicates that you're a solo practitioner, and of course it's easy to name a company after yourself, unless your last name is McKinsey, in which case you can't do that.

I would caution people on several fronts. One is, don't go crazy worrying about the URL address, the name of the company, search engine optimization, and everything else. Just call yourself something. If you go to my blog, my blog is called "contrarianconsulting.com" but the blog is Alan's Blog. We have "summitconsulting.com" for my company website, but again, that's not my brand. You can use tools like "namesecure.com." That enables anyone to type in "alanweiss.com" which most people would do just by default, and they're redirected to the website for Summit Consulting Group. That service costs about $49 a year. Nothing to it. Don't worry about protecting your company name or going crazy buying URLs held by others.

If people Google you or your company, they should find you because you have so much intellectual property out there that it increases the amount of content your name is associated with. We actually had a case on my Forum (alansforums.com) where one consultant asked to have another thrown off because his company used one word in its title that she used in her title. She said that since she had somehow protected the name of her company, others could not use the same word in the name of their companies. I told her she was out of her mind, and she eventually left in a huff. So, the moral from this is that you should pick a name, buy a URL, and create products. If someone chooses to copy you, be flattered. As long as you're providing the best service you can, you don't need to worry about another threatening your success. Also, buy stock in "huff" since so many people choose to leave in it.

Q: There is a school of thought that says you should say in the name of your company what you do. So, instead of saying, "Alan Weiss and Associates" you say, "Summit Consulting." What do you think about that?

Alan: You can have it either way. If you want to name your company using terms that have significance to you, but not to others, you can add a tag line that communicates your focus and values to prospective clients. There is nothing wrong with naming your company after your dog, but then you add the tag line, "Specialists in team building in global organizations." Even if your company has a specific name like Summit Consulting Group, there is nothing wrong with adding a tag line that says, "Improving human performance in service organizations."

Pick a name that you're comfortable with, but make sure it's not ridiculous. Some people choose a company name like "Successful Strategies on the Internet," and their email address and domain name become john.toland@ successfulstrategiesontheinternet.com. The chances of somebody misspelling that as they're typing it are huge. You want a company name that can be easily typed and to ensure that by mistyping it, you don't wind up on a porn site somewhere. Have a company name that's easy for people to remember; have a company name that you can use for the domain name; and make sure it's short enough to prevent possible errors in email.

Q: Once we have our company name, how do we get it out there in terms of a press kit? What is a press kit? When do I need it? And what should be in it?

Alan: I'm a fan of having a press kit. You might call this a presentation kit or a media kit. And I like to have them in both electronic format and hard copy. The contents are identical. A lot of people will argue you don't need anything in hard copy anymore, but I still meet a lot of buyers who like to put their feet up and flip through materials, kinesthetically bend it back, pull something out, and pass it to someone else. There is nothing expensive or unwieldy about having a press kit in both physical and electronic form.

A physical press kit should have a nice presentation folder which opens up and has two deep pockets inside and usually a die cut for a business card. Have your name, logo, and company name either printed or embossed on the outside. Try not to use a label that you stick on because it looks cheap. Have your contact information printed on the presentation folder itself, perhaps on the rear. Inside what you need is typical client results. One sheet labeled "Typical Client Results" should have a bulleted list of client outcomes. They don't have to be actual verbatim client results but more a summary of typical results people get from working with you.

Next, you should have testimonials. On your website and in your electronic press release, these can be video testimonials. In your physical press kit, testimonials should be written on client letterhead.

You should next have a page or two of case studies. A case study is three paragraphs consisting of the following:

> **Situation:** Here is what we encountered: for example, a company that was suffering from too much turnover in the field forces.

> **Intervention:** This is what we did: for example, we interviewed the field force, we interviewed customers, and we looked at comparable companies and found the factors for turnover.

> **Resolution:** This was the outcome: for example, we instituted these three changes which resulted in the drop from 30 percent turnover to 12 percent turnover which is below the industry average of 15 percent turnover.

You should include a biographical sketch. This isn't a résumé. It's a description of who you are, what you are, some of your credentials, and it can have some humor in it.

Next, you have your client list. Don't have four names and list "Sample Clients." People will know that you only have four clients. If you can list ten, twelve, or thirty clients, you should list them because it's impressive.

You should also include references, especially if you're new to the business. The more references you list, the less likely prospects are to contact them. If you're new to the business, here is a little trick. On a piece of letterhead or on a page of your website, you can fit the names, affiliations, and contact details for approximately 15 individuals—three rows across and five rows down on paper, or three columns across and five rows down on your website. If you list 15 references, the prospect is likely to contact none of them. If you just list three, the prospect is likely to contact all of them. I suggest listing 15, and therefore alleviating the need for anyone to be called.

You should also have in your press kit white papers—position papers that you've written that relate to your value proposition. You should have articles that have been published about you by third parties. Include interviews that have been done with you. If it's electronic, the interview might be an audio recording. If it's your physical press kit, it can be a transcription of that interview.

Those are the basic components of a press kit, and whether physical or electronic, it should be updated regularly. If you're engaged in speaking as a profession, you can enclose a list of your speaking topics and their results. You can also enclose a sample video and audio of some of your recent speeches.

Q: At what point does a website become critical?

Alan: You should have a website right from the outset. In our profession a website isn't a sales vehicle; it's a credibility vehicle. Despite the fact that I said a lot of people like to sit back and bend something physical over and take a look at it, I would say the majority of people I meet are searching for resources online, and more importantly, they can access this information on their iPhones, iPads, or PDAs .

Consequently, having at least a rudimentary website is imperative. You can have just three or four pages to start. Hire someone to do it for you. Don't try to design your own web presence, even if you're an expert in technology or web design.

By rudimentary, I mean the following: What you should have is a home page with typical client results, some testimonials, a photo, your value proposition, and so on. There should be a link to your full biographical sketch. Post or include links to white papers, position papers, or any articles that you have published. These will help establish your credibility.

From there, you can post the other components from your press kit or add additional materials and links. My website now is about 400 pages, but you only need a few to start. Remember, it's a site for credibility. When people hear of you, they'll go there first to check you out. You don't want to hit people in the face with a sales proposition; you want to establish credibility—that not only are you good, but hiring you will be beneficial to their organizations.

Q: Obviously, we want our websites to convey a professional image. What other aspects of our business contribute to creating a professional image to our customers?

Alan: Let's talk first about the image that you project when you're not physically present. Your website is often the main channel through which people will learn about you. And we've already discussed the importance of your physical press kit.

Next would be the outgoing message people hear when they reach your voicemail. First and foremost, it should be prompt and efficient. Callers shouldn't have to wait for seven rings. They shouldn't be told, "Please wait while we try to locate him." Be sure your voicemail is set to ring three times, at most, before your voicemail picks up. Have a very succinct outgoing message like, "Hi, this is Alan Weiss at Summit Consulting Group. Sorry I missed your call. Please leave a detailed message. I will get back to you within 90 minutes. Thank you."

Don't leave a quote of the day, "He who drops the pebble in the sand will soon see ripples in the trees." Don't tell people that you're sorry you can't talk to them because you're working with a client in Westchester on a deal to reroute the origins of the Hudson River. No one cares. Don't include details that aren't necessary. A voicemail message isn't an advertising billboard. Just quickly encourage them to leave a message, and then get back to them quickly. People will be happy.

When you're in front of a client, your physical appearance is what communicates the most about you. Your overall appearance should be polished. This may sound like a dress for success lesson, but powerful, successful people want to do business with other powerful, successful people, so you need to be sure to look the part. I tell everyone—both women and men—to have a $2,000 suit. Even if you run a more informal company, the first time you meet a buyer, you should wear a quality suit. After that you can dress down somewhat, although I always advise that you dress half a step above the buyer. If the buyer says, "We're casual," you dress business casual.

Never take out a 19-cent pen to take notes. Take out a Cartier pen, a Montblanc, or other writing instrument that communicates success. The fact that a buyer doesn't know you doesn't mean that he or she will immediately question your skill or abilities, but if you walk in there with a ratty computer bag instead of an expensive briefcase, and you pull out a leaky pen, you have a frayed collar, your shoes aren't shined, your hair isn't groomed, or your nails are dirty, you may be communicating something you don't intend. More than that, the buyer may decide not to work with you. I know I wouldn't.

These small details matter because the care you take in the details is indicative of the care and attention to detail you'll offer your clients. You also can't drive up to a client in a clunker. If you don't have a nice car, then rent a nice one for that day. You can rent nice cars for $39 per day these days. If you're traveling to an out-of-town client, you're going to rent a car anyway. Spend an extra $20 and get a better car.

When I got my very first Ferrari, a friend of mine said to me, "Now you've done it. You don't have any cars you can drive to a client." I said, "Are you kidding? I'm driving this Ferrari right into the visitor's lobby if I can." Sure enough, I drove it down to a division of Merck in New Jersey, parked it in the number one visitor space, and an executive vice president, whom I didn't know and didn't have the appointment with, said, "Is that your Ferrari?" I said, "Yes." He said, "I have a Testarossa. Would you step into my office for a minute and let's chat?" I got to know him, and I went on to do business with him. I went home and told my wife, "You see, another marketing investment." Now, three Ferraris, an Aston Martin, and four Bentleys later, I've made good marketing investments. People want to deal with successful people. So, it's incumbent upon you to demonstrate that success through your appearance until such time as you develop a solid relationship and your skills and success are realized.

Q: When they're first getting started, a lot of people have trouble prioritizing what they should use their money for. Help us understand what is critical.

Alan: If you're just starting out from scratch, you'll need about $12,000.

For about $12,000 you can equip your office with very excellent equipment and equip yourself with what you need to project a good image and to be efficient in your work. Here is what I would do. I would have that one excellent suit and a pair of shoes, and I would get myself a decent briefcase. Spend $300-400 on a really good briefcase.

Then, I would get the best computer that I could afford that would do the work for me. I'm a Mac guy; they're magnificent machines; and they're compatible with anything. If you want, you can simply get a good laptop and use that in a docking method with a larger screen for your desktop. But if you can, get a desktop computer and also use a laptop when you're on the road. Adjust to your needs. But somewhere, somehow, whether it's in your office or you carry it around, you're going to need a computer that's sufficient to allow you to write papers, write books if you're interested in going that route, track your finances, write client proposals, and interact with people via Skype around the world. You need that kind of computer capacity.

Invest in a very fast laser printer for your large text-only print jobs, as well as a color printer for when you need to print full-color documents. Get an excellent multiline phone: one line for your office line, and one line for your house line. Get a high-quality headset to use with it.

If you're going to accept credit cards, you'll need to set up a merchant account to process payments and have a credit card machine in your office. You can also get credit card software that will let you do this virtually on your computer or even iPhone.

Get a labeler, which costs next to nothing, so you can label your files and keep them in good order. Lastly, buy decent, inexpensive furniture. Clients aren't going to come to your office, so while the furniture needs to be functional, it doesn't need to be extravagant.

Q: In terms of the programs you offer, what do people tell you was the thing that really helped them get their careers started?

Alan: People need a coach from the outset. I suggest that people sign up for one of my programs as soon as they decide to go into consulting. You don't want to wait six months before you begin learning about how to create a successful business from others who have done it before you when you can have that knowledge from day one. There are a variety of different programs available. The Million Dollar Consulting® College covers everything from developing your image to acquiring business, delivering business, ethics, and life balance.

Through the Private Roster Mentor Program, people can work with me, or Master Mentors I've trained, as a coach. The program has two different levels and three programs available for each level, so you can select the program that's best for you.

In the Total Immersion program, I actually work one-on-one with consultants. In this business, you can reach plateaus too easily. It's not so black-and-white as to say you're achieving success or you aren't. Rather, it's like having a rheostat that's set too low and the light is too dim. What happens is you think you're bringing in business and achieving success, and you become comfortable and plateau. You don't journey off the plateau, you don't grow, and because of the laws of entropy, the plateau erodes and suddenly you find yourself on a downhill slope, and you can't recover. Having a source of support and advice—some external source to help provoke us and guide us—can go a long way in helping grow your business.

Q: What kind of insurance do I need to get started, and where should I get it?

Alan: Everyone should have medical insurance, life insurance, as well as renter's or home insurance. Specifically for consulting, you need the following: Malpractice insurance—technically referred to as E&O insurance, which stands for errors and omissions insurance—will cover you when a client feels you've given bad advice, they've suffered a loss, and they intend to sue you. Those suits have become more common in recent years, especially with large consulting firms. Some large consulting firms have been sued for millions of dollars by unhappy clients. E&O insurance is mandatory. If you find someone who tells you that you don't need it, walk away from them.

One thing you can do to protect your assets is to incorporate yourself, but you still need malpractice insurance to ensure that you're protected. In addition, many organizations will require proof of malpractice insurance before they hire you. It's a requisite for doing business with many major companies. The premiums for malpractice insurance are determined based on your volume of business. To get $1 million worth of coverage typically cost around $2,500. There are insurance brokers who specialize in this type of insurance.

Another type of insurance you need is liability insurance. Different from malpractice insurance, liability insurance protects you if you're conducting a workshop at a client's site or at a conference center offsite, and someone trips over the cord of your projector. That person's lawyer may sue the facility, the client, you, the person who made the cord, the person who made their shoes, and so forth. Liability insurance is inexpensive but will protect you in these types of unexpected, but potentially costly situations.

A third kind of insurance that I would certainly recommend, especially for new consultants, is long-term care and disability. Those are two separate policies. The reason to get long-term care insurance as soon as you decide to go into business for yourself is this: Long-term care is much less expensive if you sign up when you're young but goes up as you get older. However, it can be invaluable as you get older if you require full-time care but don't want to go to a nursing home or long-term care facility. This insurance provides for care at home.

Disability insurance is vital as well because you're much more likely to be disabled than you are to die in the consulting profession, and disability insurance ensures you'll keep your income even if you're unable to work. For a consultant, there are a couple of important things here. Number one is you need a policy that will provide replacement income until you're able to completely do your former job. In other words, some policies will only pay until you can do some job, which means if you can work at a library stamping books, they'll stop paying. Consultants should have the type of policy that will continue full coverage of your salary until you're able to go back to work full-time as a consultant with the travel that entails and the level of work that it entails. That's important.

The second factor is the waiting period. The longer the waiting period before coverage kicks in, the cheaper your premium. The shorter the waiting period, the higher your premium will be. You can certainly get individual policies, which are fairly expensive, but the younger you get it, the less expensive they are. You might also be able to get disability insurance through some consulting groups, although it's not very easy. I had mine for 30 years, and it's very important coverage for the security of your family.

Q: Should taking credit cards be a mandatory part of your tool kit?

Alan: It depends. I can think of few instances where you would never want to use a credit card, but on the other hand, there are many circumstances where accepting a credit card has its benefits. Somebody hiring you to speak at $7,500, $10,000, or $15,000 might have to put it on a credit card if you require payment up front.

I did an $18,000 project for the United States Air National Guard. They put $18,000 on a Visa, and they said to me, "If we put this through normal channels, and we produce a request, an invoice, your payment, and a voucher, it will be 90 days before this even begins to go through the system. On the other hand, we can put through two $9,000 charges on a special Visa card." I said, "Charge away." No pun intended to the military, but charge. If you're willing to set up a merchant account and accept credit cards, the average fee charged to you for processing credit card payments is about 2-3 percent.

I've had clients who want to charge a fairly substantial project for a variety of reasons. Some of them are privately held businesses, and the owner wants to get points on American Express to use for an air trip. Now, I feel that paying 2-3 percent for a credit card is the cost of doing business. I'm appalled when I'm in any kind of operation and they say the cash price is different from the credit card price. I don't like establishments or restaurants that tell me Visa and MasterCard only. We don't accept American Express. That's because American Express has a slightly higher interest rate, but the problem is a lot of people carry American Express and like to use it.

You can get a merchant account through your bank. American Express acts independently, but you can get Visa, MasterCard, and Discover through a solid banking relationship or through a third-party provider.

Your Dream Team

Q: Whom should you have on your dream team when you develop your consulting practice? What professional service providers do I need in place when starting my company versus when I've been in business for a while?

Alan: First off, you need a very good attorney who knows small business and professional services firms. That's a specialty. You don't want the attorney who closed on your house, might have drafted your will, or helped with some other kind of issue. You want an attorney who specializes in representing professional services/small business firms.

If you have a good legal firm, they might also have an attorney on staff who is a good trademark attorney, and you will need that eventually for your trademarks. I have one attorney who is a trademark attorney. I have another attorney who takes care of our estate. I have another attorney who is a litigator for when a business deal goes wrong. I have a host of different attorneys whom I use as the needs arise.

I have a bookkeeper who does my books on a monthly basis. She picks them up at my home, processes everything, creates computer spreadsheets, and then delivers the raw material back to me. That costs me about $250 a month at my level of business.

You'll also need a good tax firm. You'll need a payroll service, somebody like Paychex or ADT, which can electronically file your taxes by payroll and provide you with your salary checks, which is necessary now with the various tax laws on corporations. You should not be writing out checks to yourself except for expense reimbursement.

You'll need somebody who can do your larger-scale printing. This can be a franchise like Kinko's or Print Shops, which have very sophisticated production methods these days. You can even send your materials to them so that they're printed and ready for delivery or pick up in whatever city your client is in. They can also print booklets for you, sometimes even books.

You'll also need a graphic designer, somebody who can create a logo for you, and who can generate materials and dress them up so they look good. You might need a separate tech-savvy person who can work on your website and blog.

If you want someone to bounce ideas off, identify somebody who has done what you're doing very successfully and also serves as a coach or a mentor, but it can't be somebody who simply serves as a coach or mentor. It has to be somebody who has been there and done that. If you want to learn how to write a book and get one published commercially, find someone who has done it a dozen times, not somebody who just knows the theory.

Q: What are your guidelines in terms of selecting these professionals?

Alan: I use three criteria. The first is I try to get a reference from someone who has used them. That saves me a lot of footwork and a lot of due diligence.

Next, I want to see evidence of their work. In the case of a graphic designer or a web person, they have portfolios. Even an accountant can show samples of spreadsheets they set up or samples of things they put together. For a lawyer it might have to be a question of references.

The third thing I look for is chemistry. I want to meet them and talk to them, just as I would to a buyer, and I basically want to ask myself, "Can I trust this person? Will I accept feedback from this person? Will they accept feedback from me? How do I feel about them?" That's very important.

Q: What are some of the various kinds of support consultants need?

Alan: The first one I want to mention is you need an intimate support network. That can be a spouse, a significant other, family member, good friends. The most important thing for consultants, especially starting out— but also at all stages in their careers—is to have a loving, affectionate, and intimate support system. That's because this job is about rejection. It's about factors that we can't control, such as the economy and technology and so forth. It's about surprises. We have to know when we have legitimately done a good job. We have to know when we have legitimately blown it. We have to know when something bad has happened that wasn't our fault.

Second is the support of a professional community. One of my trademarks is The Architect of Professional Communities®. I create professional communities and am successful at it because they're needed. People want to be able to connect with others, but they want to connect with others within parameters. There has to be an arbiter. There has to be a benevolent dictator. There can't just be anarchy. It can't be blindly egalitarian. You want to be part of a community where there are standards where there is somebody to whom you can appeal things, where there is an overarching voice to ensure the information being shared within the community is accurate and beneficial.

A mentor has to be a trusted advisor. If you're going to someone who is a trusted advisor whom you use as a sounding board, you go to them as someone who can give you feedback, who can be candid and honest with you, not a therapeutic one but on a professional basis. That might be for free or for a fee.

In some of my workshops, I require that people create accountability partners. If you go this route, choose someone with whom you have a reciprocity, with whom you have a good working chemistry, and to whom you're willing to be accountable. This has proved to be very effective. The danger here is to make sure that the person you choose challenges you and that you, in turn, challenge them because with accountability partners, if you're not careful, it can easily turn into a relationship of commiseration. It can become, "Hey, it's okay you didn't do it, neither did I. We were both busy."

Mastermind groups are very beneficial, but let me say two things about them: The conventional wisdom is that you should never be the smartest person in the mastermind group. That's fine, but let's face it. *Somebody* has to be in that role, and if it's you, that doesn't necessarily mean you're not taking something away from that interaction. I also think mastermind groups should always sunset. They should last for four months, six months, or even a year, but there should be some point at which they sunset and you find a new, different group.

If you want really first-class, excellent help, you pay for it; and you need to get into that mindset right away. You can't expect people to help you for free. This isn't a public service. And I'll tell you something else. I would think of the team as an action team rather than a dream team because dream teams can become nightmares.

Conclusion

Too often, beginning consultants make decisions that haunt them through-out their careers. They don't associate with other like-minded professionals and make good decisions about how to set up their businesses, or they seek advice and direction from those who aren't capable of offering it.

Experienced consultants can fall victim to their own complacency when they hit a plateau and don't know how to move off it. These people overlook the resources that could help them move to the next level of success.

At pivotal points in building your business, you'll want to reassess the way you're doing business—the way you're building or maintaining your infrastructure. This sort of examination does two things. It helps to spring-board your business, and it helps you build a house that you want to live in—both figuratively and metaphorically.

Building a Brand

4

In this chapter we pursue the topic of building a brand, with the ultimate brand being your name. We'll explore what a brand is and isn't, the value proposition, and methods for capitalizing on your brand once you've built it.

Brand Identification

Q: What is your definition of a brand, and why do I need one?

Alan: A brand is a uniform representation of quality. You don't need to establish yourself as a brand in most professions. But in consulting, you need a brand if you're going to have a successful business. There are only two ways to acquire business: You go out and get it, or people come to you, which is the marketing gravity I talk about.

Having a great brand is essential to creating marketing gravity because people are attracted to consistent representations of quality. If somebody says, "Alan Weiss is absolutely the best strategy consultant you'll ever find," that third party will be more likely to go with that recommendation. They might briefly go to my website—and we have established already that a website is a credibility factor—and they'll find all kinds of credibility, but they'll come to me asking how we might work together. When they do, having an established brand immediately removes all need to prove myself, and it can diminish all fee sensitivity.

Changing that dynamic and altering that relationship where, instead of soliciting business and having to prove how good I am, clients come to me— that is the leverage a brand can provide. Whether the brand is based on your intellectual property, a particular system or model, or your name—having a brand recognized for quality products or services is important.

Q: How do I come up with my own powerful brand?

Alan: It's a confluence of three factors. Take a look at the greatest market need you're trying to satisfy, whether it already exists or you're creating it is irrelevant; take your greatest competency in meeting that need; and take your greatest passion. Where those three factors converge, that really is your starting point for defining your brand.

You can start other places. You can start with a unique idea; a piece of intellectual property; even your value proposition. One woman, Nancy Freedman, has a brand called "Telephone Doctor®." It's a marvelous brand. A lot of people don't even know it's Nancy Freedman, but anyone who works in telemarketing or with call centers knows Telephone Doctor. That's an example of very effective branding.

Q: What are some of the ideas to strengthen and nurture my brand?

Alan: In my view, there are only three steps to brand creation. The first is to develop a brand—that is, you define and create it—which we just briefly discussed. The second is to nurture and grow it. The third is to establish brand equity, which is where you cash in on it.

An extreme example of brand equity is when somebody buys a Ferrari watch. The watch has the Ferrari logo on it, it sells for a few thousand dollars, but it's made by who knows? Ferrari doesn't know a thing about making watches, but it knows a great deal about licensing the equity it has in its brand. People say you're the Ferrari of the photo business. You're the Ferrari of the florist business, indicating speed, sleekness, appeal, and so forth. Brand equity is very important as the final stage.

To successfully grow and nurture your brand, you must make it a part of everything you do; get it in front of people through as many channels as possible and on a continual basis. You should include the brand in everything you write and speak about. You should write white papers or position papers that have your brand in the title. You should have your brand prominently displayed on your website. You should have a blog with the same name as your brand where you blog about your business and your brand. That's how people will start repeating it, and that's how you make sure that somebody else can't easily supplant you.

Q: Can you articulate the importance of the "you are the brand" concept?

Alan: It's very simple. It's one thing for someone to say, "Find me a great technology strategist," and that search results in five names. You can argue that that's a very powerful position if you're one of those five. But it pales next to the following statement: "Get me Alan Weiss." You want people to know you by name, rather than as a consultant in a particular field, because that precludes any competition. And that provides a tremendous advantage to your business.

Q: What can we learn from some of the larger corporations and how they build and strengthen their brands?

Alan: Ironically, if you're talking about implementing and applying lessons, some of the lessons are counterintuitive. Some companies have actually changed their brand to match what the consumers are doing. For example, FedEx started as Federal Express, but people kept calling it FedEx. Finally, Fred Smith and his management said, "Wait a minute. Why do we keep calling ourselves Federal Express if our customers are calling us FedEx?" And they legally changed the name of the company. Similarly, International Business Machines became IBM.

People forever have been using duct tape as an all-purpose tool, which was traditionally a plumber's tape used to seal leaks on pipes. But it has a marvelous diversity of uses, and some people just called it duck tape dropping the "t." One enterprising company changed and named their brand of tape "duck tape" and put a duck on the label.

The biggest lesson for consultants—especially newer ones that don't have a strong brand—is as you hear people sing you praises, as you hear clients provide accolades, listen to what they say about you, and you might find that's where the real secret of a great brand resides. If somebody says, for example, "She is a hierarchical strategist" or "What he did is wonderful. He is a committee builder," listen to what they say.

If you hear the feedback repeatedly from various sources, then there may be something to it. There is a reason the phrase is catching in people's cerebral cortex. And most likely they're not unique. That's a great way, and one of the few ways by the way, you can take your present client experience and transfer it to prospect expectation.

Q: What can we do to distinguishing ourselves from others in our field and stand out in a crowd? How can our brand help us do that?

Alan: Anything you do should be leveraged. When you look at your brand and say, "How do I leverage it? What are the obvious ways?" one is that it will lead you to a book deal. The stronger your brand, the more likely a publisher will be interested in publishing a book about it. When you're a thought leader—when your brand is well known and is quoted and cited by others—then it's easier to get a book published about it.

It's easier to get speaking engagements when your brand is strong. I have gotten two calls just in the past week from people who said, "You know, we read *Million Dollar Consulting*. We think it applies to our firm. We think this is the strongest brand in the field in terms of what we're trying to do." Speaking assignments will come much more easily.

You also find that you can raise your fees significantly. I talk and write extensively about how fee follows value until the lines cross. At the point where those lines cross, that's where your brand really starts to be powerful and can be leveraged. (The lines cross where fee stops following value and perceived value actually follows brand power.) That's a transition point at which value follows fee.

When your brand is strong, you have to do two things. You have to leverage it, and you have to make sure it stays strong by continuing to pump intellectual property into the community so that your intellectual capital is constantly manifested as intellectual property that other people can pragmatically use.

Q: How did you decide it was time for you to increase your fees? Was it a noticeable increase in brand recognition? Was it other factors?

Alan: It was several things. One is the fact that I wanted to create real wealth, which is discretionary time. The best way to do that is to earn more money while spending less time doing it. So, instead of conducting three workshops that are about $450 each—which is what I was charging early on in my career—I conducted one workshop that is $5,000 per person.

If you go into an organization at the top—working with executive-level management, working on strategic initiatives—you can always go down the ladder, train the front-line supervisors, and go back up again. But if you work with an organization at the human resource or training level, there isn't an executive in the company that's going to hire you to work with them on strategy. So, it all depends on how your brand is originally perceived.

How much you're able to charge for speaking while still filling a room can serve as a metric of how you're doing, how you're perceived, and how strong your brand is. At the workshops I conducted in Las Vegas, over 40 people paid $5,000 each to attend. I conducted that same workshop with smaller groups in Sydney and London. There is not an inverse relationship between volume and price if you're providing great quality.

I've also found that as the lines cross, you begin to attract people more and more. My Thought Leadership conference held every October costs $12,000 to attend but is just about filled by July. Maximum attendance allowed is 16 people. I'll not take more.

I'm doing something called "Alan 101" in Denver. I had another meeting in Denver anyway, and a couple of local groups were sponsoring me. I was doing something pro bono for them so I said, "I'll do this program the day before, and I'll just charge $450, my rates from ten years ago, giving newcomers and consultants who might not be able to afford the more expensive workshops a chance to attend." I could put probably 50 or 60 people in there, and right now I have 25. This is probably their one chance to see me at that kind of a rate. Yet there is a perceived value associated with a higher cost, which leads some to believe that if something is too cheap, it really doesn't have much worth. It's important to test your market, know your worth, and increase your prices to match the value you're delivering.

Q: Can we offer some things that the client might consider a commodity, such as time management training, and still hold ourselves up to be an expert or thought leader?

Alan: There are people who have done this—one-trick ponies. But companies don't really hire people for that anymore. Buyers are interested in results. If you think of time management, the real question is, "Can you really manage time, and why do you want to do it?" The answer really is you want more discretionary time, which means working backwards.

If your goal is to spend more time on private pursuits with your family or loved ones, your work has to be less labor intensive. That's why offering services that promote life balance rather than time management is so much more powerful, plus it's so much less of a commodity. You see life coaches today, for better or for worse, doing very well. You don't see time management coaches doing well.

Q: What feedback would we get from the client that we're offering a commodity? What would be the indicators?

Alan: There are three or four tests for a commodity. First, ask yourself, are you promising an input not an output? Time management is an input, whereas life balance is an output.

Next, if the client can easily compare your service to that of another, it's almost always a commodity. If the client says, "There are three other programs like this," or "There are four other people coaching like that," then you know you have a commodity. Whereas, if the client says to you, "You're talking about wealth as discretionary time? I'm not sure I've ever heard that. Tell me more," that's an output.

Last, if you find that there is great price sensitivity, you're probably delivering a service that's easily comparable to something else, and your clients are looking at it as a price-based commodity purchase. Those are some indicators that you have a commodity. The basic thing is you ask yourself, "Am I talking about something I'm doing?" or "Am I talking about some salutary outcome, some improved condition for someone else?"

Q: You have multiple brands: The Consultant's Consultant, The Contrarian, and The Million Dollar Consultant. Do you advise consultants to create multiple brands, or is there a danger of diluting the brand if I create too many?

Alan: It depends. It's like the novelty act of spinning plates on rods. You can put more plates on top of more rods and start spinning them. The gyroscopic effect will keep them spinning, but the more plates you start spinning, the more plates you have to keep spinning. The question is how many plates can you keep spinning without any wobbling or falling?

You can have one umbrella brand and other brands beneath it, or you could have a variety of different brands that are completely independent of each other because you do many different things. I don't think that more brands are necessarily better, but I think that a good consultant, in addition to having a main brand which bears his or her name, can have several other brands as well. You just have to be sure that you can manage and support those brands.

Q: What have you seen your mentorees do to damage their brands?

Alan: The most damaging thing that they do is deliver lousy work. Some don't fulfill promises or make promises that they can't keep. Others are sloppy in their appearance or in their performance. Still others alienate their clients. Poor work of one stripe or another is the most common cause of damaging one's brand.

A brand can also be damaged by diluting it. You can't be all things to all people.

Right now the jury is still out as to whether Mercedes, which is selling its top-end cars right now at about $350,000 and its very bottom-end car is probably around $30,000, can really sustain the quality of the Mercedes brand. In my opinion, and I've owned Mercedes continually since 1978 in one form or another, I think Mercedes has diluted its brand. I think evidence of this is, up until a year ago or so, they were trying to sell a car at $450,000 and the car did not sell. You can dilute a brand by stretching too far at either end, and I think Mercedes is an example of that right now. So, if a company that strong, powerful, and global can do it, it can happen to anyone.

Q: If you have damaged your brand, is there a way to recover from that damage and go on to become a strong brand?

Alan: The Tylenol scare reinforced the brand. It didn't damage it. Because what Tylenol did, even though what happened was not its fault—the tampering—Tylenol immediately took responsibility, accountability, and didn't try to back away.

Where Exxon took a terrible blow with the Exxon Valdez accident, where British Petroleum is taking a critical hit and lost $30 billion in market value with the leak in the Gulf of Mexico, Tylenol came out of it stronger than ever. Since then, J&J which owns Tylenol has had some problems because there have been some internal J&J scandals, and they're changing top executives to try to clean house as we speak.

The ability to acknowledge a crisis, an error, or problem, and take accountability for it and try to fix it is what can't only help a brand recover but also improve the reputation of a brand. After all, a brand isn't about perfection. A brand is about a uniform representation of quality, and that means a part of quality is recovering from damage.

The Value Proposition

Q: When working with consultants, how do you help them discover and express their value propositions?

Alan: Usually with a machine gun. It's amazing how difficult this simple process is. People aren't attuned to thinking in terms of output. They're attuned to thinking in terms of input, cash, and deliverables. What I tell them is this: Picture your typical client—it could be an existing one or one you hope to have in the future. Picture your typical client, your competencies, and the need you're filling.

Your value proposition is about competency, need, and passion. After you walk away from that client, after you shake hands and disengage, ideally how is that client better off? How would you put that in a sentence? That sentence not only informs the prospect of what to expect—that is, what is in it for him or for her—it informs your behavior. When I read someone's value proposition, I ask myself, "If I were the buyer, would this prompt me to want to learn more about this person?"

If somebody said, "I run strategic retreats," which is a deliverable, it doesn't compel me to learn more. A lot of people run retreats. So does every professor in a business school. But if someone said, "I help you develop strategies that dramatically increase market share in the short term," I might be inclined to say, "How do you do that?" That's the difference between focusing on input and output.

You want to stimulate somebody to say, "How do you do that?" or "Tell me more about it." Or even say, "I'm skeptical that you can do that" because skepticism and objection are signs of interest.

Q: How is a value proposition different from "the unique selling proposition"?

Alan: It's not. It's just another way of putting it. The value proposition or the USP must be framed in terms of an improved buyer condition. A unique selling proposition isn't "Buy this camera. It has 14 different lens settings." It's "Our camera will provide you with memories you'll never forget." Nobody buys a drill because of the attributes of the drill. People buy drills because they want holes. The USP has to be around the same attribute as a value proposition, which is an outcome.

Q: Can you trademark a value proposition?

Alan: GE's motto used to be, "Progress is our most important product." You can't use something like that. It belongs to somebody else. But it's okay to have a value proposition that's similar to someone else's as long as it's a good value proposition, and it accurately represents you.

Your value proposition needs to be different from the generic. It needs to be sufficiently interesting so the prospect says, "Hmm, I'd like to know more." It can't be "unique" because there is nothing new under the sun in that regard.

Q: In your Shameless Promotion Workshops, you encourage consultants to develop what you call the "mega value proposition." How does this differ from a garden-variety value proposition?

Alan: In Shameless Promotion I help people become absolutely, if not over the top, right on top. Most people I work with have effective value propositions because they've worked with me for quite a while, but they don't have dynamite value propositions. I try to get people to talk about themselves in terms in which they wouldn't normally talk about themselves. I help them apply adjectives like "dramatic" and "exponential" to describe themselves so they can create more enthusiasm on the part of a listener.

Q: How does the value proposition differ from an "elevator speech"?

Alan: A value proposition is an intelligent way to go to market. An elevator speech is one of the most ineffective things in the world. An elevator pitch is stereotypically two minutes of what you do with benefits, features, and why the other party should do it. Nobody wants to hear that these days. Nobody. What the sophisticated among us do is develop trusting relationships by providing value, not pitches.

Q: What mistakes do you see consultants make when they write their value propositions?

Alan: The biggest problem with a value proposition is that people incorporate their methodology in it because that's their default position. Whenever you see a preposition such as "by" or "through," you know that methodology is ahead. They try to be too detailed: "We improve telemarketing performance by focusing on accurate telephone descriptors, acknowledging objection early, and teaching people never to leave messages." I teach consultants to avoid those prepositions and focus on outcomes.

Q: Why is it that people find it so difficult to transform their thinking from input to output?

Alan: I've given a lot of thought to this. I've been asked the question a gazillion times, and I'm pretty sure I know the answer. We've been inculcated in school, work, and even our homes to focus on input-based interactions. From the time we're young, we become inured with performing tasks. We're graded on tasks. We're rewarded for tasks. The first disciplinary experiences most of us have, outside of the home at least, are what our teachers reinforce: Stand in line; stand in height order; don't talk in the hall; keep your work area neat; don't run. Virtually everything, I mean probably 98 percent, was focused on input. We even learned by rote. We learned the alphabet by rote. We learned multiplication tables by rote.

That's an input-based relationship. A transaction. So, by the time we get out of school and into secondary school and then even into college, the same mindset prevails.

How to Capitalize on Your Value

Q: What are the distinctions a consultant must make to be considered an expert and a thought leader and not a commodity?

Alan: The question is what is different about a duck? And the answer to that is you really don't know, unless you say, "Compared to what?" Your brand is being established because you're pumping intellectual property into your constituent communities. You must be speaking, writing, and publishing articles and blogs, as well as being cited as an expert in articles. People who don't agree with you must still know who you are and take issue with things you have said.

Those are all signs of thought leadership, and thought leadership can be transient. For example, Warren Bennis did some seminal work on leadership 30 years ago, and I think everything he has done since has been derivative. Conversely, until the day he died, Peter Drucker continued to produce new intellectual property.

Q: Can you reverse engineer for us the process of creating a self-fulfilling prophecy and how you've created your own?

Alan: You have to increase the size of your blip on other people's radar screens. I'll give you a very simple example. I have participants do an exercise in my Shameless Promotion Workshops. In the exercise, you create your peers. Imagine a group of peers who are at the level you wish to be. Consider how they got there. What would you need to do in order to be at that level?

In my own life, I realized that Marshall Goldsmith in coaching, Marcus Buckingham in personal growth, Jeff Gitomer in sales, and David Maister in small business growth were really the thought leaders in their particular fields the same as I am in solo consulting. We were all on the same plane. We're different people, but there are certain similarities you can pick out quickly. We all write books. We all speak. We're all engaged in some controversial, contrarian, provocative kind of positions.

I just finished *Mojo* by Marshall Goldsmith. It's amazing how frequently the two of us agree on things but use starkly different examples. For example, I talk about abandoning business to be able to reach out, and most of you have heard me speak about that for 20 years. Marshall talks about subtraction. Getting things out of your life so that you can put more things in. It's essentially the same thought but arrived at by two different thinkers in two different ways.

Q: What is "the wow factor," and what creates it?

Alan: I would say it's the ability to provide people with an immediate but pragmatic way to improve their lives. One example of this would be the process of instantiation I regularly talk about—the process of taking the intangible and making it tangible, or for our purposes, taking intellectual capital and turning it into intellectual property that can be immediately utilized by someone else. I'm not referring to a feel-good, self-help book or a business autobiography. In his own book, Lee Iacocca showed us how he saved Chrysler. That doesn't help me because I'm not trying to save Chrysler. What I'm referring to is the ability to create something that transforms people; that makes them say, "Whoa, I can use that."

Another example is the one percent solution—improve by one percent a day, and in 70 days you're twice as good. I believe that I provide people with that one percent. Some people tell me it's four percent, but I'm not shooting for the sky here; one percent is fine. People often stop me in workshops, seminars, speeches, and even in random conversation. They say, "Wait a minute. Can you repeat that?" I often think that's an "Aha" moment. If you can make someone feel that, that's how you know you have the wow factor.

Either the other person's condition is immediately improved or they know it's about to be improved if they put your lessons to work. It's when I say, "Listen, you're facing conflict and tomorrow when you go into work, here is how you resolve that conflict: Separate out whether it's about objectives or alternatives." If you provide good, effective advice, they're going to say, "Wow, I was just lost there. Now I have a tool to use." It's the same phenomenon just experienced in different ways.

Q: As we see nearly every day, some brands get destroyed in a crisis, but other brands are actually created through a crisis because of the way that leaders respond. Can you give us specific examples of using a setback to build your brand?

Alan: Somebody said, "Give me a good crisis any day, or never waste a good crisis." Apple could have suffered a crisis with claims of lost calls on its newly launched iPhone 4. Instead, they addressed the claim, suggested a reason why some people may be experiencing this problem, and offered a free case that would resolve the problem. Their solutions—putting a case on the phone or holding it a slightly different way—took care of the problem completely. There are different ways to handle a crisis, as long as you acknowledge it and get in front of it.

Most consultants will face a crisis at one time or another involving a client. For example, a consultant in my mentor program, who is very, very good, called me and said, "I made a mistake with a client. My fault. Because of that, they were late with something which could cost them money." He asked, "What do you think I should do?" I said, "Get in front of it. Say to him, 'Look. You're right. It was my fault. I wish you would have reminded me of your deadline, but it wasn't incumbent upon you to remind me of it; it was incumbent upon me to know.'"

Once you acknowledge your role, the question to ask is, "What can I do to rectify this situation?" The answer is usually less than what you would otherwise offer. I reminded him of Churchill's famous dictum: "Success is never final, and failure is seldom fatal. It's courage that counts." When you face a crisis, get in front of it, be courageous, be bold, be strong, and this too shall pass. If you handle it, you'll be a better person for it.

Q: How do we recover if someone damages our brand?

Alan: If you had a fire, what would you throw on the fire to put it out? The first thing would be water. But if it were a grease fire, water would make it much worse. You have to be very careful. If somebody is slandering you, saying derogatory things, or has cast you with a negative brand, you have to be careful not to throw water on a grease fire. Let it go away. The odds are the other person doesn't have a strong brand, and they're trying to bring you down to their level for whatever kind of psychological reasons.

There is a competitor who blogs about me from time to time. This happens a few times per year—people try to take me on unilaterally on their blogs. I call this being blog-bushed, you know, ambushed. They want to be able to say, "I took a shot at the Million Dollar Consultant," or "I bested Alan Weiss." And they're saying it to the 60 people who read their blogs. Of course, the last thing I would do is respond publicly, giving them 60,000 or more readers.

You have to first understand what kind of fire you have. Not all remedies are good for all kinds of fires. Think of it in terms of a fire and fire extinguisher. Fire extinguishers are categorized by the letters A, B, or C, depending on the class of fire they put out. Some extinguishers can be used on a variety of different types of fires but aren't as effective as the extinguishers that are dedicated to one particular class of fire. You have to make sure your response to a fire will douse the flames.

If the commentary is slanderous or libelous, then it's best to have an attorney send a letter. I've found that puts a quick end to the attack. Most people don't have the resources to do battle legally. They just want to try to be a fly in the ointment.

Q: Some brands, once damaged, never recover. Others recover and even become stronger. Summarize the key practices and lessons about refreshing, renewing, and reenergizing your brand.

Alan: Your brand has to evolve and adapt to the times. For example, The Coca-Cola Company has created and launched new products. It created New Coke, which didn't work. But Diet Coke is the second highest-selling cola—second to Coke. It now has Coke Zero. But if you want to grow your brand, you have to be willing to try things, and you can't be afraid to fail.

As economies, technologies, and societies evolve, your brand has to evolve along with them. For example, in a global economy your brand can't be strictly domestic.

If you look at advances in technology, your brand has to adapt to the changes that take place there as well or else be seen as outdated. Not only do you need to have an online presence and offer your products or services online, but you also need to provide free content on your blog, connect with your clients through social networks, and update your website regularly.

Economically, your brand has to evolve consistently with what you want it to be in changing economies.

Q: What are some tips about how consultants can better differentiate themselves?

Alan: The most important thing about differentiation is that you first have to look at how you plan, define, and differentiate yourself through your clients' or your prospects' eyes. Consider the person listening to or reading it; who your very highest potential prospects are; and ask yourself what would most effectively differentiate you from others in your field in their eyes? Then work backwards to create that.

Q: What role does creativity play in branding?

Alan: Creativity is the ongoing development of new ideas either from scratch or based on the recombination of existing ideas. Innovation is applied creativity. Creativity is the birth act, if you will; it's the gestation; and it's the delivery. But innovation is the pragmatic application of that creativity.

Many people assume that creativity is some kind of blessing from the muse, that inspiration strikes you like lightening hitting a tree in a field during a thunderstorm. The fact of the matter is that creativity can be an organized event—you can make yourself more creative. There are techniques you can use. And while some people have the native abilities and predispositions to be more creative than others, a major part of it is a learnable skill, and I've seen people learn it.

For example, what if you had a fishing fleet, and the fishing fleet was catching a lot of fish, but because of storms or strikes at the dock, they couldn't always get all of their catch back fresh in time to get it to all the restaurants. Even though they were catching so many fish, they were only able to sell about 60 percent of what they caught; consequently, their profit margins were really slammed. What would you advise them to do?

Reverse the situation. Be creative. Stop worrying about taking the fish to the people and ask yourself, "How can I bring people to the fish?" Maybe you establish these large floating restaurants. Perhaps you establish your own chain of large restaurants right on the dock, and people come to the edge of the water to eat.

There are all kinds of issues like this. There is a famous case of a consultant, Russ Ackoff, who encountered a system of buses in London where there was a conductor in charge of collecting the fares on the bus. The problem was that the bus stopped so frequently, and so many people got on and off, that the conductors couldn't get to everybody.

The company came up with solutions like placing two conductors on the bus; but then it was confusing, and it doubled the cost of payroll for that position. They suggested having fewer buses. They suggested taking a longer route. What Ackoff proposed was to station the conductor on the sidewalk at the entrance of the bus rather than on the bus. As people lined up to get on the bus, the conductors collected the fares. Brilliant.

That's what creativity is about. That's how good consultants solve major problems for clients who tend not to think creatively because they're bogged down with day-to-day operations, meeting goals, and increasing margins.

How do you organize creativity? This is more than just a creative spark. One process I call "reversal" refers to the counterintuitive. You ask, "Okay, how do I reverse the situation I have here?" In other words, instead of the officer giving direction to the cars, how would the cars give direction to the officer? Maybe there is not a good answer for that, but if you apply the technique with discipline, you'll find good answers a lot of the time. But if you don't understand the process and don't apply it with discipline, then you'll never get that kind of good answer. (Many emergency services equipment have a mechanism to change traffic lights in their favor.)

There are a few things that block creativity, and one is a poor experiential base. The more you read, travel, and interact with others, the more stimuli you have. Creativity is dependent on stimuli. If you didn't have some kind of experiential base, you don't have a knowledge base to draw from when looking for option, answers, or new ideas.

You also need self-esteem. You can't be afraid of failing. You can't be afraid of someone saying, "That's the stupidest thing I've ever heard of."

Maybe it is. So what? It doesn't matter. On the one hand you have to have the cognitive input, and then on the other you need the self-assurance that you can deal with it, express it to others, and test it.

Q: What are some key practices you observe in highly creative people?

Alan: Highly creative people tend to keep trying. Things fail. They fail. But then bang, something hits. They keep trying. They don't keep a won/loss record. They don't keep track of their percentages. They don't look at it as passing and failing. They just keep trying, and most of them sooner or later will hit it; some more frequently than others, but it doesn't matter.

Most creativity isn't based on new knowledge. It's based on recombinations of existing knowledge, existing products, existing services, and that which is around you in the environment. You must have the ability to see various combinations and applications that others don't. If the combinations are the input side, the applications are the output side.

You need to see applications that make sense. One example of such application is the need for affordable transportation to and from airports. Limos are too expensive, and buses to the airport are too infrequent, so companies started these shuttle van services where people could share the ride to the airport. It doesn't cost as much, but the van driver still makes good money.

You need boldness. You can't be easily dissuaded. You can't be reliant on peer pressure or normative sanctions. You have to be willing to stand out in a crowd and try new things. If you're not willing to do that, then you're too conservative to be creative.

Q: Is creativity always an individual property, or is there such a thing as collaborative creativity or teamwork creativity?

Alan: Studies have shown that heterogeneous teams are more productive and innovative than homogenous teams. My Ph.D. dissertation was based on the fact that with three Fortune 500 companies I used, behavioral predisposition determined innovation. I used a variety of psychometric tests, supervisor evaluations, and people's performance to posit that if you hired people based on first evaluating behavioral predisposition, you could stimulate a more innovative environment. But what I wound up proving was exactly the opposite. I found that no matter what one's behavioral dispositions, *innovation and creativity on the job were a direct function of one's immediate manager and the environment.*

Q: Do you ever use your client's work as a laboratory for your own IP development and the acceleration of your own creativity?

Alan: I use my entire life and experiences to influence my creativity and fuel innovation. I'll watch my dogs and come up with a new idea. I'll watch how the gardeners outside approach the lawn as the seasons change, and I'll get a new idea. I'll watch the difference between a heron and an egret—two birds that operate in very different manners—on the pond hunting fish, and I'll draw a conclusion. This sort of stimuli can feed creativity.

Conclusion

To improve your success, take those things that could be commodity based out of your marketing toolkit. Instead, put them in the methodology section of the proposal. We all need methodology, techniques, tools, and interventions. These should play a role in the options that we provide clients, but these should never be part of the original conversation.

Remember, when marketing—be diagnostic; when delivering—be prescriptive. Methodologies don't belong in initial conversations, and they certainly don't belong in your marketing plan. Building your brand depends on making yourself a scarce resource, not a readily available commodity.

5 | Marketing Your Business

Once you've defined and created your brand, you have to make sure you get it in front of people, and get it in front of them frequently. That means that during your speaking, in your collateral, in the course of your networking, in informal conversations, on your website, and in your newsletter, you're promoting your brand.

If you have a lot of intellectual property out there, your brand may already be very well known. But if you're only getting started in consulting, your brand will not be known. To start, you'll need to understand what marketing is, why you need to do it, how to generate marketing gravity, and how you can market shamelessly.

What *Is* Marketing?

Q: Could you explain what marketing looks like for a solo consultant? People often use the terms "sales" and "marketing" in the same breath. How should consultants manage these two functions of their business?

Alan: Marketing creates need, and sales is the ability to fulfill that need. If you're a solo practitioner, you have to perform both functions but treat them separately. The more effective you are at marketing, the more people will be drawn to you. The more attraction you create, the less of a factor your fee or credentials will play in the decision-making process and the more people want to work with you. Superb marketing can obviate the need for very aggressive selling.

The reason that's true in our profession is that it's not a commodity-driven industry. We're not selling consumer products. Let's say that your brand is Samsung or Sony—the primary manufacturers of 3D TVs. Even though your brand's reputation may be strong, there is a greater level of competition with other strong brands. But in our business, we're not selling something so easily compared. We're not selling screen size, price, or delivery date.

Q: What lessons can we learn from large companies about how to market and sell our services?

Alan: A solo practitioner or a boutique firm owner should be spending more time on marketing than sales. I don't think you want to learn from large companies because most large companies don't do it well, or the ones which do it fairly well aren't at all like us. Some companies, like Proctor & Gamble, actually want to create competition internally among their own product managers and sales force for shelf space. For a commodity company, that strategy may be effective, but in our case it wouldn't work.

The beauty of what we do as solo practitioners is that we determine how we spend our time. Consequently, if you look at the amount of time you spend on sales and marketing, about 90 percent of that time should be spent on marketing and only 10 percent on sales because the sales part—the 10 percent—is reaching out to prospects. You have to tell people how good you are, but the gravity part brings people coming to you, and that lowers both your cost of acquisition as well as the need to prove yourself. That's why a website, by the way, is a credibility statement, not a sales tool.

Q: Do you find that it's easier to teach people to market than to sell?

Alan: No, because it's equally hard to teach either. The problem is that most people are never taught this stuff. Some people have more of a natural inclination towards marketing and sales than others, but it's not something most consultants, speakers, trainers, facilitators, or coaches naturally pick up.

Some people are more assertive. Some people are less patient, which is actually an advantage. Some people are more persuasive.

Q: You often say that we're in the marketing business, but how do you advise people to balance that reality with the other demands of sales, delivery of services, life balance, and everything else involved in running a business?

Alan: Everyone is in the marketing business, but not everyone is in the sales business.

Although not all marketing will lead to sales, marketing is the most important, essential function of your business. No matter how great your expertise, if people can't find you, your business won't thrive.

We have to get rid of the bromides and the rubrics in our lives that tell us we can't be marketing while we're delivering. This is nonsense formulated by people who found they couldn't do it themselves and is called transference. If I can't ski down a black diamond hill, then I tell you that you can't either, or else I believe I'm inferior to you. So, I advise you not to even try it.

There are two types of marketing gravity. There is active gravity, when you're networking and actually doing something in the moment. There is passive gravity as well, and that's anything that's in place and attracting people without any further attention from you, such as an article, blog post, or a product people have bought from you.

Many people sign up for my programs because they've read one of my books. Too many consultants are in feast or famine cycles. They'll get four pieces of business, stop all marketing, and when the fourth piece of business runs out, they suddenly look around and realize they have no business.

I met with a consultant not too long ago who joined my mentor program. The prior year she had done $450,000 worth of business. I asked her, "Why do you think you need my program?" She responded, "Because two of my clients ended the projects because of the economy, the third cut back from $125,000 to $40,000, and I'm hanging on with my fingertips to the fourth."

Q: Many of us have made that mistake. We get a lot of business, we get caught up in delivery, and we quit marketing. Tell us about the successful people that you've mentored. How do they integrate the marketing and allocate their time so they're getting it done?

Alan: *People should work towards reducing labor intensity on the delivery side, not on the marketing side.* You reduce your delivery time by transferring to the client, using subcontractors, and by streamlining your own model. You also cut back or refuse work that doesn't make sense for you any more. If you do those things, you'll significantly reduce your delivery time and reduce your labor intensity.

You want to put marketing devices in place that are passive, that you don't have to tend to, and that are working for you all the time. Then you schedule time that you dedicate to active marketing every week.

There are many ways to actively market your business that many don't think of as marketing. For example, a lot of people I've counseled have never thought of using speaking as a marketing device. In other words, they're not professional speakers in that they don't go out and give keynotes or do concurrent sessions for large fees. But they haven't considered offering free speaking to market their consulting. My advice to them is to polish up your speaking skills a bit, which is easy, and find organizations or events where the audience will comprise buyers and recommenders. If that's the case, speaking for free is a good idea.

While you're giving the speech, that's active marketing. If it's a trade association, there are myriad opportunities available before, during, and after your speaking event. The trade association may print an interview with you in their publication before the speech, provide handouts during the event, and include you in their newsletter or distribute free copies of a book or other product to their membership. This inculcates members of the organization with the value that they can get in other materials and communications that are a passive component of your active speaking. The odds of getting business as a result of those materials are pretty darn good.

Q: It sounds like it wouldn't occur to most people to use speaking as a marketing tool for their consulting. Are there any other sort of marketing secrets that people need to know about that aren't obvious?

Alan: There are other very powerful ways you can get in front of people in an inexpensive and non-labor-intensive way. Blogs, if managed well and updated regularly, are very effective in marketing because you can publish whatever you want on your blog. It's not someone else's word count or column inches. You can experiment with new intellectual property and see how people respond to it. You can invite comments, respond to the comments, and you can engage with your audience as often as you like. You can post great content in audio, video, and text format on your blog. If you do this correctly, people will read your blog regularly and will tell other people about it. (You can transfer it easily to YouTube, iTunes, and other platforms.)

Tweet about your latest blog post on Twitter. Tweet when you post a special article. Write about the best practices in your industry. Every Friday I put up a cartoon, The Adventures of Koufax and Buddy Beagle—my two dogs. Every Monday I email my Monday Morning Memo to a list of 12,000 opt-in subscribers who have signed up over the years to receive content from me. I also post it to my blog to reach people who may not subscribe but read my blog. That way I reach a wide variety of people, and if I provide great content, my audience will share it and subscribe to more. Once you establish an online presence where people look to you for great content, *you'll be mentioned in other people's columns and gain recognition as a thought leader in your space.*

If you love speaking, do that. If you love to write, create an amazing blog. If you are a great networker, then go to places where your buyers and recommenders hang out. Start with the avenue that's most in your comfort zone and expand from there.

Q: People sometimes say, "I don't know why I write this blog. Nobody is reading it." What would you advise somebody who made a comment like that?

Alan: I would advise them that it's not a matter of hits. I've been told, "Your blog isn't among the 25 most popular," or "Other people get 1,000 hits a day." You only need one reader to make your blog worth writing, if that person is a buyer! If you're providing great content, you'll develop a readership. What you have to ask yourself is, "Who is my constituency? Who is the audience I want to reach?" If they're not reading your blog, why not? Find out what they're reading. Find out what is appealing to them. Ask them!

There are over 450 million blogs right now. But why are there so many? Because they find an audience. Because people want to read about certain niche topics. The web is the ultimate repository of specialized high content, and it's the same with the blogosphere. Blogs can be written to target very narrow audiences.

It's important to track what content is being read, shared, or liked the most. If people aren't reading what you're writing—whether it's a blog or an article on your website—it's because it isn't interesting to them, or they just don't know about it. Perhaps it's not provocative, it doesn't lend anything new to the discussion, or it's the same old same old, or as I abbreviate it "so-so." Perhaps the quality of writing needs work.

You need to constantly write and produce great content if you want to be successful, and if people aren't reading you, that can be remedied. But don't just sit there and say, "They don't get it," or "It's a dull subject," or "There is too much competition." You have to stick with it, improve your craft, and make sure the content you generate becomes a must-read for the readership you want to reach.

Q: And those in your community, other than not investing enough time marketing, what is the biggest mistake people make with regard to marketing?

Alan: The biggest mistake is that they are not patient with new marketing initiatives. They try a new strategy and give up a week later. "You know, I started a blog but didn't get any readers. I sent out a couple press releases on www.expertclick.com, and I didn't get any responses. I posted a new product up on my website, but I only got three orders." You have to market and try new ways of reaching your audience, but you have to give any new initiatives some time before deciding whether they work or not. Too often, when people don't get what they want—instant gratification—they give up. They don't have the discipline necessary to continue working without seeing results.

Discipline helps you establish structure in your life. If you're disciplined in your marketing efforts, and each week you try something new, and you've written in your calendar, "Post a blog item on Thursday. Get your newsletter out on Friday. Go to a networking event on Tuesday," you'll be successful. It takes both doing the right things and doing them continually.

Q: If we have a blog and a newsletter, and we're doing all the things you recommend and still not seeing any traffic to our sites, what should we do then?

Alan: Don't worry so much about traffic. Worry about whether you're doing business. Although traffic to your web presence may be modest at first, it requires patience, commitment, and consistency to see results. If you have multiple marketing components in place—even if many of them are passive—stick with them, monitor and update them regularly, and ask yourself at the end of the month, or at the end of the quarter, "Am I getting business from this channel?"

You never know where your next client is coming from. To ensure prospects find you wherever they're looking, it's important to keep as many irons in the fire as you can. So, don't worry so much about whether something is working immediately or how much traffic you're getting. If you're not getting business and you aren't getting paid, you aren't reaching your prospective buyers with a sufficient value proposition.

If your prospects aren't reading you, it's important to know why. Perhaps you don't have the right value. Perhaps you have the right value but you're going after the wrong market. Perhaps you're not being visible enough.

How do you change that? Ask yourself, "Do I have the right value proposition? Do I have the right audience value proposition? Do they know I'm here? Am I delivering high content and high quality?" Ask others to review your offering and marketing. Do research to see what others in your space are doing. Ask clients you're working with what you can do better.

Q: For consultants just starting out, what sort of marketing should they focus on?

Alan: There is an inverse relationship in marketing where the less experience you have, the more you have to reach out, and the less gravity you have. The more your career develops and the more experience you get, the less you reach out, and the more gravity you have.

Consultants just starting out should choose two or three strategies to focus on and develop. If it's a blog, you should be posting there three or four times a week. If it's networking, you should be visiting at least one or two events a week, and so forth.

If you don't like public speaking or you don't normally do much writing, start by devoting a couple hours a week to generating content. Once your brand and work are better known, your marketing will begin to evolve and become more sophisticated and nuanced. If you already have an established client base—client testimonials, client lists, client work, and client case studies will play a larger role in your marketing.

Every week, whether you're with a client or not, you must find and implement new ways to attract prospects to you. Your life is your life. If you start to compartmentalize it too much, you're not going to be very successful.

The Gravity Factor

Q: Explain the concept of the market gravity wheel.

Alan: I developed the concept of the market gravity wheel about ten years ago at a marketing workshop for professional speakers I conduct with Patricia Fripp called The Odd Couple®. It's a two-day program we've been doing for over a decade expressly dedicated to teaching speakers how to market

Marketing Gravity

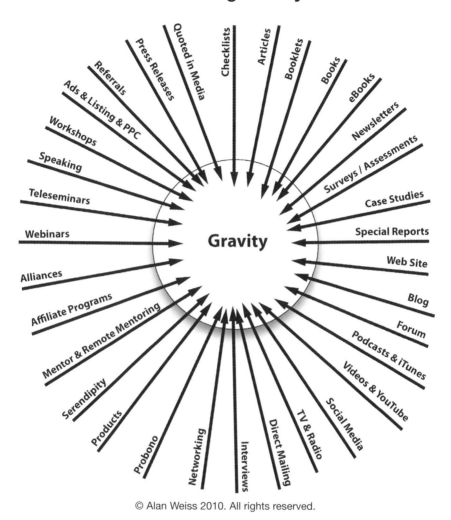

Figure 5.1: Million Dollar Consulting® Market Gravity

themselves. We created this because we saw professional speakers around us struggling with their businesses. They weren't doing as well as they could have because they lacked marketing confidence.

In one of the sessions, a participant asked me about the best ways to market and which should be priorities. I responded, "I always advise consultants to routinize inputs and customize outputs. I need to develop a routine myself to explain this. I keep reinventing the wheel." I drew a circle, and I explained that consultants should think of their business as a planet that needs to create gravity to attract things to it. I then drew spokes around the circle to represent the various activities you can do to attract people to you.

After that, I began incorporating marketing gravity in all of my work. Back then, there were 12 spokes around the wheel. Now there are many more, largely because of the rise in technology over the past ten years.

The marketing gravity wheel is meant to illustrate the various ways people can attract clients to them or create marketing "gravity." If you're just starting, you should choose two or three strategies you're most proficient in, most comfortable doing, and able to do consistently. As you gain experience and establish clients, you can incorporate other activities that may be outside of your comfort zone and require more effort on your part. Market gravity can easily calibrate how well you're doing each week, where you might be investing more time, or where you don't need to invest more time.

The most important and most powerful marketing methods are having referral business, having a commercially published book, and having high-visibility speaking appearances. Next would be a very effective and robust internet presence that includes a website, blog, and newsletter. No matter which methods you use, it's imperative that you possess the skills and abilities to do each one effectively.

Q: What is the accelerant curve, and how does it work?

Alan: The accelerant curve is a way of structuring your business so that you provide a variety of offerings at different price points along a curve. The low-cost or free offerings provide low barriers of entry for people to get to know you. Once they see the quality and value of your offerings, you can gradually move them along the curve to fee-based relationships and ultimately to more involved interactions with you that culminate in direct relationships, such as a retainer or licensing agreement for your intellectual property.

On the left side of the curve are products and services that people can get for free or that don't cost very much. It might be articles, videos, a webinar, or an ebook. Farther along the curve are fee-based offerings, such

The Million Dollar Consulting® Accelerant Curve

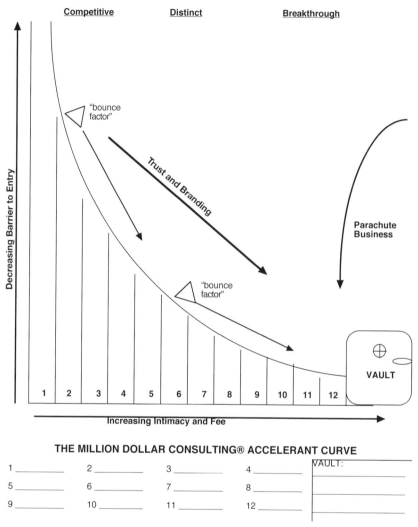

Figure 5.2: The Million Dollar Consulting® Accelerant Curve

as workshops, webinars, teleconferences, consulting work, strategy, retainers, and one-on-one coaching with clients.

Most clients don't drop into the curve at the higher price point but rather begin their relationship with you at the point in the curve from where your offerings are free or low cost. As they slide down the curve and learn more about your business, it builds trust and your brand. The farther along the curve the offering is, the more it's distinct, given your competencies and experiences. The farther down the curve a client goes, the higher the cost and therefore higher the barrier to entry. The key is not to have great chasms along the curve where there is not a next level for clients to jump to or a gap between your low-priced or free offerings and your high-priced and unique offerings.

When your brand is sufficiently established, you reach a level I call "parachute business" where people may drop in immediately on the right. In the Million Dollar Consulting® College, there are people who haven't signed up for other offerings I have but sign up for the higher-level, fee-based program because they're familiar with my free or low-fee products.

There is also a bounce factor that exists on the accelerant curve. For example, $25-purchase people may have read a book I authored, then decide to enter the mentor program for $3,500, and eventually decide to sign up for a Master Mentor program for $10,000 or attend the Thought Leadership program for $12,000. These bounce factors propel people forward.

Q: How can we use the marketing spokes on the market gravity wheel to promote the full spectrum of offerings on the accelerant curve?

Alan: You can use the gravity wheel to attract people to specific points along your accelerant curve. If you don't have an established brand, aren't that well known, or just starting out, your goal should be to get people on the upper left of the accelerant curve so they get to know you by low barrier of entry, and they'll slide down the curve. If you have a strong and growing brand, you can use marketing gravity to attract people to the lower right portion of the accelerant curve and to your higher-priced, more unique offerings.

For example, if you're just building your brand, you can write articles or guest blog posts for websites or blogs in your industry to attract people to your website where you may have more articles, a diagnostic test, a podcast, or some other free content. If you have a strong brand, you could use that article to draw people toward the right and suggest to them in the article that you conduct workshops on the topic or that you offer customized coaching in a particular area. You can use the gravity wheel in conjunction with the accelerant curve to determine where you want to direct people.

Q: How do you ensure there aren't any chasms along the accelerant curve and successfully apply the marketing wheel?

Alan: The most successful consultants are the ones who constantly restructure their business and reinvent themselves. Marshall Goldsmith has it right: "What got you here won't get you there." In other words, what has been successful for you in the past won't be successful for you in the future.

They're also not afraid to fail. They try different offerings, and if something doesn't work, they try something else. It's just a matter of finding what is right for them and right for their audience.

Successful consultants have the discipline to continue their development. Many join my mentor program just once, progress nicely, and never come back. They never engage in another activity; they never partake in another workshop or experience. You have to engage in continuing self-development.

Q: How do we create a marketing plan that's effective and successful?

Alan: Don't make it overly complicated. Consider the spokes on the wheel, and ask yourself which you want to implement and what will it take to implement them. Once you've decided, designate time to do them in your calendar.

If you want to publish articles, white papers, or books, determine where the best places to publish are, how to get to them, what resources you need, and start writing. If you want to network, find the events where your buyers are likely to be. Get yourself a little training or coaching on how to network effectively, and go do it. It's that simple, but too often people procrastinate, and procrastination is just a form of fear.

Underlying all of your efforts has to be some philosophy of business that gives you confidence that it's all worthwhile and satisfaction that you're helping others. That spark—the drive that you must have to be successful in your endeavors—is this very existential awareness of the struggle to try to find your purpose in life and exercise your talents.

The whole point is that if you believe that you have value that will help people, then it's incumbent upon you to bring that value to people's attention in every way you can for their benefit. As George Merck, founder of Merck Pharmaceuticals, said, "Do good and good will follow."

If You Don't Blow Your Own Horn, There Is No Music

Q: When did you coin this phrase? What does it mean?

Alan: That also came from The Odd Couple® workshop. In one session, the attendees were exhibiting reluctance to communicate how valuable their services could be to their clients. The room was full of speakers who are normally very confident, outspoken, and love being on stage, but they had difficulty doing this as a marketing initiative. Finally, I said to them, "Listen, if you don't blow your own horn, there is no music." Ever since, I use that phrase because my feeling about brands is that you use them consistently and constantly. The expression appears in a lot of my work today; simple metaphors like that tend to adhere to people's memories.

Music is a creative, enjoyable endeavor in most cases. But you can't have music unless somebody is blowing a horn, strumming a guitar, or bowing a violin. To create music in your own life, you have to be the musician. Just as you can't make a speech if you decide not to talk, the music here is the tune to which you move through life. My tune is very upbeat; my tunes are very simpatico with how I feel about living. But no matter what your taste is, you're in charge of making your own music.

Q: Why do people feel hindered then and reluctant to blow their own horn? Is it an issue of self-esteem, or is there more to it?

Alan: It's an issue of self-esteem, and one of guilt. We're inculcated from the time we're in grammar school and even preschool not to stand out in a crowd. We're told not to brag. We're told not to boast. We're told it's better to be modest. We're told to be gracious losers and not boasting winners.

Life is competitive. Every day, people win and lose, and the good thing is that you can lose today and win tomorrow. It's not a permanent condition, but it can be if you feel that you're a victim and that you can't win.

What you have is this inculcated belief that we're not supposed to stand out in a crowd. If you look at innovators, leaders, and people who create, *they're never average.* They're exceptional. You have to be willing to take that mantle. There is a great quote from Frank Lloyd Wright, the wonderful architect. He says, "Early in life I had a choice between hypocritical humility and honest arrogance. I chose the latter and have seen no reason to change."

You can't just be good. You have to believe that you're worthy. You should have excellent confidence so that you're not just bragging. But you must also have high self-esteem because that creates resilience so when you have a setback, a defeat, or something doesn't go your way, you bounce back. Resilience is a key feature of any kind of entrepreneur, leader, or great consultant.

Q: Can you give us some effective ways to better educate our buyers about what we offer?

Alan: Most buyers are educated incorrectly. That is, they're educated incorrectly by prior consultants, so they believe that they should pay by the hour. They believe they should look at deliverables.

They have often been miseducated by their own human resources department. So with the best of intentions, they're thinking all the wrong things. Since they've been educated improperly in most cases, what you have to do is educate them about the proper way to form this relationship. How to get the most out of it, how you work and why, and why it's best for them. You always have to convince people it's in their self-interest, and that education process could take five minutes or it could take two meetings. You can't build a trusting relationship unless you've educated the buyer as to the best kind of partnership the two of you can have.

The buyer will probably simultaneously be educating you about the best way to work with his or her company. That includes details about the corporate culture, past experiences with consultants, expectations, and objectives. This mutual educational process is part of that relationship building.

Q: Many consultants suffer some form of impostor anxiety or impostor syndrome. They feel undeserving of success. What is your advice when a consultant experiences this?

Alan: This is chronic. If you have high skills, don't feel worthy, and fear being found out, first deconstruct what you do. You have processes that are successful because the results you've generated are successful. A lot of clients and executives say, "I really don't know what it is, or I really can't tell you; it's in my gut. I have good intuition. It's a visceral feel." And I tell every one of them that that's crap. Nobody, *nobody* succeeds consistently at what they do by gut feel and hunches.

What is actually happening is that they've developed highly effective processes that they either can't or won't articulate. You have to do the equivalent of creating the picture of what their processes are. You must deconstruct what you do. In your last project, why was it successful? What did you do? What do you do consistently that creates these kinds of results?

Once you understand the processes and recognize your strengths and abilities, you'll no longer feel like an impostor. But the combination of not blowing your own horn, not standing out in a crowd, and not articulating why you're good can lead to huge feelings of low self-worth.

Q: What recurring themes or problems are related to not having enough self-esteem?

Alan: It's a problem within society. Many people who have chosen to be consultants come from a background where there was some sort of adversity. In one of my sessions, I asked the ten people in attendance how many of them came from a home where their parents were either divorced, had an alcohol or drug problem, or were abusive. Seven out of ten people raised their hands.

When my daughter was an undergraduate at Syracuse University, she was required to live in the dorms her freshman year. There were about 70 women on her floor. One night during one of their floor meetings, somebody asked how many of the girls grew up in traditional families with their original mothers and fathers still living together. Danielle looked around as she raised her hand. Only two other women had their hands up. So, one of the problems that we have in terms of self-esteem is that many of us are still carrying baggage from sometimes disastrous childhoods.

We all have a story. I was raised in a traditional home. My parents are still alive. Growing up is never easy, but sometimes it's more difficult for some than others.

It's true that everyone has some sort of baggage. Where the problem lies is that many people don't take time to reassess the baggage they carry. We need baggage. You don't get rid of all of your baggage. You need your history, challenges, experiences, and failures to influence your decisions and behaviors down the road. The idea is to have appropriate baggage for the future. We should check that baggage on a regular basis, repack our bags, put in what is relevant for us now, and that's the baggage we carry around.

In my book, *Thrive: How to Stop Wishing Your Life Away*, I explain that we have to throw the old baggage off the train; otherwise, it's going the same speed we are. Throw it off the train; kill a couple cows in the countryside if you have to. If we aren't careful, the weight of the baggage can pull us into depression.

One of the effects of clinical depression is that low self-esteem and guilt dampen talent. That's what a lot of people are facing, and they don't have enough of a support system to help purge them of this horrible stuff that they carry around, which lowers their feelings about themselves.

One other thing I'll mention is that you have to watch the people with whom you associate. People who are energy suckers can deflate you slowly and insidiously.

Q: Why is this a big problem for solo consultants?

Alan: Consultants, architects, accountants, interior designers, attorneys, and anyone who has a solo practice are left to their own devices. In a large or boutique organization, you're part of a team and can count, to some degree, on others to help you get things done. There is a momentum. You go along with the flow. If you have a busy day, somebody else can pick up the slack. You have colleagues who commiserate with you, and the overall forward momentum of the organization helps carry you along.

In large organizations, you have these people being carried along by the few people still manning the oars. But when you're on your own, you have no such support. The ship can't propel itself without you. So you need a great spirit, a lot of energy, and a ferocious intent to move through each day full speed ahead because nobody else is rowing but you.

That's what you have to do to adapt to normative pressures. That's why I've been a contrarian for virtually my entire career. I'm not about to submit to normative pressures because what do they tell you in our profession? You charge by the hour. You deal with human resource people. You don't boast or brag. You don't drive an expensive car to the client. Who wants to live their life that way?

Sometimes I've talked strategically about taking a sharp right professionally. Find a different way. March to your own drummer.

Q: What is your advice to get past procrastination?

Alan: Procrastination is the expression of fear. It's the fear of moving something forward. You might fear rejection. You might fear failure. You might fear critique. You might fear ridicule. There is a lot that people fear; however, if you're fully engaged, eager, and ready to go, you would move things forward. You wouldn't procrastinate. The fear is often expressed incorrectly or hidden. Find the real fear and deal with it.

Q: How can we become shameless promoters?

Alan: Shameless Promotion came out of Alan's Forums (alansforums.com). Somebody was asking about how to promote better.

The whole premise is to let go of faulty preconceptions. For example, we start off the workshop with something called "the super value proposition." It's not sufficient that people have a value proposition. A super value proposition is something you would otherwise almost be embarrassed to talk about. You can see real transformation taking place.

Shameless Promotion means doing things like creating press releases, writing articles, making speeches, creating podcasts and teleconferences, creating product, and even having casual conversations that are shameless in their promotion of your business and services. By the way, I got this from Patricia Fripp, along with her permission to use it. The idea isn't to be obnoxious, offensive, or for you to be ashamed. The idea is for you to be shameless in helping people understand the tremendous value you can bring to them. What it calls for is reassessing the wording on your materials to reflect a more compelling offering and a more powerful result for the client.

Q: You've often said that logic makes people think and emotion makes them act. How can we better use both logic and emotion in our marketing?

Alan: You have to synergize them and understand that you might have an idea that intellectually makes sense—cognitively it makes sense—but if you really want to sell it, to convince or influence others, you have to strike an emotional chord. You have to get an emotional reaction. That's the key to connecting with your prospects.

When planning the marketing campaign for the Self-Esteem Workshop, I asked myself, "What can I say that will appeal to the audience this offering is for?" In the promotion for the workshop, the headline read, "Do you have the self-esteem to attend the Self-Esteem Workshop?" It was an emotional trigger that resonated exactly with the prospects that the workshop was for, so it was effective. This is how you should organize not just your approach to your clients but your approach to your life, so you're more efficient, more productive, and you feel like you control your own fate. That's an emotional appeal.

If you believe that logic makes you think and emotion makes you act, then you want to think of what you need to do, which is the logical process. If you want other people to take action on it, you have to convert that. You have to metamorphose that into an emotional appeal that they'll respond to, and that's why you hear people say, "Last day only," "Last day for this price," or "We'll never offer this again." They're creating scarcity, and scarcity creates an emotional reaction. "Gee, I wonder if I really can never get this again; maybe I should do something."

Q: You spoke of the fear of rejection and the fear of failure in relation to procrastinating. What about the fear of success? Is that something that holds us back sometimes?

Alan: Absolutely. Being afraid of success fits right into what you originally asked me about. It's the impostor syndrome. You don't want to be found out.

I actually worked with someone who followed my instructions and finally started to meet with buyers, finally used the right wording with buyers, and finally had a buyer say, "Hey, here is what we would like to do. We think you're the one." This person put up so many roadblocks and so much resistance that nothing ever transpired, and I realized that this person really didn't want the job. This fear of being found out comes when people with low self-esteem feel that any expectation of them isn't going to be met because they're not worthy.

Procrastination is the fear of success because you never get around to it. Why didn't you send the proposal in? "It's not ready yet." Why didn't you call them back as promised? "The timing wasn't right." There are plenty of excuses, but the key is getting beyond the excuses and focusing on the action.

Q: What is the distinction between fear of failure and fear of success?

Alan: They're two sides of the same coin. Some people will resist doing something; they'll procrastinate; they'll undermine their own efforts. They'll find excuses because they're afraid of failing and because they're afraid if they succeed, they'll fail because they won't be up to it.

A fear of success is the same thing as a fear of failure expressed a different way. If I fear success, it means that if I do what they ask me to do, if I do what they believe I can do and don't do it, I'll fail. It's all based on the same set of emotions.

Q: What are some tips for consultants to engage a buyer emotionally?

Alan: As you build the relationship, listen to how the buyer speaks. If the buyer talks about "What we want to achieve—we want to be leading edge, and my team wants to introduce new products," then the buyer is really engaged in the limelight, recognition, and things like that, which is fine. If the buyer instead talks about "Get it done fast—let's not waste time," then the buyer is very task oriented and goal oriented and wants to get things done quickly.

If the buyer seems apprehensive and asks, "Who else has done this? What kind of precedent is there?" then emotionally this person is looking for guarantees and assurances. If the buyer says, "Let me see the detail here. What would the numbers look like? How many people? Which cases?" then the buyer is very analytic, and that's going to appeal to that buyer.

Be sure to listen and find out what your buyer's hot buttons are. Engaging the buyer in conversations will help build a relationship. Inevitably, the buyer will say things that reveal emotional positions, emotional needs, and emotional interests, and where appropriate, address those needs.

Conclusion

Should you keep doing the same things if they're the right things but not getting results? My suggestion is keep doing those things, and add things to them. Diversify: If you're sending out press releases, keep doing that but also begin networking. If you're networking and sending out press releases, keep doing that but also begin speaking. Add things to the mix, and you'll find there is a synergy that takes place, and that they'll probably help each other. You'll build a self-reinforcing body of work. But whatever you choose to do, start now.

Growing a Business and Acquiring Clients

You Think You're in the Consulting Business, but This Is the Marketing Business

There comes a time in every consultant's career when a need arises to pursue new business and wrestle it to the ground. For some, that occurs when you hang out a shingle and print stationery; for others, it happens after several years when the highly successful consultant has exhausted the fuel supply. No matter what your situation is, you'll need to identify opportunities, prepare for success, gain market share, and guarantee repeat business.

Getting Your First Client

The way you get your first client can vary. If you're leaving a company, if you're a refugee from a large organization as so many consultants are, your first client is often your prior employer. Since that's very common, it's a good reason to plan how you depart and refrain from blowing up bridges. Other ways to get your first client are to let everyone around you know what you're doing. You can't be bashful. You have to be able to say, "This is what I'm doing now, and this is the kind of value I provide to these types of people, and if you know of anyone who can use this kind of value, please let me know."

You need the basic resources to begin networking. In other words, you need a business card, an address, and a value proposition. Then you have to begin reaching out to people because this isn't the consulting business. It's the marketing business.

Q: How do we decide whom to say this to?

Alan: You should reach out to every contact you have. Your Christmas card list (viz.: "holiday card" for the politically correct) is a great place to start. If you're embarrassed about talking about what you do to friends and neighbors, it means that you don't have enough confidence in what you're doing. Your mindset has to be, "I have genuine value to deliver to people, and I'd be remiss if I don't offer it to as many people as possible because I can help them."

You can't start in this business thinking about making a sale or hitting a quota. You have to start by thinking about how much value you can bring to the maximum number of people. Start with the people closest to you—the people you know socially, individuals in the civic community, people you've worked with professionally, and anyone you think may be a potential client or reference point.

Q: Should I get my website up to speed and get all my marketing materials together, or should I just go after the clients?

Alan: Well, the two options aren't mutually exclusive. It's like asking, "Should I look for air before water?" The answer is to do both. Go after clients, but be sure to have a website underway. For a consultant, a website is a credibility statement. It's common for someone to hear of you and then go to your website to learn more about who you are.

Q: Who is my ideal client? Is it anybody who can write a check to me, or should I be picky even at the beginning when I really need the money?

Alan: Although it's ideal to have six months of reserves in the bank when you go out on your own, if that's not possible, any business can look like good business. If you want to go after certain clients more aggressively than others, prioritize the ones you feel would constitute ideal clients. Those may be the ones who will benefit the most from your value proposition, who have a history of using outside consultants, who are doing well and are able to pay, or with whom you have an existing relationship so it's not a completely cold approach.

Q: Is anyone willing to write a check an ideal client?

Alan: An ideal client is one who can pay and who has the most need for your value; but if a client comes along that might not be ideal, you should still accept them. The other question here is "What clients do I turn down?" The clients you should turn down are these: problematic prospects. A horrible prospect never becomes a good client. The behavior you see is indicative of how your future interactions will go. If somebody doesn't meet commitments or deadlines; if they're distracted during meetings or take calls while you're sitting there, these aren't good signs.

Q: In order to establish credibility with new prospective clients, should we consider pro bono work? If so, where do we draw the line on pro bono work?

Alan: As a new consultant, you may want to consider doing some pro bono work. You would only do this type of work for a nonprofit, though—never do free work for a for-profit organization. There are plenty of nonprofits which could use the services of a consultant, so find a nonprofit in which you believe and offer your services. It might be for an organization that raises funds to support research or education about a particular disease or a human condition of suffering, or a social group, civic group, or even a political group as long as you believe in the cause.

Be sure the project you work on is relatively brief. Don't commit to a long-term pro bono project that will pull you away from building your business. Even if you're helping with long-term projects, such as strategy work, explain upfront that you'll consult on a short-term component of the larger project.

Also, have an arrangement beforehand where the executive director agrees to give you a testimonial and a reference at the end of your arrangement if things turn out the way you both expect them to. That isn't something you negotiate later. Be clear about your expectations upfront. "I'm doing this because I would love to have you endorse me."

Make sure you are in contact with influential people within the organization. One of your criteria may be that you meet with the board members because the board members in these organizations may be buyers for their own companies. Maximize the number of influential people you meet.

Q: You often speak about focusing on the "fourth sale first" with a client. Why is the fourth sale significant?

Alan: The acquisition of new business is extraordinarily difficult. It's the most time-consuming and expensive thing we do. The perpetuation of existing business is one of the easiest and highest-profit things we do. I'm talking about not being too greedy the first time you're hired by a client. Don't look at work with a client as a snapshot. Look at it as a film. Think about a relationship. A typical client might constitute a two-, three-, or five-year relationship that results in seven figures instead of five figures within the first two months.

Q: What does it mean concretely and pragmatically when we're developing the relationship with the buyer, thinking about the fourth sale?

Alan: You want to have an understanding of what the buyer's long-term interests are. If you're dealing with a buyer who tells you, "This is my last year before retiring, but I want to go out in a big way," it will be difficult to think of the fourth sale first. What you are thinking is, "I have to make sure I make lateral connections here because the buyer just told me he is leaving." If the buyer says, "This is a transitory stop for me. They've asked me to fix this mess, and then I'm going on to other things," this is an up-and-comer who could be helpful to you and you helpful to him for the next ten years.

You should show interest in your client's personal and professional aspirations. Listen for what that client needs, and provide effective resources and solutions.

Q: What is the first sale? What is the second sale? What is the third sale? And are they important for us to recognize?

Alan: All sales are important. The fourth sale is just a metaphor, and what it's meant to convey is you want to prepare yourself for a long-term relationship. I worked with Merck for 12 years, and that probably resulted in $2.5 million of business, not counting the spinoff business from Merck. I worked with Hewlett-Packard for ten years and with Calgon for five years. For a consultant, those are long-term business relationships, but even a two-year relationship is a wonderful accomplishment because the terms of most consulting projects are a month, three months, or nine months.

Focusing on the fourth sale creates a mindset where you're open to seeing other opportunities, expanding business, finding lateral buyers, and all the kinds of other possibilities to provide services to new clients. So, even while delivering, you should be marketing. It's a myth that you can't market while delivering.

Referrals: The Platinum Standard

Q: Why are referrals the most important spoke on the gravity wheel? Why should we consider referrals so important?

Alan: The buyer-to-buyer referral is the platinum standard in consulting. Many business transactions rely on cold calls and direct mail to reach buyers. If you think of the way executives buy, they generally make decisions by listening to peers. They won't go to the Yellow Pages, look at an advertisement, or contact a trade association. They'll ask somebody they respect for information on businesses or services they've used.

Consequently, the ability to generate buyer-to-buyer referrals is invaluable, and what you have to do is pursue it assiduously because many people don't think to automatically do it. To ensure clients remember to refer you, as you near the end of the contract, you should ask the buyer, "Would I be accurate in saying this project has preceded the way we both hoped it would? I'm wondering who we might share the results of our work together with."

When I was first married, I was working at Prudential Insurance. An agent was assigned to me from Prudential to sell me insurance. His name was Hal Mapes. Hal said, "Look, I'm here to sell you insurance." I bought an insurance policy from Hal. He would come every six months like clockwork, and he would see if our condition changed, if we needed more insurance, and then he would ask, "Can I have three names of people I can contact?" I would answer, "I have no names." He would respond, "Of course you have names. You went to school with people. You know other people at Prudential. You have friends. Give me three names!" I gave him three names. Six months later, he came to the door. I opened the door and said, "Hal, here are three names. See you in six months." Hal had about 300 clients when we met, and he visited his clients twice a year, totaling 600 visits. So, if he got three names at each visit, that's 1,800 referrals. If he closes 10 percent of them, that's 180 new clients. The next year he doesn't have 300, he has 480.

Q: Once you ask for a referral, then what? What do you find to be the most powerful form of contact?

Alan: There are three ways you can do this. You can ask for an introduction. You can ask for contact information and contact this individual yourself. However, if your client prefers to keep his or her name out of it, you contact the referral without revealing the source.

An in-person introduction by the buyer is the ideal situation. But if the buyer is 2,000 miles away, and you know your client has passed your information along, a phone call is fine. As soon as the introduction or referral is made, you should call. If you get sent to voicemail, I recommend saying, "I was referred by your friend, Kathy. Here is my number. If I don't hear from you, I'll call you at 10:00 tomorrow morning." You want to establish a definitive time and date. Also, be sure to keep the individual who gave you the reference in the loop and give updates on your progress in case you may need help to make the connection happen.

Q: So, your first choice is a person-to-person, face-to-face meeting, and then if they're too far away, you'll call them. Does email play a role in this?

Alan: No. Too many people use email in place of a phone because they have a fear of rejection. Email engagements can be less threatening, but they're also less effective. On a phone call, there is inflection, intonation, and threat because the rejection may seem more personalized. You have to get over that.

Q: Could you walk me through the script that I'll use initially to open that?

Alan: I would say something like this: "Linda, Aviv referred me to you. Has he mentioned that I'd be calling?" You would respond, "Yes he has, Alan. He told me you would be calling." I would say, "Well, Aviv told me that you could use some of the value I provided to him and his company. He seldom refers people to me, but when he does, it's usually extraordinarily valuable for me and for the person he recommends. I would like to sit down with you for 20 minutes, learn a bit about what you do, and see if it does make sense for us to get into further discussions."

You respond, "Well, you have me now, just talk to me now." I say, "I would like to do you the same honor and the same service I did to Aviv when we first met. I also prefer meeting rather than doing this over the phone. I would be happy to come see you. Of course, there is no obligation or cost to you. I'm going to be passing through your area three times over the next couple of months. If any of these times are good, we can meet at your office or whatever makes sense."

Q: When a client says that they'll refer you personally, how do you control that conversation, or what tips would you have?

Alan: What you say is, "I really appreciate that. That's great. Who are you talking about? What is the best way to do this, and when should we communicate again about this?" You want to push this forward because people with the best of intentions often don't follow up on their promises because of other priorities arising.

Q: What do you say when asked, "I want to refer you. What are your executive coaching fees?"

Alan: A good response to that is, "My fees vary depending upon the needs of the individual. If you connect me to the person you have in mind, I can prepare a proposal for him or her."

Q: Let's say I'm a starting consultant, and I want to increase my business dramatically. What is some of the low-hanging fruit I can focus on?

Alan: The low-hanging fruit for anybody are people you know and people who know you. For example, if you belong to a club, ask the manager or the board of directors if you can host a free "enrichment session" for the members of the club. It's a way of demonstrating your services to ideal clients. Some who attend may contact you later to consult with their businesses.

Another option is to focus on the micro as a path to the macro. There was an insurance brokerage for Northwest Insurance—one of the finest insurance companies in the country. The manager of the brokerage said, "I have ten salespeople reporting to me, and you're an authority on sales. Would you come in and talk to us? We have a $500 honorarium." I responded, "I'll come in and talk to your team. Make the check out to the Animal Protection League." He went on, "Did I mention that I'm on the program for the Northwest Insurance National Conference? We look for speakers for our events." About five months later, I was sitting elbow-to-elbow with the CEO of Northwest Insurance in New York making the keynote at their national conference for my full fee.

You can look for local branches of major organizations and make connections that way. Start with individuals you have some association with. Who knows you the best? Where are you most comfortable? How can you make inroads?

Q: Why do you think most consultants don't ask for referrals? Is it a self-esteem issue? Is it skills? Is it both? Or some other things?

Alan: Usually, it's self-esteem. People are afraid of rejection. They're afraid of clients saying "no" even though they'll probably say "yes."

As I demonstrated, everyone gives referrals: "Go to my dentist, he hurts less." That's what usually happens, but they're afraid clients will say something negative about them. This is rarely the case.

Q: How have you personally used referrals in your business, and how do you use referrals to further grow your business?

Alan: This is going to sound very, very simplistic, but when you just do a great job, people begin to talk; they begin to brag. Buyers have egos and may say things to past colleagues or peers like, "You should see the guy I'm working with. You should see what we did the other day." When you do great work, people want to work with you and refer you to other people.

Q: When is the right time to ask for a testimonial or a referral?

Alan: Two-thirds of the way through a project you should ask for a referral. If you wait until your work is done, the probability is that without you there, there is little motivation to create the referral. If the client asks for a week to think about it or needs time, you can give them time because you're still going to be there.

Q: What is the difference between generating referrals in the corporate wholesale business and the retail business?

Alan: It's easier in corporate business simply because there are larger networks of buyers. On the retail side, you can reach a lot of people at once through the introduction of intellectual property; for example, a book that everybody is talking about. On the wholesale side, the typical size of the sale is larger, and so that's when the reference, the referral pays off in a greater way.

Q: Say the buyer—a senior executive in a large company—promised referrals to two of his peers but hasn't acted on it. What can I do to get the referrals?

Alan: "I know you're busy, but I have you on the phone right now, so let's take three minutes and just get this done." But you have to pick up the phone. Email is too easy to ignore.

Q: When I ask my buyer who else in his network can benefit from my value, I initiate the contact, but it's almost like a cold referral. When buyers take the initiative and speak to their peers, they're leading the conversations, and they're warm referrals. When a peer of the buyer reaches out to the buyer urgently saying, "We have this problem," and the buyer replies, "You must check out my consultant because he can help you," this is what I call a boiling-hot referral. What can we do to generate more of the boiling-hot referrals instead of the cold referrals?

Alan: You can make the fire higher. Stoke the flames. In other words, the reason that the buyer receives the query from a third-party company and refers him to you is really timing. The buyer is working with you. You're a proven variable. What you need to do is stay in front of people who can make those kinds of instant referrals. Even if you're not actively working with them, by dint of a newsletter, a membership, a value you send them in the mail, or some kind of follow-up meeting, you need to keep your face and value in front of people so that you're the first resource they think of when somebody comes along with that boiling-hot need.

The more you create a dependency, not a co-dependency, for help and value—even if it's not paid for—the more people will turn to you for your services. If people see you as a good source of information and help, they'll come to you no matter what, and you can choose which clients you work for and what you charge.

Q: You've spoken in the past about your work with Hewlett-Packard. The beauty of the story was that you had a connector, a maven there referring colleagues to you. So, this really is the secret formula of referrals: having somebody that enjoys putting the word out for you. What can we do to identify these people, to develop such relationships with them that they enjoy putting the word out about your work?

Alan: Well, I'll tell you something that's not in any of my other books, and it's something I virtually never speak about because I don't want to confuse people. I'm relatively low on human resources departments and gatekeepers. I think it's good to have that attitude when you're targeting executive-level buyers. However, there are occasionally people in human resources positions or knowledge management positions who have the best of intentions, good skills, and superb connections, and they become unique multipliers.

Over the years, I've had a couple of contacts who created millions of dollars for me because they referred me to their buyer networks. They would find a need with buyers they were connected to and connect me with those buyers. They would also take credit for making the connections. And the more they did, the more the internal buyers they worked with relied on them, and the more they relied upon me and people like me because they knew they would get top results, and it would reflect favorably on them. This spider web of incandescent help throughout organizations became as strong as tensile steel, and that's how I came to work with those organizations for so long.

Q: How did you cultivate these relationships?

Alan: The majority of the people I worked with were people who didn't have any kind of ego. They had to be responsible; they had to make decisions. They saw themselves as fulfilling a noble role in being support people. They had the right attitude, the right perspective, and tremendous credibility, unlike so many others.

They could set up meetings for me with vice presidents or presidents of firms. They set me up with Roy Vagelos who was the CEO of Merck at the time I sat in on his executive council meetings. Art Strohmer was the absolute key guy there, and we're still in touch today, over a decade into his retirement. I met Art through a training program we put on. He felt I had a lot to offer.

The woman at Hewlett-Packard—they were changing their consulting and sales operation to a more consultative role, not just a technical role—Marilyn Martiny, picked up *Million Dollar Consulting*, read some other books, and invited five of us out there to audition, to try out in front of her groups, and I hit a home run. When people joined Hewlett-Packard after that point, they were given two books: *The HP Way* and *Million Dollar Consulting*.

These were exciting, marvelous places to be. They wanted consultants who shared the same mindset. Hewlett-Packard used to have an exercise called the burning platform. The burning platform was meant to excite people to do something—to create rapid, effective movement. They also had something they called the straw man—the test of the ideas. This was occurring daily.

Q: If another consultant calls and says, "I have a client who needs help with succession planning. I would like to refer that client to you." What are my obligations to the consultant who did this referral? What are the ethics about paying for this kind of referral?

Alan: If you don't have an agreement with a consultant about referral fees, you have some options. Without a pre-existing arrangement, referrals may be considered a professional courtesy, and you may choose to reciprocate when the opportunity arises.

If you're referred, it's a good idea to keep the referring consultant abreast of the progress. You can let him or her know the client accepted your proposal and thank him or her for being so gracious to recommend you. A written "thank you" note is also a good idea. And don't forget. You can reciprocate with a corporate client. It depends what you're selling.

When a consultant refers a client to you, they usually say, "I'll expect a referral fee" or "What is your referral fee policy?" If they don't, it's a professional courtesy. My referral fee policy is as follows: If a fellow consultant gives me the name of a buyer and I close the deal, I'll give the referring consultant 5-10 percent of the first year or immediate project business. If a consultant introduces me personally to the buyer, I'll give the referring consultant 10-20 percent. If the consultant closes the sale, and I just come in and make sure I don't embarrass myself, I'll give the consultant 20-25 percent.

A referral fee never goes to an employee within an organization. But you can do that with another consultant, with this exception: If you're working with an organization, and you tell your buyer that you can recommend a consultant who offers a service you don't provide, and you bring me in as the consultant, you can't accept a referral fee from the consultant you referred because your client thinks he or she is getting an objective opinion. Unless you disclose the financial arrangement, it's an unethical arrangement.

Q: What if a consultant wants to subcontract with me? Is that a different arrangement?

Alan: A subcontractor is generally paid on some basis, and that basis is usually time. So, unless you become an actual partner in the project, you're just being asked for a specific level of support. Subcontractors are asked to step in and do something: write code, fix this system, perform a task. Often, you're a pair of hands, you're not a brain, and consequently you're going to get paid based on the tasks you provide.

Q: We all understand the concept of referrals, yet most here aren't doing a fabulous job of referrals. Give us some tips when they get back to the office to become effective in doing referrals or handling referrals.

Alan: I would go through my database, do some triage, and take my highest potential referral sources and give them a call. Make a list of the second highest referral sources, and send them an email to see what business you could stir up. I would ignore the bottom third for the moment because time is an element here.

Next, make sure that people know that you could use the business and that you're accepting referrals: "If you know somebody who can help, let me know." Be sure to make that part of your vernacular, part of your lexicon.

Q: What are some of the most costly mistakes consultants make in their efforts to acquire clients?

Alan: The difficulty is that they don't exploit all the avenues available to them to acquire clients. Consultants are often reluctant to aggressively pursue all of the avenues available to acquiring clients because they feel some guilt doing so. They feel that they're discomforting people. You have to have the opposite mentality.

One of the benefits of building a brand and building a strong, thriving practice is that you get to a point where you're attracting people, and you don't have to do all this outreach. It's important to be aggressive at it when you're starting out or when you see business slowing down.

Q: You often ask, "Who cares?" in response to questions of factors that don't really matter. You clearly are compelled to say this to help us break through the paralysis of over-caring. What are the things we should care about profoundly in our business?

Alan: You should care about your ability to do a quality job for people to help them grow, learn, and prosper. You should care about learning as well so that you're not stagnant.

We grow. We change. And we have to embrace that change. I've had a long career, which is good and bad—it's a little bit frightening—I keep reinventing myself, and I plan to reinvent myself mightily in about four or five years. Just because you're really good at leadership or strategy doesn't mean you should focus solely on those aspects of business.

You have to continually evolve and change to continue to be valuable to your clients. That not only enables you to profoundly help other people, it allows you to take some of the risks for them by learning and testing new models and strategies because you can afford to. You can afford to fail. But it also gives people a reference point for how to act as you continue to evolve as a professional and as a leader.

Q: What are some tips or secrets to accelerate learning integration and application?

Alan: The best way to accelerate integrated learning is to use it immediately. It's not unlike learning a new word—you should use it immediately, you should use it in varied context, and don't worry about what others think about it.

If you want to integrate learning, you have to be discriminating about what learning will be most beneficial for you at the moment. Not everything you learn will be immediately applicable or even relevant, and so you have to understand what to take on. The third thing, which I think is sort of a nice crucible, is ask yourself, "Can I use this to help others? Can I use this immediately and others will profit from it, or is it something that's going to be sort of on my back burner or help me?" Any change you make that can't be perceived by the customer is useless. That's why I hate this back office, quality control nonsense where people are moving desks around, changing rugs, and all this nonsense. When was the last time a customer said, "I'm going to renew my membership because you've changed your back office considerably"? The changes you make must be visible to and appreciated by the client and provide more value to our clients.

Q: You say that most successful people continuously reinvent themselves. If your practice is doing well, and you're content and enjoying your lifestyle, should you step out of your comfort? Also, what are some ways to reinvent yourself?

Alan: You should step out of your comfort zone—even if just one foot at a time—and you don't completely abandon your past, but you need to find more things to bring into your future.

The way you reinvent yourself is by developing new talents. When you develop new talents, what invigorates people, what excites people is the exercising of their talents at work. Don't just rely on old talents. If you develop new talents, they're going to need an expression, and that expression is reinvention.

Q: When a person feels unsafe, they tend to grab and hold onto something; they become rigid, rather than becoming flexible or nimble. How can you help others find that sense in themselves?

Alan: There was somebody in the mentor program who asked me, "How is it you're so unflappable and not scared in pressure situations?" I answered, "I'm not afraid of failure. I'm simply not afraid of failing." I get up. I dust myself off. I'm resilient. On with my life. You can't be afraid to fail. It's part of life. It happens to all of us. It's usually a growth experience. It's not damning. It's simply another experience.

If you have more failures than successes, you have a problem, but you can reverse that too. You have to understand that life is short, and the horizon for all of us gets closer and closer. But when that horizon is closer, you start to create some priorities in life, and the priorities are never really material things. It's about what you create—the legacy you leave for others. You want to be, I think, as aggressive as you can comfortably be. But too many people are deterred by the fear of failure rather than being motivated by the thrill of success.

Building Relationships

Q: You say the more time you spend on relationship building, the quicker your business will grow. Tell us about the importance of creating relationships, and how instrumental is that to business growth?

Alan: The more time you spend on establishing relationships, the faster you get the business. Marketing creates demand, and it's easier to create demand with people with whom you have good relationships.

To build relationships, you must have trust. Trust is the belief that the other person has your best interest in mind. If I trust you, I'll listen to feedback and take it to heart. If I don't trust you, I'll listen to a compliment and wonder what your motivations are. You can build relationships in a variety of ways.

Q: You often say if you're given 90 minutes of dedicated one-on-one time with a buyer, you'll fly across the U.S. to see them. In a 90-minute period of time, how do you quickly develop a relationship of trust?

Alan: I'll travel anywhere for 90 minutes with an economic buyer. I was mentoring a woman and she told me, "I have an opportunity to meet a buyer, but I'm not sure it's worthwhile."

I asked, "What kind of business is it?"

She said, "Well, it's $250 million."

I asked, "Is that your target market?"

She said, "Yes."

I asked, "Are you seeing somebody you think can buy from you?"

She said, "Well, he founded the company. He is the president."

I asked, "Then what is your hesitancy?"

She said, "It's a two-hour drive."

You have to be willing to hop on a plane to a different time zone, a different season, in order to meet with a buyer. That effort shows the buyer you're looking to have a relationship.

There is a direct proportion between distance and reception. I live in Rhode Island. If I tell someone in New York I'm going to buzz down to New York from Rhode Island on the Acela—a two-and-a-half-hour trip—they'll usually say, "Fine, if I can meet with you, I will." If I tell someone in San Francisco I'm going to fly five hours to be out there, they'll say, "Great, I'll put it on my calendar. What time is good for you?" If I tell someone in Hong Kong I'm coming, they'll host me.

You want to impress upon the buyer that you're making this effort, and the farther the better. If you're able to get a 90-minute meeting with a buyer, you should set the agenda in advance. You can explain, "Here are my expectations while we're together. I know you have some expectations too; let's share those and set an agenda." Instantly, you present yourself as a peer of the buyer. A buyer's time is valuable; your time is valuable.

In 90 minutes you want to go through the points on the agenda, establish a relationship, and have a goal for what should come out of that meeting. You should have minimum/maximum objectives. Your minimum objective might be that you establish a good relationship or that you agree to meet again or follow up by phone with the objective of establishing conceptual agreement. Your maximum objective, during that 90 minutes, may be to achieve a high-quality relationship, a conceptual agreement, and enough information to send a proposal within the next day or two.

If you're never meeting your minimum, you're not performing very well. If you're always surpassing your minimum, perhaps you should be even more aggressive. If you're surpassing your maximum, then you're not setting the right expectations.

Q: I'm a firm believer that the more value I provide on my blog and website, the more I give in a relationship, the more it comes back to me. Marshall Goldsmith believes in giving all of his intellectual property away, knowing that where he makes it back is on offerings such as speeches for $35,000. What can we do as consultants to give, with the goal of eventually reaping what we sow? Where do we draw the line so that we don't give too much?

Alan: The easiest thing for a consultant to give away is intellectual property. You don't have to give material things like books, jewelry, or liquor, although that sometimes works. What you want to give is information on best practices, rules, patterns, or trends that you see. You want to give insights. The intellectual property you provide will suggest new ways of thinking to your buyer. That's the easiest thing to give.

As far as the line, it's hard to say you can give too much. One possible line you may draw is telling people what they need to do, but refrain from telling them how. When people ask, "Well, how would I do that?" you can respond, "Well, the first step would be to hire me."

Q: How have you leveraged relationships to create this dramatic success in your business, both in the wholesale environment and now in the retail area?

Alan: At first, I wasn't very good at it, in all candor. When I worked for a consulting firm in Princeton, New Jersey, there was a fellow in the strategy unit who had the stereotypical black book of contacts. He had every contact he had ever made in school and after school. But, if you said to him, "I'm looking for someone who is an expert in the beverage distribution industry," he would say to you, "I know four people, just a minute." He was always my standard for developing relationships and contacts.

I'm not bashful about purging lists because it's not about how much information you have, it's about how much *quality* knowledge you have. I would rather send something to 40 people who are high quality prospects than 5,000 people who are irrelevant. When I started *Balancing Act*—my newsletter, which now has 14,000 subscribers—people asked, "How did you start that without spamming people?" I actually picked 40 people in my database who I thought would accept this without getting upset, and that's how *Balancing Act* began.

Q: In reference to networking and the "nexus" concept and unique multiplier, how can we leverage that concept to strengthen relationships with future clients and existing clients?

Alan: A unique multiplier is someone who can introduce you to a variety of important people who may become important to you as well. They might not themselves be buyers, but they can put you in touch with buyers. What motivates unique multipliers is that they want to add to their own network as well. If you have your own network of contacts, or if you bring entry for them into a new industry, it's interesting to them.

The nexus is somewhat different from the multiplier in that this person usually knows one person, but the one person they know is superb. You'll hear a nexus person make a statement like, "You have to meet my…" and then you fill in the blank: my boss, my brother, my sister, my ex-boss; but they know someone who can immediately use your value.

Q: Most people have far more experience building personal relationships than business relationships. What are the similarities and differences in the two kinds of relationships? How do we transfer what we already know to the new situation?

Alan: Most of us are not adept at building personal relationships; we build personal acquaintances, and there is a difference. In a social setting when we make acquaintances and perhaps develop relationships, what are they about? They're about common interests, and they're about creating new interests for people. We've all heard, "Wow, she is an interesting person. I would like to see her again." And, it's about enriching your life.

Business relationships aren't much different. The context is different, the meeting place is different, the issues are different, but the process is not essentially different. In other words, you're enriching my life, you're a person of interest, and you can bring us value that we don't have right now. They're analogous types of situations. The contextual background changes, but not much else.

Q: You've said before it's not a great idea to be mentored by a friend or to work with friends. What are the boundaries on how we should keep these separate?

Alan: There is a word for it; it's called sanity. The boundaries are pretty clear. You should never take on a friend as a client. You don't want a friend owing you money. You don't want to have to collect money from a friend. You don't want a friend saying, "I'm not quite sure the job was done well enough." You should keep friendships and business relationships separate.

When developing a relationship with a client, be sure to keep it on a professional level. It's difficult to give candid feedback and maintain a professional relationship when you're dealing with a friend. You have to maintain boundaries.

Q: How do we handle it if we're visiting the client at their location, and they want to take us to dinner? Should we refuse? Go along graciously? What advice do you have?

Alan: If the client would like to take you to dinner, it's usually a group dinner to meet some of the people you'll be working with. The rationale is that you get to meet the people you'll be sitting down with the next day; that way you won't have to spend time on introductions later. That makes sense. But I dislike social dinners solely with a client because of potential problems: alcohol, lack of privacy, confidential issues mistakenly revealed, spilled food, and so on.

Q: Could you give us some tips on how to quickly gauge a client's personality and know how best to interact with them?

Alan: I hate labels. Too often, they're used to explain away rather than to understand. There are, however, some behavioral and environmental things you can look for to see who you're dealing with.

It's important to match your behavior to the comfort zone of the other person and not try to force them into your comfort zone. For example, if someone is assertive and says, "Nice to meet you, what's the best way to proceed?" that's not a person whose time you want to waste. If somebody else, though, says to you, "Tell me something about yourself, I would love to know where you're from exactly. I use to live in your part of the world," you don't want to say, "Yeah, yeah, yeah, I'm from Boston. Now here is what you can do for me." You want to adjust your pace to suit the pace of your client.

Also, look for environmental cues. Some offices look like the bridge of the battleship: everything is in its place, it's neat, anything can be retrieved in five seconds, and you know what is going on. It's sort of scaled back for action, and there is nothing loose. You walk into other offices and there are mementos and paintings, and you know this person is going to have some stories to tell you.

There is not one perfect style of communicating. There is no perfect behavioral style. The key is flexibility. The more flexible you are and able to accommodate a wide variety of personalities, the more successful you'll be.

Q: In consulting, what are the elements that build trust?

Alan: The elements of trust are being free to suggest things without fear of rejection and without fear of one-upsmanship. Trust requires tucking away your ego. The fragility of ego is the downfall of many people. The ego is a wonderfully recuperative entity, so we shouldn't worry about it getting bruised, damaged, or knocked around, nor should we be carrying it on our sleeve. We should tuck it away safely.

Trust is about feeling free to offer advice, feeling free to receive advice, and viewing people with two clear qualifications. One is, this is a healthy, undamaged person. The second is, this person is a peer and has good things to offer.

Q: The journey from prospect to buyer is about overcoming objection filters and converting a series of "no" into a series of "yes." Explain that process and give us some tips to accelerate the process of the journey of "yes."

Alan: Many people think in order to get next door, they need to go around the block. When you ask, "Why don't you take a right and not a left and just go next door?" they say, "I never thought of that."

There are all kinds of filters that naturally intercede between the relationship and the actual buying decision. The filters that are the easiest to get rid of—or maybe the hardest, depending on how you look at it—are your personal filters. These filters may tell you, "I'm not good enough," "I've never worked in this industry," "This is the first time we're meeting," or "I've had a bad experience in this business." You have to get rid of those.

The filters that aren't your own are more difficult to remove. It could be that there isn't a history of hiring consultants. It could be that there is a resistance to using outside help because of past bad experiences. It could be that the decision-making process is flawed. The ideal thing to do is to circumvent that. The whole nature of a relationship is to circumvent it, go right to the buyer, and if you establish a trusting relationship.

You can also fight your way through them, but it requires a tremendous amount of time and discipline. *The reason some people are able to close business more quickly is they simply ignore the buffers.* They ignore the blockers, and they go right to the buyer. When you keep your eye on the obstacles, you head to the obstacles. But when you keep your eye on the goal and stop looking at the obstacles, you stand a better chance of getting to the goal.

Q: Last week I had a conference call with my buyer and her peer who is a prospect. She introduced us and spoke highly of the benefits of our collaboration. The prospect asked for a meeting where he intends to learn more about the work we've done. What are the key steps, questions, and tips to turning this meeting from introduction to engagement?

Alan: Stack the deck with questions about the buyer's needs, goals, and objectives. You can open the conversation saying something like this: "I'm curious—I always ask this question, and I would love to hear your answer, and I'll tell you what other people say if you'd like—what has prompted you to be at this second meeting? Why are you interested in working with me?" Whether that response is 20 seconds or five minutes, it's going to be invaluable.

Ask what she sees as the ideal outcome of the meeting. No matter what the response, it will help inform how you should proceed. He might respond—like a lawyer might—"Never ask a question to which you don't know the answer." She might volley the question back and ask, "What is your idealized outcome?" A good response to that would be, "I would like to learn enough about you to put together a proposal where I can be a tremendous help to you."

A mistake many consultants make is not having control of the conversations or interactions. It can by like herding cattle. A young calf wanders away, and the cowboys have to drive it back. They keep the herd on the trail. It might take them three days, it might take them a week, but they're going to drive the cattle. That's what you have to do with these discussions; you have to keep them together and headed towards your goal.

Q: Do you recommend having a conversation at the completion of a project to summarize and wrap up the project? What are the elements of this conversation, and how can you use this conversation to generate new business?

Alan: There should be regular debriefings with the buyer along the way. You and the buyer should be agreeing on the exact nature of the progress, what objectives were met, and which still have to be done. This last conversation would be a sort of final debrief. During the final 30 days, or ten days of your work together, depending on the overall length of the project, you should be agreeing on what the client needs to continue to do once your work is over. The buyer should provide you with references, testimonials, endorsements, referral business, or whatever you're asking for to the extent possible Then you should determine what your continual relationship or communications will be.

If you don't see an opportunity for more work there, what you can ask is, "Would it be permissible to include you in my database of newsletter subscribers? Would it be permissible for me to call you once a quarter and offer some best practices I've heard?" Provide them with a few different options. If you offer enough menu items, your client will choose some of them.

Q: In our professional relationships, what is the essence of a mutual exchange of value?

Alan: When somebody asks, "What is your billing basis?" I explain, "My fees are based on my contribution to the value you receive from this project which represents a dramatic return on investment for you and equitable compensation for me." That's my standard response. I don't bill by time units. In any consultant/client relationship, both parties should walk away feeling that a great job has been done. Ideally, the client should be left thinking, "I got a bargain." And the consultant should be saying privately, "What a windfall."

Q: If having confidence in the value that we offer and asserting it with conviction and courage is integral to achieving success, why is it so difficult for so many to be confident? What can we do to develop more confidence?

Alan: What it boils down to is fear of the unknown. In many of my workshops, I start by asking for a volunteer. There might be 500 people in the audience. I would ask from the stage, "Can I have a volunteer?" You could hear a pin drop. Nobody moved. I wouldn't move.

When somebody finally volunteered, I would ask them to come up on stage and shake their hand. You could see they were tense and nervous, and I would give them a gift. I would give them books, some recordings, or a gift certificate to a restaurant, and I would say, "Thanks for volunteering." The volunteer would stand there staring at me like, "Now what happens? Do I get hit with a paintball?" I would say, "That's it." The volunteer would go back to his or her seat. The whole audience would be surprised.

Next, I ask, "Why didn't anyone else volunteer? What are the odds that I would embarrass you in front of your bosses at a corporate function? What are the chances that I would get rehired if I had a habit of making fools of my audience? The odds are you were going to gain something here." Then I would ask, "Now, can I have another volunteer?" And 499 people would raise their hand, and I would yell, "Get out the paintballs!"

People are afraid of the unknown, and instead of looking at the unknown as high potential, their innate response is to fear it. Procrastination is a form of fear; delaying things is a form of fear. You have to ask yourself, "Historically, when I've tried new things, what has happened more often than not?"

Q: If I've had a professional conversation at a networking event and I feel I've blown an opportunity—I didn't take charge, I lost control of the conversation—should I just let it go, or is there some way I can redeem myself assuming I have the person's card?

Alan: Never beat yourself up. You can spend your whole life recovering from faux pas, gaffs, and everything else; don't worry about it. Tomorrow is another day, and you'll have another chance. Contact them. What is the worst that can happen?

Q: You say that we shouldn't do business with friends. With some of my clients, I develop very strong relationships. For those of us who desire to create deeper relationships with our clients because it strengthens not only our friendships but our business relationship as well, is this a bad move for our business, or is this a subjective matter?

Alan: In the retail business, closer relationships are the norm. I have two reactions to what you just said. The first is, it's an important distinction, in terms of my retail business, in terms of mentoring, and things like that. I don't consider that the same as wholesale business in terms of relationships.

You can get a lot closer with people with whom you have one-on-one relationships in this kind of business than you can with corporate clients. I'm still not saying they should be intimate friendships, but friendships will inevitably develop out of it. Then you have to use your judgment about how to proceed with that.

When somebody calls you with a question and calls me with the same question, you're dealing with it on a relationship basis, and I'm dealing with it on a business basis.

The difference is what I'm answering in two minutes, you're taking 40 minutes to answer. You're allowing the other person to add peripheral information, to suggest other things, to wander into other areas where I'm just saying, "What's your question? Here's your response. Anything else?"

Even when I have good relationships with people, they know when they're approaching me on a business basis, it has to be pithy and concise and to the point because that's what the relationship is set up to be. The client is looking for an answer; thus, once the answer is provided, the exchange is over.

Kicking It Up a Notch—Reaching the Summit

Q: What are some ways we can kick it up a notch in our businesses in order to go from $0 to $300,000?

Alan: Interestingly, growing a business from $0 to $300,000 isn't that difficult. It's much easier than going from a six-figure to a seven-figure business. Going from $0 to $300,000 means changing some basic habits and developing other basic habits. It means allowing yourself the freedom to fail because nobody is going to rapidly increase business unless they're willing to fail. It means having the wherewithal, the personal integrity, and willingness to step out of one's comfort zone and try new things. If you do that and if you're aggressive enough, two large projects can equal $300,000. One super project can be worth $300,000.

I don't mean having thirty $10,000 projects. With that type of volume, we would be working on two or three projects per month. I mean becoming a major player in consulting by being fearless about your value and what you charge.

Q: If we want to go from a six-figure to a seven-figure business, what are the key changes we need to make to our mindset to move in that direction?

Alan: When I say it's harder to go from six to seven, it's metaphoric. For many people, a $700,000 per year business is their goal. It means a great life, and so I'm not insisting a seven-figure income is the be-all-end-all; but as a point of comparison, going from six figures to seven figures requires two key elements that are difficult to achieve.

You have to let go. When I started Million Dollar Club, one of the characteristics common to all of the members of the club, even at that level of success making seven figures, was that they were all carrying around stuff that they had to let go of.

I use the analogy of playing on the monkey bars on the playground. I can remember, as a kid, grabbing the first rung, holding on, and looking down at the approximately 2,000-foot drop below me. What I did was instinctual; I held on more tightly. When I held on more tightly, my knuckles turned white, my arms cramped up, I lost my grip, fell two feet, and hit the ground. I did that repeatedly. Finally, after watching some of my friends make it across, I realized what I had to do was to counter-intuitively let go, reach out, and generate the momentum to traverse the monkey bars.

In the same way, you have to be willing to let go in your business. You must let go of some things that were dear to you, let go of things comfortable to you, let go of clients who were there when you first started out. You must do that, or you won't have a hand free to grab the next rung.

You must also change your thinking pattern. You have to think big, and establish thinking big as your standard thinking pattern. Pessimism and optimism are philosophies of life—not moods that strike on a particular day. You must choose to be optimistic; to face each day with excitement; and you have to choose to regard your career in the same way. Your mindset every day has to be, "How can I make the biggest impact today? How can I attract the most attention? How can I create the best results?" If you ask yourself those questions every day, your behavior will reflect your thinking. Our self-talk informs our behavior. Changing your attitude creates a different internal language which, in turn, informs your behavior and influences your actions.

Q: Do you have some pointers on how we can change our mindset so that we're constantly thinking bigger?

Alan: There are a variety of techniques you can use. Here are a few: Instead of focusing on getting one new client, think about what broader strategy you can implement that will attract a dozen clients. Instead of visiting prospects, think about how you can draw prospects to you. Instead of improving your website, think about creating a broad Internet presence that's unique and creates a sense of community. Perhaps it's a repository for the best of leadership thinking, a series of videos on the best innovative ideas and thinkers, or an online community where individuals can connect with others in your industry and have access to valuable content and resources.

Those are ways to immediately start thinking differently. Most people decide to tweak their websites, post another position paper, or upload another video testimonial. Most people target a company, and they want to try and make inroads in that company. Why don't you target an industry? Why don't you target a country? You have to think like that.

Q: You tell consultants to raise our fees regularly. How do we know it's time for us to raise our fees, and how can we know if we're raising fees too high and eliminating customers by doing so?

Alan: Not all clients are good clients. What you want to do is determine which clients are of the highest value and focus on them. You should raise your fees when you start noticing that your industry perceives you as highly valuable, when you're producing intellectual property, when you have copyrighted, trademarked, patented-protected your work, or when people refer to you as an expert or authority. It's not that you're either here or there; it's a gradual. As these things happen, you raise your fees.

It's all about the value—not that you perceive, *but the value your perspective customer perceives.* When I do strategic profiling with people—as you know in the mentoring program and so on—it's always about what does the perspective buyer perceive in terms of your value to them? That's when you raise fees. If you lose customers by raising fees, that's okay. The real issue is how many customers do you gain and at what fee level.

There comes a point where value no longer drives fee. That is, fee doesn't follow value; value follows fee. People expect to get what they pay for because buying is an emotional decision. People believe if something comes at a very high price, and there is a strong brand, you get what you pay for.

Q: Most consultants experience slower times in the course of their careers. What should you do when you find yourself in a lull? How can you use it in a positive way?

Alan: If you find yourself in slow times, welcome to the club. What happens in slow times? People stop spending. That's the nature of this profession; there are peaks and valleys. During the slower times, you should focus on doing things you can't do during the faster times. Slow times may give you an opportunity to write more, prospect more, create more intellectual property, and engage in self-development.

In one of my books, I explain that you don't sell the conference table. I've dealt with some people who, when times were tough, kept selling everything. They eventually arrived at the conference table, and one partner asked, "If we sell the conference table, where will clients come to sit?" The other guy replied, "We have no clients."

You can't save your way into growth; you can't cut your way into prosperity. When things are slow, that's the time when you should spend more money and invest in who you are and what you do.

Q: Often, we unknowingly sabotage our own growth and success. What advice can you give for dealing with and overcoming these tendencies?

Alan: We sabotage our growth in a lot of ways. One way we sabotage ourselves is by withholding information from others thinking we're protecting them. That is, often we don't want to burden people with our grief, our failure, our frustrations, or news of the decisions we face. We all need other people, though, and if you don't ask people for help, advice, or support, you wind up communicating with another person, namely a therapist. We all need emotional support. It should ideally come from loved ones, it should come from family and people close to us, but it can come from friends, colleagues, or deliberate support systems such as mastermind groups. We need emotional support systems, and to cut ourselves off from that under the guise that we're protecting them can be detrimental to our business.

Q: What is the difference between someone saying, "I have to do this," and them saying, "I'm going to do this tomorrow morning at 8:00 a.m."?

Alan: This is a difference between the intellectual and the emotional. The difference is when someone says, "I need to" or "I should," the real question is, what are they feeling about the task? I may feel like I have to finish this book. I may feel like I have to start another book. I may feel like I have to get something done. But does that mean it will get done? When you need to do something, you tend to put it onto a "to do" list that never quite gets done. When you feel that you want to do something, you tend to get it done faster.

Q: You say that volatility is here to stay. How do we turn volatility to our advantage?

Alan: With volatility comes ambiguity. If you're comfortable sailing around in a storm, enjoying the turbulent winds, that's an ideal place to be. Nobody knows what is going to happen next; nobody knows what the outcome of every situation will be. The most successful entrepreneurs are adept at operating in situations with high degrees of ambiguity.

You have to be nimble. Things are constantly changing, so you have to be able to say, "Either this will happen, or that will happen. Be prepared for either. Be prepared for both." That's the kind of advice you have to give to your clients as well. Business isn't black and white anymore.

Q: How should we look at problem solving versus innovation within our industry?

Alan: What most companies are seeking to do is restore a past level of performance. If you watch great companies and great individuals, they're constantly raising the bar. When companies or individuals are so far ahead of the competition that they have no competition, there is no urgency and nobody gaining on them. They need to find ways to motivate themselves and raise their own bar.

You have to think big. Innovation requires that you raise the bar. In problem solving, you know the past standard can be met again because we used to do it, so you know it's safe. With innovation, you don't know that your new standard can be met; it's never been done. However, even if you don't get there, if you just get half way, it's still a higher performance than you're currently achieving.

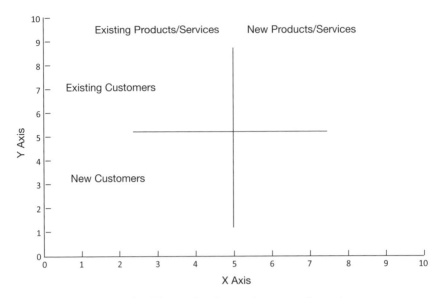

Figure 6.1: The product/service/customer dynamic.

That's where consultants become very important, and that's also where what we can do for ourselves becomes very important. What we have to say to ourselves is, "I've written a couple of books. That's pretty good. It's probably better than most consultants, but how can I express myself in other media? How can I express myself in other languages? How can I express myself in multimedia? What else should I be doing?" Or, "I'm going to reinvent myself as a speaker, and instead of dedicating more time to writing, I'm going to grow my speaking business." Or, "I'm going to become a coach." Or, "I'm going to start a new discipline entirely about organizational productivity."

Q: Can you tell us how we can use the Double Access Chart process visual to give us some ideas about kicking it up a notch?

Alan: In the Double Access Chart, clients are on the top: the left being existing and the right being new. Products and services are on the vertical: the top being existing and the bottom being new. But, this has changed. The figure illustrates how we all must evolve, reinvent ourselves, and create intellectual property. Traditionally, the easiest quadrant was selling existing products and services to existing customers. It was the easiest thing: they know you, they love you, you've already got the stuff, so you introduce more of the same stuff.

But what is happening is existing clients are cutting back on the budgets allocated to the same old stuff, whether ours or somebody else's. They feel that they've done the same thing for a long time. They're pretty good at it, but they can't do this same old stuff anymore if they want to grow their businesses. So, you need to offer new products and services to existing customers. This puts you in a different quadrant, and now what you must communicate is, "You know, you need some new direction, but we have a solid relationship, we still have trust, we still have the creditability of having proven results, so I'm in the perfect position to provide you with new products and services. I would like to discuss this new product with you. People are raving about what it has done for their businesses. I would be remiss if I didn't offer this to my best clients." That's how you can use these quadrants in a volatile time to understand how you should be adjusting your business.

Q: What must consultants do if they want to go in a new direction with a different offering?

Alan: A consultant who has been in business for a while has a web of contacts, a brand that's built up, and experience in introducing a new product or service to their existing clients. They have a client base. It might be a new product or a new service, but it's certainly not as tough as being a brand new consultant. The toughest thing for anyone is to introduce new products and services to new clients. (Which is why cold calling and buying prospect lists is silly.) By definition, that's what a new consultant is doing because they don't have clients. But they have the option of producing new products and services for existing clients.

Q: You use this metaphor of a bike to illustrate the importance of setting your direction: "If your bike's front wheel is one degree to the right, you could end up in a whole different universe." Explain the applicability of this concept to achieving success.

Alan: On a traditional bicycle, the momentum comes from the rear wheel. The power in your rear wheel is your skills, experiences, ability, and all the great stuff you bring to bear. But all those elements are what propel you forward, while the front wheel, or your navigation wheel, steers where you go. So the real trick is the delicate, nuanced art of guiding this front wheel to get the power you have to the right place, at the right time, at the right speed.

You have to have good navigation, the ability to determine what your value is, what your market is, and how best to get there. That's the trick of the bike. Power alone isn't enough, nor is navigation alone. If you have the skills, expertise, and ability but are delivering it to the wrong audience, your business won't succeed. Similarly, if you get to your marketplace, but you have nothing of value to offer them, you're not going to be successful either.

Q: How important is it for us to formulate communities around our world to reach higher levels of successes?

Alan: Communities are important to your business because they provide another opportunity for you to connect with your audience, and members derive value without your needing to be actively involved all the time. To develop thriving communities, however, involves a lot more than smart marketing. It involves a lot more than pumping intellectual property. You have to grow and inhabit a larger psychological, emotional, spiritual space because one way or another, you're taking people into your life.

Community is about people coming together to speak directly to each other, but knowing that you're the reason they're together and able to engage with others in a way that helps them grow their business. Also, the more people you draw to your community, the more influential the people who come into your community, the more influential people they will draw, and it becomes a sort of self-fulfilling prophecy (not unlike the iPhone and its apps, by the way).

Community can be achieved at any level. The key is for people to both be able to contribute to it with a sense of gratification and to gain education and empowerment from it.

Q: What are some insights into what make a consultant successful?

Alan: One is that you should never be satisfied with what you've accomplished. You should always want to accomplish more. Possessing a genuine and legitimate hunger to do better and to do more is a sign of an active and inquisitive mind.

There is no room for defensiveness. You don't need to accept everything, but it's better to listen to what people have to say and decide what is good for you.

You need to have confidence, and be okay with yourself, be okay with failure, and feel good about yourself so that you can face the next challenge and face the next situation without the added worry about protecting yourself. Those are some of the attributes I see in successful consultants.

Q: What are some of the structural defects consultants have in our businesses, and how do we recognize and eliminate them?

Alan: Any kind of structural or systemic defect means there are flaws in your business that are costing you and hurting your business. We often don't recognize them as such because we accept things as necessary evils, and they become inculcated. Most of these necessary evils can be addressed, eradicated, otherwise squashed underfoot, but you have to have the volition to do that. Often, we don't see them because we're blind to them, and we need other people to point them out to us.

One of the benefits of being part of a community, whether large or small, is that other people can point them out. So, we perform work, we have aspects to our companies, and we get involved in situations which we shouldn't be doing any more. Even if they made sense at one point, they don't make sense any longer.

Conclusion

The more successful you are and the longer you're in business, the easier it is to acquire both the wrong kind of business *and* the right kind of business. Why settle for the former when you can select the latter?

The most economical "new" business is repeat business. "Thinking of the fourth sale first" means considering a client relationship as a longstanding process, not a finite project or "event." Selective acquisition of clients requires you reject inappropriate business, ask for referrals, manage new accounts rigorously, and understand that people believe they get what they pay for. Therefore, you must understand that value will actually follow your fees as you escalate them. When this happens, you'll be the ultimate consultant.

7 | Value-Based Fees: Creating the Win-Win Dynamic

Buyers don't shop for the best price or negotiate with the salespeople. They choose brands based on their pragmatic and practical virtues, but they also want the satisfaction of knowing they have chosen the best brand *for them*.

The majority of buyers who want to find the right vendors, partners, and resources for their organizations pursue value—they don't shop price. Therefore, whether seasoned or new, you'll want to increase your credibility and then charge accordingly. To do otherwise is to deprive yourself of a fair price for your services.

There is another adverse consequence of low fees. They promote doubt with the buyer. Once buyers are told a price far less than they expected to pay, they begin wondering if there is value in your services. You can't afford for your buyers to have these doubts about you.

The Genesis of Value-Based Fees

Q: Where did the concept of value-based fees come from?

Alan: After being fired in 1985, I went out on my own. I made a lot of mistakes, but I also made two decisions that were really crucial for me. The first decision I made was that since this was a relationship business, I would focus on forming the right relationships with the right buyers. The second decision I made was that my fees would be based on the value of my work.

Earlier in my career, I had worked at Kepner-Tregoe, a training company in Princeton, NJ. We sold training materials and hosted public sales training seminars where we charged by the head. Essentially, we were charging $250 for a set of materials that cost about $25 to put together, and

$300 per person for public seminars. We had goals for the fiscal year, and we were responsible for moving more and more boxes and selling more and more tickets to the seminars.

I knew I didn't want to be in that business. I didn't want to be in the time-and-materials business. I didn't want to be in a business where I was selling commodities. It was terribly labor intensive, terribly impersonal, and the focus was on all the wrong things. The focus was on the deliverable and the thing you were providing rather than the thing you're creating. We were driven by our printing presses.

Value should follow fee. People feel the more they pay, the more the value. If you're at a stage in your career where these factors play a role in a buyer's decision process, there is a value in that, and buyers are willing to pay for it.

Q: Why do you feel that billing by the hour is unethical?

Alan: We're in this business of improving the client's condition. Any client you're working with will be best served by having his or her issue resolved quickly. The more quickly you resolve the issue, the better you're serving the client. However, if consultants are compensated based on the amount of time they spend with a client, that business model is in conflict with the consultant's objective of resolving issues quickly.

If you look at large firms like McKinsey, they all have an accounting "mentality." If a firm is paying one of its consultants $300 an hour, they're billing the client $500 an hour to cover the overhead and make a profit. That whole notion is a production capability strategy and has nothing to do with markets served. It has nothing to do with products, services, or relationships. It's production capability and is no different from a paper mill or a steel mill. If you can improve a client's business in 20 minutes, think about it: You're much more valuable than somebody who takes 20 weeks to accomplish the same thing.

Q: What is the difference between saying a project will cost "X" dollars and this project will not exceed "X" dollars? Are these pricing structures different from having value-based fees?

Alan: You're asking about the fee and not the basis here. When you say a project is going to cost say $150,000, the basis for that is your contribution to the client's derived value. Let's say it was a 10:1 return. The client is deriving over $1.5 million of benefit.

In the second instance, "The project will cost no more than" suggests that the basis of your fee is a sliding scale which has a cap on it; but what is that basis? Having a set limit implies that there is a time in which the goal will be achieved and is thus considered hourly billing. How else are you deciding whether it costs $150, $100, or $75 without some kind of time component as a factor?

In the first instance, "Here is your fee" is true value-based billing. If you're considering the hours and giving a client a price based on your hours, you're not truly embracing value-based fees.

Q: When you set your own fees, do you consider hours at all or do you consider that as one of many things in the formula?

Alan: Many who claim to charge a project fee or value-based fee are simply backing into it trying to estimate how much time they're going to spend on it. Aside from the ethical quandary of why would you get something done faster when you charge by the hour, charging for your time implies that your time is 100 percent productive and valuable. That is, you would be working 40 hours a week straight; so, if it's not going here it's going there, it's a zero-sum calculation.

But it's not your time that's valuable. It's the results that are valuable. If you had your choice, would you rather be working 20 hours a week making a couple of million dollars a year, or working 60 hours a week making $500,000 a year?

Q: Should we consider hours at all? How about factors such as travel, whether it's a project I specialize in, or whether or not I like the client?

Alan: I don't consider travel or time at all. I do consider my own well-being. I'll increase the fee if a project requires more from me. I'll increase the fee if the project requires international travel.

Some projects have more wear and tear than others. If a project is estimated to take a week, but it turns out four or five extra days are required, the fee doesn't change. The margins are so high, additional time doesn't matter.

Also, what I include in my fee are things like my brand. That is, people want *me*.

Q: Why is it better for the buyer, the consultant, and everybody involved to use value-based fees, the ethical factors aside?

Alan: First, the client is much more prone to get their issue resolved quickly because there is equal onus on the consultant to get it solved quickly. That is, if you're going to pay a consultant $100,000 to take on a project, and the consultant can get it done in ten days, it's much better for both parties than taking two months; so, that's the goal the consultant should work towards.

Using this model, the client also doesn't have to make an investment decision each time they contact you. It's a deterrent if a client must consider, "Gee, I need Alan for this, but I know he is going to charge me $2,500 a day."

Thirdly, what if your employees have questions? Do they have to request permission to meet with the consultant because that time will be charged to the project?

Lastly, the fee that's quoted is also the cap. The client knows exactly what the cost is going to be. There are no hours involved. There is no time that's going to accrue and accrue and accrue.

As a consultant, you have to be able to confidently make these kinds of arguments and defend your fee structure. Many buyers have been taught to accept an hourly model by consultants who make an erratic living charging by the hour.

Q: It almost sounds as if the more a buyer makes and the more profitable a buyer becomes as a result of a consultant's services, the more the consultant is going to charge. Is that true?

Alan: No. What is more accurate is that the more that you save your clients, or the more that you improve their business, the greater a fee you can demand. That's an equitable compensation for the kind of results you can produce for them. The size of your business doesn't matter. What you're charging people isn't based on the size of their company or how successful they are but rather on how much they improve due to your direct contribution; that's an equitable transaction.

There is a thread on www.alansforums.com about capitalism and its relationship to business and commerce. Capitalism is based on a very ethical transaction that says, "I'm going to deliver a certain product or service, at a certain quality, and at a certain time in return for certain value that you provide for me in terms of compensation or other benefits that we also agree on." If both you and your client agree on that, you have an ethical capitalist transaction.

Converting to Value-Based Fees

Q: What do I need to do to convert my fee structure to value-based fees? How do we move away from hourly fees and truly embrace value-based fees?

Alan: First off, all new business—clients with whom you're dealing for the first time—should be billed using the value-based system. Never talk about hourly rates, time spent, or materials. If the client brings these factors up, disabuse the client of these notions.

Next, go through your current client list and work on converting the highest potential because otherwise you're going to get bloody in a futile battle. Focus on clients with whom you can do a lot more business; clients who have a highly profitable business; clients with whom you like to work; and clients who can give you a lot of referrals. Convert them over to a value-based system by demonstrating it's in their best interest to do so.

You could broach the topic by saying, "Chad, I've been working with new clients on a new system that they've just loved, and it has worked out very well for them and for me. You've been such a good client I would be remiss if I didn't at least explain it to you so that you can make a choice as to whether you would like to continue with our current arrangement or switch to this newer one."

Q: What if their response is, "I've worked with consultants in the past, and they charge me based on the amount of time a project takes. I don't understand this other rationale. How do I know for sure? I get this okay, so of course if you'll deliver that value, I can see that it makes sense. But how can I be sure that we'll actually get these results?"

Alan: You can say something like, "Well, I can understand that because the consultants you worked with in the past may have taken advantage of you as a client. The fact is that I want to enter into a relationship with you wherein we agree on the objectives, the metrics for success, and the value delivered to you. We agree on how I'm going to help you do that, and then I receive equitable compensation.

Let me ask you a question: Of all those consultants you worked with, how many of them actually sat down with you and established objectives that were business outcomes; metrics to measure progress which you would hold them to and they would hold you to; the value brought to your organization by meeting them; and then provided you options to get there? How many did that as opposed to simply giving you a letter of agreement or a list of their deliverables?"

Q: In the mentoring community, which consultants have the most difficulty transitioning to value-based fees?

Alan: IT consultants have a difficult time because they're used to being hired to be a pair of hands rather than a brain. They come in to do things for the client in place of the client hiring employees. So, any kind of technical consultant tends to have trouble with this. Many IT consultants successfully change if they commit to incorporating it into their business consistently.

As far as what type of personalities have the most difficulty, consultants who will implement the new fee model consistently are those who don't feel threatened, those who haven't feathered a nest so deeply that they don't want to leave the nest. Many consultants say they would love to employ value-based fees, but they say they can't because their clientele isn't right, or they aren't set up for it, or some other unfounded reason.

Q: How do I know if I am undercharging my clients?

Alan: You probably are undercharging your clients. That's a pretty safe assumption. But if you want a calibration, if you want some kind of test instrument, I would tell you this. Provide three different options in the proposals you submit to clients and see which they choose. If clients are constantly choosing the most expensive package, you're probably under-charging. If clients are vacillating between two and three, that's probably a sign you're close to where you should be price wise.

Be aware of what your clients are communicating to you through their words and body language. If they agree very quickly, or say you're a bargain or other things like this, it's nice to hear, but you're probably not really pushing the envelope.

Also, consider the amount of intellectual property you have put into the environment objectively, consider the degree to which you're seen as a thought leader by others, and ask yourself if you're near the top of the pyramid. Similarly, are you charging as if you're at the top of the pyramid, or are you charging as if you're still climbing?

Q: Is my assumption correct that if clients are often selecting option 1, that I'm overpricing?

Alan: If clients are too often choosing option 1, you haven't sufficiently differentiated the increased value in options 2 and 3. If they're buying option 1 for $100,000, they could certainly buy option 2 for $120,000. They can find another $20,000. If they found $100,000, they can find $120,000; but they haven't chosen that option because they feel option 1 will satisfy them, and they don't see enough extra benefit in option 2.

It's incumbent upon the consultant to make sure that option 2 and option 3 are sufficiently increased in value so that clients see the value of the larger proposals. Buyers hate to spend money, but even more than that, they hate to lose value.

Q: Some clients are very aggressive in their requests and are looking to change a lot on an ongoing basis. Some clients would just like to tweak their business. The challenge I run into is regarding post-project, ongoing mainte-nance. How can you project what the requests may be over the next year? I find the best way to do it is think hourly for that part of my business. Am I making a mistake to segment that part of my business and think hourly there versus try to think value-based?

Alan: Offer your clients three options and say, "We have three options here. One is the major change option, if you envision you're going to be making frequent major changes, which happens with the best of sites, with the best of implementation because you have a dynamic business and conditions change. We'll make unlimited changes for you for $50,000 a year. And if you want to renew that for the next year, it's $35,000 and it declines.

The second option is the minor change program, and that is if you believe that you'll be making minor changes, and by that we mean no more than one a month and no more than one page is worked on. We're happy to do that, and that fee is $15,000, and the fee is reduced to $10,000 the next year.

If you don't want to pay for either of these programs but you want to pay by the instance, then we'll charge you an hourly fee for that, and our fee is $500 an hour." You can charge an aggressive hourly fee because it can serve as a deterrent.

So, there they have their choice. If they don't select the bulk amount for either of the major or minor changes, then they're going to have to pay $500 a shot as they want changes. If you think about it, if they make one change a month, suddenly we're talking $6,000. That's if the change only takes an hour.

Q: One aspect of that business could be interpreted as commodity based, not the high-end strategy type conversations. In a commodity base, the challenge for consultants is to push what would be the additional value so it's not presenting itself as commodity based. Is that right?

Alan: You have to take people out of a commodity mindset because in worst case, there are commodities out there, and there are instances where you have to compete on price. Now, that's not a place I ever want to go, and it's not a place I think consultants ever have to go. There are things that you buy every day—whether it's staples, rubber bands, bread, or milk—where people make decisions on price. But we're not in that situation.

Q: On the Million Dollar Websites, we publish our prices for the three packages offered on the site. So, what is the answer for those coming out of there and saying, "But wait a second. Why are you deciding to put your prices on your website where you're recommending for us not to establish prices on the front end?"

Alan: We established prices for that, just as there are prices for the mentor program, because what we have there are three different programs. What we're saying is that you can have a dramatic and very comprehensive website created with all kinds of follow through for one price, or you could do it more modestly for a second price, or you could do it even more modestly for a third price.

Don't forget that a website for most people is a credibility statement, not a sales tool. Consequently, we're helping them create these great credibility statements, but it's hard to put a value on how much new business is being derived or how much new business that it's helping to close. In the case of the Million Dollar Websites, we're giving people options in terms of what they want to invest and what kind of help they think they'll get from it.

Q: Are there any situations when value-based fees don't make sense? When you should just put a price tag on something?

Alan: Value-based fees don't make sense when you simply have been asked to do a speech or an event. For example, if you're asked to do a keynote, be sure to offer your other services: "Would you like me to do these five other things as well?" If a client wants to opt for that kind of menu, then suddenly you have a value-based fee. But if a client just wants you to show up and speak, then you charge a speaking fee for that.

Q: One of the obstacles to value-based fees and to converting clients is convincing the clients that we can really deliver. If we don't have a long list of testimonials or a long history, how do we do that?

Alan: You show that you're credible, if you don't have a large client list, by providing all kinds of intellectual property and initiatives with new ideas. No matter what your area of expertise, you also have to have an original, creative, compelling approach that will help people say, "I need to hear more from this person." Do your homework about the business and industry so you're conversant in the prospect's environment and you can say things like, "You know the reason you're ranked number four in your industry is that you haven't identified yourself as having a particular specialty, but you're just following the footsteps of one, two, or three. Let me give you an example of a change you can make quickly and easily to address that problem."

No one needs justification for value-based fees based on the amount of time they have been in the profession, their age, their gender, their specialty, or anything else. Value-based fees are simply payment terms within a business relationship between the client and the consultant as equitable partners.

Your credibility comes from being able to assure your prospects that you have value independent of the number of clients you've had, the number of times you've done this, what your background is, or where you went to school.

Q: If you don't have a robust client list and a prospect asks you for the references, what do you do?

Alan: If you first work at developing a relationship, the probability is that you won't need references. If you've reached the proposal stage, you've shared things, chatted, and discussed the proposal. At that point, the client is probably not going to ask you for references. If they do, give character references. If they ask to get references from your clients, you can respond, "As it would be with you, my clients insist on complete anonymity; and I'm sorry, but I can't give you their names. However, I can give you the names of people who can attest to my voracity, my honesty, and my ethics."

Q: Do value-based fees have any kind of relationship to self-esteem?

Alan: Self-esteem is really the underlying factor behind people's ability to change, to be courageous, and to overcome objections. It's not directly related to value-based fees. If you have low self-esteem, you're going to say, "What makes sense to you, or what can I do to persuade you, or how would you prefer to work?" But when you have high self-esteem, you aren't afraid to speak your mind, question a client, or critique an organization.

Q: There are many people in your community whose focus is on training. They offer a variety of programs. How do you help them take the training deliverables into a value-based framework?

Alan: Training is noble work, and most people who are making money in speaking are also trainers. Very few of us are able to sustain ourselves as keynote speakers if we chose to do that alone. Very, very few.

The orientation for training has always been on the input side. How many people, how much material, and what is the duration? People who provide training should discuss what should be happening prior to beginning the training. In other words, what is the preparation for the culture? What is the preparation for the participants? What is the preparation for their managers?

Then have a variety of experiences for them—not just a single event but several events over the course of time. Then have follow-up for them so that you're doing email coaching, phone coaching, or a session for their direct superiors. You're measuring their progress in terms of what their superiors have found; you're doing benchmarking studies, internal best practices, and so on. Instead of a two-week training program, you're in a six-month process; and instead of charging $25,000, you're charging $125,000.

Q: Should training professionals also embrace this platinum rule: focus on the output rather than the input?

Alan: They should because otherwise they can go on training forever, but there are two huge problems with that. One is that you can only charge so much because you're a commodity, and the buyer will always be somebody in human resources or training who is focused on trying to find the lowest price; they'll always look for somebody who can do it cheaper than you can.

Second, if you work with clients that way, it's terribly labor intensive. Not only are you faced with lowering your income because you're in a competitive commodity product area, but you're also decreasing your wealth because training is so labor intensive if you do it in the conventional manner. A lot of people get started that way, but the goal should be to evolve out of it.

Q: When you're speaking to trainers and they want to know how they recover the costs of materials such as printing the participant's manual, mailing the books, and so on, should they separate that out or fold it into the value-based fees?

Alan: The companies that need to focus on those expenses separate it out. They charge for materials. That's why time and materials are so noxious to me. It's the cost of doing business. Just like a telephone, a stamp, or FedEx is a cost of doing business.

You should be charging so much in value-based fees that your margins are so high you absorb that. But every time I see somebody charging for telephone, gas mileage, or things like this, I know I'm looking at an amateur.

Value Formula

Q: How do I figure out what my value is?

Alan: It's not a question of what you're worth; it's a question of what your contribution to the project is worth. If you ask the right questions, set the right objectives, measure the necessary results, and provide obvious value, you'll get the client to commit. There is a very nuanced and subtle way to get the buyer to say conservatively what the solution they are looking for is worth and what role you're playing in contributing toward it.

There are three questions consultants should ask themselves at the time of setting fees: "Why me? Why now? Why in this manner?"

- **Why me?** If you have a particular piece of intellectual property, a reputation for being an expert in a particular area, or experiences that make you perfectly suited to a project, and there aren't many others who can do this as well as you can, that certainly is a reason to charge more.

- **Why now?** Is there a certain urgency? Is there a window of opportunity that's going to close? Is there a problem that's growing significantly worse where the client is really moved to action? In that case, you should also charge more.

- **Why in this manner?** Has the client tried to resolve the issue but failed? Did they hire a different consulting firm that failed? Have they just let the issue fester and thought it would go away by itself?

By asking yourself the questions why me and why now and why in this manner, you can also get a feel for how aggressive you can be with your fees. A good formula is to try to demonstrate a 10:1 return for the client, but I have a couple of qualifiers for that.

I was consulting with a boutique New York consulting firm. This one was in manufacturing, and they told me that if they can get their client a 2.5:1 or 3:1 return, the client would be ecstatic. Don't forget all returns are annualized, and that's the second aspect that's very important.

There are three components to consider when you're setting fees:

- **First**—what is the tangible result times its annualization? What is the amount, let's say, of market share increase or extra profit or increased revenues? Multiply the tangible results by the annualization because not only should the results continue once they're established, but they should multiply.

- **The second factor**—what are the intangible benefits times the emotional impact? What does this mean to us in terms of reputation or aesthetics, and multiply that by the emotional impact for the buyer. That's an important consideration that too many consultants overlook. It's not easily quantifiable, but it's highly qualitative.

- **The third factor**—peripheral benefits. That is, even though it isn't an objective and even though it isn't expected as a tangible outcome, if as a result of this project the client is able to attract talent more easily, reduce recruitment costs, or retain people longer and reduce attrition costs, those are important peripheral benefits to at least note in the proposal and adds to the heft of your fee.

Q: Should I try to put a price tag on the peripheral benefits? If the client tells me that their recruitment costs are a certain amount, should I try to quantify that in a proposal?

Alan: You should put a fee together, but you don't put a price tag on each and every item. If that wasn't the objective of this project, but the objective is to reduce recruitment costs, then you would quantify it, and you would say, "What are your recruitment costs right now?" "Well, we find that middle management is about $65,000 a person." "What do you think, if we achieve the objectives of this project, we would be able to reduce your turnover by?" The buyer says, "I think by at least 30 percent." I say, "Let's take half of that, 15 percent. If we reduced it by 15 percent, how many fewer people would you need to be hiring?" "Well, probably 30 a year." "What is 30 times $65,000?" Now you have a tangible and a quantitative result. So, it depends whether these things are directly the objectives of the project or they're simply peripheral benefits.

Q: How do you measure intangibles in the proposal? How do you talk about them with the buyer?

Alan: You don't have to measure them because what we do is art and science. The science is the objectives, measures, value, and quantifying what we can. The art is understanding the buyer's ego, the buyer's personal objectives, and the importance of the peripheral and intangible benefits to the buyer.

Q: When considering the annual return on a project, do you look at the next year, the next five years, or into perpetuity? How far out do you project the effects of your work will be felt?

Alan: Ask the client, "What will this look like in the year ahead or whatever the timeframe is if we achieve this?" I usually cut the client's projections in half—I'm archly conservative—so the client can never accuse me of overestimating the numbers. Then in the proposal, note that these will no doubt be annualized benefits. It enforces A) the tremendous value that's accruing, and B) the fact that my fees are based on the most conservative aspects of that value. That's what provides the client with the comfort, really, not to question fees when the results look so positively attainable.

Q: What about proposals and engagements where it's difficult to define the tangible in terms of bottom line—like a leadership training program?

Alan: That's a very good example, and you have to be careful of broad requests; these can be red herrings. When clients say they want a leadership training program, there are two things happening: One is the client has already arrived at an alternative. Secondly, the client is asking you to deliver the alternative, in effect completely bypassing what has generated that alternative.

The question to ask immediately is why does the client want a leadership training program? The client will likely say something like, "We find that people are being promoted here without sufficient preparation on how to deal with former colleagues who are now subordinates, how to deal with financial matters when they haven't been prepared to read balance sheets, how to deal with the press, and so forth." Then you say, "What are the repercussions of their not being prepared, and what are the advantages of their being better prepared?" The client will say, "We'll have less turnover in these leadership positions, we'll have better relationships with the press, we'll have more productivity from people who don't feel that they've been bypassed for promotion, and so forth." You always have to seek the "why" which is behind any preordained alternative.

Q: Do you return at the end of the project engagement to review the value that you promised in the proposal?

Alan: Yes. First of all, as the project continues you should be interacting with the buyer on a regular basis, and it might be more frequent at first. It might be weekly, and then it might be twice a month. It depends on the length of the project. But you should be debriefing with the buyer regularly, applying the metrics. The proposal is an organic document; it's not something static on a shelf. Use the metrics to agree that you're making progress and the correct progress; or to fix things that are wrong because you have joint accountabilities, so if something is not happening, whose accountability is it?

Then toward the end of the project, you should sit down; and assuming that there is no repeat business or nothing else you're going to do there, you should prepare for the disengagement. The disengagement is about taking another look at the objectives. Were they met? Yes. How do we know? By these metrics. Was this value delivered? Yes. So, the return you're getting on your investment here is X, Y, or Z. That's a good thing to do because it will prompt the buyer to think of you in the future if you're needed. To refer you to other people. To provide you with a testimonial. To serve as a reference, and so on. It's almost *de rigueur*. You don't just walk away from a happy client.

Q: You advocate being paid in advance whenever possible. Why is that so important?

Alan: When you get paid in advance, it takes a lot of concerns off your mind! It takes concerns off your mind that somebody might be unhappy with you, try to interfere with the project, and so forth.

It also completely eliminates the possibility that the project will be canceled because you're not going to give the money back. Projects are canceled sometimes because of external circumstances, the buyer changes, or unforeseen events, but *your* project can't be canceled.

The third thing about being paid in advance is that it gives you the freedom to be candid and honest and not have your work challenged by subordinates or others in the organization. They can't easily disrupt the project or root you out of there because the buyer has a vested interest now in making sure the investment that has already been made shows dividends. It's really a win-win situation to get paid in advance, and I think you're quite right in feeling that way.

Q: Regarding tangibles versus intangibles, how do we uncover the intangibles in a project?

Alan: There are a few ways. All buyers have personal objectives that are going to be met by a professional objective whether they're in small companies or large companies, middle managers or senior managers, for-profit or non-profit, government, or education.

Ask yourself these types of questions: What is the personality of the buyers? Do they love to lead teams—they want to be seen as being in the forefront? Are they highly task-oriented and results-driven—they just want to get things done rapidly? Are they people who want to prove something to others? Do they have very strong upwardly mobile aspirations within the organization or elsewhere? Do they prefer to play a role not solely in their company but also in their profession and take a leading role in trade associations? What kind of person are you dealing with, and what will be personally important to them? You're going to get a lot of intangible benefits from those questions.

The second area to think about is what I call interstitial. Interstitial refers to the details between the larger objectives that tend to benefit from the work as well. When you look at the objectives and the tangible benefits, you ask yourself, "What changes are going to result from that? What else is going to happen as a result of this?" You can suggest this to the buyer: "If you did that, then this should also happen, correct?" The buyer might respond, "It is, and it will, and that would be an added benefit." And you have increased your value.

Q: What are some examples of the intangible when we're talking about web-type projects or IT-type projects, and we're talking to technical people?

Alan: I don't need to know the project; what I need to know is who the buyer is. So, the buyers are web and IT buyers. Some of the intangible benefits would be being seen as state-of-the-art; having the potential to almost immediately go global when they're ready to, with the proper infrastructure in place; having the ability to quickly inject additional products and services into their client base via electronic means; having the ability to communicate better with customers and receive feedback more rapidly; or possessing the ability to involve their customers, and their vendors for that matter, in their own design work and critique of new products and services.

Those things may not be part of their original intent to have a new website or new web presence. But once you present the potential of these outcomes, while it might be hard to quantify because they don't know when they'll introduce new products and services, the option and the potential of being able to do that rapidly is appealing.

Q: Is it possible that the owner of a small business isn't fully realizing the potential value to him or her, and asking that question early on may actually shoot myself in the foot because we haven't uncovered the value yet?

Alan: You have to use your judgment, and you have to get a feel from those owners fairly early about what they're willing to commit. You have to make sure you're dealing with people who have a particular level of intelligence and ability to run a business well.

You can find out by looking at what other investments they've made: Is the business failing, or have they invested in the physical property and physical plant? Are they careful about collecting client names and providing their clients—especially a good client—with great relationships; or do they just treat clients as if they're an interference? You can look for those kinds of signs and determine how much you think the owner is going to place faith in your kind of value and your kind of help.

Q: For the consultants who focus on smaller businesses, what can they do to determine whether they should go into a full blown OMV discussion—objective, measure, value—or if they should find out the budget early on?

Alan: Any time you're talking to a small law firm, a small accounting firm, a medical practice, or a design firm, you need to know early the size of the business, the revenue generated, and the number of employees. You're better off getting a $100,000 project than ten $10,000 projects, and you're much better off getting a $10,000 project rather than ten $1,000 projects. You owe it to yourself to check these things out early, and again try to get a feel for how much the organization is willing to invest.

Conclusion

One of the fundamental problems besetting the consulting profession is quite simply how to charge the client. If you're charging by the hour or day, you should move to a value-based fee system. The "traditional" approach of charging for the time spent solving the client's problems comes from the "sister professions" of accounting and law, where the approach has served to seriously delimit the ability of accountants and lawyers to earn money and create real wealth.

This business is about value, not about fees. If the discussion is about fees, you've lost control of the discussion. Collaborating with the buyer to establish project outcomes, measures of success, and *value* to the organization will result in higher fees than any other approach to billing you've ever employed.

8 | Doing Well by Doing Right

There are ethical gray areas that require analysis and even introspection. But they are the minority. It's important to remember that what is legal might not always be ethical, and what is unethical might not always be illegal. That's why ethics should be within the purview of consultants and not the legal department.

Most ethical transgressions are committed on behalf of the organization, not for individual gain. That makes them no less serious and can, in fact, create peer pressure to engage in the same acts in a sense of distorted loyalty. Consultants need to do better. They need to understand the nature of ethics and the challenges they can present in order to arm themselves with the skills to do ethical battle.

What Are Ethics?

Q: Can you define "ethics" vs. laws for us?

Alan: Laws are easy. Laws are codified legislation which a governing body decides is appropriate for social and commercial interactions. So the law is written. It's not black and white. If it were, we wouldn't need judges and juries; the law has shades of gray. The bromide among attorneys is first argue the facts; if you're losing on the facts, argue the law. With the exception of Louisiana in the United States, we follow English common law. (Louisiana follows the Napoleonic code.)

Morals to me are the underlying belief systems which permit a society to function daily without anarchy, rampant thievery, and chaos. Of course, we see countries that operate without morals. There was a time when in Lagos, Nigeria it was hard to walk down the street without stepping over bodies. There was a time where Colombia was reaching anarchy. Greece has come close more recently. Somalia is anarchic. Afghanistan is close.

Ethics are values that people agree to live by that help them in their daily lives and daily interactions, and so personal ethics tend to vary. Morality concerns the overreaching agreement of society on how to operate. Occasionally there are differences in morality amongst good people. Abortion would be one case in point; vivisection would be another. I think we're reaching that position with the climate change, global warming, and so forth. I think there are good people on both sides who have different views.

You can go to extremes. I am against vivisection. But I'm also against the actions of PETA—People for the Ethical Treatment of Animals—which goes to extreme and violent lengths to protect animals, many of which I think are completely inappropriate.

Ethics, though, are much more situational. They determine how people react and act in certain situations. Anatole France said, "The law in its majestic equality forbids the rich, as well as the poor, to sleep under bridges, to steal bread, and to beg in the streets." That's the difference between ethics and law. It's illegal to steal, but what if your family is starving? Ethically it's right to feed your kids, it's not legal to steal the bread, but you can see the quandary.

Ethics has three primary factors. One is awareness. Are you aware of what constitutes ethical and unethical behavior in your environment? The second is volition. Are you willing to do something about it? And third would be skills. Do you have the capacity to do something about it? I think those three things, if they're all present, represent someone who can consistently act ethically. If any one is missing, you'll have very situational ethics.

Q: We've all heard you say, "Who certifies the certifier?" Who sets the ethics when they aren't clear?

Alan: That's a great question. I was an expert witness in an ethics case at one point. What had happened was a very large search firm had a major client, the client was looking for a replacement CEO, and the search firm talked them into getting the job to evaluate not only external candidates but internal candidates. They gave a test to one of the leading internal candidates and determined after the test that the candidate wouldn't pass muster, wasn't acceptable, and, of course, they went and found an external candidate, which paid them a lot more money.

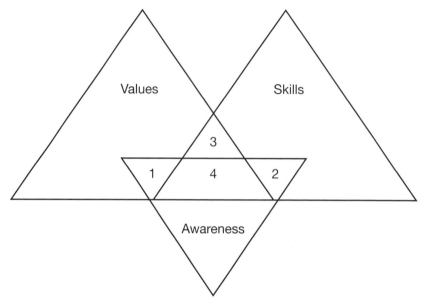

1. "Would act" but can't, because of lack of skills.
2. "Should act" but won't, because of lack of values.
3. "Could act" but doesn't, because of lack of awarness.
4. "Will act" because all elements are present.

Figure 7.1: The factors in ethical conduct.

An ethics problem right there. But the lawyer for the defendant—the man who was passed over who felt he had to leave the company after that harsh assessment—called me in and asked me to take a look at what went on. What happened was the search firm used two of its people who had no background in psychometric testing, no background in assessments—one was an engineer and one was a manager of some sort—and they gave this test that had never been validated to this poor guy and reached their own self-serving conclusions that he wasn't effective. From my point of view, all they were trying to do was get the external work which paid more.

I appeared at a deposition at this huge law firm in New York which the big search firm had chosen to defend themselves; eight floors full of lawyers—you want to start to get some air freshening spray in the place. This very, very aggressive female attorney came at me and pressed me about what constitutes ethics, how would I know, and what about the fact that ethical behavior is set by the prevailing society? You could have the culture of a neighborhood, the culture of a nation, the culture of a school, the culture of a department, and the culture of a company. A culture is nothing more than that set of beliefs which govern behavior. That's where ethics come in.

What most people would ascribe to as an effective way to conduct oneself business-wise and socially is the prevailing ethical behavior. Does that vary and does it vary in circumstances and among different people? Of course it does. But I can safely make a case to you that getting two people with no testing experience administering a test that has never been validated, the result of which is to get a higher commission than choosing an internal candidate who up to that point had brilliant internal reviews, *is an unethical practice*! After a lot of fireworks and a lot of shooting across the table—in depositions it's not about validity or truth, it's about trying to destroy the other expert—the search firm had to settle out of court.

Q: Does common sense reign when we're looking at an ethical question?

Alan: No. Common sense, though, is in the eye of the beholder. Most people have heard my story about being in a warehouse in Pittsburgh and wandering back there because I was doing a project for a very large company at the time, and the project was about something else entirely, but I always toured the grounds.

In this warehouse where officers of the company never ventured, there was an old-fashioned nude calendar which said, "Miss March," and I said to one of the people, "What is that?" He said, "Miss March. Pretty good, huh?" I said, "Okay, where is the supervisor?" He said, "In the office."

I said to the supervisor, "Do you know what is out there?" He said, "Yeah, Miss March. Wait 'til you see Miss April." I said, "You know, this creates a hostile work environment. You can't do that." He said, "Alan, it's a warehouse." I said, "I can see it's a warehouse, and I know that you probably only see men back here, but nonetheless you can't do that." He said, "Well, we have done it forever." I ran into the manager as I was leaving, and the manager said the same thing, "It's Miss March, Alan. It's a warehouse, give us a break."

I went back to the president, who I had a debriefing with at 6:00 anyway, and I told him what was going on. Then I told him about this. I said, "You know Fred, this isn't in my purview, but here is what I found." And of course, he was rightly horrified. I said to him, "You have three problems.

You have these people putting up Miss March who don't know the difference. You have no monitoring; nobody found this except me wandering back there. And your human resource people are obviously asleep at the switch."

That's a normal condition, but it still shouldn't be. Go back to common sense. Do any of these people have common sense? They'll claim they did, but it certainly didn't strike me that they did with relation to Miss March. Miss March had more common sense than all of them.

Common sense is often too common and not very sensible. Other than that, it's fine. It's like conventional wisdom. It's seldom conventional and seldom wisdom, but there you have it.

Q: Who makes a decision whether something is ethical?

Alan: Ethics is a personal matter. That's why I said morality pertains to society at large and prevailing conditions. Ethics are usually situational and personal. And the question is whether you're mainly consistent with others or not. Nonetheless, you have a personal responsibility to make ethical decisions. If you need help deciding whether something is ethical, you can go to a colleague or group of colleagues and see what kind of advice they give you.

Many organizations have corporate ombudsmen who help with these matters. There are experts just like there are in the law; there are ethicists. (I wouldn't advise the one who used to write in the Sunday magazine section of the *New York Times*. He is a former writer for David Letterman, and his advice is just hopeless. How he got this contract is beyond me.)

You can go to a university and find somebody teaching ethics courses, and ask them about it. You can hire them for $150 an hour, or they might just be kind and give you an answer. So, there are places to go.

You're right, though, that different cultures have different ethical bases. For example, in many places in Asia there is a belief that any human idea belongs to the masses, belongs to everyone. You can't safely copyright, patent, trademark, or service mark an idea. That's okay because even in the United States, even in western cultures, you can't really protect the concept.

However, in Asia it's often extended to the intellectual property itself, and some of my books have been copied word for word and put out by other people. Articles are simply appropriated. That's the prevailing culture. You'll periodically see the Chinese, South Koreans, Indonesians, or Malaysians bulldoze 450,000 CDs that were simply pirated. You'll see people in movie houses over there shooting videos of the movie which they then sell on the internet, and this is quite acceptable. So, there are very different ethical bases in different cultures. Some of them are simply formalities and social mores, but some of them go much deeper.

You have to adjust to the social and business environment in which you operate. I'll give you a quick example of that. When I was with a consulting firm in Princeton, I was in charge at one point of Asia and Latin America. I calculated that I had 32 million square miles of ocean alone in my domain. My Venezuelan general manager, who was having a tough time meeting budget, put in his next year's budget figures, and I saw in there $32,000 for "commissions." We didn't pay commissions. Everybody was on salary at the time, and people received bonuses at the end of the year for their performance.

I immediately saw through the commissions and realized what they were—they were bribes. I said to him, "Jorge, we aren't paying bribes. I'm telling you right here and now, you take this out. I'm not authorizing the $32,000, and if you find it somewhere else, we're still not paying bribes. If I find you're paying bribes, you'll be fired."

He said, "Alan, we can't compete here without paying bribes. All of my competitors pay bribes. We have to pay bribes to get business."

I said, "There are a lot of companies competing here and a lot of services and products not paying bribes. If you're not smart enough to figure out a way to do that, I'll find somebody who can because I'm not accepting that. That's not the way our company does business, and if we have to close the Venezuelan office, we'll do that."

Well, he found a way to do business without paying bribes. You'll have people claiming these kinds of ethical distinctions, but are they really distinctions or just an easy way to try to take a shortcut?

Q: Why do we need ethics? And why should we care?

Alan: Capitalism is based on ethics. Capitalism, which if you haven't looked, is the prevailing economic system in the world. Socialism has lost. Capitalism has won. Communism has lost. Capitalism has won. Fascism has lost. Capitalism has won. Capitalism is about 10-0 right now. It has a much better winning percentage than the New York Yankees.

The fact is that I agree to provide you with a certain product and service at a certain time and in a certain way. We talked about this earlier. You agree to accept it in return for a certain remuneration paid in a certain form and at a certain time. That's the ethical underpinning of capitalism, and that's why where you have people trying to cheat each other, you don't have effective capitalism, and you have more anarchanistic and more anarchy. You have more anarchy than you would have elsewhere. You have more breakdowns in commerce and more shakedowns than you would have elsewhere.

Why do you think people get so outraged when a politician is on the take? They get more outraged by that than when a politician has a mistress. The reason is the mistress undermines ethics to the extent that the politician's family is caused harm, but the acceptance of bribes hurts the entire community. That presupposes that the politician has made decisions which can negatively impact you financially because they're disproportionately giving advantage elsewhere financially.

That's why ethics are important. They underlie our entire system, and our kind of pluralistic complex country couldn't be possible today without, believe it or not, most people following common ethical and moral guidance. The Judeo-Christian belief system was certainly acknowledged by the founders of the United States in their creation of this country, and most people in the United States today by survey would claim that they're religious and/or spiritual. I'm not saying that if you aren't religious and not spiritual you're not ethical; you certainly can be.

However, people are in need of guidance, and people like to receive guidance. When you stop at that red light on a deserted street at 2:00 a.m. and you wait, you're not staying there because of the law. The probability of your being captured—found out for going through that red light—is nil. You're doing that out of an obligation to society. That's what is really happening, and society takes responsibility for certain checks and balances. In other words, at the end of the store aisles there are cashiers. You're not expected to pay the money and then take your own change. However, there are things that happen on the honor system that happen quite successfully.

Q: Can you tell us some other classic ethical issues that you have encountered over the years?

Alan: I was approached by the senior vice president of human resources of a large insurance company in New York. The human resources department had about 40 people in it. He said, "My people are cheating on their expenses. I know they are. They're putting down lunches with clients when they don't really have clients, but I know they're just eating with each other or people in the company. I also see supplies disappearing, and I've personally observed them taking the supplies. I have a lot of circumstantial and situational evidence, but I'm more concerned with you getting to the cause of this. Why is this happening in HR?" I thought that was a pretty laudable project.

I began to poke my nose around. It was a small, $35,000 project. I found out within 48 hours that the senior vice president of human resources was entitled, by company policy, to fly first class. But he would take a first class ticket and cash it in, fly coach, and keep the difference. Everybody in the department knew this because he talked about it, and he bragged about it. It was an additional source of income. Here is a guy making $175,000 a year at the time getting another $25,000 a year by doing this. Since people saw that, they figured all bets were off, and they could similarly try to take advantage of the company.

I told him that after 48 hours. I said, "I have good news for you. We can solve this right here." He listened and he said, "I didn't hire you to tell me that I was the problem." I said, "Well, no matter what you hired me for, you're the problem." And we parted company. I parted with my money, and he parted with his falsified expenses.

GE used to have a program called "Work Out," and I was a faculty member for two or three years and had the highest ratings. One of my sessions was on ethics. I would give people this challenge: "What if you found a superior cheating on his expense reports?" And people would ask me—these were up and comers, high-potential people in GE—"Well, it depends. Did they bring me on board? Did they hire me? Do I like them? Do I not like them? Is it $50? Is it $500?"

In one of these sessions, a very small woman, about five feet tall, who was from accounting, stood on her chair in the back of the room to be seen and said, "Hold on. In for a dime, in for a dollar. If somebody is cheating, they're cheating. The amount doesn't matter. Wake up." I was always impressed by that woman, and I hope she went far in GE.

Q: As a consultant, is it your responsibility, and an ethical responsibility, to report your economic buyer to the powers above him?

Alan: If I find the economic buyer acting in an unethical way that materially damages or puts in jeopardy the company, yes, I should report the economic buyer. Stealing is a cause for doing that. Falsifying documents is a cause for doing that. Not giving fair evaluations but rather playing favorites is a cause for doing that. Taking money from a vendor is a cause for doing that.

An economic buyer who simply complains about the boss has probably inappropriate behavior, but I wouldn't consider it unethical behavior. An economic buyer who consistently agrees with the boss to do something and then deliberately undermines the boss, that's unethical.

Q: What do you feel are some taboos for consultants? Are we bound by the same code of conduct and ethics that govern, say, psychologists?

Alan: No, because there is no bond of confidentiality. There is no equivalent with consultants of the "Priest's Confessional." There is, however, an ethical cannon amongst priests, psychologists, and psychiatrists that they can reveal confidences if there is imminent harm to others or to the person himself. If a terrorist were to say, "I'm going to blow up Grand Central Station tomorrow," that can be reported. If a person says, "I'm going to commit suicide tomorrow and take my child with me," that can be reported.

I have a stock phrase I use in my consulting because for 25 years, I've been approached with this: "Alan, can you keep a secret? Alan, can I tell you this in confidence?" And my response is always the same: "My responsibility is to my client. If you tell me something that in my sole judgment indicates to me that it will materially damage my client, I'm obligated to tell my client. So, before you tell me this confidence, consider the fact that I might feel that I'm forced to divulge it, and I'll not be responsible to you if I do."

That way whatever they tell me, I can make a judgment about. I think we're obligated to report clearly unethical conduct. I think we're obligated not to accept confidential information without some kind of disclaimer, and I think that we should violate confidences in certain circumstances. If somebody sent you an email and says, "This is in confidence," we should violate confidences if we find that the content presents a danger to our client.

Q: What do you do if your morals don't match those of your client on controversial topics?

Alan: It depends if it's business or personal, and it depends how much it differs. For example, if I happen to disagree with a client on abortion, no matter which side each of us is on, that doesn't really matter unless the client engages in public displays and public endorsement of one side or another within the company and within the project for which I'm engaged. In that case, I won't accept that. I was called down to a Christian college in Virginia to talk about a project, and the buyer constantly proselytized everyone in sight and felt that there was no redemption for anyone who wasn't strictly part of this particular sect. So, I just left there and washed my hands of that.

On a business basis, I'm concerned about values. I won't do and historically haven't done any kind of consulting work that involves downsizing because I've found almost without fail that downsizing is the result of errors made in the executive suite. It punishes the wrong people. It causes tremendous harm to people in the company, and the proper people aren't being punished.

Q: Would you consult the Iranian nuclear agency?

Alan: Absolutely not.

Q: Would you consult the U.S. nuclear weaponry system?

Alan: Absolutely yes. The ethical issue is simple. The Iranians have publicly said that they feel that the state of Israel should be annihilated and doesn't have the right to exist. The Iranians have been found factually to provide resources, money, and arms to terrorist organizations. While the United States has made political errors and often hasn't used good judgment, I believe the United States morally and ethically is a force for good in the world, so I would consult. I don't think there is a need for the French to have nuclear weapons, but I would certainly consult with the French nuclear authority or the French nuclear military operation as I would for that in the United Kingdom. I can make clear determinations about what I see ethically as intent.

Q: Coming back to your original distinction and delineation of moral and ethics, what is the core framework or the core belief that guides you in considering and framing your ethical position? Is it the grace of God, is it the Ten Commandments, is it religious conviction, or something else?

Alan: Over the years there have been various schools of thought about this. When you say the greatest good for the greatest number, it's the utilitarianism which Jeremy Bentham and other philosophers advocated. Others would say that it depends on the outcome. If the outcome is good, it's moral. If the outcome is bad, it's immoral. That was a position the writer Ernest Hemingway advocated.

There are a lot of schools of thought of morality. My own is that there is a prevailing ethos in any culture that dictates what is right and wrong on large-scale issues, and there are personal ethics that dictate what is right and wrong on very specific issues, and I follow my conscience in both morality and ethics. I would say that the Ten Commandments would play a very strong role. I happen to be a practicing Catholic, and I think that tolerance and redemption (by redemption I don't mean salvation, but I mean the fact that people can improve and that none of us is perfect) are very important issues in my life. I find forgiveness to be very important.

But I will tell you that nowhere in the Bible have I ever found, and in fact nowhere in any ethical system have I ever found that while you should forgive someone, you should also let them continue to do the same harm to you. So, if someone is harming you or hurting you, forgiveness is one thing, but allowing them to continue is another. Those are the kinds of distinctions that I can very easily draw.

Q: You've said that traditional imparters of ethics are disappearing. How so?

Alan: If you look at the last quarter century, what you'll find is that the traditional sources of guidance on ethical behavior were the family dinner table where a child would sit there without going to soccer practice, without getting on the internet, and without being distracted by 100 different things. You would have a one-income family, so the mother in most cases would prepare dinner, the father and mother and children would sit down, and the children would listen to their parents deal with ethical concerns.

In other words, the father might say, "I think I was passed over for a promotion by someone who didn't deserve it but had cozied up to the boss." Or the mother would say, "I don't know what to do; I think the neighbor's children are smoking. Should I go tell their parents or not? I have seen them during the day." Even if the resolution weren't perfect, and even if the parents didn't have a good answer, the point is that the children heard it discussed. They heard good and bad discussed, what should be done about it, and they received in most cases some ethical grounding. In some cases they may have received a horrible example but in most cases a good one.

We had the schools of a quarter century ago where we still had lifetime professional teachers who were viewed with respect and who wouldn't put up with unethical behavior in the classroom. Copying, plagiarism, cheating, and looking at somebody else's notes was simply not allowed. Rutgers

University took some surveys years ago and found that 88 percent of all college undergraduates admitted to cheating, and the worst cheating—the highest percentage of cheating—occurred in the business major. Public education has declined as has its impact on correct ethical behavior.

A third area was religious, and no matter what denomination you belonged to, they were all consistent with how you comported yourself. Since then we've had scandal in the Catholic Church. We've had scandal in the Jewish faith. We've had scandal in the Protestant sects. We've had churches formed by these fire-and-brimstone preachers who have been found to be having affairs, cheating on their taxes, and committing all kinds of incredibly unethical acts. We have one pastor who runs a church which openly talks about the love of money.

What does that leave? For the first time it has created a generation of people entering business without the traditional foundation of ethical principles instilled by the family, the schools, or religion. That's like asking someone to swim who has never seen water.

Q: How do you tell whom you will trust?

Alan: Can I trust you with my wallet? That's a criterion I've always used when I enter into a partnership as I have with Patricia Fripp (The Odd Couple®), or the way we're collaborating on this book, or one of my clients, Jarvis Coffin at Burst Multimedia. My greatest assurance that I think somebody has the highest possible integrity and ethics is that I can trust them with my wallet. In other words, I say to them spend what you have to spend, and you know my share will be my share.

When you interact with someone over time, you can understand, you can see, and you can observe and feel that they're always erring on the side of doing the right thing. If there is a question about whether something should be returned, whether somebody should be given some leeway, or should someone be allowed to use something, you always err on the side of the right thing because you really trust them.

Q: How do you handle challenging or even obnoxious clients or HR persons in an ethical way?

Alan: I would like to think I handled them ethically by confronting them. In other words, I don't try to go around their back unless they become intransigent. I don't try to undermine them. I just confront them and say, "What you're asking me to do is stupid. What you're asking me to do is bureaucratic. I won't do what you ask me to do and here is why."

In one famous case at Hewlett Packard in Loveland, CO, the purchasing manager got in touch with me, and she insisted that the deal I had with the general manager was null and void, and that he didn't have the authority to negotiate with vendors! I told her I'm not a vendor, I'm a consultant. She said, "Well, you're a vendor to me." So, I knew this was going absolutely nowhere. When I told the general manager, "We can't get started" and he said, "Why not?" and I told him, "Because of your purchasing manager," he fired her. I have no remorse about that. Her job is to support front-line management, not to subvert things because of her bureaucratic needs.

This is going to sound horrible but there is a reason that these people are in human resources, in purchasing, and in training. There is nowhere else for them to go. They don't have a large view of life. They're not pragmatic, and when you find people who just want to put numbers in boxes, that's what you get.

Q: In all of these stories and in the story you just told about the HR person, the key that I hear in your story is courage. The courage to tell it as it is, speak with confidence, and assert your position.

Alan: You have to have courage, and you have to believe in what you're doing. I get criticism occasionally from people, unsolicited criticism that I'm arrogant. That I'm out of touch. That I'm too ideological about something. I take on all the controversial positions I can because it drives more and more attention to me. This morning I received an email from somebody who said, "I'm curious. Why don't you have an email access on your cluttered and verbose landing page?" I sent back a note to him and said, "I have forwarded this to my technical expert. When you say 'cluttered and verbose' you're making a gratuitous, nasty comment, and what you need is an exercise in interpersonal communications."

I simply don't accept that kind of crap from anybody. If you're going to deal with me, you can deal with me on an intellectual level, and you can try to change my mind, which people have been successful doing. But calling me names, cursing at me, or making insinuations isn't going to work because I'm confident that I operate with a process of integrity that's sincere and intellectually honest.

Q: Let's talk for a few minutes about ethical breakdown. We live in a time of great moral relativity. We hear constantly about CEOs and politicians who have done something that would be considered unethical. Why is this happening? What has changed?

Alan: There are quite a few reasons. Let me just hit three or four. One reason it's happening is it's more public. It has always happened, but now people are more aware of it. For example, President Kennedy had various and numerous dalliances with women, but the media had a tacit agreement not to report it. Marilyn Monroe was famous for sneaking up the back steps of the White House. You can imagine how many people were in on that, but it never made the press; and if it did make the press, if some gossip columnist reported it, it was hushed up. In those days, it was considered okay. In these days it isn't. Things are more public today.

A second issue is that we have lowered the bar, and what we have determined as a society with this crazy egalitarianism we strive for—trying to protect everybody's self-esteem by lowering standards instead of raising them—is that it's okay to use your fingers to push your food onto your fork, and it's okay to use profanity on Facebook.

Just the other day this unfunny comedian and terrible co-host on The View, Joy Behar—who has no reason for being on television that I can imagine—gets up with Whoopie Goldberg and walks off the set because Bill O'Reilly was saying something about this mosque that has been proposed at Ground Zero. They didn't agree with him, and so she stands up and walks off. That's not intellectual behavior. That's not even pseudo-intellectualism. That's barbaric. It's like sticking your fingers in your ears and saying, "ya-ya-ya-ya-ya-ya" so you don't have to listen to someone else. These people are on television. These people are role models. What we have done is lowered the bar having to observe this behavior from "TV personalities."

There is another factor at work, which I've mentioned here, and that is there is absolutely aberrant narcissism, if that isn't redundant, that attaches itself to power these days. I'm convinced these people don't think they're going to get caught, and Elliott Spitzer, the Attorney General of New York at one point, doesn't think he will get caught with $4,000-a-night prostitutes using his credit card. He is an attorney. What is he thinking? He has dealt with the media for 25 years. Of course you're going to get caught. They all get caught sooner or later. Everybody gets caught sooner or later when you have that kind of high public profile. This narcissism says it's going to happen to other people, not me. Look at Bill Clinton.

All of these factors create this lowered bar, this limbo we're doing in terms of ethics. When that happens people say, "Well, if he can do that, if she can do that, then it's okay for me to cheat on this or to steal that."

Q: What you describe as this narcissistic culture I also perceive as the gospel of pleasure and the gospel of instant gratification. What is your view of this, and why does the gospel of pleasure and instant gratification continue to gather great following? Which aspects of this pleasure and gratification culture do you agree with and which aspects do you reject?

Alan: I'm all for immediate gratification. I wrote on my blog the other day: The older you get, the more your horizon becomes closer, and the more you want instant gratification. When you're 25, you think you'll do everything there is to be done in the world. When you're 35, you think you might have to narrow it a bit. And when you're 65 you think, 'Okay, which part of the world is going to come to me?' There is nothing wrong with instant gratification.

I had an electric train room up here for about ten years with all of the Lionel trains I couldn't afford as a kid. I had two layouts. I tore it all down over this past year, and now I have a gorgeous library there. Who knows what I'll do in another three or four years. But instant gratification is fine so long as it doesn't come at anyone else's expense. I think it was Thomas Payne who said, "Your freedom stops at my nose."

There is nothing wrong with taking a suite on the Queen Mary II and sailing the ocean. There is something wrong, though, with using connections to acquire something that other people have to wait for a long time when you haven't rightfully earned it. All of these things are on a continuum, and instant gratification, just like money, isn't inherently good or evil. It's something that's available, and it depends how you avail yourself of it.

Q: We spoke earlier in this chapter about capitalism. It seems that after 150 or 200 years, we have found perhaps the weak point of capitalism—the terror of the short-term. How much of the breakdown we're witnessing in recent decades in corporations has to do with and directly relates to the compulsion of the short-term?

Alan: I don't think that the real terror of capitalism is the short-term. I will address that in a second. I think the real problem with capitalism that we have learned is that it doesn't distribute wealth very well. It generates wealth in amazing amounts, but it doesn't distribute and redistribute it very well where society needs it.

To get back to your issue about short-term, it's all about reward. Look at the American car manufacturers pre-recession, going back to the '50s and '60s. Ask yourself how were the top executives at Ford, General Motors, and Chrysler rewarded? Their pensions—their retirement—were based on the average profit of the company in the five years prior to their retirement. So, if you're that CEO, you're not about to invest a half a billion dollars in R&D that might not come to fruition for ten years. You're going to invest in things that you can make money on in the next five years because that's what your pension is based on.

The problem with the short-term is if you reward people that way, that's how they'll react, but that's not intrinsically an issue of capitalism. That's an issue of poor management, lousy leadership, and poor governance for that matter.

Q: So, the capitalist system does need to find a solution or an answer to embracing the long-term—the sustainable results—rather than just the next quarterly earnings?

Alan: I think it has the answers; it's a question of whether or not they're used. I'll give you a sports analogy. If you look over a period of time at a team like the Boston Celtics in basketball, the New York Yankees in baseball, or the New England Patriots in football, what you find is an inordinate amount of championships over a finite timeframe that sometimes is 10 to 20 years long because the managers and the ownership were planning for the future.

As we speak, the New England Patriots are 7-1. They have the best record in professional football. They're 7-1 and they have something like five or six first-round draft picks next year which is unprecedented because of the kinds of trades they made this year. They traded away talent, they're still 7-1, and they have all of these first-round picks for next year. They're going to be around for a long time with championship teams.

Similarly, if you look in the private sector, there is a reason that Apple has been so successful for so long. There is a reason that FedEx has been successful for so long. There is a reason that Jack Welch at GE, who was really running 12 separate companies and one of the last true conglomerates, was successful for so long.

Q: Would you share with us a couple of examples when you faced an ethical dilemma in a client situation, and how did you come to the choice that you finally made?

Alan: Well, I made a bad ethical decision in the '70s that never left me. It was worth it for having had the experience.

I was a client service guy at a consulting firm in Princeton, and I reported to a guy who was a regional manager. We were all striving to make our money and to hit our quotas at the end of this calendar year. IBM was a client in our region. Every year in December they ordered 100 sets of materials for the first quarter, and we sold boxes of material—that's one reason I got out of that business—and I put through the order. IBM received notification and the IBM guy told me, "Alan, don't ship the order this year. We don't want it until next year for our purposes."

We didn't get credit unless that stuff left our loading dock. My boss put pressure on me—we really needed that $10,000 or $20,000 IBM order—and I never voided the order. It landed on their loading dock in December, and I hoped they wouldn't notice it. The contact called me and said, "Alan, we're going to pay for this, but we're extremely disappointed." I never forgot that. I decided I wouldn't do that ever again. I just didn't even want to be in that business any more.

I was advising the president of Calgon. The sales director had authorized an employee who bought a fax machine for their home to write it off using fake lunches. The employee had already paid for it, but the sales director said, "We ought to be providing these fax machines in your home, so just write it off." Of course, word got out, and the vice president of sales said, "Hey, it happens. It was for the good of the company, not personal riches. Don't worry about it." The vice president of human resources said, "Fire the sales director, and fire anyone involved."

The president said, "I have to decide on this tomorrow." It was Sunday night. "I would like you as a sounding board; what do you think?" I said, "Nobody profited personally, and the employee paid for it herself. The problem with the employee is when the director said 'put in the fake lunches' and she agreed. Your director didn't profit at all, he has a spotless record, but this is a terrible decision he made. It's terrible judgment, and it sets a terrible precedent.

If I were you, I would tell everybody in the company what happened because word is leaking out. I would chastise your sales director and deny him his bonus this year, even though his region is doing well. I would say to the salesperson that she has to reimburse for those free lunches, and I would give her a notice of reprimand. I would spell out to everybody in the company that here is why this isn't done. I would use it as a learning experience."

Ever since, it's fairly easy for me to ask myself certain questions. Did someone profit personally? Was there malicious intent? Does this break a clear ethical code? Is it a gray area? And so forth. You can answer those questions fairly quickly.

Q: Backing up to your example about shipping the products. If you had to do that over again and felt yourself in that sort of tug-of-war between what the client wanted and what the company was asking of you, how would you have done it differently?

Alan: I would have found a different way to make the money. I wouldn't have shipped that to IBM, and I would have said, "Okay, this puts us $20,000 down. Is there another account that we have where I could convince them to take more materials than they had anticipated by giving them some good break, good price, or whatever? Is there something I can do to make up for that? If I can't, I'm going to have to tell my boss I'm going to be $20,000 short on my estimate, and if that impacts my bonus, it impacts my bonus."

Q: Let's talk about the role of confidentiality. Many of the people listening to this and reading this are involved in coaching. I know that this question of who owns material and whether or not I keep the secrets of the person I'm coaching becomes one of the things that's of concern to everybody. Who owns the information, and how should we set this whole thing up?

Alan: Specifically in coaching, there is a buyer and a client. Sometimes they're the same person and the buyer says, "I'm hiring you to coach me," so that buyer becomes your client. Confidentiality isn't an issue. You don't repeat anything that's said to anyone else.

Sometimes the buyer isn't the client. The buyer says, "I want you to work with my subordinate," in which case you say, "Fine, let me know what the ground rules are. What are the rules of engagement? Do you expect me to brief you on what is happening? Do you expect the client, your subordinate, to brief you on what is happening? Or do you expect that we'll maintain confidentiality, and you'll know nothing? What are you expecting?" And the buyer will tell you.

When you see the client, you say to the client, "Here is what the buyer stipulated. The buyer will learn nothing, or the buyer will hear from you or from me. Is that agreeable to you?" So, everything is out on the table. The one thing I would say in addition to that—and I write about this extensively in *Million Dollar Coaching*—is I'll never ever observe a confidence if harm is going to be done; material harm to the organization, to another person, or to that person who is telling me.

Q: When we're thinking about ethics, is there a different level of ethics when I think of how it applies to me? In other words, should I be adamant about certain things and maybe just let other things go?

Alan: Jefferson had a great quote. He said, "In matters of taste, swim with the tide. In matters of principle, stand like a rock."

There are core values and operating values. A core value is "We're going to bring the greatest in scientific research against the greatest areas of human health suffering." An operating value is something like "I'm not working past 5:30 in the evening because I owe that time to my family." It really depends what you're talking about here.

Q: You talked before about how you confront ethical breakdowns. When we encounter such betrayal of ethical behavior with clients, partners, or even staff, what is the effective language to confront it?

Alan: First, you want to verify what is happening. You would say, "It looks to me like you're picking up this lunch bill, and you're writing it off as if I'm a client, but that's in violation of company policy. There is no client here. Is that what you're doing because I don't want to be a party to that?" So, the first thing is to validate it. Because you might say to me, "Alan, you've got it wrong. I'm not writing this off as lunch. Because this is on my personal credit card, I'm just making notes about what we were doing here and why so when it shows up on my bill, I know what it was." The first thing is to validate, not to jump to conclusions.

The second thing—if you do find it is, in your opinion, an ethical violation—is you want to be very calm about it, but state the facts and positions. If it impacts you, what has to be changed? If it impacts the company, the client, or whatever, what has to be changed? Sometimes you'll see an ethical violation doesn't impact you so much, and you shouldn't get all upset because it doesn't help. You see somebody breaking into line, jumping a line, but you have a reserved seat, so it's not like they're taking your seat. I see somebody who has an electronic device during takeoff and landing. I don't jump up and down about that because I don't think it matters. I don't think there is any impact on safety in the air at all because I see it happening all the time.

However, when the seat is reclined in front of me on takeoff, I politely ask the person to put it up because that's for my safety. If there is a short stop, I'm going to hit their seat. It's not for their safety.

We're all making decisions like that every day, but you'll see people who I call TPO—the terminally put-out. The TPO people are those who get exercised over every transgression. Somebody doesn't use their turn signal in front of them, somebody doesn't say "please" and "thank you" loud enough, somebody is whispering during the beginning of the church service, or whatever it is, they take it as a personal affront. That's an absolutely guaranteed express lane to a heart attack.

Q: We had quite a few permutations of this following case study on Alans-Forums.com. I'm coaching an executive, and I see him kissing a woman who I know isn't his wife. Do I address this as a separate engagement from our coaching engagement, or do I confront it directly?

Alan: In the case you just gave me, I know he is married. I know he was kissing someone. I assume it wasn't a kiss on the cheek. I assume it was a passionate kiss from what you said. If that's the case, I would say to him, "John, by the way, at 4:30 yesterday I was leaving the building, and I saw you near your car in an embrace with a woman who works here, and you seemed to be kissing her passionately. I'm making no value judgments other than to tell you I saw it, and if I saw it, I'm sure other people saw it and can see it. I just want to pass that on to you for what it's worth."

He is going to say something to me like, "Alan, thanks, I appreciate it," or "It wasn't what it seemed," or "It's none of your business," or "Oh, my God, I need your help with this!" Who knows what the response is going to be? All I'm doing is reporting the facts, and it's very logical to assume that if I saw it, other people will see it. It's logical to assume if I saw it, that isn't the first time it has happened nor will it be the last. No less than my saying to someone, "Your wallet is sticking out of your pocket. It would be really easy for someone to grab it." I'm doing them the same kind of service.

Q: At times my right foot presses the gas in the car a little bit too hard, and I see the speedometer going past where I'm supposed to. Am I in an ethical quandary?

Alan: That has nothing to do with ethics. That's a question about the law and how intelligent the law is. If you look on most highways, what you really see isn't a speed limit; you see a reciprocity.

Let's say the speed limit is 60. What you'll see is most people doing 70 or so. Because they're all doing 70 or so, nobody stands out in a crowd. When you see somebody really moving fast compared to that reciprocity, they're probably doing about 85 or 90, and that's the person the cop is going to see first. Theoretically, the cop could pull over anybody who is doing 70 in a 60-mile zone. Occasionally you get the short straw, and they pull you over.

You have to decide, for your own sake, whether you're going to obey every technicality of the law. For example, many times we're all standing at a red light. There isn't a car to be seen for two miles, and it's a sweltering hot day or a bitterly cold day. Theoretically, if you cross against the light, you're jaywalking, and that's a crime in a lot of cities.

I always walk across the street. I'm a New Yorker, and I'm not waiting on the sidewalk. I don't do it dangerously. I don't jump between moving cars. If the street is clear, I see no reason, absolutely no reason, to stand on that sidewalk. On the other hand, if I'm in a store and I see something just sitting there, and I could take it and put it in my pocket, I don't do that. You make these decisions every day.

Q: You talked earlier about us lowering the bar when it comes to ethics. Yet, you also commented that the behavior JFK got away with in regard to Monroe, he wouldn't have been able to get away with today. Is the world becoming more ethical or less ethical?

Alan: I don't think it's becoming more or less ethical, but it's becoming more public. One thing the mass media have done, including social media platforms and a more desperate press, is engage in a desperate scramble for stories because of the competition. Things are much more transparent, sometimes even naked, and I don't mean that as a pun. Consequently, things that were readily hidden years ago are no longer readily hidden.

As we speak, there are people trying to catch a person who is responsible for leaks of military documents. I forget the name of the website, but years ago there was no clandestine kind of release. When Ellsworth released the Pentagon Papers during the Vietnam War in the hard-print media—the *New York Times*—many called that traitorous. It was considered unbelievable. How did he get them? Now you see these kinds of leaks all the time.

Today's teenagers and preteens are texting—they call it "sexting"—nude pictures of themselves to each other. You have the bizarre situation of some 15-year-old kid being arrested as a sex offender with something that's going to stay in his or her file for many years. This is the kind of nuttiness that arises when we have such blatant and easily accessed mass communications.

Q: Let's speak about the ethics of living large. You mentioned earlier you often encourage people in your communities to enjoy life and to live large. Explain the ethics of living large.

Alan: It's strange to me that while people have such trouble with ethics, they also have such trouble with guilt. It doesn't make sense to me, but I think if you find an ethical clarity for yourself, then you alleviate the guilt that tends to haunt so many people. My feeling is that society makes certain things available to you that are legal and ethical. If they are legal and ethical, you should feel free to avail yourself of them.

Let's say that you don't believe in using internal combustion engines, and you should only drive electric cars. That's fine for you. But don't enforce that on me because neither the law nor ethics commands that I do that. There are some people who remove all fat from their foods, religiously. To me they look like they're ill. That's their right. But don't demand that I do it.

I understand that people have aroma allergies, although you hear a lot more about that today than you ever did before. But don't insist that I don't wear cologne unless you have some personal appointment with me, and it makes sense for you to make that request of me.

There are things that are legal, and there are things that are ethical that society makes available, and you can use them. Look at tobacco. Cigarette smoking has been demonstrated to be a known killer. It's taxed like crazy. People have cut down on smoking seriously except, ironically, for teenage women. However, tobacco is legally and ethically available in this country.

I remember sitting in a place once where cigarette smoking was allowed, and a woman at the next table said to me, "Do you mind if I have a cigarette?" I said, "You know, I do. I'm still having my dessert. Thank you for asking." She said, "Oh, no problem," and she put it away. You know that's ethical, civil conduct.

When I was working out this morning, I was on the treadmill watching the "Today Show" and they had a major piece titled "Is there a breakdown in civility?" Of course there is a breakdown in civility because what you're seeing on television are crazy shows where people are encouraged to attack each other. Reality shows that bring out the worst of humanity. As long as those are placed on the air by people who have the legal and ethical right to do that, you're going to find that it sets a standard for people which continues to deteriorate civil behavior and discourse. There is a local blog in East Greenwich, a very upscale community, where I live. But there are some people who can't comment on any issue without launching an *ad hominem* attack. They're nasty and brutish, but they feel that kind of behavior is appropriate today. I think they're troglodytes.

Q: You just mentioned guilt, and indeed for many people the idea of ethics is coupled with guilt. Why is that, and is it wrong?

Alan: I think people are subject to guilt from the "should" that's on their shoulders—you should do this, you shouldn't do that—that's inherited from antecedents. It's inherited from family. It's inherited from environment. It's inherited from nurturing. It's inherited from close friends, experiences, and normative pressures.

A lot of those have nothing to do with ethics. Don't try to sing in public, you have a terrible voice. Don't stand up and deliver a speech, you stutter and can't communicate well. Don't play baseball because you have terrible coordination. That guilt has nothing to do with ethics. If guilt and ethics were more closely related, we would have a lot less crime.

Q: I think it was Warren Buffet who said, "Live and act as though everything you do will be reported tomorrow morning in the *Wall Street Journal*." In other words, don't do anything that would embarrass you in front of your children. Isn't that good advice to live by?

Alan: Well, hold on. That might work for business dealings. It doesn't work in the bedroom does it? My kids are embarrassed just to think that they were conceived. They say, "I think Mom and Dad were doing it." Probably so.

I think Warren's advice is probably good under certain circumstances, but not all.

Q: He does imply in his brief that embarrassment is a good guidance for you in terms of making choices, the right choices, in terms of ethics. Do you agree or do you reject the idea that embarrassment is a good guidance for ethics?

Alan: I would tend to reject it for several reasons. One is some people are embarrassed by things they shouldn't be embarrassed by, and some people are not embarrassed by things they should be embarrassed by. I would also maintain that some people don't consider embarrassment to kick in unless it's on the front page of the *Wall Street Journal,* but if it's less than that, they don't consider themselves embarrassed. Some people are embarrassed just to stand up and make a resolution at a board meeting. That doesn't mean it's unethical; it just means that they're shaky and not so confident. I don't think embarrassment is a sufficient judgment. I think it's terribly uneven, and while it's a nice cliché to me in the breech, it doesn't work.

Q: Very important delineation. You spoke in a previous discussion on ethics and redemption. This is one of the greatest things about America, particularly how the American spirit and culture have this readiness to embrace the ethics of redemption. A good example is the person you mentioned earlier, Elliott Spitzer. He resigned in disgrace from the governorship of New York, but he is now launching a new show on CNN that seems to be drawing praise. What defines whether redemption works or not? I don't mean redemption in the afterlife sense, I mean in the public eye sense.

Alan: Separate redemption from salvation. In other words, I've maintained that I think the capitalist system is based on Judeo-Christian ethics, and one of the most appealing things to me personally about that ethic is that it talks about redemption in your lifetime. That is, you can be forgiven. You can make good. You can atone. The Jews have a day of atonement. Every day the Christians are saying you know you're forgiven, but understand what you did and don't do it again. I think that this aspect of being redeemed and this aspect of people forgiving you is extraordinarily important.

Take a look at presidents who are revile during their lives. Yet Lyndon Johnson and Harry Truman are held in much higher esteem today. I would project that this will occur with the second George Bush as well.

People tend to forgive. PeeWee Herman who was oriented toward children's shows—PeeWee Herman Playhouse and so forth—was arrested for indecent exposure in a theater in Florida. Obviously, his career just flattened out, but he started doing some TV and movie work in minor roles; and just yesterday in the *New York Times* there was a huge article that he is bringing back PeeWee's Playhouse 30 years later. He thinks he can do it. He thinks it's time. He thinks people will have forgiven him for what he believes was an unfortunate transgression that he is atoned for.

We have parole boards. We have rehabilitation centers. Rehab has become a verb in our lexicon. I think that people do tend to forgive, and it's an important part of capitalism and is an important part of the ethics that underlie our system.

Q: How have you spoken about ethics to your children at different stages of their growing up? How did you introduce it when they were very young, and what kind of conversations can you recall with your children about ethics at different stages?

Alan: The best thing that worked for us was that we would deal with their situations as they came up. In earlier conversations for this book, we talked about the disappearance of the family dinner table. We always had a family dinner table. My wife ran the household. I traveled a lot, so I wasn't always at the dinner table. When I was home, the four of us always, always had dinner together. If there was an extracurricular activity or something they wanted to do, it was after we had dinner together. Whenever I was home we ate together, and we would have that opportunity to hear what was going on.

In addition, I was often at home on a Wednesday afternoon or Tuesday morning. I would go to school activities, dance recitals, and various teacher conferences. My kids went to an excellent high school here, Moses Brown, which is a Quaker school. They had Quaker meetings where everybody was encouraged to stand up and just speak. It was a fascinating experience at Moses Brown.

What we found was that dating, liquor, drugs, peer pressure, raging hormones, driving, and everything else had to be dealt with. At one point, my daughter was driving. She was 17. She was driving our SUV, and one of her friends had had some beers, and he got in the vehicle with a six-pack of beer, he offered her one, and she refused. She drove him home, and she told us what happened.

She said, "You know, I drove him home because he needed to get home, and he shouldn't have driven himself." I said, "Yes, fair enough Danielle, but he should never get in your car with alcohol. You could have been arrested for that, and you were enabling him. You were telling him it was okay to drive, he'd be taken care of, and he could even drink in the back of the SUV." We talked about what she did there in terms of what she thought was a good deed but maybe wasn't such a good deed. Maybe if he had to call his father to come pick him up, it would have been a whole lot better for him at the time. Those are the kinds of things we talked through. It wasn't perfect, but I think it worked awfully well.

Q: Are you thinking about a *Million Dollar Parenting* book?

Alan: Well, I would be happy to run that by McGraw-Hill, but I…

Q: Interesting idea.

Alan: I don't know that they would be in the mood for that. Don't forget, my ethics book was the one that never sold much!

Conclusion

Passivity is the same as endorsement of unethical acts. If you're not opposed to them, then you support them. Neutrality doesn't exist in ethics. As consultants, we need to act as ethical exemplars. Might taking a stand effectively end your career? Only if you look at your career as a static thing rooted in a particular organization and culture. Your career—and your life—are larger than that. Your career can be blunted, ruined, and sullied by *not* taking a stand, even when that means you'll lose a valued client.

9 | Writing Proposals: How to Create Proposals That the Client Can't Wait to Sign

Written proposals are formalized arrangements of ideas and actions for consideration and acceptance by the prospective client. They aren't inanimate documents which occur at some point in a business deal. Effective proposals are based on conceptual agreement between you and a prospective client about *what* is to be accomplished, *how* it will happen, *when* it will occur, *where* it will occur, *who* is accountable for its occurring, and *the degree to which you will confidently know it has occurred.* It all starts with…

Determining the Economic Buyer

Q: How do I get to an economic buyer, and how do I know that I'm talking to one?

Alan: The best way is to have them come to you. If you write a book, if there is tremendous word-of-mouth about you, if people are referring you to their peers who are buyers, if there is media interest in you, these buyers will come to you. If you need to go to them, then you need to aggressively and assertively network. You need to get your repute and your success track in front of them.

I don't think that cold calls work in professional services firms. If you're selling consulting services, I don't advocate direct mail, cold calls, or anything like those. I think it's a huge waste of time; and even if you hit one, it's going to be 1 in 10,000 and will direct you all the wrong ways.

The second part of your question was how do you know you have an economic buyer in front of you? Very often you can do it by hierarchy. In other words, if someone owns a small business, they're the economic buyer. If someone is a senior vice president in a Fortune 500 company, they're probably an economic buyer. But sometimes you don't know, and so you ask questions.

First of all, you listen to the kinds of things they say. If they say, "I have a budget that I need to invest before the end of the year" or "I've been trying to get this initiative done for ages, and I just haven't found the right person, and the money is burning a hole in my pocket" you know they're a buyer.

You can always ask them something like, "Could you explain to me what the decision making process is?" Suppose they say to you, "Well, if you and I agree and shake hands, we can go forward." You say, "In other words, if we shook hands, we could begin tomorrow? You have the money, and there is no other approval required?" And they say, "Yes." That's a pretty good indicator. If on the other hand you get things like, "Well, it would have to go to the committee" or "My boss just rubber stamps this for approval" you know you don't have a buyer.

Q: In what circumstance does it make sense to wait for them to take the first step?

Alan: It doesn't make much sense unless the buyer is overseas, and he or she is on an airplane from Macao to Katmandu, I would suggest it would virtually never make sense to me. Think of this pragmatically. First of all, you offer tremendous value to the company. Why delay the value? Secondly, if they can profit from working with you, why delay the profit? Thirdly, things come up all the time and whenever somebody says, "I will get back to you," it means you're not the top priority. If you're the top priority people say, "Let's do it now." So, you need to accelerate that.

Finally, you need to find out if you're just being blown off. You need to find out if somebody is just making an excuse. I said some things never change, and the age-old excuse in this business is "We love you. We'll get back to you." We've all said to people, "I'll get back to you" because we don't want to say "no" to them.

For all of those reasons, I'm always for pushing the throttle to the firewall. I'm always for full speed ahead, and let's make this thing work; and if it doesn't work, I would rather know now than having put that on my forecast, thinking I have money coming in, or having to follow up. I would rather know now that you're not interested and that it isn't going to work rather than take three more weeks to know that.

Q: What are some other techniques you use to get through gatekeepers to the economic buyer?

Alan: I tell the gatekeeper my preference is to appeal to their enlightened self-interest, and I'll say to them, "Look. We both agree that this makes sense. You have identified this buyer is the one that would make the decision. Why don't we collaborate on how best to go there, and if you want me to go by myself because there might be some blowback, there might be some adverse consequences, I'll be happy to wear the black hat. However, if you want to be seen as a key collaborator and someone who has helped to create this, I'm happy to go with you there. What makes sense?"

If that doesn't work, then I use guile, and I'll say to the gatekeeper, "Ethically, I need to see the person with the fiduciary responsibility to make this investment decision because unless I hear from his or her lips what their expectations are, as you can imagine, it's folly to go forward with this. Unless they're happy and we know what they're expecting, there is no way to make sure that no matter how happy you and I are, that this won't blow up in our faces. And of course your career is invested here and mine isn't."

The worst kind of conversation to have is, "Well, listen. I understand you feel you've been tasked to do this, and I understand your comment to me that I'm not going around you, but I have news for you—I'm going around you. I'm going to contact the buyer, and if the buyer wants to go forward, we will. If you want to throw a monkey wrench, you're welcome to try; however, I really don't think that's in the best interest of your organization. That's your ego I'm hearing."

Some people are afraid that if they don't romance the gatekeeper, once the project is assigned, the gatekeeper will cripple the project. The fact of the matter is that if an economic buyer gives the go ahead to a project, there is no gatekeeper in the world who is going to do anything but jump on that bandwagon.

Q: After you finally meet the economic buyer, how do you structure the conversation to lead around to talking about a proposal?

Alan: Once I get conceptual agreement, I'll submit a proposal. But the real conversation I'm having is in listening for areas where I can help; and as I hear the areas where I think I can be of most help, I'll say to the buyer, "May I ask you some questions?" which I call "rhetorical permission." Because we have a good relationship, they're never going to say "no" to that, and I'll try to get agreement on what the objectives are, what the measures of success are, and what the value is for that particular project.

When I do that, I would say to the buyer, "I have enough here to give you a proposal with some options and your investment. May I do that, get it to you in a day, and call you on Friday at 10:00 to see how you would like to proceed?" It's a question of finding the buyer, establishing a trusting relationship which may take time, gaining conceptual agreement on a legitimate and appropriate project, and then submitting a proposal.

Q: Let's back up the conversation. You've just met the economic buyer, and your goal is to build the trust and start building towards conceptual agreement. How do you actually begin that conversation after you say, "Hello. I'm Alan Weiss"?

Alan: I would say something like, "Linda, it's a pleasure to meet you. I'm curious about what prompted you to want to talk to me. I always love to hear that from people whom I've just met. Why is our conversation of interest to you?" By doing that, I immediately turn the tables, get the other person talking, and get some feeling as to why they're even interested in spending time with me. Nine times out of ten that will lead me down a road to something of value to them.

Q: How do you define conceptual agreement?

Alan: Conceptual agreement means that you and I have explicitly agreed, overtly agreed, on what the objectives for a project are—that is, the business outcomes. What the metrics are—that is, what the measures are that indicate we're making progress and we're successful. And what the value is—that is, what the impact is of those business outcomes in your operation for you and the company. If we agree on those three things, that's what I call conceptual agreement, and that's the heart of a proposal. Once you have that from a buyer, you can go ahead.

That, by the way, is why you should never do a needs analysis. Never allow yourself to be delegated elsewhere without coming back because if you have a buyer in a room—a true buyer—that's where conceptual agreement takes place. Not with anybody else, and not with information gathering.

Q: We've had the conversation for whatever reason that has gone before, we've built some trust, we've gone through objectives, measures, and values, we have conceptual agreement, and we're at the stage of writing the proposal. What is the purpose of a proposal, and why are they so important?

Alan: A proposal is a legal and ethical agreement as to what I'm going to provide for you and what you're going to provide for me. I'm going to perform certain services which will produce certain value which you're going to participate in and cooperate with to whatever degree we've established, and you're going to pay me for that. You're going to remunerate me for that in a degree to which we've also established.

The proposal protects both parties, documents and codifies what happens, and is organic, in my opinion. That is, it's used as a template throughout the project. It doesn't sit on a shelf somewhere, nor is it merely a legal entity. That is, I don't use any boilerplates, I don't have my lawyer create these, and I want to keep them the heck out of my client's legal department. This is an operating agreement between the client—the buyer—and me.

Q: You just said keep it out of the legal department. How do I do that?

Alan: You say to the buyer, "I'm going to submit this to you, indicate the option that you prefer, sign it, and send it back to me. Alternatively, if you simply send me the payment which is either a deposit or full payment, that will constitute agreement as well." I don't put any legalese in there. Once I put "The third party shall hold harmless," I'm dead. That's going to the legal department. So, my proposal is 2½ pages no matter how big the project, and it has absolutely no legalese in it. It's a conversational report of what the client—that's the buyer—and I agreed to.

I've managed to keep those out of legal departments 98 percent of the time. The 2 percent I haven't is when there is simply no alternative. For example, when I dealt with the Federal Reserve. Nobody could sign an agreement without it going through their legal department. They delayed the project two months and turned my 2½ pages into 32 pages that really didn't alter anything about the entire project. Sometimes you have to put up with that kind of nonsense, but I prefer not to if possible.

Q: I remember when I took the proposal writing workshop, you mentioned that you'll sometimes put in there "Payment of any part of this constitutes acceptance." Are you still advising people to put that kind of language in?

Alan: Yes. I had a buyer in New York at an insurance company who agreed to a $250,000 project. He paid $125,000 upfront and $125,000 in 45 days. I had $250,000. I finished the project in four months, and he never sent me a signed proposal. When I asked him about this later, he told me that he had authority to sign a $125,000 payment. He did not have authority to sign a contract, and he wanted to keep it out of his own legal department because he was very eager to get this project underway, and he knew it would delay it by 90 days. I allow people to simply pay me, indicate which option they want, and that constitutes acceptance of all terms above.

Q: In that proposal writing workshop, you talked about the steps of the proposal. I believe there were nine. Could you walk us through what those are?

Alan: The first step is situation appraisal which is a paragraph or two at most about why you're talking. The company wants to improve its brand. The company wants to make an acquisition. The company wants to expand into Europe. The company wants to accelerate the sales process. It's a general sense of why you're talking. In other words, why have we even come together? And you want to start the buyer, when the buyer reads the proposal, nodding his or her head up and down—"Yes, that's right, that's what we talked about."

Steps two, three, and four are conceptual agreement: objectives, measures, value. For objectives I'll say, "The objectives we discussed include" and I'll put them down in bullet points. "The metrics we discussed include"— bullet points. "The value we discussed include"—bullet points.

Step five is methodology and options, and here I talk about the different options the client may choose to go forward. I don't mention fees, but I mention different options, and I usually mention three—although there is nothing magic about that—but that's what I like. Step six is timing. How long will each option take? When do you prepare to start?

Step seven is joint accountabilities, referring to what the client does and what I do. The client is responsible for making certain documentation available, making certain personnel available for providing the administration for the project, and so on. I'm responsible for adhering to nondisclosure agreements. I'm responsible for maintaining confidentiality. I'm responsible for doing certain things personally. And then of course, the client is responsible for paying me as agreed on dates specified, no matter what.

There is a line in there that says we both agree that we inform each other immediately of any developments which might materially affect the success of this project. I put that in because often partway through, I found out that the client knew—my buyer knew—that there was going to be a divestiture of the division but hadn't told me. Or I'll find out that three vice presidents are actively looking for work outside the company, and the client needs to know.

Step eight is terms and conditions. This is the first place where the client sees the fees, and in terms and conditions I say, "The fee for option 1 is X, the fee for option 2 is Y, the fee for option 3 is Z. Payment is 50 percent due on acceptance, 50 percent due in 45 days. Alternatively, if you pay the full fee at acceptance, you may take a 10 percent courtesy discount."

Then I state our policy for expense reimbursement. "Expenses are billed as actually accrued and are due on presentation of our statement each month." I don't offer net 10 days and net 30 days. "Due on presentation of our statement." I'll give the client 30 days leeway, and on the 31st day, I come down like the wrath of God; but if you put net 30, the client will take 60 days. I tell the client what I'll charge for—reasonable travel, living, and so forth; and what I don't charge for—FedEx, postage, phone, and so on.

My ninth and final category is acceptance. It says, "By indicating the option you choose below and by signing this agreement, you accept the terms and conditions as specified. Alternatively, by providing us with either the deposit or full payment with discount, you accept the terms and conditions specified for the options you've chosen."

So, in 2½ pages that's what I've done. There are no resumes. There is no background information. There are no credibility statements because all of that has been accomplished when I built the relationship with the buyer. It's short and sweet. That's how I can get these out so quickly, and I'll FedEx these within 24 hours.

Q: You say 50 percent at the time of acceptance and then the other half within 45 days of acceptance of the proposal. Do you ever have people say, "Wait a minute, Alan. This means I'm going to pay you before you do any work for me?"

Alan: "Well, how can that be? If you're going to pay me on acceptance, I'm ready to start work. But if you're telling me you want to get my time, you agree to this, but you don't want me to start for three months, that's your decision. But you still have to pay me to secure the time, to secure my preparation, and so forth. That's your commitment. My commitment is I'll put the time aside, and you'll have my top priority on the date you're ready to begin. Your commitment is to make your investment."

Q: "Well, I don't want to do this until January, and if I had somebody build a deck on my house, I wouldn't pay him until it was finished."

Alan: "Well, why don't you have somebody who can build a deck help you? Why don't you have a carpenter come in and do the strategy for you?"

Q: Do you usually have people pushing back on that—of paying before the work is finished?

Alan: No, almost never. The reason is I've dealt with Fortune 1000 companies, and the kind of projects I do even though they're expensive—even though they're six-figure projects—doesn't even equal the money they're paying to have the plants watered. That's not the money they're paying to have the windows washed. That's not the money they're paying to have the parking lot maintained. So, $150,000 to a Fortune 1000 company is nothing. Nothing.

That's why you need to find a true buyer who doesn't have to go up the line, who can personally approve these things. Marshall Goldsmith and I talked about this when he was my guest for my Thought Leadership Conference in West Palm Beach. We agreed that $100,000 today to a major business isn't a gnat on the windshield if the ride is about value.

When you're dealing with a small business, that's tougher. The buyer is going to be the owner, and so you have to convince the owner on an emotional basis. If the owner says, "Look, it's September. I would like to start this in January. That's when I want to pay you." You say, "Well, fine. Come back in January, but I can't guarantee you I'll have the time then."

The fact is whenever you want anything in life, you put a deposit on it. If you say to an auto dealer, "Look, I want this brand new model. When is it due?" "Well, it's due April 1." "Well, put one aside for me." "Sure, where is your deposit?" They're not going to put it aside without a deposit. Consequently, you need to have policies just like Hewlett Packard, JPMorgan Chase, or Walmart. You're allowed to have policies.

Q: Just to clarify: They give the deposit, and then you start shortly after. You do part of the work before you've been paid the other half?

Alan: Yes. You start when you get your deposit. And then in 60 days, whenever you specify, you're going to be paid the second half. Now, if the project is only a month long, then you change the payment terms; but most of the projects at this amount last for several months. But if you're doing a $15,000 project, and let's say it's a three-week project, you either get paid in advance or you get paid half of it now and half of it in ten days.

You never, ever want to wait until the end of a project to be paid, under any circumstances. I don't allow people to pay me when I speak or after I speak, only prior.

Q: You get all that up front?

Alan: I get the money up front when the date is booked.

Q: No exceptions to that rule?

Alan: Get paid up front, and if it's a nonprofit whining they have no money, remind them that there are corporations in the community that might be happy to sponsor the project. There are people on their board who have the money to underwrite the project. There are people who are donors to them who have traditionally underwritten projects, so let's use a little initiative here.

Q: How have people in your program learned this the hard way?

Alan: Well, they haven't been paid! What they've done is they've either dealt with non-buyers kidding themselves, or in a small business they've agreed to get paid at the conclusion, and the buyer says, "No, not until you do more work for me." Of course, the buyer then has all of the leverage.

Q: I'm the owner of a small business, and I really want to bring you aboard. My sentence to you will sound like this, "Alan, I really like what you have to say. I really want to make it a win-win here. I'm okay with the 50 percent deposit, but for goodness sake, you have to appreciate my viewpoint or my side here. I never pay until completion. Why now?"

Alan: "Chad, tell me something. Why didn't you pay until completion in the past?"

Q: "I guess I needed, number one, to hold some leverage over whomever I was doing business with."

Alan: "And why is that?"

Q: "That gave me the piece of security that it will force them to complete the work."

Alan: "Because you didn't trust them to do a good job or to do things that you felt still needed to be done. Correct?"

Q: "If you're asking for the ultimate trust, maybe there isn't 100 percent trust, but I trusted them obviously enough to hire them…"

Alan: "But you didn't trust them enough not to think you also needed leverage over them."

Q: "That's right."

Alan: "And what I'm suggesting to you is that we have a relationship where I'm trusting you to do your part and to pay me as planned. And I'm sticking my hand out and guaranteeing you that I'll deliver what is needed, and if you're unhappy, within the boundaries of this proposal, I'll make you happy. I haven't established the client base I have through making people unhappy. Moreover, the difference to you of paying me 50 percent now and 50 percent in 60 days versus that final 50 percent in 90 days is negligible. So, I'm sorry that I have to break your streak here, but this is the way I do business. If you're telling me you can't trust me enough not to hold some leverage over my head to make sure this job is completed, then we've missed something somewhere in our conversations thus far."

Q: You just completed the writing and publishing of *Million Dollar Coaching*. Give us some examples of conceptual agreement that would typically appear in coaching with a CEO, with a senior executive.

Alan: Objectives for coaching are behavioral objectives, and so those might be something like "Provides more frequent and candid evaluation of subordinates to improve their ability to perform" or "Doesn't lose temper when confronted with contrary opinions. Allows other people to contribute even antagonistic opinions in a productive and constructive atmosphere." It might be "Organizes work better so that more time is spent on customer issues and less on administration." Those are all behavioral things that are typical of coaching. They can be more specific. They can be more general. The measures are based largely on observation, but they can also be based on things like

360-degree assessments which are a form of observation, customer feedback, and things like that.

Q: When the request from the buyer is to engage in a retainer, would you still include a conceptual agreement in that proposal?

Alan: No. If I'm doing retainer work, there are no objectives, measures, and value because a retainer is access to your smarts. That's a true retainer. Consequently, the only three variables that are important are how many people have access. Is it just the buyer or is it other people besides? What is the scope of the access? Is it 9 to 5 western time or 9 to 5 eastern and western time? Does it include weekends? Are there personal meetings expected? Then there is the duration. Is this for a quarter, a half a year, a year, or whatever? So, there are no objectives, measures, and value, but those are the three variables to look at.

Q: For the benefit of those where speaking is the major focus or a major focus in their consulting practice, how do we frame objectives, measures, and value in speaking proposals or proposals of speaking engagements?

Alan: If it's just a speaking engagement, if you're doing a keynote, you don't really need them. If you're doing something that's sort of more in depth than that—you're doing a three-day workshop—then you could use them. However, if you're following some of my advice in *Million Dollar Speaking* and elsewhere that you're looking at things prior to the speech, during the speech, and after the speech—telephone interviews, coaching, assessments, handouts, whatever—then you can get closer to objectives, measures, and value because you have more of an opportunity to do it.

The trouble with just looking at that for a single-hour speech or a half-day speech is that you don't have enough time to accomplish a lot of objectives, and there are no metrics. The only metrics would be back on the job, but you don't have enough time to transfer a lot of skills. So, the metrics that occur by default are these stupid smile sheets where people say, "What did you think of the speaker? How was the lighting? Did you like the lunch?" Those are just dumb.

I wouldn't worry about it too much in simple speeches. If you can successfully move the speech into more of a process so it's a semi-consultative engagement, then you might be able to do it.

Q: How do we talk about or how do we get the buyer ready to avoid sticker shock? In other words, through the entire conversation the buyer has in his or her head this is going to be $5,000, whereas you have in your head it's going to be $50,000. Then when you send the proposal, you get rejected because the buyer thinks you're way out of sync with him.

Alan: That's the purpose of objectives, measures, and value, and that's why it's such an intrinsic part of my process. If you establish value correctly and the buyer agrees to it—which is conceptual agreement—let's just say that the value is quantitatively and qualitatively in the neighborhood of $500,000. If your proposal says $50,000 as one of the options, that's a 10 to 1 return. Right there you're establishing ROI.

If you're dealing with a real buyer, then price isn't so much the issue as value. The more low-level people you're dealing with, the more they're going to be concerned about a budget they can't overcome; but real buyers find money. They move money from other places. Pseudo buyers—human resources, training, and so forth—have strict budgets that they don't dare go beyond.

If you're dealing with senior people in Walmart, Exxon, or Ford, you know that these things aren't going to be a problem. But if you're dealing with a small business, and I think we talked about this before, it's quite appropriate to say, "So as not to waste your time or mine, what are the paradigms you have? What are the parameters you would like me to stay within?" Which is in essence asking, "What is your budget?"

If they say, "It's $500," you say, "Unfortunately, it can't be done for that. You're better off getting better coffee and donuts in the morning." If they say, "I was thinking around $25,000," then you might say, "Okay, that might work at the lower end." Or you might say, "You know something, I haven't put this together yet. I have to give it a lot of thought, but I can tell you right now there is no way to even get this minimally done for under $15,000."

You can test the waters right there before you walk out, and that's a useful thing to do. The owner of the small business could say, "I think this is so important, I would be willing to move more money toward it, but you would have to show me a good return." Or they might say, "I'm sorry, I just can't do that." Owners of small businesses are so price sensitive because emotionally they're wondering whether they should put money aside for your project or their kid's orthodonture or college fund.

Q: You often encourage us not to fall in love with our methodology, yet when we get to the option stage, we have to have some methodologies that we feel confident will meet the objectives. Can you walk us through how to arrive at those methodologies and some language and guidelines for designing them?

Alan: Well, no! How could I help you here design methodology? The fact is that given your specialty—whether you're an OD consultant, an expert in compensation, a coach, an expert in sales, an expert in service—no matter what your expertise is, no matter how general or how broad, you need to have a tool kit, and your tool kit has to be developed over time. I talked to a guy this morning who sent the most amazing email. He said, "When we talked yesterday on the phone, you told me to observe the client as part of my coaching. I never realized that was a methodology, but of course it's a methodology. Where else can I get these things?" Questions like that just floor me.

If you're in this business, you have to be reading, experimenting, trying, and discussing. That's one reason to belong to my communities. But for goodness sakes, you have to develop methodologies that work for you, some of which are standard methodologies like a 360-degree assessment, which is common, and some of which you create yourself. You have to decide what works for you. I could spend the next four hours describing methodologies. I'm not going to do that.

Q: In other words, have a tool kit. Develop some things that we trust that get us the information we need. For example, 360-degree assessments if we're doing coaching, but don't fall in love with the process. Keep our eye on the objective.

Alan: That's exactly right.

Q: Listening to this discussion it becomes clear that when you are there with the buyer, you don't know yet the range of options you'll offer. These will actually become clear as you sit and write down the proposal. Or do you have clarity already in your mind?

Alan: No, I don't, because I don't know what my options are until I know what the objectives are.

Q: The options become clear in your mind when you write the proposal, not before?

Alan: Yes. The options become clear when I've left the battle zone, when I've left the arena, and I'm back home, I'm on the plane, or wherever I am and can sit down and carefully think about what happened. I can replay the tape in my mind. I can think about what happened. I can think about this buyer, the environment, and what is needed. I can take a look at the value and how I'm going to restate that value to its maximum impact because even though the buyer comes up with the value, I'm the one who is going to restate it in the proposal.

I'm going to come up with fees, and the most time I spend on any proposal is on my fee levels, and that for me takes a few minutes to think about. The options then become clearer to me in terms of what should be in option 1, what should be in option 2, what should be in option 3, should there be an option 4, or should there only be two options? What is involved with them? What do I need in option 1 to make sure all of the objectives are met because even option 1 has to meet all of the objectives? Those are the kinds of things I'll review.

Q: My guess is we're unearthing something important here. For many in the communities, many of your mentorees, this is an area of struggle of specifically having the confidence in: Do I have enough information? And when I'm a day away reflecting on all of the data that I received and what we were able to discover in this conversation, that will indeed be sufficient for me to articulate the options that would generate enough value to justify my fees. Correct?

Alan: I dealt with a woman yesterday who has a proposal where option 1 is $100,000 and they go up from there to about $190,000 or $200,000. My critique was that the separation and the differentiation of the three options were insufficient. There wasn't enough substance in terms of their differentiation and differing value, and I doubted that the client was going to buy into the escalating options.

She said to me, "Well, what do you think I should put in the options?" I said, "I don't know. You're the one who has the content. It's your content. It's your client. You were there. I wasn't there. But here are some categories to think about: Timing, Technology, Growth, Demographics, Superiors, Parent

Company, Customers, and so forth. Think of those areas. But I won't do this for you."

This is a woman who spent a lot of money with me, and she came back this morning having redone the proposal overnight, and it was magnificent. It was superb. There was great differentiation. She put a lot of thought into the options. I said, "Now you're cooking." And she said, "Thanks for this. It's what I needed."

That's how this has to work. Now, once she has done that, she can replicate that. She can do that again for herself or for other people whom she coaches. If I did it for her, all she would have was a fish—not the ability to fish—and that wouldn't work.

Q: In the beginning of this book, we spoke extensively about the importance of being a generalist. Yet many of the consultants that you coach and mentor came into consulting from a particular area of expertise. Is this another challenge in the proposal writing because many people have a particular solution or methodology in mind, and they try to build the proposal around that?

Alan: It's the greatest problem. It's Maslow's question really. They have a hammer, so they keep looking for nails. That's a much more effective advisory than his hierarchy of needs. Much more pragmatic. That's why I advise people never lead with your methodology. It's delimiting. It stunts your growth. Not everybody needs it. You become obsessed with it. And it severely narrows the panoply of possibilities for you.

Your methodology is simply an implementation device, and you should be constantly adding to it and changing it. The most boring people I meet are people who just do one thing. If they have a six-step process toward better sales, it could put you to sleep. "I have a 12-step, three-month strategy process." Yawn. So you need more flexibility than that, and your value to people isn't your methodology. Your value is how they are better off when you walk away.

Budget and Objections

Q: We're going to wrap up the chapter on proposals and focus on identifying the budget and overcoming objections. We started to talk about the budget in our previous segments, and you shared with us the value equation. Talking about the value equation and with that in mind, give us a little bit more feedback of how do we best identify the budget range?

Alan: It depends upon the organization with which you're dealing. For example, if you're dealing with a large organization and a significant buyer, you don't really have to worry about it because that person will find money. The concept of value-based fees is based upon dramatic results, and buyers—true buyers—love to invest in dramatic results.

If it's a small organization, no matter what kind of buyer you're talking to, it might be prudent if you were to check a budget. You can say things like, "It seems to me that these are important plans, and the scope of this is of high impact to your organization. Have you budgeted for this? Have you considered an investment in this?"

They might say, "Yes we have. We've put aside X amount of money," and then you can decide whether it's going to be appropriate or not even for your lowest option. Or they could say, which isn't uncommon, "We've never thought of doing this, so we haven't budgeted for it." If you have any suspicions or doubts at all, you could say something such as, "So as not to waste your time or mine and to be totally candid, it seems to me that the minimum amount of investment is going to be $50,000 or $60,000 (or whatever). Of course, your return is going to be well into six or seven figures, but that's the investment that would be needed to launch this. Is that something that you're willing to consider?" You could also ask people a question such as, "What parameters would you like me to stay within?" and so forth.

So, long story short, in large organizations, significant buyers—you don't have to check. Smaller organizations, no matter how significant the buyer, if you're at all uncomfortable, there is nothing wrong with checking that out, just as somebody will ask you what budget do you have in mind when you're looking to purchase a home, purchase insurance, or anything else.

Q: We'll talk about objections shortly and give different case scenarios of different objections, and we're interested in your feedback there. The language you just shared to lead to the budget, how critical is that to set up the right expectation in the buyer's mind? Is that the language we need to use, or do you have some other tips on other language to prepare the buyer from the budget discussion?

Alan: I think that language is appropriate. It's not rocket science. You just need to ask two or three questions, and if you have a history with the organization, you don't have to worry about it. If you know of other people who have done projects for the organization, you probably don't have to worry about it. But if you're at all doubtful, before you go into the energy and time of creating a proposal, you want to have that very brief discussion.

I was talking to a woman in Connecticut on the phone, and she wanted me to speak, and it seemed like karma. My speaking fee is $25,000, and I asked her what her budget was and she said, "$500"! These things happen.

Q: Last week I met with a prospect, and in the course of the conversation he said, "I'm not sure but I think I can sign up to $150,000." Yesterday we reviewed the proposal and he said, "You know what? I actually realized that above $100,000 I need the CFO's signature." This is a Dow Jones company, a multinational corporation, and he said there is a policy that consultant engagements above $100,000 need the CFO's signature. We reworked the proposal and agreed to amend it with a new option that was larger than the original second option, but smaller than the third option which did not exceed $100,000, and we just agreed on it.

Should I have done anything differently? Do you have other strategies that you can recommend to bypass something like that $100,000 trigger?

Alan: On the assumption he wasn't dissembling, he wasn't just engaged in a little bit of braggadocio where he had less authority than he wanted to let on, if he were honest and he just discovered this limitation, I think what you did is pretty good. It was probably A-. A+ would have been, "Why don't we go to your boss who can approve this and see if we can get the full-fledged option 3 going? It's not that much more money than your limit, and with your endorsement, your boss might just go for it."

There is certainly no harm in that, and if you were to say, "Geeze, I really don't want to do that, I don't feel comfortable," then you could have reverted to Plan B. Or if you went to the boss and the boss said, "I just don't have budget for that right now," then you go to Plan B. So, it seems like you did a pretty good job. You got a nice project, but I'm not sure I would have stopped pursuing the top option if there were alternative routes to do that.

Q: What would you do in this situation? You're the consultant. I'm the buyer and say, "I've read your proposal on strategy. It looks really good. You gave me a lot of ideas that I hadn't thought of before, but you're really a lot more expensive than anybody we've ever used before. I used this marketing firm a couple years ago to help me with strategy, so I think we're just going to go with them."

Alan: You can't be a mendicant. You can't be there with your hat in your hand begging for the business. I would elevate the discussion and say, "Listen, if you used that firm years ago, why are you even talking to me now? If we take a look at the results that you can achieve here, and by your own admission in our discussions you indicated that these were the results, and your return is "X" and your benefit is "Y," why is it that now you're just looking at the investment side and thinking of going back to a firm you used years ago which you didn't automatically call but rather came to me?"

When that situation arises, I don't think you have a very good relationship with the buyer. As you know, I think this is a relationship business, and a trusting relationship comes first.

If you have a trusting relationship, you're probably going to hear something more like, "Gee, this first option here, $125,000 is more than I anticipated because we're only getting about a $500,000 benefit, and that's only a 5 to 1 return." Then you can have a discussion and you say, "Well, it's not $500,000. It's annualized, and we agreed it would be $1.5 million probably in 18 months." That's a rational discussion in a trusting relationship.

Q: You've often said that there are no new objections. That we should be ready for them. How do we do that? How do we get ready for the objections that aren't new?

Alan: Objections only fall into four categories. People will tell you they "don't have enough time" which is specious because time isn't a resource, it's a priority. Everybody has the same amount of time. If somebody says they don't have enough time, what they mean is "I have time to think about this, I have time to do this, but I'm not going to give it to you, I'm going to give it to somebody else."

The second category is "no money" which means that again you have a priority problem, not a resource problem, because there is always money. The lights are on. The insurance is being paid. People's benefits are being paid. But they just choose not to give the money to you.

The third area is "no need" which means "I love you, but we don't need what you suggest." That doesn't work for me because a consultant's job is to establish need, and we talked in earlier interviews about the fact that there is either preexisting need, need you create, or need you anticipate. That's your job as a consultant providing professional services.

That leaves one category which is "no trust." And that one is legitimate. That's why I keep reinforcing the fact you need a trusting relationship. If you trust me, then you'll find the time, you'll find the money, and you'll appreciate the need. That's why I've said that ironically, paradoxically, counterintuitively, the longer you take to establish a relationship, *the faster you'll get the business.*

Q: The prospect tells you on the phone, "Alan, this sounds great. I really want to proceed with this proposal. However, I'm swamped right now. I'm working on a major initiative in my business. It wouldn't make sense for me to start on this project until April of next year.

Alan: First of all, you shouldn't be doing this on the phone. As I've said, email is one-dimensional, phone is two-dimensional, but your presence is three-dimensional, so I would advise against that.

The second thing, I would say, "Well Chad, I'm glad you made the decision to go ahead, and let me suggest that since it's now November and April is about a quarter of a year away, there are some things we can begin now on a low key. Why is it you think that it would be too difficult to start now with some aspects?"

This actually happened to me with a client in North Carolina—a manufacturer of pool equipment. I was talking to them in March, and they were gearing up for their busy season. There were seven of us around the table, and the president says, "Alan, we want to do this. I've discussed it with my team. We think it's fabulous, but we want to put it off until the fall when our business slows up so there is minimum distraction here."

I said, "Why do you feel that it wouldn't be appropriate to go forward now?" And he said, "We're gearing up for our busiest season, and the place will be a mad house. There will be people rushing hither and yon. There are orders to be filled. There is a lot of overtime. There is customer demand. There is dealer demand. This place is like a battlefield."

I said, "What better time to really fully understand and appreciate your operation at its most critical point than when it's fully engaged? If we start this in the fall, what we're going to be looking at is an organization working on a much lower profile, and if I had to bet, you would have no temporary employees then. You would have no overtime. The phones wouldn't be ringing. We'll have a false sense of how to implement this, and it will fail when your busy time comes again."

A vice president in the room said, "That makes so much sense. I'm convinced we need to start this now." And everybody came around, including the president. So, you have to be prepared to turn these objections around in your favor.

Q: How do I make the distinction—and I realize it may be subjective—when to get on the plane to see the buyer, especially when I deal with smaller-type projects?

Alan: I don't know what you mean by a "smaller-type project," but I would tell you this: In my world, if you're dealing with a project that's going to be $25,000 or higher, I would get on a plane to see people. If you don't have the cash for the airfare, then find the money. Put it on a credit card and pay it off, use frequent flier points, call any decent travel agent and get a greatly reduced fare, or go on Orbitz or any of these online sources.

If you're talking about $7,500 for a speech or an $8,000 product order or something, okay, stay home. But at $25,000 and up, you ought to be in front of your buyer, especially if that's just the tip of the iceberg. I always talk about thinking of the fourth sale first, and if this organization has long-term benefits in terms of revenue and/or referrals, you need to go see people. It's a cost of doing business.

Q: Personally, I wouldn't think of getting on a plane for a project probably short of let's say $75,000-$100,000. You're changing the mindset here that I should consider getting on a plane and seeing someone for projects below that minimum?

Alan: Let me put it this way. $25,000 is nothing to sneeze at. If you're spending, let's just say $1,000 on the airfare, that's four percent of the project fee you would get. But you're still up $24,000 because the client will pay the expenses in the delivery aspect of the project. And let's say the client gives you a renewal project for $25,000, gives you three referrals that result in $60,000 of business, or serves as a reference for people who bring you another $65,000 of business. I could go on and on.

In my book *Million Dollar Referrals* for McGraw-Hill, I look at a client as having all kinds of varied value for me, a multiplicity of value. The revenue is just part of it. If you look at a client as that kind of jewel, as that kind of potential income source that you can leverage, that's scalable, it's silly not to go to try to close that piece of business in person.

If it's a small business in Bismarck, ND, and it's a $10,000 piece of business, but the buyer has four dry cleaning stores, stay home. But that's seldom the case. I would really tell people that you need to put a premium on getting in front of buyers who not only can do business with you but can provide all this ancillary business.

Over the course of a dozen years with Merck, I made millions of dollars not solely from Merck's coffers, not from Merck's treasury, but from other companies' treasuries because of my ability to do business with Merck, Hewlett Packard, the Federal Reserve, Mercedes, Toyota, or JPMorgan Chase. I could go on and on. Some of those were fairly small projects to start, but nonetheless I wanted that company on my client list.

Q: I'm blown away. I never thought about that.

Alan: No one has ever asked me that question before, so I thought I would give you a number.

Q: Thank you. It's a huge reality check. Now, you're talking to the prospect, and throughout the conversation they're saying, "Alan, we're a leader in our industry, and we're doing just fine." What is your response?

Alan: "Well, I'm happy to hear that. What are you doing to create a killer gap so you're doing superb, and the people who are in second and third place have no chance whatsoever of catching you? I don't think that IBM ever sat back and said, 'We're doing just fine. We can coast.' I don't think McKinsey, Apple, or FedEx ever sat back and said, 'We're doing just fine, let's coast.' I can guarantee you Google has never said that. Why should *you?*"

Q: I'm talking to a small organization based on the standards that we established today. I hear from the small organization, "Alan, budget isn't an issue." How do I respond?

Alan: Well, if budget isn't an issue, why would you respond at all? If they tell me budget isn't an issue, then don't worry about it.

Q: Fair enough. The buyer says, "You come well recommended, but you don't have experience in our industry."

Alan: "Well, that's why I'm so valuable. You have industry experts dropping out of the rafters here; in fact, I tripped over three of them in the hall on my way to your office. You need to sweep some of them away. They're getting in the way of things. The fact is, what you need is expertise from outside your business. You need fresh air. You're breathing your own exhaust. You need best practices from other places. You need somebody who isn't buried in your own content, in your own retirement plan, in your own fringe benefits, and in your own succession planning scheme.

Q: To which the buyer replies, "Okay, my worry is it will probably take you two to three months to get up to speed and even learn what is going on here."

Alan: "Well, I hate to disappoint you in that, but there are two fallacies with that position. The first is I'm a really quick study, and historically it has taken me about 48 hours to understand the client with whom I'm dealing. Now, that doesn't mean that I become an expert to the point that I can sit down and do the jobs of the various people here. But that's not why you're hiring me, so that's irrelevant.

"Secondly, I can make a case that the processes I use are so powerful that a deep understanding of your business is totally unnecessary to apply these processes, and your position isn't unusual. Everybody becomes so impassioned about what they do in the content of what they do that they seem to feel that everybody has to share that same depth of knowledge to be able to give advice about the business, and frankly, that isn't borne out in reality. If you look at the best advisors in the world—people like Peter Drucker, Marshall Goldsmith, and so on—they have very little content knowledge about the organizations in which they deal. They have a huge amount of *process knowledge* that's applicable to any organization."

Q: Here is another objection. In this case the prospect says, "Alan, these are great ideas, but I just hired two new people to do this internally for me."

Alan: "That's fine, and it's not mutually exclusive. First of all, you have two new people, so the benefit to you is that they're here long-term, one would hope, and that they can carry on and retain expertise. Of course, the benefit that they provide isn't as great as you think because they don't know the culture any better than I do. They don't know the politics any better than I do. They will probably have to look for the restrooms, as will I, for the first couple of weeks.

"Consequently, there is no big benefit there. On the other hand, I can actually accelerate their progress and the investment you made in these new people. I can enhance geometrically, exponentially, by drawing them into this project so that they embrace not only the content of the company they have to learn but a fresh approach to it that's provided by these outside best practices and not people who are already here who would normally orient them."

Q: You're demonstrating to us the key to any objection that comes your way is you turn the direction as a platform, as a springboard to make your point.

Alan: Linguistic martial arts. Use the other person's momentum. And that's exactly right because what it gains you is a stunned silence. When you have a stunned silence, that's when you can move in and influence the discussion the way you like because most people aren't expecting that. They're expecting a different line of argument.

Q: To continue on, "Alan, we're having this conversation in November, and your proposal looks really good, but my leadership team is spread all over the world. They aren't going to be together again until March, so it makes sense for us to just push this to after the first of the year, and put it on the 2013 budget."

Alan: "We could certainly do that. Do you mean that you want to implement this in March when they're together? Is that your idea?"

Q: Right. Team building.

Alan: "I think that's a good idea, and I'm all in favor of it. So, since this is November and that's March, we need to have them do some prep work. If we're going to maximize the time they're together—you must be spending something like $250,000 on airfare and lodging to bring them together, never mind their lost time on the job running your operation—to maximize this we need to put some things in place now. There is a book they need to read. There is some material they need to digest. I want to take a look at their backgrounds. I want to run some case studies by them in advance. We should actually begin now."

Q: "Alan, you come with really good references, and you have some good things to say, but I would like to just turn you over to the VP of HR now."

Alan: "What do you mean, turn me over? I feel like a pancake."

Q: "You're talking about succession planning, and that's really under the purview of HR isn't it?"

Alan: "Actually, no. The implementation and the monitoring of the administration are done by HR here, and that's what you've chosen to do. But the guidance, the strategy, and the fit into our business are done by you. Succession planning by definition is strategic. Consequently, if you want me to talk to your vice president of HR, I would be happy to do that. But the decision to do this and the way that we go forward is your decision, so if you want me to talk to her, fine.

"Let's you and I agree to a date when I'll come back and debrief with you. I want to remind you of something. Whenever anybody is responsible for something internally, their immediate response—their immediate stimulation when somebody is brought in from the outside to deal with it—is defensiveness. So, I'll find out whatever I can, I'll debrief with you about what seems to make sense or not make sense, but you and I are the ones who will have to decide how we go forward on this. Then HR will be brought in as we deem appropriate to help administer it."

Q: In my situation, we're both very, very busy. You're a consultant, and I'm the CEO of my organization. "I would like my CFO, whom I trust tremendously, to handle all of the details both on a strategic and technical level. I would like you to work directly with him."

Alan: "I would be happy to work directly with him. That's no problem. However, you and I have to regularly talk. That might be in person, or by phone, or by email, and I have access to you when I need you, just as you have access to me when you need me."

Q: You and I had a discussion in a situation regarding the budget establishment. I was totally off base thinking this project that I'm about to put in a proposal was in the range of somewhere between (option 1) $28,000 and (option 3) $70,000. As you shook me up, option 1 became $150,000 and option 3 became $375,000.

Alan: You were in a different universe.

Q: Help us better understand how to establish these budgets. Why was I so off base?

Alan: The reason was you hadn't fully digested or calculated the return this buyer was getting. I don't think you had looked at a sufficiency of factors that constituted short- and long-term benefit. You hadn't looked at the annualization potential. You hadn't looked at all of the emotional impact. Consequently, you were too focused on too narrow a set of benefits.

Once we discussed that, you readily agreed that the buyer indeed was getting much more than you had first described, and an increase in fees made sense. You were smart enough to do that with me before you put anything in front of the buyer in writing, and that's why consultants need sounding boards. That's why they need a mentor, a coach, a mastermind group, or something that helps them do that.

When I first started the mentor program, I worked with a woman who sent me three proposals that were rejected over three weeks. One, two, three. Bang, bang, bang. I told her in each one what was wrong with them, and after the third one I said, "Barbara, how about you send me the next proposal before you submit it?" Conceptual breakthrough here. And she hit that for $80,000. The same principle applies here. We need people we can bounce things off because once I pointed that out to you, you immediately saw it.

Q: "We're looking for the best of the best to coach our CEO. Obviously, we're talking to you. We're talking to Marshall Goldsmith. And we're talking to Marcus Buckingham. Why you?"

Alan: "I don't know. You're talking to good people. I would have to meet your CEO to tell you. I would have to see if he is right for me and if I'm right for him. I would have to see how the initial discussion goes. What his or her expectations are. Whether they're reasonable. Whether I can meet them. Whether I have the skill set. Then I can tell you if I'm the right person or not. But I think anybody who would say to you right now that they're the right person without meeting the CEO, without meeting the client, is doing a song and dance."

Q: Now I'm the CEO, we're having our discussion, and my last question to you is similar. "Alan, I'm very impressed with what you have to offer me. Why you?"

Alan: "Well Chad, I'm impressed also, and I think we can work together, and I think we can make some beautiful music here. All the people you're talking to, from my understanding, are superb people. I think the choice for you is a combination of how good the chemistry is but also how blunt and candid you want the feedback.

"My style is to do things rapidly and to give you candid feedback that's both pro and con and to move as rapidly as you're prepared to move. My style is also to hold you accountable and not to let you get away with things. I don't care how busy you are. I don't care how many demands there are on you. Now, if that's a style you're comfortable with, then I think I'm the guy for you. If that's not a style you're comfortable with, and you prefer someone who is more laid back, and you prefer someone who is more tactful and political, then you might well find somebody else more to your liking. So, I think that's a decision you have to make, but if you choose me, I would be happy to work with you."

Q: We just covered a number of objections, and the rule of thumb that the mindset that you coach us to is that objections are a sign of interest. Let's differentiate and make a distinction between an inquiry of interest and a rejection that will lead you to say, "Okay, I don't need to follow this up. This is the end of the line. There is no further conversation."

Alan: First of all, what you said is exactly true because if somebody bothers to argue with you, it shows that they're interested. The worst kinds of people we deal with are those who stereotypically never get back to us. The people who don't return phone calls, don't return emails, and suddenly they disappear. Those are the apathetic people or the completely uninterested people, and you have to give up on them. But people who raise argument—raise objection—are those who are interested in what you have to say. *An objection is a sign of interest.*

If I understand your question, even among them there are some who will give you the sign clearly that it's silly to pursue things. When you get a sign like that, then you should really stop. One sign would be "Look, we've looked at four different people. We think you're very good, but we've chosen this one because they have an office only half a mile away." "We've chosen this one because they've done business with four other clients in our industry." "We've chosen this one because my vice president's brother-in-law is a member of their firm."

When you hear things like that you say, "Thank you very much. If I can be of help in the future, let me know." They've given you the courtesy of a formal "No." Some people will say, "I took a look at your proposal, and I didn't like it." You might have had an excellent relationship, but you did a lousy job with the proposal, or you did a lousy job creating expectations or not creating expectations. That happens too. I used to miss 20 percent of my proposals. These things happen, and as I've said before, *you have to accept rejection and reject acceptance.*

Q: In conclusion, we've tried to address these four major categories of objections that clients have to our proposals and to working with us. What do the people in your mentor program tell you are the objections that they're hearing most and having the most difficulty with?

Alan: My observation over the last 15 years is that they have the most trouble with no money. But the etiology is off. They're having the most trouble with no money because they're often not dealing with a buyer. They're dealing with a feasibility person. They're dealing with a human resource person, a trainer, or a learning and development person.

The second issue is that since they haven't established conceptual agreement, that's an easy out for the buyer to say, "We have no money," and the consultant folds his or her tent and off they go into the night, stealing away like a discovered thief! So, it's not quite a legitimate objection, but it's one they fear the most, and it's one they have the most trouble dealing with. In all honesty, the one that gives them the most trouble is no trust because they're not spending the time investment on developing that key and very critical relationship.

Q: In summation, the top three things are be with the economic buyer, get conceptual agreement, and spend some time to get the trust?

Alan: Yes, but not in that order. Find the economic buyer, develop a trusting relationship, and develop conceptual agreement.

Q: We conclude this chapter and one follow-up question on a completely different level. This is the week of Thanksgiving. In a few days we'll all be celebrating Thanksgiving. Alan, what does Thanksgiving mean to you, and how do you intend to celebrate this year?

Alan: Well, I give thanks every day. We're fortunate in a lot of respects. We're fortunate that we live in this great experiment called America where freedom, liberty, and human justice—while imperfect—are nevertheless the prevailing value system of the country. We're fortunate we live in a land (and this is obviously not confined to the U.S.) of great resources where we've been able to help other people around the world from a scientific standpoint, from a humanitarian standpoint, and from a military standpoint.

We're fortunate that this is the land of innovation and that all of us on this call—and presumably most of the people who are reading this or listening to it in the United States—have the great capacity and latitude to be innovative, creative, try new things, and to take risk in a society that not only allows it but rewards it. Those are the kinds of things I'm thankful for, frankly, every day. I'm a spiritual person, and that's in my prayers every day.

On a practical basis, Thanksgiving is wonderful because it's an excuse to get together with your family. Thanksgiving is about family, food, and football! It's a wonderful tradition, the food is plentiful, and if you're careful about it, it's actually good and won't kill you!

Thanksgiving is the major secular holiday in the United States. There are few like it in the world, and in the U.S. I think it has gone beyond its original meaning which was of the Pilgrims and the settlement of the country (though formalized much later by President Lincoln). I think it really represents the fact that we're all, by the grace of God, fortunate to be here—either born here or have immigrated here. All of us alike as one appreciate the great beauty of being able to live here.

Conclusion

Proposals that you send to anyone other than the economic buyer are the equivalent of leaving on the landing lights for Amelia Earhart: a nice gesture but ultimately futile. Proposals—and their acceptance—from a true buyer, on the other hand, are critical to your success. They're based on trust, not legalities. Sign your copy and agree to proceed on even a telephone approval.

The discussion should never be about fees. It should always be about value. If it's about the former, you've lost control of the situation. This is your fault, not the buyer's. Stop doing that.

The Consulting Engagement: Proposal Acceptance

10

Just as we should prepare the environment and culture for the acceptance of a proposal, we should set the stage for acceptance of our interventions. Probably the most critical factor in the eventual success of our implementation is the role of the buyer.

With rare exceptions, the buyer should be the champion of the project. The buyer may delegate accountabilities to lower-level people, but the buyer must be the point person who leads the charge. Implementation is a partnership. If clients don't pull their weight, you'll all sink together. That's why next steps are so important. You'll need to address those things that need to change and also preserve those traditional approaches that should never change. Some of these issues will be strategic, others tactical. The client will rely on you to help them walk the talk and talk the walk.

The Buyers Signed the Proposal. Now What?

Q: In previous conversations you've recommended FedEx or using a courier service to get the proposal to the buyer. Do you still recommend that, or is it okay to just email?

Alan: Previously, I recommended using FedEx or a courier service to deliver the proposal—which I still recommend—but a lot of buyers want it electronically today, which is fine. I used to be concerned that the proposal might be opened and read by somebody inappropriate, but if the buyer requests it, the buyer is an adult. I would suggest that when the buyer requests an electronic copy, you send it electronically on your letterhead so that it looks good. It's not an email. In other words, it's an attachment to email on your letterhead, but concurrent with that, you also send a hard copy via FedEx so they have both hard copy and electronic.

Of course, whenever you submit a proposal, you tell the buyer, "I'll call you Friday at 2:00 (or whenever) to discuss which option you would like to choose." If the buyer doesn't call you first, you call the buyer at 2:00 on Friday and say, "I'm calling as promised." So, that's generally the scheme of things.

Q: Now you have the signed proposal in your hand. You've agreed on the start-up date, and the buyer has agreed to the 50 percent up front; however, the buyer is very eager to get started on this. Is it a good idea to go ahead and start work before you have a check?

Alan: I think if you have a good relationship with the buyer, it's a legitimate company, and you're not working with somebody out of a basement somewhere, I think that's fine. Let's just put some concrete terms on this. I think if the buyer calls you on Friday and says, "Listen, I've decided to go with option 2, and I'm going to get a check issued immediately for the 50 percent payment in advance. But I would like you to start next week, if you possibly can, because there are some things happening that I think you really should be seeing, and they might not occur for another three months."

I think your response to that is, "Fine. I would be happy to be there. I assume you're drawing a manual check so that you can give it to me while I'm there." When people say they're having a check drawn immediately, they often mean that they're putting it into their company's payment system, their payment cycle, and some of those cycles are 45 or 60 days. Just be specific about what you're expecting and then start work.

Q: So, it's realistic to expect that they would get that check to you immediately and not put it through the normal processes?

Alan: If their normal process is they can pay a check in three or five days, that's fine. I'm certainly willing to wait a week. But if their normal process, which is far more likely, is that it goes on some kind of check request form to accounting where it sits on somebody's desk for 29 days and then the computer spits out a check, that's unacceptable.

Q: What is your advice for getting this off on the right terms—some tips to create goodwill and momentum at the start of the engagement?

Alan: At the start of the engagement, you shouldn't go racing through the hallways of the building telling everyone they're doomed. Basically, what you should do is start slowly. If you met some other people in the course of marketing and discussing things with your prospect before the prospect became a client, reestablish contact with them. If you haven't met many people or you need to meet more people, start to meet them. Start to talk to them. Interview them. Get to know people gradually. Get the lay of the land. Make some observations.

You're right, these projects can be complex, and they can be complicated, and I've never, ever, ever started a consulting project where I had all of the information or where the project went merrily along exactly the way I thought it would. There are always changes, and that's why "needs analyses" and all of these upfront, information-gathering things are worthless because things are going to change anyway. Start fairly gradually but then plan to build up speed. Accelerate considerably.

Q: And obviously, keep the buyer involved with all of the changes that are going on.

Alan: The buyer, at the beginning of a project, should be involved on a regular basis. You might debrief weekly, and then as the project unfolds, you might debrief bi-weekly, and then you might debrief monthly. I would never debrief less than monthly, but you can get to a point where once a month is fine. If you do things monthly, I would suggest that they be in person. If you do things once a week, you could have two meetings in person, two meetings by phone; but the very least you should do is by phone, never by email. You can use email to document the debriefings, but you have to keep the buyer apprised.

One of the major reasons is if you keep the buyer apprised, you can give the buyer good news. You can tell the buyer, "We're making progress. According to these metrics, we've made nice advances here." That way, inevitably, when you have to give the buyer some bad news—somebody isn't holding up their end of the bargain, a given area isn't performing the way it should—that bad news is in perspective with all the good news. The buyer can take that and act on it in a much more positive manner.

Q: What mistakes have you seen your mentorees make at the beginning of the consulting engagement?

Alan: In no particular order, there are four or five. One is that they try to implement their own methodology irrespective of what is needed. If you think there are seven steps to effective acceleration of sales, you want to check to see if the client is using any of them. So, the client might already be doing three of them better than you are. Don't implement the seven, just implement the four the client needs, if that's what is needed.

A second thing is that there is too much time spent—let's say there is an inappropriate amount of time spent—data gathering. So, rather than starting to move things forward, the first several weeks are wasted just gathering data. The fact is you can gather data and concurrently move things forward. Success, not perfection. You're never going to have a complete picture. Move when you have a picture that's good enough that it's recognizable.

A third thing is they get engaged accidentally or even advertently in politics. People are pointing fingers, and suddenly you find yourself taking sides, and there is communication shutdown. You should always be a neutral, impartial, objective intermediary.

Fourth, you get yourself tangled up in human resources. They, of course, want to do things 15 ways from Sunday, implement all the latest fads and buzz words, and administer the thing to death. So, you have to stay away from them.

The final thing is that they're not light enough on their feet to handle the inevitable changes that we alluded to just a few minutes ago. Suddenly, they sort of become a deer in the headlights, and deer are caught in headlights like that because their eyes dilate so much that they are virtually blinded. Consultants should keep their focus, they should squint a little bit and not let all that light in there, and be much more focused on what they do so that they don't freeze when suddenly they get hit with light from a different direction.

Q: The buyer decided to take advantage of the 10 percent discount and engaged immediately on a number of pressing issues, and we already created value. It's credible and we have mutual trust. It now appears that payment will be coming in 30 days. What are my options?

Alan: You have to say to the buyer, "Look, this discount I'm giving you—in fact my entire fee—is based on use of my money. That means that I'm expecting to be able to have the money and use it. I understand that you have your own processes, your own procedures, and so on, but nonetheless, that's the basis of my fee, so we have a couple of choices.

"One is that you issue a manual check, you get it to me in the next two or three days, and that will take care of everything. I don't mind waiting for part of a week. But the second thing is, if you can do nothing but put this through your system—so instead of commencement I'm being paid in 30 days—then I'm going to have to charge you the regular fee and not allow the 10 percent discount. A third thing to do is simply delay the start of the project until I get the check, but you seem to want to proceed now. So, which of these three options seem to make the most sense to you?"

Q: So, once again you actually present options?

Alan: I love to present options because it puts the onus back on the other person to choose something that they feel is workable and not for me to come up with the magic solution.

Q: In addition to what you shared, what are some practices you developed to accelerate the engagement to create momentum and specifically to build a sense of confidence and optimism about the success of the project?

Alan: You want small victories quickly, and so I might go back to the buyer and say, "We were talking about getting all five of your direct reports to commit to make presentations to their people, and I've already heard from four of them. I'm confident by the end of the week, we'll have all five." Something as small as that shows the buyer progress. It shows you're working on the right things. And that you know full speed ahead.

I think you also want to give people credit, and as early as you can, you want to share credit with client people and say, "Congratulations. The sales force has already set up an input device on the intranet of the company to provide knowledge sharing about new clients commensurate with what we were talking about in this project, and it's much faster than we anticipated."

You have to show small victories. You want to share credit quickly. And you want to be very visible. You want to make everybody aware of what is happening. It's not important to show major success early. It's just important to show that you're willing to communicate and willing to listen.

Q: How different should we engage in terms of the tactics of engagement when the buyer is directly involved in the process, or as is often the case in large corporations, when the buyer is somewhat remote from the process and the project?

Alan: It doesn't really matter. The answer to the question is the buyer has to be involved to the extent that you need the buyer for several purposes. One is to sort of walk the talk and talk the walk as explained at the beginning of this chapter. The second is that you might need the buyer's clout to help move a previously immovable object. The third is you might need the buyer's advice or insight on some things that you're encountering, and so on. So, whether the buyer wants to be at arm's length or hands-on doesn't really matter so long as the buyer is fulfilling the needs that you have.

Let me answer a question you didn't ask me. If the buyer is so hands-on, and the buyer is starting to interfere with the project, intimidate people, or cause them not to be candid because the buyer is in every meeting and everything, then you have to pull back on that. But I would tell you that's a pretty nice problem to have as opposed to the buyer who suddenly disappears.

Q: What should consultants do if we sign a proposal but already have a great deal of work going on at the same time? What should we do to get things moving even if we feel swamped with other projects?

Alan: That's a great question, and I'm asked that a lot. It's an issue, a challenge that successful consultants have; and unfortunately, some of them decide to turn down the work, which is ridiculous. I remember one year I had 36 projects going on during the course of that year. I don't turn down work.

What you can do is stagger it. So, at the beginning, let's say your time is pretty much taken up for the next month, and you bring on a new client. Schedule it so that the first month with the new client, the client is doing most of the work. Circulate a survey. Make your interviews by phone. Ask the client to develop certain data, or get permission from the client's customers for you to visit. So, get some of the administrative and organizational stuff done early.

Another technique is to put in a day or two, and make yourself very visible. You come for two days during the week, you carve that out of your time, and you show that you're there. Now you tell the client you have to go back and analyze, give the client some feedback, get the next steps, and there are all kinds of things like that you can do.

The key is that you're the consultant, and don't let the client determine how you consult. If the client says, "Aviv, we're happy to have you joining us, we're happy to be your new client, and for the next two weeks we would like you on site," obviously, you can't agree to that. Even if you weren't doing anything anywhere else, you shouldn't agree to stipulations like that.

The Distinctions Between Content and Process

Q: How should we keep in mind the distinction between content and process as we begin the client engagement?

Alan: Let me refer to sort of a kindred spirit here and someone who was doing this long before I was. His name is Edgar Schein. He wrote a book called *Process Consulting* long before I wrote my book called *Process Consultation*. He is a distinguished professor, a great consultant, and writes well. I have a lot of respect for Edgar Schein, and if you ask him what process consulting is, he will tell you it's the ability to deal with people in terms of how they do things, not what they do. I've adopted that because I've found that I can consult with almost anybody in anything given those criteria

So, in answer to your question, I would very much focus on the processes and the "how" in terms of what you see and the manner in which things are getting done rather than the what. I wouldn't tell them that the car ought to be painted blue. I would tell them that the car is taking too long to get painted, and here is why. Those are the kinds of separations that are going to make you a much more effective consultant. The exception would be the equivalent of a legal expert witness who is an expert on car painting and can come in and talk only on car painting, but that's a very limited value.

Q: It almost sounds counterintuitive, to start slowly and create quick success.

Alan: Actually, it does sound counterintuitive. But it's not because if you accept the quick successes or advancements and not necessarily finalities, you're in good shape. Let's just say, arbitrarily, that one of the things you're going to do is to set up focus groups, and you're going to conduct focus groups in concurrence and accordance with the project's guidelines. Telling the client, "Good news. We've already set up six focus groups, and we've involved two of your remote locations," is a small victory. If you say to a client, "We agreed that I talk to at least a dozen of your customers, and 14 of them have already agreed," that's a small victory.

The small victories at the outset are about the implementation, not the result. As the project unwinds, at the end of the day, the victory is going to be about results. So, I would suggest to you that in the course of a project, especially a large one, the victories will start with implementation, input, and tasks that go well and gradually metamorphose, change into victories about results, outcomes, and goals.

Q: As we now move into "Content and Process," give me some more indicators. Sometimes I find it vague—the fine line distinction—between where content starts and process stops, or vice versa. What are some of the indicators for me to easily distinguish whether I'm looking at content or a process?

Alan: What and how. "What" is content and "how" is process 99 times out of 100. Content is the *what* someone is doing. They're approving insurance claims. They're manufacturing brake pads. They're driving a high speed transport.

The process can be any number of things in terms of how these people are selected, how they go about their work, how they organize their work, how they are rewarded, and so on. At the conclusion of the project, the customer still wants to make brake pads and still wants people to drive high speed transports, but they might want them to do it better, more safely, with better publicity, or with less stress, and so forth.

Q: You talked about focus groups. In the option the buyer selects, it includes a series of focus groups and a 360-degree assessment. What are some of the tips you can give us to do this rapidly? How do you maximize the impact of the focus group on the success of the project?

Alan: Focus groups have advantages. They're live. You can ask follow-up questions. The groups are self-sanctioning. In other words, somebody could say, "This place has the worst benefits of anybody in the industry," and four other people could say, "We've worked at competitors. The benefits here are as good, if not better, than anyone." So, all that's positive about focus groups. You can also mix and match. In other words, you can mix new employees, old employees. You can make cultural, racial, ethnic mixes. Gender mixes. You can really test out a wide variety of things.

The disadvantage of focus groups is that there is a confidentiality problem, and even though you say you're not going to reveal names, you know 19 people in that room hear what the 20th person is saying, and whether or not they choose to honor confidentiality is really up to them. You can't control it. What you can do is make sure there aren't direct superiors in the room, set ground rules, and things like that, but ultimately there is always a confidentiality issue.

So, those are the pros and cons of focus groups. My advice about focus groups, if you're gathering information, is to always use them in conjunction with other kinds of inputs.

Q: How do you determine that you have enough interviews with focus groups and you're not going overboard?

Alan: Patterns emerge. Let's say that you're trying to evaluate the role of compensation in retention of employees, just for argument's sake, and after four focus groups, you have very, very clear patterns. The focus groups have been diverse.

People are telling you that they aren't there for the money; they are there because the company affords them latitude of freedom. They believe in the company's mission. They love the environment. They love the CEO. And as long as the money is competitive, they're happy. You don't need to run another five focus groups if that's what you've heard, and they're diverse cross-sections of the population.

Q: We want to understand what is the place of art, what is the place of science in the engagement with the client in delivering results?

Alan: It's like when people ask me about research for my books, it's almost embarrassing to hear that word applied to my books. The science of an intervention includes methodology, technology, tools, and instrumentation which are tried and true and work. We've been talking thus far about things like focus groups, surveys, interviews, 360-degree assessments, psychometric testing, observation, and so forth and so on. There is a lot of methodology out there.

The art form, however, is in adapting it and sometimes even creating it on the spot for your purposes. Every organization's culture is somewhat different. Every organization's complexion, its attitude, its values are somewhat different. Its leadership, of course, is different.

I mentioned Edgar Schein before, who I have great respect for, but he and I disagree on corporate culture. Edgar's approach to culture, last time I read it, was something like this: He said that culture is really a residue of where an organization has been; it's sort of a culmination of an organization's history. So, you don't worry about culture change because any time you invoke change, you're creating new culture. I hope I haven't done him a disservice there, but that's my understanding.

I don't believe that at all. I believe that culture is really that set of beliefs which govern behavior, and if you want to change an organization, you have to change the belief systems. I'm not talking about religiosity or even spirituality. I'm talking about how people believe in their mission, how people believe in their values, what people believe about the customer, what people believe about their own roles. So, part of the art that goes with the science is the artistry of understanding how you can effectively persuade, cajole, and influence belief systems, self-worth, and such issues to create the organizational change that the science will support.

Change and Innovation: For Ourselves and Our Clients

Q: Would you give us your definitions for innovation, evolution, and reinvention?

Alan: Let me define innovation first. Innovation to me is applied creativity. Creativity is simply good ideas and people coming up with them. You've seen some of my process visuals where I show how you actually can monetize creativity. *Creativity is applied innovation.*

Evolution tends to occur through trial and error, and species-wise it occurs through the best adaptations, but those can take a long, long, long time. So, evolution is a slow process as opposed to revolution.

Reinvention is an intent. But reinvention can only be effectively created through innovation. You only have two real issues in organizations. If you look at this in a macro sense, one is you have people trying to fix things. That is, you have people trying to restore past standards of behavior, performance, and so on. Or you have innovation where people are trying to raise the bar and create new standards of performance, behavior, and so on. For my money, the first one, the problem solving has been more than taken care of with quality procedures and "lean and mean" going on for decades.

Companies are pretty good at it themselves, but raising the bar is different. It's much harder because there is big risk there. In problem solving, you know that the performance once was successful; in raising the bar, you don't know if the new standard is ever going to be successful.

My first book, with my co-author Michel Robert, was *The Innovation*

Formula, and it's still being sold. It was on the curriculum of the Wharton School for quite a while and Temple and Villanova as well. When we "researched" that book—and again, research is a little bit of a strange word for me—we were getting into the background of what we were going to write about. Joseph Schumpeter, who is quoted all the time, called innovation "creative destruction." A lot of caché there. I like that. But what you want to do is you always want to try to raise the bar.

The way you don't become complacent is you constantly innovate. And if you call that reinvention, that's fine, but the heart and soul of reinvention is innovation.

Q: What are some of the best ways for us as consultants to, number one, bring innovation to our own organization, and number two, bring innovation to our clients?

Alan: You never, ever can extrapolate from the present to the future, if you want to innovate, because you'll always have a straight line, rather shallow progression. This is what is wrong with the planning process in most organizations, which delimits your future. If you want to innovate, you have to think outside the box.

That's the stereotypical phrase. You have to break the paradigm, another stereotypical phrase but accurate. The point is that you have to think in different terms, in different dimensions, if you want to innovate. If you're worried about how you get fish to shore fresh from boats far out to sea, innovation means you think about how you get people to the fish.

Let me give you a very contemporary example, which always bemused me. Airports are basically built for airplanes, not people. They made a big extension in Boston at the Delta/Continental terminals, but the big extension involves you actually having to go through security, down escalators, across moving walkways, up escalators, and across something else to get to the planes. They should be bringing the planes to the people. They used to bring the old Concordes in London right to the Concorde Club. The plane's nose came right up to the club, and the steward would take your hand baggage and bring it on the plane. You bring the plane to the people.

Right now you have this new A380—this monster that Aerospace Industries has launched—with a lot of problems. It can hold about 500 people with a first class, and without a first class can hold about 800 people. But people are still entering through a bottleneck. They're still entering with somebody taking their ticket, scanning their ticket, or whatever at one or two boarding areas; two if they're lucky, otherwise one. And the same thing about every plane in the sky right now, whether it holds 150 people or 300 people, you're going through this one entry point. Planes should open from the side so people can march on *en mass* instead of walking on through a bottleneck down the aisles with the flight attendant screaming, "Please get out of the aisle; let people behind you get on board." Planes aren't built for people, they're built for airlines. They're built to be flown, and they're built for pilots. They aren't built for the customer.

If you take a look at anything regarding air travel today—whether it's security, customs, or immigration—they aren't built for people, they're built for their own sake. That's the place where innovation could be wildly success-ful once somebody decides to shake loose of all the paradigms that are freez-ing people into these unsuccessful models right now.

Q: When we're thinking about evolution and reinvention for ourselves and for our clients, what do you feel is the importance for our survival and our continued growth?

Alan: Without growth there is no excitement. There is no energy. There is no investment, and I mean psychic investment, emotional investment, and so forth.

We were at the Million Dollar Club out in Bora Bora. When we were going around getting feedback from the group, one of the group members said that I had said, "I don't need to make more money. At my stage of the game, $2.5 million or so is just fine, that's a nice lifestyle, and I want to do other things." He said to me, "You have to stop saying you don't want to grow." But he misinterpreted.

Just because I don't need to make more money doesn't mean I'm not growing. I might well be growing more than he is because my growth is spiritual, my growth is emotional, my growth is intellectual, my growth is in terms of my legacy and ability to help others, my growth is my intellectual property, and I can go on and on and on. Growth comes in a multitude, in a myriad of forms, and the key for us is to keep growing because the growth is what fuels the kind of impact we can make on the world.

Q: Let's go back to Edgar Schein for a minute. Many people know his work with organizations and organizational culture in particular. What many people may not know is he introduced the word "influenceability," which I've always loved. He based this on his research with the Korean POW's and how some of them were brainwashed or overly influenced. As consultants, when we go into a new engagement and we're looking at innovation and change, is there a positive way of looking at brainwashing and how some of it can be appropriate?

Alan: First of all, using research in terms with Edgar Schein is appropriate, so that's an appropriate use of the word given his work and his rather profound influence on consulting. I wouldn't use "brainwashing." What I would tell you is this. If you look at psychology today, most psychological authorities who are experts in behavior change will tell you that the way you get behavior change is to replace old beliefs and old behaviors with new beliefs and new behaviors and not to try to chip away, erode, and gradually persuade those old beliefs and old behaviors to change.

I believe that people, organizations, countries, you name the entity, all act in their own self-interest. To expect a country not to act in its national self-interest is insane. To expect an organization not to do it is insane. Sometimes they're forced not to do it by the government, regulation, or inept leadership, but all things being equal, organizations will act in their best interest, and people will act in their own self-interest. So, if you want to change organizational people, you want to create a self-interest goal that will cause them to change their own behaviors. I wouldn't call that brainwashing. I would call that enlightened self-interest—just the opposite as a matter of fact.

Q: That sounds more like Edgar Schein's influence, doesn't it, than brainwashing?

Alan: Yes, I agree with that. If you look at Roberto Cialdini who wrote *Influence*, the name of his book and what he says are essentially the same thing. Most of us who are engaged in this—especially engaged for some time and with major organizations and powerful people—will tell you that you have to change the self-interest. You're not going to change them through coercion, carrying a big stick, or through normative pressure because they're either too mature or too large for that. The best way to get people and large organizations to change is to change their self-interest.

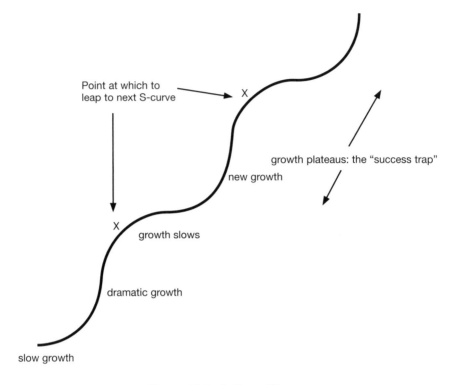

Figure 10.2: S-Curve Theory

Q: What happens when people don't continue to innovate? In other words, they don't take that upward "S" curve to new paths. Rather, they sink first into complacency and then into some other things that I haven't heard you talk about before—protection, entitlement, and desertion which finally leads to abandonment. Could you walk us through what happens there?

Alan: If you don't innovate and you keep clinging to what used to make you good, your visceral reaction is to try to protect it more and more. You don't want people to erode it. You get paranoid. You see enemies. You see people who are taking your ideas and taking them somewhere else.

When you're innovative, you're climbing, you're out of your shell, and you're vulnerable. You can fail. But when you're protective, you develop these defenses and steal mechanisms and you sue people.

When protectionism doesn't work, decline occurs because the protection isn't enough. Your market erodes, your good customers leave, your name declines, your brands are no longer powerful, and your protection—your trademarks—mean nothing, and then you're abandoned. People abandon you in the marketplace. You're no longer of interest. Osborne Computer and the Saturn car disappear—that's what takes place. Organizations and people driving organizations really have no choice but to keep growing because the alternative is to disappear.

Q: One of the things that also struck me in the Change Management Workshop is that one way or another, consultants are all in the change management business. If I'm accurate in that, how should consultants adjust their mindset to think of themselves as change agents?

Alan: You're accurate, and it really doesn't matter how they consider themselves as long as they consider themselves people helping their clients to improve their condition. I could make a case to you that the true change agents are all internal. I'm no change agent because I don't stay there. I have no accountability, no responsibility once I leave. I'm being paid for a specific set of results. I have no influence over people's performance, income, or anything else. That's a matter for management. That's a matter for executives.

The true change agents are always internal. I don't think it's as important as how people regard themselves in terms of what they do as to what they create and what they affect. I think that's the much more critical aspect of it.

Q: In what situations do you prefer to use individual interviews over focus groups?

Alan: I prefer to use both. I seldom ever have used just one or the other, and I also use surveys. The reason is I like to see if I get the same patterns using three different, basic inputs. I also accompany that with observations as I wander around. If I get patterns that are consistent and basically the same over those different approaches, those different interventions, I know I have something really valid. Each of those things has pros and cons. Each has advantages and disadvantages. So, for me, the way to make the most of the advantages and to mitigate the disadvantages is to use a combination of them to get my patterns.

Q: What best practices do you use in the reporting?

Alan: My practice has been to talk to the buyer interactively—to meet with the buyer and give the buyer feedback—and then give the buyer an executive summary of what I discussed. I like to do the feedback part first, the interactive part first, because it's very fresh. There are no preconceptions. Then I like to give the buyer something in writing so the buyer doesn't have to have taken notes, and there is clarity about what I said. I won't disseminate that further unless the buyer asks me to. I keep everything very brief.

Q: In reporting, less is more works as well?

Alan: Correct. You're better off changing three fundamental issues that can profoundly help the organization than having teams and committees addressing 40 issues that would just be moved from one easel sheet to another. It's another reason that I virtually never, ever use PowerPoint.

Q: A typical engagement begins with diagnostic elements that we just discussed and follows into prescriptive elements, solutions, the intervention, and so on, and these often follow a divergent into convergent phases. Do you make a clear distinction here? What practices do you use to inform, to coach, to instruct the client, the buyer that we're now moving from the diagnostic phase into the prescriptive solution?

Alan: It becomes self-evident, and you're quite right. The further you go into a project, the more prescriptive you must become. I've had clients tell me point blank, "You said earlier, 'I'm always giving options.' At this stage of the game, we don't want options; we want your best piece of advice." So, I'm very careful, once I get pretty far into a project, that I'm giving clear advice as to what I think is best. The further you go, the more that advice has to be specifically prescriptive. Do this and not that. Do seven of this and not six. It's these nine people and not these other sixteen. That way you've worked to the head of the arrow. You have a nice sharp point on things. It's this and not that. The more the project unfolds, the more you learn, the more you should be properly prescriptive because you have the ammunition to be prescriptive.

Q: Following on the culture change conversation. You said that it's a belief that governed behaviors; therefore, if we're to change and impact the culture, we have to change the belief and the enlightened self-interest which will ultimately guide behavior. I find in a couple of recent engagements that what the organization needs is a very concrete, pragmatic description, actually written in concise statements of the new behaviors. Does this make sense?

Alan: The model you just provided is a very good one, if you can obtain agreement with the client on the behaviors that you want to see manifested. For example, a server in a restaurant always asks at the end of the meal would the people want an after-dinner drink or dessert. A teller in a bank always asks a customer, "Would you like to see our new low-cost checking account that might be appropriate for you?" A repair person visiting in a home always asks, "This is now fixed. Please sign here. By the way, would you like to purchase a warranty that would cover you if this ever occurs in the future?"

If you agree that those are the behaviors, then you can monitor them. You can spread the good word about them. You can reward them. That's absolutely the best way to go because they're manifest. You can see them. There is no question about whether they're occurring. It's an excellent way to do business.

Q: What often sabotages interventions and change, and how do you mitigate resistance?

Alan: There are two or three probably highest risk land mines here. One is the fact that the people who are most visible and who are the avatars don't walk the talk. That might be hierarchical leaders, but it might also be informal leaders whom people respect, top sales people, union people, whatever. They have to adapt and display the behaviors that you're trying to get others to display.

A second is that you get cognitive dissidence. The reward system isn't consistent with the behaviors, so what you need to do is to create a rational reward system—not just financial but also non-financial rewards—which encourage the behaviors you're trying to create and discourage the behaviors that used to be there that you want to have subsumed.

A third thing is that they disappear after you leave because you've been the catalyst. You're not really the change agent, so you have to make sure that there are people internally who take the ball and keep running with it. This is why I've always talked about transferring the skills so that the impetus and the focus remain on this new set of behaviors until they're entrenched within the organization.

Q: In your book, *Process Consulting*, you say that change management is an oxymoron. What did you mean?

Alan: Change management, if you think of the words, is like stress management. Change isn't something you manage. Change is something that you create. Change is something that you rejoice in. Change is sometimes something that you bat down because it's inappropriate change. It's like these stupid titles that come up: chief executive of knowledge discovery, chief executive of customer experience. These are basically titles in lieu of pay raises.

For my money, change management is simply a phrase we use today without people thinking about it too much. We really aren't into change management. What we're into is a focused change. We're into constructive change. We're into a strategic change. Some change isn't good, some change is good. It's up to us to implement the good stuff, and beware of the bad stuff.

Q: How do we help organizations shift from incremental change to visionary, breakthrough change and growth?

Alan: You have to paint a picture of the future as to where you would ideally like to go and work backwards. Visionary change—just think of your phrase—means following a vision, which means you create a vision *first*. Visions aren't created from what you're looking at today. They're created from something new that you develop, that you construct. So, extrapolated change—change that comes from where we are today—will never be visionary. You have to think of a new future and work backwards.

Helping the Client Develop Strategy and Tactics

Q: Is there a danger with becoming more prescriptive at the beginning and not towards the end?

Alan: Yes. If you recall the conversation we had, you walk into a doctor's office and say, "I'm not feeling very well. I feel sort of achy. I have a headache." If the doctor says, "I'm going to prescribe Zoloft," that's not a very good prescriptive device because the doctor hasn't taken your temperature or blood pressure, hasn't asked you questions about when this began, hasn't observed you long enough, and Zoloft is basically used for depression and mood swings. As a consultant, you need to be more like a doctor and not make your diagnosis and then prescription until you know enough.

Q: The other concept we talked about was change management is an oxymoron. What goes through your mind to take a position like this—whether it's your contrarian approach or not—that you just break the mold and totally reverse it? What goes through your mind to do that?

Alan: That's a good question. I could cop out and say, "It's the *gestalt*." I asked a psychologist once—a Ph.D. from the University of Rhode Island who was an advisor to a firm I was heading—how he made his assessments based on psychometric tools, and he said, "It's the *gestalt*." I said, "Peter, I understand *gestalt*, but when you pick up this documentation, what do you look at first? Let's start with that." He said, "Well, I look at this first." I said, "It's not so much *gestalt* then." So, I'm not going to cop out.

A friend of mine who you know, who is in the Million Dollar Club and a Master Mentor—Andrew Sobel—said one of the most valuable things he has learned from me is my ability to take something that sounds similar and show how different it is. For example, I draw the difference between coaching and mentoring. I draw the difference between cause and effect. I draw the difference between problem solving and innovation. I say things like strategic planning is an oxymoron. And he says, "I've used that. I've copied you and used that in rooms of high-level executives, and the whole room has stopped breathing."

I find these tremendously important techniques, and the way I do it is my mindset is such that I look at life in two ways. I look at life always with the sense of healthy humor. I have a certain perspective about life—this whole aspect of residing on a rock traveling at 85,000 miles an hour around an exploding star and remembering that the dinosaurs that lived for 200 million years were wiped out by a random space debris.

The second is I look at life and things around me with a very healthy skepticism. That is, I'm not a cynic. I don't try to knock down for the sake of it. But I do look at things somewhat skeptically, my basic diagnostic approach. So, when somebody says "change management," I simply don't accept the phrase. I think of the words, and I'm a writer, so words are important to me. Change management, like stress management, is utterly ridiculous.

Just like the classic "managing diversity." You don't want to manage diversity. So, the booklet I wrote is *Rejoicing in Diversity*. At given times, at given junctures, and at important points I'll bring people to a screeching halt by pointing out the very structure they're using—that is, their cognitive structure which of course informs their behavior—is shortchanging them. It's not giving them proper latitude, and that creates a tremendous awakening. That's probably among the most valuable things I do. Although I can't charge for that separately, it's intrinsic in the value I do provide, and I do charge for it.

Q: As change-management consultants, how do we help our clients think about creating a new future?

Alan: Let me give you some specific examples. Yesterday afternoon, I met with the artistic director of a Tony-award-winning theater in Providence, one of the four or five top regional theaters in the country. I used to be on their board, and he and I meet once a month in his office, and he asks me whatever is on his mind and I respond. Not only am I an excellent consultant, but I'm an avid theatergoer in New York, here, and elsewhere.

He said to me they're running three world-premier plays, and he wanted to create a magazine, a glossy brochure of the playwrights' inner thinking: three different playwrights, how they change the plays, how they improve them, and he wanted to sell this to people who attended the plays. He said, "What do you think of the idea?"

I said to him, "How many people are going to attend these three plays?" He said, "Probably around 6,000." I said, "How many of these people do you think would buy something like this?" He said, "About 10 percent." I said, "How much would you charge for these?" He said, "Uh, oh. I know where you're going. Maybe $5." I said, "You have 600 people paying $5, which is $3,000, which is not worth even discussing it further, except for this: What if you took this glossy magazine idea you had, and instead of printing it and spending that money, you put it online. You offered it to your entire constituency, not the people buying tickets or your subscribers."

Under his plan, only people walking in the theater would have access to this. I said, "Put it on your website in all its glory electronically, and encourage the greater Providence community—which is 400,000 people, never mind Boston and Hartford—to download this. Let them download it to see how playwrights think. If you have 400,000 people and 1 percent of them download it, that's still 4,000 people and probably 4,000 people who are above and beyond the 6,000 you're going to have coming into this theater. That might encourage still more ticket sales, and so forth and so on." That's the way I deal with clients.

Another thing I do with clients is to stop them from extrapolating from the present and saying, "If we're doing this today, what could we reasonably do next month, next quarter, next year?" Instead, I have them paint a picture of the future. "In a year, where would you like to be?" That's one of my first questions to anyone who enters my mentor program. "In a year or two, where would you like to be? Describe it." Then you work backwards from that. If your expectations are unreasonable, you can adjust them, but the question about thinking big is to paint the picture that makes sense to you. But if you extrapolate from the present, you wouldn't be talking to the guy who wrote *Million Dollar Consulting* right now, and you certainly wouldn't be interviewing for a book called *Alan Weiss on Consulting*.

Thinking big is a mental set, and it's a discipline, but there are some pragmatic skills you can use to help you get there.

Q: Look at the following words and give me the differences: Problem solving, decision making, and planning.

Alan: These are three interesting concepts. Problem solving refers to something that has happened in the past must be either corrected or ameliorated. In problem solving, something has occurred, and you either want to remove it or you want to ameliorate the effect of it. So, if you have a car that's leaking oil, you either want to fix the leak or put oil in it once a week if that's easier. Years ago we owned a Jaguar, and you simply put more oil in them than you did gas; that's how they ran.

Decision making is in the present. In decision making, you're choosing among options, and you're deciding what is the best course of action given the relative benefits and the relative risks. You might be deciding that in reaction to a problem, or you might be entering the picture there for the first time.

Planning is for the future. In planning, you want to implement something and protect it from going wrong. It's a protective activity.

The way I look at these three—problem solving, decision making, and planning—is past, present, and future. When you reach a client or when you're dealing with a personal issue for that matter, you need to ask yourself, "Am I responding to something that has happened in the past? Am I trying to make a decision in the present? Am I trying to protect something in the future?" The difficulty is that a lot of people, including consultants, tend to use these phrases interchangeably—like they'll use imply and infer—and they all have different starting points.

With a problem, you have to find the cause. With a decision, you have to create the objectives. With a plan, you have to understand what your preventive and contingent actions are. If you confuse them, you'll be at the wrong starting point, and you won't be successful.

Q: When we talk about planning, at times I've heard you talk about the fallacy of planning. What did you mean by that?

Alan: Planning should be an execution process when strategy is set. But when you talk about strategic planning, that becomes an oxymoron. The way most companies look at their plan is like this: They'll tell the sales force to come up with what their quota should be for next year. In other words, if you sold $500,000 this year, what should you have next year? They'll take a look at the territory. They'll take a look at new products. They'll take a look at the competition. But the fact is that the sales force is rewarded on overage from the prior year for their bonuses.

They're going to try to lowball that, so they'll say, "I did $500,000 last year. I should do $550,000 next year." That goes up to their management, and their management will say, "My bonus is based on this, so instead of $550,000 each, I think they should do $530,000 each." So, by the time it gets to senior management, it has gone from $500,000 to $510,000, which is just a few percentage points increase because the planning process puts handcuffs on you. It's a bottom-up process, full of conservatism.

The strategy process is a top-down process. When you look to the future, you should always be strategic, and once you agree on your strategic goals and their realism, then you create a plan to put them in place.

Q: I'm still unclear about how you feel about SWOT (strengths/weakness/opportunity/threat) analysis, but let me push back just a little bit. If someone has always done that, and you're saying that won't differentiate you, it's too simple....

Alan: No, no, no. What I'm saying is it's crap. Simplistic crap. Worthless.

Q: What would you encourage this consultant, who hasn't on his or her own come to that conclusion, to substitute to dig deeper, to get to the information that's really critical, instead of engaging in something like SWOT?

Alan: Get off your rear end, put the beer down, crawl over to the computer, Google "strategy," and read some books. Read Peter Drucker, Ben Tregoe, and John Zimmerman. Read some of my work. Not that I put myself in Drucker's category, but if you want to read something simpler than him, you can read me!

The fact is there are a lot of great approaches to strategy out there. If you ask seven experts—I mean true experts on strategy—about the discipline, they'll give you 12 different answers. So, if you want to be adept to strategy, then do a little homework and start reading on the subject. Apprentice yourself to someone who is doing it. Convince someone to take you on a project so you can learn, and you do the scut work. You do some of the collation work, you do some of the group facilitation work, but have someone show you what it's really like. Doing a SWOT analysis for strategy is like telling me that you would like to get involved with me in a highly conceptual game, and I bring out the chessboard, and you bring out tic-tac-toe. It's crap.

Q: Let's go back to looking at the strategy as we're helping our client look into the future with their strategy and what they want to do. How do we help them see the options and develop optional futures for themselves?

Alan: My chosen way, the way that I've always felt was best—and I got this from Ben Tregoe who writes about this in his book *Top Management Strategy*—is to help determine what their driving force should be. Most companies have nine, ten, or twelve strategic areas, it depends whom you read and listen to. Traditionally, I've looked at nine of them. For example, markets served, products and services offered, technology, method of sales, method of distribution, return, profit, and things like that.

Interestingly, most organizations and most people will have a default position that they're driven by profit, and they're not. A driving force means that strategic area dominates all others, and few organizations are dominated by profit. For example, General Electric, which is one of the last of the old-time conglomerates, right now has 11 or 12 startlingly different businesses. Light bulbs and railroad engines have nothing to do with each other, except trains might carry light bulbs. THEY may be driven by profit (number one or two in every market, forget about the NBC purchase!)

Profit is seldom the driving force. It's seldom the predominant strategic area. So, what you do is you say to a client, "Let's pick three or four strategic areas that could be your driving force and test them. Let's see which most fulfills the future that you want to paint for yourself." That becomes a very diverse, dynamic, and disciplined exercise.

Q: Once they've identified the driving force and everybody on the leadership team has agreed that that's what it is, then what?

Alan: Once you've identified what your driving force is, you start to assemble your strategy and your accountabilities, and you look at critical issues that need to be addressed to implement that driving force to make it a reality.

GE even under Jack Welch had an operating principal that said you have to meet your business goals, but you also have to do it consistent with the GE belief system. This was in reaction to some terrible scandals. There was a scandal with Israel's defense department. There was a scandal with the diamond industry. There was a scandal with the NBC unit, which was guilty of blowing up a Ford to try to prove it was vulnerable to gas tank explosions. Welch said, "Sorry, you have to achieve results within our value system."

Once that's in place, and you say your driving force is going to be products offered, markets served, or whatever it is, then you start to work your way down through the organization and say, "Who is going to be accountable for what?" So, if markets served is our driving force, who is accountable for getting the resources together to build our markets? Who is accountable for plugging more products into those markets? What are the critical issues we need to acknowledge and overcome in order to get that desired future?

That's the kind of conversation you have. Strategy should be organic. It should be a living document against which people judge their progress every day and not something in a three-ring binder gathering dust on everybody's bottom shelf.

Q: We've often heard that most companies fail at execution rather than at strategy. They have their two-day retreat, they establish the strategy, and then things fall apart after that….

Alan: They fail at strategy, but what they fail at is the implementation and not the formulation.

Formulation is always conceptual and looks beautiful, but when they go to implement it, which is the question you just asked me, the implementation of the strategy fails. That's quite right.

Q: How do we make ourselves valuable to our clients for the implementation stage?

Alan: You have to apprise your clients of what implementation requires. For example, in no special order, it requires key accountabilities right down to the front line. It requires that the evaluation system of the company be oriented around the tasks, deliverables, and input that will create the output leading to that strategy. It requires that compensation reward the right efforts to discourage the wrong ones. I just gave the example of GE where the values were as important as the performance.

It requires that the feedback system be monitored and altered so that the proper communication is going to the right people, at the right time, and the right place, consistent with strategy. And it requires monitoring so that you're sure that nobody has simply abandoned it and jumped ship because they can do something better for themselves independently, off the radar.

All of those things and more constitute key milestones that consultants can create so that management is a lot more confident. We not only have the route, we have the route lighted, and we have guideposts to tell us we're still on the route. You can look at implementation almost as a GPS system where you've created a navigation for the client.

Q: Then we can offer each of the things you just listed in our options for helping them in the implementation.

Alan: That's correct. The client might feel that they're already good at some of this but not others. You want to help them where they need the most help, but you also want to take a look at where they think they're good just to validate for them that it's true.

Q: You're engaged with a client to help the company develop strategy, and you just indicated the range of elements that are likely to be included. What are the signs of good outcome? What is the typical conclusion of an effort like this?

Alan: A typically successful strategy project will involve all the key stakeholders and get their commitment—not merely compliance—to the nature and direction of the business. Moreover, they'll commit to make decisions consistent with that nature and direction, and they'll be held accountable for their role in doing so. You'll achieve with them consensus—not unanimity, but consensus. *I define consensus as something you can live with, not something you would die for.*

You'll always have competing interests. You'll have the R&D experts who feel you're going too fast. You'll have the sales people who tell you that you're going too slow. Yadda yadda yadda. But they'll reach some agreements within which they can all operate successfully, and they'll realize who is accountable for what, and then they'll begin to communicate this downward. One of the signs of success is that as it's communicated downward, it's successfully translated into operating beliefs, into specific tasks, jobs, and accomplishments that people at lower levels have to do. If that happens, then the strategy is being successfully implemented.

Q: What would typically be the product of a strategy effort? Would it actually be a documented, agreed upon, or even signed action plan with accountabilities as you indicated?

Alan: It could be, but that isn't the outcome so much as the byproduct. The outcome is that all key people have their marching orders and accountabilities that they've committed to abide by, and they're now taking their own groups and organizing them at subordinate levels to reach that strategy. That's what you want to see happening. What is documented, what appears in writing is simply a byproduct of that kind of an action.

Q: Is there a direct connection between strategy and innovation?

Alan: I did my Ph.D. dissertation on innovation, and I nearly got bounced right out of the program because I used Hewlett Packard, Marine Midland Bank—which is now part of HSBC—and Merck for my research. This was a nontraditional Ph.D. I tried to prove that by testing behavioral predisposition—which I knew how to do because I was the president of a psychometric consulting firm at one point—I could prove that if you hired certain personality types, you could foster more innovation irrespective of your environment. What I proved in these three companies was exactly the opposite; that no matter what your behavioral predisposition, innovation was a function of environment and your management.

I remember my retired professor from Harvard saying to me, "Your science is good, but your reasoning is completely wrong. You better change this." I went home grumbling and said, "I'm done with this program," and my wife said, "Sit down and do the damn dissertation, or I'll throw you out." So I did.

Q: Are you saying that your initial theory of the case was proven differently through your dissertation effort?

Alan: Yes. This is a classic example of researcher bias. When I talked about companies being driven by what some other company is doing, because of my bias—my background was in behavioral testing—I felt it was all about personalities, and so I set out to prove that. But when I got these unpleasant things called facts, look where I was working. I had free access to Merck, Hewlett Packard, and Marine Midland Bank because I was working with top-level executives there. They gave me *carte blanche*, and I was doing questionnaires, interviews, we were measuring progress in the companies, and I was getting supervisory feedback about behavior change.

It was fascinating, but what I proved was that innovation is a factor of management and environment. It has nothing to do with personality. Consequently, getting back to your question, if you want to create a far more innovative culture, what you have to engineer, what you have to deal with is the environment and the management.

Q: Brilliant. In which of your commercially published books are the insights of this dissertation captured?

Alan: I have written so much I can't remember, but I probably talked about it in my book for internal practitioners, *Organizational Consulting*. I'm trying to think if I talked about it in *Good Enough Isn't Enough*. I can't remember, but I've certainly spoken about it widely. It was a great learning experience for me, and it was just an eye opener that you can take people who are assertive and aggressive, or you can take people who are much more reticent and amiable, and make them all more innovative. You can take people from vastly different backgrounds, and if the environment is right and the management is right, you can create or discourage innovation.

As an example of that, if you take a look at Yahoo! or Apple or Levi-Strauss—it doesn't have to be high tech—they've encouraged tremendous innovation. At the British Standards Institute where I was working on an innovation project years ago, senior management there did everything they could to discourage innovation, even though they didn't realize that's what they were doing. So, you had some very, very assertive and creative people there who just gave up. They couldn't get anything done because of the environment. It's an interesting phenomenon.

Q: At which stage in your career did you do this dissertation? What is fascinating about this is you acted in the field in your earlier stage from one paradigm, and then through this dissertation, you completely changed your paradigm about change, about suggesting change, about bringing change in an organization.

Alan: I change quite frequently. You've heard me say I'm constantly surprised at how stupid I was two weeks ago. When I was in my 40s, and this would have been in the '90s, I decided to pursue my Ph.D. because I was hearing from human resource types in organizations things like, "How does this compare to Mortzberg's 3D approach to modular introspective effectiveness?" and I just got so tired of it. I knew why things were working, but I needed some more grounding and underpinning.

I wasn't about to take two or more years off to get a Ph.D., so I found a nontraditional school with a very good course approach. It was two and one-half years to get my degree. I nearly got thrown out twice. I did my oral defense in front of professors from Harvard, Southern California University, and so forth. It was very rigorous and I enjoyed it, but I didn't have to show up except for my oral defense and one or two other times. I served 200 hours on a suicide hotline, I was on the board of a shelter for battered women, I did this dissertation using three clients, and I did some research at Brown University. I did a lot of work I'm very proud of, and I don't care—traditional or nontraditional—at this point.

What I learned in doing this is that there is a lot of misconception about what makes people change and what makes people tick at work. There is a lot of emphasis on the wrong things and not enough emphasis on the right things. Just to give you a simple example, too many managers feel that if you increase the pay, people will respond well; but in fact, if you pay an unhappy worker more money, what you have is a wealthier, unhappy worker.

If you take a look at the literature and at least in my experience, people perform best when they have gratification in the work they're doing. They perform best when they have a latitude of action. They perform best when the decisions they make influence the outcome of their work. So, I took that and used it as my definition of empowerment. When I started to talk to organizations thereafter about empowerment—which I was always talking about anyway—I started to use a new definition and said, "Empowered people can make decisions which influence the outcome of their work." Now management had a criterion, they had a metric—not just a feel good sense— to see if we were really empowering people, and they can even decide who can be empowered. They realized that letting people decide where the Coke machine should go isn't empowering people, and this held management's feet to the fire because empowerment was previously about making those kinds of decisions.

This was a tremendous benefit for me and constitutes, I don't know, five to eight percent of my effectiveness. People are always asking me, "Do I need a Ph.D. to be successful?" You don't. Nobody cares. I could legitimately today put 19 initials after my name. A woman just asked me this morning—I'm appearing at a conference—she wanted to get FIMC, CMC, CPA straight. It doesn't matter. This adds to my effectiveness of that degree, but I basically use Ph.D. to get reservations in restaurants.

Q: You were talking about your dissertation and your findings. What are some of the things that the best companies did in terms of environment and management to encourage innovation?

Alan: They did a few things that to me were really revelatory. One was they rewarded behavior, not victories. That was critical. I'm the one who coined that phrase, but that's what I learned they were doing because I really had to think about that a long time, and I finally realized what was going on.

As a result of that, post-Ph.D. I was working with Calgon in Pittsburgh, and they had an awards ceremony every year. We implemented an award the president and I talked about. The president handed out a trophy for "the best idea that didn't work." Everyone got up and applauded, and I said if the same person gets it eight years in a row, you have a problem, but that didn't happen! The president, the people, and management loved the idea. My insight was that you reward behavior and not only victories. Here is this big trophy for the best idea that didn't work, and that gave people permission to try things irrespective of whether they were successful.

A second key about these innovative environments is that there are avatars, and people can look to see successful examples. There is the freedom to fail. Innovation is rewarded, and people aren't always trying to cover their rear ends. You see a lot of organizations where people are trying to stay off the radar screen entirely; they take their name off the door, they unplug the computer, they leave the phone off the hook, and they sit under their desk on the premise if you can't find me, you can't hurt me.

I'm talking about organizations, the *Hartford Current* for example, where the editor would take the previous day's newspaper and chop it up.

He would put things up on the board that every reporter had to walk by to get to a cubicle or keyboard, and it would say, "Great Headline," "Fabulous Lead," "Wonderful Recitation of Fact," "Nice Reporting Without Opinion." This was the positive board, and this board showed people what the editor was prizing and how people who took certain risks and innovated in the newspaper business were appreciated. That provided a constant uplifting spirit to that newsroom about the risks they could take in reporting stories and investigating stories.

Q: When we're looking at consultants who focus on strategy-type work, what is the key distinguishing factor or factors between a great strategy consultant, to a mediocre, to a terrible one?

Alan: I think great strategy consultants have to have a discernible and communicable methodology. They have to inform the client as to how they're going to operate and why, and they just can't play it by ear. That's what I don't like about life coaches. They sort of listen, and then suggest things, but there is no real methodology. There is no discipline. I think there are a lot of bad approaches, like SWOT, but there are also a lot of good approaches.

I would recommend that the outstanding consultants would be ones who A) have a discipline, and B) have done it before. If you say to me, "Well, everybody has to start some time," yes, but they can start as an apprentice. This shouldn't be the first time you're doing it. No client should be a strategic guinea pig so to speak.

You deteriorate from there, but consultants who use simplistic devices—simplistic personality assessments, simplistic problem solving devices, simplistic tools—and who try to pass these off as a strategic approach, they're just trying to get money. They're just trying to demonstrate they can try to do something, but it's the old Maslow example. They have a hammer, so they're looking for nails.

Q: For those who want to dramatically improve their ability to become a strategic consultant, short of reading the books that you mentioned earlier, what should they consider doing?

Alan: I would recommend three things. The first is, I would read those books. I would read Peter Drucker's *The Effective Executive*. I would read Drucker's *Managing in Turbulent Times*. He has written a lot of books, but there are two, and they're ageless. I would read Ben Tregoe's *Top Management*

Strategy: What It Is and How It Works. You might want to take a look at my book *Best Laid Plans*.

The second thing I would do is participate in strategy, and find someone who would take you under their wing. Establish a *quid pro quo* and have them help you understand the process and how they go through it.

The third thing is I would try to practice this in a low-threat environment. You might offer a *pro bono* strategy approach to a nonprofit, a charity, or an arts group. Get some experience under your belt, and get some testimonials from people. Only the gifted few can wing it, and there are precious few people who can walk into the top tier of a billion dollar Fortune 1000 firm and start to help them with strategy. Those are some very smart people sitting there, and they're going to need intellectual capital that represents additional value to what they would otherwise be doing.

The Consulting Engagement

Q: A key message you shared with us was how you continue to learn, continue to change, continue to evolve, and that this means never being dogmatic about anything, being prepared to embrace new ideas and new ways of seeing the world. In the context of consulting engagements, is this one of the coaching and re-educations we need to offer the buyer; namely, to let go of dogmatic views and beliefs, and embrace fresh ideas?

Alan: I think for anyone—a buyer, colleague, friend, family—the fact is that we don't grow and we don't change unless we're willing to let go. You can't reach out unless you let go, whether it's a new type of food, a new vacation experience, a new market place, or a new relationship. That would be my advice to anyone, under any circumstances.

Q: Focusing on this, when you coach and work with your mentorees and you run into dogmatic beliefs and behaviors, how do you coach? How do you help them let go and gain the confidence to see things in a new way and take a pragmatic approach to life?

Alan: I try to find out what is the basis for them holding that dogmatic view and why they're being so doctrinaire. Usually, not all the time, it's because they're seeking safety or they're lazy. They're just falling back on the tried or true. They're following the course of least resistance, and what happens is that what is otherwise a pleasant, effective, or reliable stretch of ground becomes the sole highway they'll travel. So, you have to explore and prod and find out how they got there to begin with. Most of us, in actuality, change every day. We encounter traffic tie-ups, and we take an alternate route. We encounter an undue, unexpected piece of resistance, and we try to overcome it. Change is the norm, not the exception, and we have to embrace the fact that the more resilient and more flexible we are, the easier it is for us to improve.

Q: Let me explore a few specific elements in the consulting engagement. In this situation, the buyer himself is in a new role, and just a few weeks into the project the parameters are still very ambiguous because you're helping the buyer build his team, design his work, and there are many moving parts. What are some ways to accelerate a project filled with ambiguity and unknown dependencies?

Alan: The best way to do that is to agree on what the end result or even interim results are, and throw yourself in the direction of those results. In other words, you might not know what lies in store for you on the path, but you do know the results and the end destination. It's important to know your port of call. You might decide we're going to Dublin. You can go to Dublin a lot of different ways, and you might encounter some storms and some rough weather, but you know where Dublin is, and you're going to get there.

You lead the way, you light the way, and you say, "Follow me." The combination of you and the buyer both saying to people "follow me" is pretty powerful. The buyer knows the content and culture of the organization, and you know the process of change. You're going to find some hiccups, some obstacles, and some disruptions, just as a plane encounters sudden air turbulence, but that happens.

If you're not going to something pre-established like Dublin, but you're creating Dublin from scratch, creating a Shangri-La, then you identify it. You say, "That's where we're going, that's the picture we've created, follow me." So, the question really isn't the fact that things will be ambiguous; you know that. The question is, do you have the confidence and the wherewithal to light a beacon and have people follow you?

Q: That's beautiful imagery, and I suppose part of whether you're going to Dublin or building and creating Dublin is to always know that there isn't just one right way. There are many ways to get to Dublin or to build Dublin.

Alan: That's true, and let me say two things here. The first is that if you know your destination, if you know your objective, there are many alternatives that will get you there. The problem is that people, instead of looking at objectives, look at alternatives, which goes back to that doctrinaire aspect you started with, and so they're stuck on this arbitrary alternative. People are doctrinaire about procedure. They're not doctrinaire about results. It's the input side that tends to be doctrinaire.

The second thing is that there is a country song by Donna Fargo that says, "You can't be a beacon if your light don't shine." Your own beacon has to shine. You have to shine the light out there, and then people will follow you. If you extinguish your own beacon, nobody is coming. They don't know where you are.

Q: You're engaged with a buyer, and it's midway through the project. What are some practices you use to reduce labor intensity?

Alan: The most obvious one for me is to transfer what I'm doing to the client. The reason I believe that consultants shouldn't only help clients with the content of their issues but transfer process skills to the client is that not only are you providing more value to the client and making them self-sufficient, but you're also reducing your own labor intensity dramatically. The duality of being able to reduce your labor intensity while also providing value is highly attractive.

Some consultants will tell you—the poorer ones—that by transferring your abilities, expertise, and processes, you're giving away your intellectual property, and you'll be less valuable in the future. *Au contraire*. I believe that the more you give to the client and make the client self-sufficient, the more the client will be prone not only to call on you in the future but also to call on you under your own conditions. That's the most elemental way to reduce labor.

I'll say one more thing in light of what we spoke about a few minutes ago. This doctrinaire aspect of focusing on alternatives: Another excellent, but harder way to reduce your labor intensity is to streamline your own process. So, stop falling in love with your methodology. Stop pouring cement on it like it ought to be made into concrete, locked in stone. Use the bromide you like and disassemble, deconstruct your methodology so you can make it simpler and less burdensome.

Q: So many powerful distinctions in what you said there. Specifically, this idea that we need to empower the client rather than to preserve or maintain dependency upon us, and that actually is likely to generate more business rather than the other way around.

Alan: It's counterintuitive, but it works. That's why I write so many books. The more people read my books, the more they want me. Nobody says, "Oh, I've read his book. I don't need him." People say, "I've read his book. I would love to meet this guy." And the same thing when you do things for the client, the client says, "Look at what this person has given us. Let's see what else we can do with them."

Q: In your OD years, did you have a rule of thumb for what would merit you traveling to the west coast from your home on the east coast, to the client's location?

Alan: It depended how hungry I was. When I first started out, I would go anywhere for anything. I needed to put bread on the table, and it was before I had the brand, the expertise, and the confidence to really start to push back at clients as to how some of this should work. But once I learned the ways of the wise, I started to realize that being on site wasn't a testimony to my expertise or my effectiveness. So, I would try to make intelligent decisions—politically and pragmatically—about what to do. It's important to be seen at a client, especially a new one to a certain extent. But it's also important to educate the client that your presence isn't commensurate with your value.

With a mature client—this is just three or four years ago—Hewlett-Packard came to me for their 20th project with me. We hadn't done anything for about a year. They came back to me, and they needed something done in the short-term, very quickly, which they knew I could do, and so they came to me. There was no question that I was the one for them, and I figured I could do this in about 30 days, and it would be around $50,000 the way things worked out.

I remember it was the end of November, and my buyer at Hewlett-Packard said, "We're in agreement. Just send me the proposal. I'll sign off. Can you start immediately?" I said, "Absolutely." She said, "So, we can count on the first or second week in January we'll have what we need?" I said, "Absolutely." She said, "When will we see you?" I said, "You won't." She said, "What do you mean, you won't? What does that mean?" I said, "I'm not coming." They're in Mountain View, CA. It's their headquarters, and I'm in Rhode Island, so you can't get farther away in the United States. I said, "I'm not going to be there, Marilyn. You don't need me there. Here is what we're going to do. You don't need me present. You know how to reach me if you need me." She said, "Well, yes, but shouldn't you put in an appearance? We have some line executives concerned…." I said, "Who do you report to?" She said, "You know who I report to. I report to Hugo in Brussels." I said, "Who does he report to?" She said, "He reports to Chuck in Hong Kong." I said, "How many times do you see each other?" She said, "Never." I said, "I'm just trying to fit in."

I never did go out there, they paid me $50,000, and they were ecstatic.

With a mature client, you can get to that point of reasoning where they understand the value is the output, and if you're convinced that the output won't be deleteriously affected by your not being there, fine. If you have to interview people and you know you have some senior people and some client customers, you make a judgment and say I have to be there in front of them. It won't be as effective over the phone. That's fair enough. On the other hand, if somebody is in Melbourne and is the only person in Australia to be interviewed, you do that by Skype or something, and that's the way it goes.

Q: Let's focus for a moment on the times you do go to the client's location, headquarters, another plant, or wherever. What practices do you use to maximize your time when you're at the client's location? For example, how do you use the lunch at the company's cafeteria and other tips for that?

Alan: I used to go to Chicago to see a client. They were in Mundelein, IL, which is about an hour north of Chicago. I used to catch about a 6:30 or 7:00 a.m. flight out of Providence. This is the days when airlines had a lot of flights, and it was a 90-minute flight, plus you picked up an hour. I would get in there about 7:00 in the morning, and I would drive up and be there at 8:00 or 8:30 by the time I picked up my Hertz car. Hertz delivered their car to me, which made it easier, and then I would catch a flight home around 4:00, which means I would leave the client around 2:30 and get here at 6:30 p.m. So, it was a 6:30 a.m. to 6:30 p.m. day, without an overnight, and I would be home to have dinner with my wife.

The way I did this was I would have two or three appointments set up ahead of time. My appointments were always brief; in other words, they would be about 30 or 45 minutes. I would never let somebody put aside an hour or 90 minutes because I was busy implementing. These weren't market-ing meetings. I wouldn't allow meetings back-to-back because you could never tell when one might run over, but they were pretty close together. If I were running focus groups, I would include a focus group or two while I was there, and it would be adjacent somehow to the other ones. I would use the interim time to wander around and look at things. In other words, I would pay my respects to people who should know I'm around. I would watch things happening.

I've always been ambivalent about lunch, and I try not to involve my lunches with clients if I can help it. I would either pick up a burger, a hot dog, or a salad in the cafeteria, or I wouldn't eat at all. That really didn't matter to me.

That's how I would use my day, and I would make sure I left in time. I would never schedule anything close to my departure time so that nobody could delay things, and I didn't want to miss my flight. People got in the groove of doing that.

I worked for Calgon in Pittsburgh where the flight was only about an hour. I used to regularly travel as a daily commuter there and beat people who were commuting from where I live here in Rhode Island into Provi-dence, and I certainly beat the people who were commuting back and forth to Boston and have a whole lot less stress. I got clients in that groove, and the way I scheduled my time was such that most of them were highly flexible and willing to do this. If I found that somebody was going to be out of town or somebody was going to be wrapped up in some other meeting, I would change my meeting date until they were free along with the other people I needed to see. I was very productive that way.

Q: What is and isn't appropriate in terms of exploring new opportunities inside the buyer's organization and also with peers while you're working on a specific project?

Alan: If your mindset is truly that you provide tremendous value that you would be remiss in not expressing and providing for people, then you should be doing that on a regular basis. It's nothing but a myth—a stupid, dysfunc-tional myth—that you can't market while you're delivering. In fact, I would submit to you that the ideal time to market is while you're delivering because people see your quality. You're often on site. You're usually in touch with key people, and it's an ideal time to market.

There is nothing unethical, illegal, or immoral about marketing while you're delivering. Consequently, while you're wandering around, make friends, make acquaintances, suggest things to people, provide people with free value, and let them say, "Who was that masked man, and how do we get him back in here? He just saved the bank from being robbed." That's the kind of dynamic you want to create among clients and other interested parties within the client.

Q: Has there ever been, or can you see a situation where engaging with two peers on two separate projects would create a conflict of interest in the way you need to coach and consult each one of them?

Alan: I've never found that, but what I have found is that there is often a political context that you have to keep in mind. I was consulting with the Federal Reserve in New York, and the executive vice president had hired me, and two senior vice presidents were very key in this project. They headed separate entities, and they were warring entities because the two senior vice presidents were at war. He said to me, "They don't get along, but they can. See if you can work with them."

I soon found out that the enmity between the two couldn't be reconciled by me on the outside who had no control over their income, their bonus, or how they acted. I finally had to tell my buyer, "Here is the situation, and here is how we have to resolve this. The four of us have to sit down together, and if they agree—even if they agree not to love each other—to perform in certain ways, we can get this done."

He said, "What would be an example of that?" I said, "We have to have a presentation to your staff about these new changes, instead of her presenting to her people and him presenting to his people. Why don't we get all their people in one room, intermingle them, and have them both present together?" He said, "That's brilliant." He told them that's what we're going to do, and I helped to script it.

Q: What are typical things that can derail a project midway?

Alan: There are a lot of things that can derail a project midway, from the ridiculous to the sublime. The buyer leaves. The buyer gets fired. The buyer gets promoted. The buyer gets transferred. The buyer retires. The buyer gets sick. The buyer dies. That has happened. If your key sponsor—your key source—is no longer there, that's going to be a big problem.

A second is that you've worked on the incorrect assumptions. Either you've accepted assumptions from a client organization that you shouldn't have, or when you attempted to honestly verify them, you didn't verify them accurately, correctly, or sufficiently: What the competition is doing, what the customers are expecting, or what the technology is capable of is simply insufficient.

Thirdly, a major derailing factor is that people's self-interests get all balled up, and that could be real or perceptual. So, if you perceive that something happening—and unions are famous for this—is going to adversely affect people's incomes, their job security, or their status, people start to resist things with no further information, with no further facts. You have to carefully manage perception, and that's especially important in change management initiatives and in strategic change. It's important with merger, divestiture, or acquisition. I could name another 40 things that will derail a project, but those are the three that come to mind, so let's stay with that.

Q: Can you give as a concrete example, a story, a case-in-point of a project that nearly got derailed, and you intervened successfully to complete the project?

Alan: I was working for a very large bank—at the time one of the top dozen in the country—and it was siloed. There were four or five key silos in the bank, each headed by an executive vice president who reported to the CEO. Four of the five were collegial and got along. The fifth executive, who headed an investment area which was at the time the most profitable part of the bank, just sailed along to his own tune, and he would give lip service to priorities but then not do them. So, rather than fight at the meetings and be seen as the outcast, he would always agree and then he wouldn't do it. His operation would be odd man out, and without that key part of the operation, the projects wouldn't be successful.

I recognized the fact that it was a question of trying to change his behavior. When I met with him, he was really surly. He had this beautiful office overlooking this gorgeous view of the water, and he had seats in his office taken out of a ballpark that was torn down that he had purchased at auction. He was a real character. I tried to stress to him the importance of his coming along, and he didn't want to hear that.

I finally said to him, "It seems to me that the CEO has five direct reports." He said, "Yea, that's obvious." I said, "It seems to me that he is going to leave here, retire before the five of you leave." He said, "Well, that's true." I said, "And it seems to me that two of those direct reports, given who they are and their backgrounds, are in no way going to be considered by the board for his spot." He said, "That's true."

I said, "That leaves three of you. I don't think that you would be among the leader of the three, despite the size of the operation you're leading, if it also turns out that you were resistant to every initiative he tried to create, some of which have the board's blessing." He finally came around on that basis because it was about a 48-month period at most before the CEO retired. As a postscript, ironically, before the CEO retired, the problem executive was actually dismissed from the bank for some unethical practices.

These are the kinds of things that happen at the very highest levels that you have to take issue with, and you have to deal with them, and not always successfully. As I said in the example before, sometimes you have used the CEO's clout to get things done because you simply don't have the authority to get it done.

Q: What are some practical ideas that we can bring to our own practice in order to create breakthrough, innovative ideas, visionary thinking that we can implement in our own business?

Alan: If you want to be more innovative as an individual, you have to have triggers that will help you do that. In other words, you have to ask yourself where does innovation originate? If you read some of my books, innovation originates in a relatively few areas. Drucker would agree with this if you read his material as well.

I would advise the following: Where have you had the most success? What has been successful beyond your wildest dreams—unexpected success or dramatically high growth—and how do you build on that? As you know, I believe that you build on strength. You don't build by correcting weakness. So, if you want to be innovative, you have to look for things that are already going well, and then exploit the hell out of them.

I think a second thing you look at is unexpected events. Those events could be political, regulatory, competitive, or technological, but you ask yourself what is going on here that I can capitalize on? As an example, if you take a look at airports today, you'll find that with the new security issues and hang-ups, people bemoaning the fact they're being patted down and the lines at security. On the other hand, you have very upscale restaurants, excellent shops, and boutiques because they built them since they know people are spending a lot more time in airports and will shop there. That's very innovative given a problem in society, an unexpected event, but nonetheless, they can capitalize on it.

Another area is to look at combining technologies. The iPhone is one of the greatest examples of combined technology you can possibly think of. You have a communication device by phone and email, you have a place to take notes, record, check your stocks, play games, text message, track your expenses, and I can go on and on. So, you have 45 or 50 things you can do with this depending upon your own proclivities. That's an example of combined technologies in a single platform. It's dramatic. You can combine technologies through your own company and be dramatic.

Another thing to look at, in terms of your own practice, is demographic change. How do you perceive your value—and the buyers who partake of that value—changing in terms of distribution, their income, and their education so that you can capitalize on that? Does it send you overseas, does it send you to retail rather than wholesale, or wholesale rather than retail? Does it send you up or down the hierarchy? What does that mean in terms of your market? The final thing is perception, and perception is controllable. You manage perception, so do I really need $120 racquetball shoes to play racquetball when I can play in my sneakers? I don't; however, they claim you're a better racquetball player with them, and the court won't let me on unless I have racquetball shoes, not sneakers.

People stopped smoking over the past several decades because of the clear perception and education that their health will suffer, the health of their loved ones will suffer, they won't get to see their grandchildren, and so forth. On the other hand, people haven't stopped drinking because that case has never been really made. Drinking is seen as a social nicety and as a relaxant. True or false, that's the perception. So, the way you manage your customer's perceptions will have a great deal to do with your ability to innovate with customers as well.

Challenges

Q: You have a great relationship with the economic buyer, the trust has been built, and we have a proposal with some clear outcomes. Then we run into somebody on the senior person's team who isn't happy that we're there. How do we handle that?

Alan: I would go through a brief series of escalated encounters. My first encounter would be to try to convince them what is in their own self-interest. In other words, "The buyer's team is for this, you're the only holdout. You might think you're giving us 'lip service,' but you and I both know you're not supporting the project, and I'm going to report that factually back to the buyer. It's really in your best interest to do this, you'll be a member of the team, and you'll gain the credit that accrues when we achieve this." I'll try for self-interest.

The second thing I'll try to do is to create a direct connection with the buyer. I'll say to the buyer, "Paul here is holding out. He isn't being effective. The three of us need to talk this through, and you need to specify to him what his behaviors need to be to make this effective."

Number three is, try to isolate and flow around the resistor. I'm not a zealot, I'm a persuader; so, if I can flow around these pockets of resistance, I know they'll eventually fall. But if this is a resistance so important that the project can't succeed, then you have to threaten, and you simply say to the buyer, "It's him or the project. *Not him or me.* It's him or the project. You make the choice. But we can't flow around him. He is holding up the entire game. He has the key resources, and he has the key clients, and clearly he doesn't feel the need to comply or even especially commit to what you want to accomplish."

I have that escalating approach. I have to tell you, it has very seldom been necessary, but occasionally it has been.

Q: In other words, you start by addressing the behavior with the individual, but then you don't waste much time before you get your buyer involved?

Alan: No, because I don't know about you, but I can tell after one meeting whether I'm going to be successful. I can tell by listening to what the nature of the objection is, what the tone is, and I can certainly tell in the next two days whether any actions that were promised were taken or not.

I know when I'm being told the truth, and I know when I'm being lied to. I just did a Friday Wrap session about how to tell whether someone is disingenuous with you or not. Whether it's hype or whether it's real. So,

I can tell that fairly quickly, and once I know, I'm not going to let that rest. I'm not going to be afraid.

Q: Another challenge that we often face is "scope creep." Would you explain what this is, why it's risky, and what we can do to avoid it?

Alan: Scope creep occurs when the scope of the project is subtly and nonetheless deliberately increased because the client asked you to do things that weren't in the original agreement. Hewlett-Packard used to call this "undocumented promises." There would be a $2.5 million project with Citibank, for example, and the people who were low level in the project would be approached by other low-level people from the client. They would be asked to do favors, and rather than—in their perception—jeopardize the project, they would do these favors. At the end of the day, the project took twice as long because of all of these undocumented promises, and the profit margin was shot to hell. So, Hewlett-Packard needed to end that. We needed to create a system to end that.

With an individual practitioner, the solo consultant, or professional services provider, you don't have the complexity of other people making promises, but you do have a problem of you making promises or being afraid to reject a request by a client. My response to a client is, "I can do that for you. I would be happy to do that for you, but it's not within the parameters of the current project. I'll write you an addendum so that we can do this in a way and in a manner that's fair to both of us. Is that okay?"

Q: Who usually introduces the scope creep? Do consultants who are worried about losing favor do this, or does the client usually try to introduce this?

Alan: When the consultant initiates it, I call it "scope *seep*," which is a coinage that I originated. That occurs when the consultant is feeling low self-esteem, not worthy, and insists on doing more and more to justify his or her presence and fee. It can come from either direct scope creep or scope seep, different sides of the same coin.

Many times, when it comes from the client's side, it's not malicious. It's just the client asking for a favor or an additional service that the client thinks is a small request but turns out from the consultant's point of view to be a serious drain on time and energy, and something for which the consultant isn't being compensated.

Q: In your work with large companies, did you ever make an exception to these rules?

Alan: Sure. Take a company like Merck where I worked for 12 years, several million dollars, and several million more in referral business. If Merck needed a favor done, I would do it. They didn't need to ask twice. I was on a retainer for five years for Calgon, and I was asked at one point if I would come out on a weekend to help with an emergency session. I never talked about a proposal, a fee, or anything. I just boarded the airplane. So, for good clients, all of us have to use our judgment.

I've always told people that you should use positive, productive, and validated practices whenever you can, but you should have the good judgment to know when you have to make an exception. If the exceptions happen with regularity, they're no longer exceptions, and you're caving.

Q: You aren't anticipating enough in your proposal if this happens very often?

Alan: That could be or it could just be that because you're good, you're asked to do more and more because the client wants to get what the client perceives to be more money's worth. Instead of educating the client correctly, you don't like the confrontation and you give in. That's just dumb.

Q: Aside from the obvious that we're not getting paid for what we do, are there any other risks or problems for the client if we allow scope creep and seep?

Alan: The problems for the client are that the client becomes defocused from what the real goals are, so the point of the arrow gets blunted because all these other things are underway. The second thing is that the client's own resources become scattered, so instead of all of the energy, attention, and monitoring going into the basic project, its objectives, and the value those objectives provide now, it's being frittered away and scattered about all these other things that are happening, and you have all these other interest groups involved.

Picture a fast car that's about to go down a straightaway, and just before the driver hits the gas, 15 different people with different interests say, "Let me on too, let me on too. I need to get on." Suddenly, the car is overloaded, and somebody wants to stop in 100 yards, another wants to take a left turn, still another wants to do something else, so the car is neither traveling on the fast track nor to a common destination. That's what ruins the journey here.

Q: It sounds as though one of the other risks to the consultant is if you allow the client's focus to get scattered or resources to dissipate, you jeopardize the success of what you started to do in the first place.

Alan: That's true. Whenever you defocus, you jeopardize the project. That's why I say when you're marketing—while you're there—if you find something else that you can help with and the client agrees, you create a separate proposal. It has a separate focus. It has different accountabilities. There is nothing wrong with two or three concurrent proposals. As long as each one has a sharp point, is focused, and the client is supporting each one appropriately, that will work.

Q: Regarding scope seep, let me just go back to this. In a conversation I had in the past with one of your more successful people in your mentor program, he said to me, "I always deliver more than I promise. I like that style, and it creates great successes for me." Bad decision? Good decision? Or is it just a matter of personality here?

Alan: I think it's a bad decision. He and I have talked about things like this, and I don't think he does that as much any more, believe me. I think when you over-deliver and under-promise—which is the bromide—it basically is a position of insecurity. So, you figure I had better not promise too much, and I had better deliver even more so the client likes me, respects me, and will have me back again.

If you do an accurate job of gauging the client's objectives and of stipulating what the value of meeting those objectives is, and you meet them, the client should be delighted. You might exceed them, but I don't like this whole over-delivery philosophy because it's terribly labor intense, and it creates the wrong precedent. If you think of the fourth sale first, the second sale, the third sale, the fourth project, the fifth engagement, the client is going to have unduly high expectations. So, I think you have an honest-to-God transaction with your buyer as a peer.

When I go to buy a new car, the Bentley dealer doesn't throw in a Porsche. "Thanks for spending $300,000. We're going to throw in a $100,000 car as well because you're such a good customer." If I take the car in because I need the brakes adjusted, they don't repaint it. They might wash it, but that's hardly over-delivering. When I go to get coffee in the morning, as I did this morning, the guy who runs the coffee shop doesn't say, "Take a free donut," nor do I expect one. The transactions have to be appropriate.

Q: Isn't there some light or slightly gray line where you possibly do over-deliver? I'm not talking about the big things but the small things.

Alan: Sure. Like I said, you use your judgment, but you can't let it become a way of life. You have to be judicious about it.

Q: I realize that every client's situation is uniquely different, but if my goal is to absolutely delight the client, what can I do in the engagement in order to make sure that I stand out from my competitors?

Alan: Put yourself in the client's shoes and ask, "What would really knock the socks off this client?" Too many times we're asking about what would knock our own socks off, so we create a recourse, we do something ridiculous. Ask yourself what would really knock the socks off the *client.* A lot of times it's the client being able to be less involved and get the same results. It's being able to do something faster than anticipated, or the client being able to brag to the board or to his or her superior, or just spending less labor on whatever is going on. You have to look at each client somewhat differently to see what will delight them, make a reasonable judgment, and then see if it's possible.

Q: In large organizations, let's say that your point of contact is actually one or two steps away from the buyer. What is the advice that you would give others in order to constantly stay in touch with the key buyer, and how often should we do that?

Alan: In any project, you should have debriefing points with your buyer. We talked before about the fact that the earlier in the project, the more frequent these are. They should involve good news as well as bad news to keep the bad news in perspective when it occurs. They should be irrespective of whom else you are dealing with. So, even though the CFO might be your key contact, the key implementer—nonetheless, you're meeting with the buyer once every other week, you're talking by phone twice a month, or whatever it happens to be to keep the buyer apprised. You never give up that relationship, no matter what.

Q: When you facilitate a strategy effort, and one person on the team sees his role as the one responsible to explain to you why every idea you propose can't work, how do you respond? How do you manage this situation?

Alan: I've encountered those. Along about the third or fourth demurral, I'll say, "Oh, wait a minute. Lou wants to say something. Lou, what don't you agree with now?" I'll say, "Okay, Lou, you've said three negative things. Is there anything at all positive going on here?" Lou will say, "No, I think these three things are awful."

I'll say, "Fine. Let's test that with the rest of the group. Does the rest of the group think these three things are awful, and can the rest of the group not find anything positive at all as well?" I'll use group norms to sanction him. I won't allow that to go on, and the longer you enable that—the longer you allow it through passivity—the more you enable it. So, you have to strike back, and you can usually identify those people fairly quickly.

Q: So, you never allow it to become a conflict between you and the person, you shift it to a group to the person dynamic?

Alan: Yes. The example you gave me was in a group, and so you want to use the group norms, the normative behavior of the group to sanction this guy. Now, if everybody in the group says he is right about that, then I'll accept that. I'm not going to let personality overwhelm fact. On the other hand, if people say, "That's not right what he is saying; he just feels that because of this," then we're going to have to deal with that.

If it's a one-on-one situation where I find somebody that negative, I'm going to be direct and say, "Lou, I must tell you something. You're the fifth person I interviewed, and you're the only one who has been consistently negative about this. So, that leads me to believe it's not me, and it's not the project, but there is something about you. So, how about explaining to me why you're so negative about this?" I'll put it right out there, and we'll see what happens.

Q: What are some of the best ways to develop alliances with key influencers that can accelerate or have the power to sabotage the project? Can you give a concrete example?

Alan: You have to make sure that you're really dealing with a key influencer. For example, I never care what the human resources people think. They'll claim that they're the implementers. I don't care what they think because once something is decided by senior management, they're going to go along with it. They're never going to undermine it. Once they know I have the ear of the buyer and will say, "These people are undermining it," they're cooked. So, I'm not concerned about that.

However, if you think about our earlier examples in terms of concrete examples, when you do have these people who lead significant areas, once again, I would look at their individual, rational self-interest and see how to bring them around.

I like to deal with people as peers, I like to deal with people professionally, and then I like to adjust to their styles. If somebody is all-business, no-nonsense, task-oriented, let's get this done, I'll adjust to that same style. I'll make the best use of time. I'll make the best use of their energy. If somebody else, though, is highly interactive—wants to have lunch, get to know me, and do things like that—I'll do that if it means I can foster a better relationship and get them to do what they need to do to make this project successful.

You have to adapt to people. You have to give people the benefit of the doubt. You can't assume that they're damaged, and you need to work on observed behavior to correctly evaluate what your next course of action should be.

Q: We've spoken at length about the project, the midway of the project, and we're now coming to the completion of the project. Take us again through the key elements of the closing conversation and how to best conduct the discussion that will also possibly lead to next opportunities, and at the same time clearly bring that point of disengagement and completion of the project.

Alan: If you're talking to the buyer near the completion of the project, you should have already done several things. You should have sought out references, referrals, and testimonials. You should have discussed additional business, repeat business, expanded business, and lateral business.

As this project concludes, separate out the project concluding from the relationship concluding. Ideally, in decent-sized companies, a project concludes and a relationship continues, hopefully augmented and improved by the success of that project.

You would debrief with the buyer on the results of this particular project. You would revisit the objectives, which you've done many times to this point. You would revisit the metrics of success and show that the objectives have been met or are in stages of being met. You would talk about the value that the company is benefiting from as the result of meeting those objectives. Then you talk about any follow-up work that the client should be doing to reinforce and to ensure that the project has traction, takes hold, and so forth.

In addition to that, I would talk about things that perpetuate the relationship, if that's at all possible, and where you go from here. I tend to shy away from some kind of final report in a three-ring binder or a PowerPoint presentation to the top team, which to me is too much of an ending rather than a continuance of the relationship.

Q: We've tried to highlight some of the universal challenges that consultants face when they go into projects. What do the people in your mentor program tell you are other kinds of challenges they're facing?

Alan: I think the biggest challenge that I hear from the people in my mentor program while they're consulting is covered by a lot of the questions you three raised. In other words, I often hear something has changed. How do I deal with this? The buyer wants to do something different. The company has had a change of course. There has been a development that was unexpected. I have an area of resistance I didn't expect. The kinds of questions you've been asking have been very, very accurate in terms of what people encounter.

What I don't hear as often, but I wish I heard more of are: I found these opportunities—how do I exploit them? I have ideas for this client that can significantly go beyond what we're doing—how do I create a new proposal in a politically and pragmatically correct sense?

Q: One of the things you're seeing is that we're overlooking too many opportunities?

Alan: There are these blinders that are put on, just like a horse's blinders. Horses wear blinders because, unlike a human or a dog, they don't see forward together, which is called stereoscopic sight. They see to the side, as many animals do that are configured like that. So, horses see right and left, not directly ahead stereoscopically. You put blinders on a racehorse—so they can't look right and left simultaneously, get distracted—and force them to focus on the track ahead.

A lot of consultants are wearing these blinders, and they're not looking around at opportunities. They're just looking at the objectives that are there at the moment and don't even look for anticipated problems. If a problem comes up, they'll deal with it

Opportunities seldom slam you in the face and say, "Here I am, stop, pay attention." You have to be more nuanced and subtle than that. The difficulty is they're racing down the track with the blinders on. You have to look around and understand that if you truly believe in your mindset that you provide unremitting value for a client, *then it's incumbent upon you to look for ways to provide that value and bring the client in on it.*

Q: Finally, as we conclude this chapter on the "Consulting Engagement," talk about the client engagement in terms of the chess game. In chess you have the opening, the middle game, and the end game. Give us some final overview tips for the opening, the middle game, and the end game of a successful consulting engagement.

Alan: A lot of people are lousy at the end game of chess because they never get there. That's a rather important consideration. I remember playing with a guy once, and we got to the end game and he said, "Now I'm in trouble." I said, "Well, you've never gotten this far before."

He said, "That's my problem. I don't know what to do now." I think in chess you know there are several things that are important. One is, you have to think three or four moves ahead. The grand masters think 25 moves ahead, but I'm not that smart, and I'm not that interested really, but I like chess as a pleasant diversion. If you think three, four, or five moves ahead, you'll win most games.

The second thing is each piece does different things. You have to understand a knight has a peculiar kind of movement pattern that's different from a bishop which can cut diagonally across the board. So, which tool are you going to use? Which approach are you going to use? Which piece are you going to advance that has the most import at the moment? And I would remind you that even a lowly pawn can become a queen. So, the most insignificant pieces on the board can become the most powerful *if you play your game right.*

The third thing about chess that's important isn't unlike racquetball, and that is you have to control the middle of the board. It's very difficult to be successful if you don't control the middle of the board. When you're playing racquetball, it's almost impossible to win if you aren't controlling what they call the "T"—the middle of the court—so you can move with a minimum of exertion and motion, still reach the ball, and cause your opponent to move more and exert himself or herself more. So, when you look at a consulting project, you need to think ahead, you need to have the right pieces, you need to control the sweet spot, and you'll more than likely win the game.

Conclusion

There is a profound difference between consulting and codependency. At some point, you must leave. This may mean you move on to another project and repeat business with the same client, but all individual engagements must end. Sometimes that means departing. That's particularly true with smaller clients and highly specialized projects. The entire point of our profession is to improve the client's condition. Make sure they recognize and endorse the improvement. Referrals are a win-win way to do that. You must plan for repeat business in as many categories as possible.

Waiting for the client to instigate it is like sitting home waiting for your phone to ring. You wonder if they've lost your number. Don't do that.

Using Technology: Naisbitt Was Right About High-Tech, High-Touch

11

Technology interacts and intervenes with most of our marketing in one form or another. The key is not to allow it to also interfere. Social media platforms, websites, branding, and accessibility all influence how we do business today—but these and others will shape the course our businesses and lives take. The key is to use 100 percent of the 30 percent of technology most relevant to you. That will ensure that you control it, and it doesn't control you.

What Did Naisbitt Mean by "High-Tech, High-Touch"?

Alan: Thirty years ago John Naisbitt talked about high-tech, high-touch in *Megatrends.* What he meant was that the more you use technology as part of your business and life, the more high-touch is needed.

One example is Amazon pioneered automated distribution and ordering on a large, global scale. If you have a problem with Amazon—a shipping problem, somebody just reviewed one of your books that's slanderous, or they've done something inappropriate or wrong—if it can't be solved automatically the first or second time, an Amazon representative will call you. The first time a rep actually called me on the phone, I fell over. I thought that was just a marvelous use of people, and it showed that they weren't doctrinaire and just married to this high-tech interaction.

Then there is a company called Richard Solo. This is the guy who used to run one of these big catalog companies, and he went on his own. His company went bankrupt, so that's why he called it Richard "Solo." The problem is you can't touch him. In other words, when you have a problem, there is no phone call. There is no phone system. There is no customer service. So, that is high-tech, no-touch and why his first company probably failed.

Another example is when I worked with Hewlett-Packard years ago, I helped them transform one of their call centers which was handling about 50 percent of inquiries automatically and 50 percent with human representatives to 90/10. The technology got so good that they made it 90 percent automatic and 10 percent human; but the issue was a very sensitive one because for that 10 percent, you couldn't just take the 50 percent of the people handling the old customer transactions. You had to have very special people for very complex, convoluted, delicate, sensitive, and tricky problems. The objective was customer satisfaction. Ninety percent of the time, the system took care of you, you're happy, you go on your way, and it's fair. But 10 percent of the issues required you could talk to somebody who was sort of a 360-degree technologist and could take care of what your issues were.

That kind of combination is what Naisbitt was talking about all those decades ago. The more we've gone into higher and higher levels of technological ability, the more he has been right.

Q: What technology do consultants need to be successful?

Alan: I'm going to answer that question two ways because right now, as we're doing this book, it's a very transitional period. I've had the benefit of hearing the great thought leader in technology—Walt Mossberg—in person. One of his superb and insightful comments is that people don't get up and say that they're plugging into the electric grid when they use their hair dryer or electric razor, they simply do it, and he said people are going to stop saying, "I'm on the internet" because it's just part of our lives.

If you think about it, you use an iPhone, an iPad, wireless Bluetooth technology in your car, and so forth. It's just part of our lives like the electrical grid, and so in the one sense—on a generic or even strategic sense—a consultant has to get used to using technology as a part of his or her life and in an appropriate way. Just like the telephone is a tool that you want to use effectively and efficiency, so is technology a tool you want to use effectively, efficiently, and automatically in your life.

On a more specific basis to answer your question, ironically, one of the most important things about technology is to be able to type fast. And the one thing that technology requires is input, which is usually typing (though it can be voice recognition technology). And it generates output, which is usually paper. Forget about the paperless office. It's never going to exist. So, if you want to use technology well, you have to be able to type rapidly. I type

60 words per minute. You have to be able to organize well because you're going to get a lot of paper.

I tell people when they're speaking to tell people what others need to know, not everything you know. The same thing with technology. You need to use a computer, a sophisticated phone, a PDA, or whatever it is to the extent that it really helps you. So, I use high-end Apple equipment. Every platform I use is Apple, high-end. But I probably use only 20 percent of the capability to about 98 percent effectiveness. The other 80 percent I use either in a rudimentary manner or I don't care about.

For example, I use word processing ferociously. I could probably do it blindfolded. However, I've never tried to create a slide. So, you have to be selective in your uses. And just like a consultant would never say to a client or prospect, "You could consult yourself. You don't really need consultants from the outside," I would say to consultants, "Why are you creating your own slides when there are people who can do them better on the outside? And even if you can do them, that's not how you spend your time."

Q: You just made a statement there in your explantation that you don't believe the paperless office will ever come to be. Explain that a little bit more.

Alan: If you take a look at the entire process of which technology is a part, what you said before is right. You said something about technology not being an end but being a tool. So, if you look at the context, the sequences, and the processes in which technology is a part, there is always an input and an output. The issue on the output side is that you often get paper produced, and the paper you do something with. It's not all virtual. It's not all electronic. It's not all on the screen. It never can be.

Consequently, the paperless office is about as accurate as the checkless society—despite the fact that people pay more and more stuff online, despite wire transfers, and everything else. I think in the last year or two, Deluxe check makers—one of the largest in the U.S.—probably had their biggest year ever. More and more people are writing more and more checks.

Technology hasn't reached the point of removing these physical things in our lives. What it does is it replaces some of them, which we can do very well, and it needs to play the proper role. *But if you aren't organized in terms of the output of technology, then you'll be swamped by it.*

Q: Many strive to become global consultants. You've operated this way for years. What technology tips can you share with us to help us operate anywhere and also globally?

Alan: On a global basis, what have been the main problems for any consultant to operate successfully? There have been just three or four, but they were almost insurmountable. One was time shifting. Australia—from the east coast, U.S.—is antipodal. It's a diametric opposite. Consequently, it's not only a different time and day there, it's a different season. If you travel to Australia, you leave on a Friday, you get there on a Sunday, and there is a huge time-shift issue if you try to communicate by phone. There is a huge acclimation issue if you go there in person, which is the second big problem with international travel—it takes time, you have to acclimate. Thirdly, it's expensive. Fourth, there is a cultural issue.

My colleague, Omar Khan, and I co-wrote a book *The Global Consultant* because both of us have operated globally for years. What technology enables you to do is time shift. So, when I open my computer at say 7:00 in the morning, I have emails from Germany, Australia, the UK, and so forth. If I launch something new overnight here, the first people who buy into it are usually in Europe because it's six, seven, or eight hours ahead. So, the time shifting is great.

The second advantage is you can do things remotely. You can use Skype. You can use email. You can use video and so forth to deal with people on a remote basis so you don't have to get on an airplane. When I was running the Far East and Latin America for a consulting firm in Princeton, every quarter I had to go both places. But now you can go once, then pick up in the middle with all of these technological remedies, and maybe only go twice a year. It doesn't have to eliminate, but it can reduce the hassle.

It's much easier to get to know people, culturally, to communicate. Let's face it, we're very fortunate in the United States because English is the universal language, and American English has become the universal type. So, you can start to communicate with people, understand who they are, and get acclimated culturally on a remote basis. It's much, much easier to do business. If you do decide to go there, you have a much better preparation for being effective when you're there. In other words, your learning curve is already taken care of.

Q: Technology can also be a huge time waster and also be used ineffectively or even, I would say, foolishly. We both have seen consultants waste much of their time endlessly surfing the web, participating in meaningless social media discussion, or even using PowerPoint presentations in the buyer's office. Share with us what your thoughts are about stupid use of technology, and how and where one should draw the line.

Alan: Meaningless time on social media is redundant. Technology should be used to further your goals. Now, I'm talking about a business sense here. Ask yourself, "Is this going to further my goal or not? Is it better if I call someone, email them, or go visit them? What is going to further my goal?" I keep telling people that you can't establish relationships by telephone. You can't establish relationships by email. Email is worse than phone. Email is one dimensional; phone is at least two dimensional. You've got to be there in person. You've got to be three dimensional.

What happens is that consultants procrastinate. They avoid making some tough decisions and performing actions that give them discomfort by using the excuse that they have to do things technologically, upgrade their technology, or do something on the computer, and it's just absolutely ridiculous. For recreational purposes, we're all playing games now that we would never have played before, and that's fine. This morning I think I've just hit 5,000 followers on Twitter. I've got, I don't know, 900 friends on Facebook and 2.5 million contacts on LinkedIn. So, I've been engaged in this stuff. I've been knee deep in this stuff. I'll tell you that even for recreational use, these can be huge time dumps for any generation, any age, and for all the world.

Twitter reminds me of sort of a flea market with people yelling random things to each other. Facebook reminds me of these loud Irish bars in Boston around closing time where nobody has any manners, everybody is getting kind of nasty, and everybody thinks that they're smarter than they are. This whole notion that you can take sort a college sorority or fraternity experience and put it online isn't appropriate for anything else.

Q: Many have to deal with software upgrades, how best to actually use the technology, and which technology to use. Should I maintain it myself or should I get an expert? Technology changes and improves very rapidly. What are the best ways that you would suggest for the average consultant to reduce their technology frustration?

Alan: If you want to reduce your technology frustration, what are four or five things you can do? Number one is find the technology that best suits you. Not what everybody is using, not what you feel is trendy, but what best suits your needs. That's why I recommend Macs to everyone because they're intuitive. They don't require complex steps, they're just about idiot proof, and they're also fairly virus proof. What technology best suits you?

Secondly, use the technology only to the degree it helps you. Just because there is a newer version of something doesn't mean you need it. I'm a professional writer. I've written 20-40 million words, whatever it is, and I'm still using Microsoft Office and Word. I haven't upgraded to the very latest one because it doesn't have that many advantages for me, and it has some things I don't like. Use the technology that's comfortable for you.

Then thirdly, when you're having trouble, understand that there is a sequence you can go through. It's no different from being on an airliner—something is wrong, and the pilot says, "Let's go through the checklist." Number one, you might want to go to the site of the software or hardware you're having trouble with—just look at Frequently Asked Questions, the latest bugs, or something like that—and see if somebody has written about it.

Number two, have a friend, a technical advisor, or someone knowledgeable who you can talk to. You're my business technical guy, and I go to you if there is something I can't figure out. My son-in-law is an excellent recreational technical guy, and I talk to him about 3D TVs and things.

Finally, don't be afraid to pay for an expert. Get in the Geek Squad or somebody like that who is very, very good at this stuff, and have them help you do what needs to be done. So, go through that kind of a checklist, but don't spend hours trying to remedy a technology problem, and always have a backup plan. In other words, if my main computer goes down here, my house is wired; I could just open my laptop. If for some reason I lose internet here, I'll go work on a different project that doesn't require me to be online or use my Verizon access card or my iPhone hot spot. Always be prepared to have a backup, and don't be wedded or enslaved to a single option at a single point.

Q: There was a survey that asked people how much time they spent online, and they asked that through different age groups. When they came to the 12-year-olds, they found that these youngsters didn't actually understand the question. As you said earlier, for them there was no off/on distinction; it didn't exist because they were born into the time the internet was already there, and so they don't see the internet and not being on the internet as separate realities. It's one meshed reality.

It seems to me that part of what you're coaching us here really relates to a transitional phase. This generation born around the beginning of the 21st century won't have the challenges that some of the people in your community—those in their 40s, 50s, and 60s—have in terms of being slower to adapt, and some of them still feel overwhelmed by technology and the internet. What is your advice to the people that do feel overwhelmed by technology and the internet?

Alan: Let's take the issue you raised at the start of this question. The fact is the question that they asked in that survey is a silly question. "How much time do you spend on the internet?" is like asking, "How much time did you spend on the electrical grid?" per Walt Mossberg. Now, if you ask someone, "How long do you use your hair dryer in the morning? How long does it take you to shave with an electric razor? How long do you listen to a radio that's plugged into the wall?" they could probably answer that. So, asking somebody how much time they spend on social media is a legitimate question. Asking people how much time they spend on Google or Wikipedia, those are questions that are easier to answer and probably more useful.

I think you're talking about generational differences there in the latter part of your question, and I've never gone for generational distinctions. I think we're all individuals, and we've had different experiences generationally. Nobody else can know what it's like to be an elder baby boomer, which I am, and to have been born right after World War II and what that was like in the United States. However, my exposures to technology are the same as someone who is 25 years old. The same technology is in front of us just like there are 24 hours in a day in front of both of us. So, using a generation, as some people do, to explain differences I think is neither here nor there.

I would tell you that people must get used to technology and get comfortable with it. It's like telling me you don't choose to use the telephone. It's ridiculous, so you better get used to it. If you choose not to, to be a luddite, to be primitive, that's your business; but you're not going to succeed.

Q: Let me approach it one other way. The technology companies like to talk about these psychographic groups. They have the early adopter people that jump on any new technology to be first to get it and demonstrate that they have it. The second category is the utilitarian people that you describe that perhaps use the 10 or 20 percent of technology that really is functional and creates value for them, and they aren't too interested in the rest. The third category is technology adverse. I think one of the messages I'm getting from you is, if you're going to be in business for yourself as a consultant, first you can't be technology adverse. Then you can choose whether you're going to be the early adopter or somebody who just finds a part of the technology that you like to use. Is this a fair conclusion, or would you coach and advise differently?

Alan: I would say two things in reaction to your proposition there. The first is, you proved my point in that early adopters, utilitarians, or whatever, are cross-generational, and it's not unique to any one generation. I know people who are in their 60s, 70s, and above who are the first to use some new technology, and I know some people who are relatively young who wait and see what other people are going to do.

The second is, you can't be technologically adverse. That's true. However, you don't have to be an early adopter; you can be somebody who wants to see what is out there, watches how it's used, and then makes some intelligent decisions; I think that's a smart way to be. So, I put in my request for the new iPhone at this time, and I received it about two or three weeks subsequently, but I didn't have to be the first in line and have the very first one. I had a perfectly good iPhone at the moment. I think you make decisions based upon where you are, and I think in some things you might be an early adopter, and in other things you might not be, even within the technological realm.

Q: We want this book to be relevant in the coming decade, and it seems to me that one of the next evolutions in technology is going to be speech recognition. Can you imagine speech recognition replacing typing, or is your typing as fast as you speak?

Alan: In the first place, they've been talking about speech recognition for at least 10-15 years, and it's very difficult to perfect. I would agree that they're going to get there. I don't know how soon. I think there is a danger and an advantage.

The great danger in speech recognition is that people are pretty bad at communicating today. They've lost touch with grammar. They've lost touch with punctuation. They've lost touch with inflection, meaning, metaphor, and analogy. People aren't good writers any more. They're worse than they were during the Civil War, and consequently, speech recognition will make it even worse. Picture what you see on Facebook, which is the most common denominator of the basest, lowest form of communication. Or worse, go to YouTube where it's common to see obscenity and scatological references by people who are functionally illiterate. Picture that being the primary way that people establish writing. That's kind of frightening. Who knows what that will lead to?

The advantage, of course, is that if speech recognition is used with discrimination, it will be great. By discrimination, I mean this: I might use it to dictate a proposal because a proposal has a given format. I've acquired the information, and I need to plug in the content. I could easily dictate a proposal anywhere and be confident of what it's going to look like, and I have a command of both written and spoken language.

All language is verbal; the question is whether it's oral or written. However, I would never write a book or an article by dictation. People tell me I write the way I speak, and that's because I convey what I'm thinking both orally and in writing the same way. Nonetheless, it's much more effective for me to type, write, and see, than it is merely to dictate. You could always go over what you dictate and re-read it, and I'm sure that some accommodations will be reached that way, but there are pros and cons to voice recognition.

Q: Do you perceive your speaking voice and your writing voice to be very similar or the same?

Alan: Throughout the years—I published my first book in 1988, and I've written 47 books right now—people have told me consistently and frequently that I write the way I speak. They say that when they read what I write, it's like they've been speaking to me. It's like I'm writing for them; it's like a conversation. I take that as a compliment. So, my writing and speaking are very close.

However, there are nuanced differences that would take a keen eye and ear to see and hear; there are things I do differently when I write than when I speak because of the different forms of communication involved. However, if there were a percentage here, they would probably be 90 percent the same.

Some people are very dissimilar. The analogy would be that if you listen to somebody who is in politics speaking to you at a cocktail party, they'll speak one way. If you listen to them make a speech, all of a sudden they start orating. Ted Kennedy was like that. He took a big breath and off he went. He sounded like he was just pompous, yet he had good ideas. I met Ted Kennedy in a bar. He was an easy guy to talk to, but when he got behind a lectern, he was awful. And most politicians are that way.

The same thing with writing. Some people pick up a pen or go to the keyboard, and they tend to become rather pompous. They tend to feel it's a more formalized medium and consequently, they pontificate, and that's unfortunate. I think the more you can speak and write with the same level of inflection, influence, conviction, and so on, the better communicator you are.

Q: I know you said there are no writing blocks, but this self-view that you need to have a different voice when you write may be a blockage for some.

Alan: There is no question. The problem is that when most people sit down to write, they think they're writing *War and Peace*. They think they're writing the "Gettysburg Address" (which Lincoln wrote on the back of an envelope). All they're writing is an article on why a team should be self-directed. You have to keep perspective.

When you don't have a real feeling for history, geography, and language, it's hard to retain context. It's hard to understand and to have perspective. And that slows up everything you do. It either makes you inaccurate or ineffective. Neither one is a happy ending place.

Q: Technology, in my mind, can be used to drive and improve our business and at the same time make life easier, better, and fun. You often talk about the fact that we don't have a business life and a personal life, but we actually have one integrated life. Does the same rule apply to technology?

Alan: I think you have to use your own comfort levels in everything you do. Let me just give you a few examples based on your question. I acquired an iPad slightly before you did, and when you got your iPad, I had about 40 apps on mine. You showed me your iPad, and you must have already had 100 apps on it. You were much more inclined that way because it's your comfort level to pursue what you could put on there and look at it just for the sake of seeing how it would work. In my case, I'm much stricter, and I'll pursue an app only when I'm convinced it's going to make my life better. I don't do it just for curiosity.

The *Wall Street Journal* is a great example. The *Wall Street Journal* has become the most widely distributed newspaper in the United States and maybe the world. It has surpassed all others in daily circulation, yet the *Wall Street Journal* is something I read in hard copy. I like to put my feet up and hold it in front of me, and I find it a little bit more difficult on the iPad to follow stories and to browse around. I look at the headlines on any two pages I open. That's how I read it. You can't do that on the iPad. However, the iPad is very user-friendly with the *Wall Street Journal*, and the resolution is magnificent, so are the photos, and so on. So, I can understand you doing that. What the *Wall Street Journal* has done brilliantly is it appeals to you and it appeals to me. That's how it has got to be—so that your comfort level is probably the same in your business and personal life the way you use technology.

I know if you're driving to a restaurant, you'll use your Bluetooth in your car, and you'll probably give a voice command that says, "Italian restaurant in Cleveland" or something, and the thing will talk back to you. I'm more prone to punch in on my memory GPS a restaurant I want to go to or simply call 411 hands-free. We're both doing something that's comfortable for us.

That's the secret to any kind of innovation, and that's what will make it most useful. Now, whether people ruin their lives or not by putting too much time into it goes back to what we've been talking about for the last 35 minutes. You have to adapt this technology to your best interest and not the other way around. You can't adapt your best interest to technology.

Q: Could you walk us through your personal growth, evolution, and readiness to embrace and leverage these amazing technologies, and what influenced your decisions over the years?

Alan: This might be surprising. My feeling is that I owe it to not only my business but also myself. This goes back to your point about personal versus professional and there being just one person. I owe it to myself to stay immersed in what goes on around me. I need to be conversant in a lot of things. First of all, that's how I enjoy life. But secondly, that's how I've become an object of interest to others. Just this morning on Facebook, I had four or five posting exchanges with a guy about great restaurants in New York. As you know, I know wine. I know restaurants. I know travel. We are up-to-date on Broadway plays, and so forth and so on.

We were in Summit, New Jersey, 30 years ago. Tandy, which is Radio Shack, came out with a color computer, and I said to my wife, "This computer stuff looks like it's catching on, and I need to go do something, and this looks like a simple machine that might be good for the kids as well and that I can fool around with." And she said, "If that's what you think, go do it."

I drove to a Radio Shack, and I paid $1,800 for the Tandy color computer, keyboard, screen, and whatever it came with. I taught myself a little bit, started to fool around with it, and started to even get email, which I ignored because I wasn't interested in email and didn't need it at the time. As I read more and more about people using computers, Apple came out with—I forget which model it was—but it was a tiny screen and sat up there—I still remember the tiny television screens we had in the '50s—and one thing led to another. I kept upgrading through the years with Mac, always Mac, as they came out with newer and better models because I wanted to stay abreast of the field. I've never owned a PC in my life. Then I started to integrate it into my business and realized the areas of my business where it could make a huge difference.

Move the clock forward, and I met you [Chad Barr], and you knew much more about technology than I ever would from the standpoint of how it works, what its potential was, and so forth. I found that the technology became an entirely new universe for me to use to pump my intellectual property into all of these various communities. I think that you probably admit as you showed me one thing or another, I carefully analyzed it to see if it made sense for me, and if it did—it was embraced. I didn't do anything half-heartedly. So, it took you a while to convince me to have a blog, but once you did, I don't think I've ever failed to post there three, four, or five times a week, every week, in multimedia.

Q: What about the difference between one's using technology versus leveraging technology?

Alan: Let me give you a very simple example that I think makes your point. To use technology is to write a proposal on the computer and send it to your client electronically. To leverage technology is to have a proposal template on your computer where you can just plug in the content, send it to clients, and you never have to recreate that work. To use technology is to send an email to someone apprising them of what is coming up. To leverage it is to create a database of people to whom you can provide value on the basis of 10,000 people and not just one person at a time.

Q: Many look at your online digital empire and are inspired to get there and try to implement similar concepts in their business. Yet, at the same time, they just get overwhelmed. Is it as simple for a consultant to just move three things a mile technology-wise, internet-wise? Give us some tips for consultants. How can they get there faster creating that kind of internet success that you've created?

Alan: First of all, you need somebody to help you. I've been very fortunate I met you. You need somebody who can help because it's not something you can do yourself. You need an expert—just as a client shouldn't consult for himself or herself, you shouldn't do the technology work yourself. You need someone to help you do it, someone you trust, and someone with whom you have a partnership.

It would be rather natural then to morph from a website into a blog. Then I would say you should look at something like a newsletter. The difference, of course, between a blog and a newsletter is a blog is someplace people come to. They leave commentary. It's interactive. A newsletter is something that goes to them. You might want to think about some kind of a chat room. Some kind of a community. This is much more difficult than the first three, so that's why I'm putting them in this order of evolution where people can come and meet other people, you form a community, and you're providing value just by dint of your hosting ability for them to be there.

Then somewhere as you go down this path, depending on your proclivities, you might want to start doing teleconferences, podcasts, videos, or some kind of interactive question and answer kinds of things. It depends on what is comfortable for you.

You can't do everything at once, but they do build on each other. Once you have a website, it's easier to do a blog. Once you have a website and a blog, it's easier to do a newsletter. So, I think you have to create some rationale for yourself and move down that path. I have to say one thing. I've been astounded, just appalled, by the people who tell me somebody has been working on their website for nine months. If somebody has been working on your website for nine months, they're stealing your money.

Q: Looking into the future—whether it's the next 5, 10, 15 years—what do you think the future holds for consultants in regards to technology and its importance in their business?

Alan: It's a vital part of their business today, and it will be a vital part of their business in the future. To go back to your questions that opened this segment, it's going to be high-tech, high-touch as Naisbitt predicted. In other words, the more that you're interacting with people remotely—the more you're using email, audio, video, and so forth—the more you have to personalize things. The more you have to be willing to pick up a phone and call people. The more you have to be willing to visit people. The more you have to make yourself accessible.

Don't forget, in the midst of all of this technology we're talking about, one thing we haven't mentioned is that I'm very accessible. If you look at thought leaders in various brackets, I'm probably near the very top in terms of accessibility. "Monday Morning Memo"® is one of the things we put out every week, 52 weeks a year. And people write me, they hit "return" and will ask me about Monday Morning Memo, they make a comment, or they share a story. I respond to every single one of them. "Balancing Act"® goes out every month, first of the month. People respond to that. I respond to every one of those people.

I'm highly accessible, especially if you're in my inner community, the mentor program, the Forums, and so on. You can deal with me on a pretty regular basis. That's going to be very important for consultants, and it's going to be very important for consultants who want to leverage what they do, leverage their intellectual property, and go beyond having to be physically present. The old style that your value is only in being physically present not only is dying, but it's going to be as ancient as giving people these silly workbooks where you fill in the blanks. The height of idiocy. People still do that. But the world is changing.

Website, Blog, and Other Internet Platforms to Market Yourself

Q: How does a consultant best choose his or her domain for the web address?

Alan: I've never been fastidious about matching a URL to certain names. If you can get them, great. For example, a friend of mine happened to have www.contrarianconsulting.com. But the blog is called Alan's Blog because that's the brand we wanted to build. I think too many consultants choose to name their company or to brand themselves based on the URLs they can get, and that's the tail wagging the dog.

I think what you want to do is think about the names, the brands, the positioning you want with the public that will best help your business, and then get a URL that makes sense. But at this stage, there are a gazillion URLs out there. Some people are even in the business of simply securing the names and then reselling them at a profit. I wouldn't worry too much about what URL you choose. I would worry much more about your brand, your positioning, what you call your blog, your website, your chat room, and so forth.

Q: If www.contrarianconsulting.com was not available, would you have gone then simply with www.alanweiss.com?

Alan: You can do these things easily through organizations on the web like www.namesecure.com. In my case, there is no such site as www.alanweiss.com. But if you type in www.alanweiss.com, it automatically directs you to www.summitconsulting.com. That costs about $45. It's very inexpensive. If you're ever concerned about these things, you can use what I call redirection devices to make sure that people get to the right place. Because intuitively, someone might say, "I'm looking for Alan Weiss. I don't know his website. Let me type in www.alanweiss.com."

Q: You talk about the importance, when it makes sense, to create passive income products in your business. In the context of the internet or your website leveraging these tools to help drive passive income products, give us some tips.

Alan: I think the best way to create products is to ask yourself a few questions first. One question would be "What is the value that I want to try to convey?" The second is "What is the best vehicle to convey that value? Is it text, audio, video, live over the internet, combination?" Then ask, "Who is my most likely market to purchase this?" That might influence the prior question because if your market is high-level executives, they might not be as willing to use the internet to learn as some younger people. I don't know, but that's a consideration. Then ask, "What would be the easiest and least expensive thing for me to design?" And that's how you start to put things together.

If you aren't certain about things, don't worry so much about the media, and try different approaches. People ask me how do I know whether I'm going to put something in my blog, on my website, in a commercially published book, in an article I write, in Alan's Forums, in the Monday Morning Memo, or whatever. I tell them I really don't care. I just think about what it is and start to write it somewhere, start to record it somewhere, or start to shoot it somewhere. Sometimes my stuff is recycled, sometimes it overlaps, but 85 percent of it's new. Consequently, I don't get all wound up over where it should appear.

I think if you want to create products as a newer consultant, the key would be to find the value being conveyed, who will receive it, what the best form would be for it, and then how you can do it rapidly and inexpensively. And see what happens and experiment. That's why it should be rapidly and inexpensively so you don't invest a whole lot of money. I know a guy who came out with a commercially published book—from not a great publisher, sort of a bottom-level publisher—and without telling me and without telling his wife, I think he invested $80,000 in promoting this book. He might as well have gone to Vegas. He would have stood the chances of a better return. The book sunk in a week to 1,500,000 on Amazon.com.

Q: How best do you leverage a website, newsletter, and blog?

Alan: For a veteran, you want to pump as much intellectual property and new value as you can into your communities. So, your website is always going to be a credibility statement, and it should grow with your credibility. Accolades, new testimonials, new intellectual property displayed, and things like that. Your blog should be more and more provocative and should be building your brand. So, you should keep talking about the brand you have with the new brands you want to create or your name, as well as introducing provocative intellectual property. Your newsletter should back up those first two by doing that on a quick-hit basis every month if that's the period of your newsletter.

Don't forget, the web is the ultimate repository of highly specialized content. Unlike anything in the past, if you're a left-handed fly fisherman, you can find left-handed fly fishing equipment on the web. If you're the collector of 19th century New Zealand stamps, you can find 19th century New Zealand stamps for sale or at auction around the world using the web. So, for people even with a very limited kind of scope or for limited markets, the web is still highly useful because it targets exactly those people you need.

Instead of being broadly advertising, you place an ad in the newspaper, and 90 percent of the people who get the newspaper don't read the ads; and 90 percent of the 10 percent of the people who do don't need that stuff—that's a long-shot proposition. But when you're using the internet, you're able to find targets of opportunity that are much more aligned, much more focused with what you're trying to promote. Consequently, that's how these things should be used. Your newsletter should be targeted at those kinds of groups.

In terms of a blog, it's no different from a veteran consultant. Every week—three, four, or five times a week—you're putting things on there in various media that establish you. In fact, it's probably more important to a newer consultant than a veteran, and then the newsletter serves the same purpose as well. It backs up those two, and you can reach very targeted audiences.

Q: How different should a website be when your focus is the corporate buyer versus the retail buyer?

Alan: Let me just say a couple things in preparation to really answer this. The first is that I didn't make such a conscious decision. Sometimes it's better to be lucky than good. What I found was that as I began publishing books on consulting like *Million Dollar Consulting,* the retail market grew around me; and as I advised elsewhere in this book, when you find need growing, cater to it. As I did that, retail grew as a percentage of what I was doing. Then it grew some more, and I realized it had benefits that the wholesale—the corporate side—didn't have, and the corporate side had disadvantages such as travel and boredom which the retail side didn't have. Then I made the shift more dramatically and moved my accelerant curve to retail.

In terms of a website, what we're talking about here is a corporate purchase versus a self-help purchase: wholesale/retail. And we used to think that when wholesale was down, retail went up. In other words, if economic conditions were down, people were laid off, there weren't as many jobs, it was harder to get promoted, and the retail side went up because people were looking for more control of their destiny, and they wanted to be entrepreneurial. But when times got better, a lot of people who couldn't make it as an entrepreneur went back to work for large companies and so forth.

That's no longer true. That old hydraulic system is kaput. What happens today is that the two of them move independently. So, the retail market could go up and down, the wholesale market could go up and down, sometimes they both go up together, and sometimes they go down together. So, if you want to make a difference on your website, what you have to basically remember is that your buyer is different, but your website is still a credibility statement, and so that underlying strategy doesn't change.

For a retail market, you can offer more for sale on your website. The retail purchase of books, video, audio, albums, newsletters, experiences, workshops, all of that is perfect for a website with a retail market. It's an individual purchase. People can go there and do it.

With a corporate market, you're not really trying to sell products, especially not on a website. What you're trying to do is simply establish credibility for somebody who has heard about you, or seen you, or talked to you and just wants to check you out. So, the emphasis on a corporate basis isn't on product sales at all. You might have a book or two that you sell there, and that's fine, but the real emphasis is on testimonial, endorsement, and credibility.

On the retail side, you also want endorsement and credibility, but then you want to provide a raft of things people can engage in. So, let me put it this way. On the retail side, your accelerant curve is much more manifest on your website than it is on the wholesale side.

Q: The more my focus is on the corporate, senior executive, CEO type engagement, the more I should really ask myself not just what should be on my website but what should I possibly *not* put on my website because it may diminish or take away from the focus and the credibility that I'm looking to create.

Alan: It's very important because we spoke a little while ago in this interview about the web being this repository of highly specialized content, and that when you're on the web, you want to find it easily. The same thing with people trying to find you. If your website tries to be all things to all people, then you've given up that targeting that people can do.

I've actually coached people, mentored people who want to put on their website the fact that they do team development work and nutrition. I tell them that if you're actually in fact adept to both of those things, you need two different websites. Otherwise, it's going to do what you just said; it's going to compromise your credibility if you accept the fact that your website is a credibility statement.

Q: With this in mind, your blog is very personal. Let me put to you hypothetically. If you're now doing what you were doing in the mid-'80s and early '90s—your OD work—how would your blog be different?

Alan: My blog would have far, far less personal things on it. I wouldn't be talking about my grandchildren, and I wouldn't be talking about my travels. I might occasionally be talking about favorite restaurants because corporate buyers like to hear that as well. But the predominance would be about corporate benefit. It would be about how you improve implementation of strategy. How you avoid being driven by your competition. How you best expand overseas. So, given whomever I determined my audience was—and let's say it was executives in Fortune 1000 companies—I would orient my blog toward what I believe would be in their best self-interest.

The reason that my writings today aimed at retail are so personal—the reason I mention the Bentley, suites, first class travel, the Queen Mary, and this kind of stuff—is that I'm a thought leader at the top of my profession. People are drawn to me because they want to learn how to be better at what they do.

Q: There is a point where showing off isn't showing off at all?

Alan: You have to blow your own horn, and when I look at my ski instructor, I want to see that ski instructor traversing the double black diamond doing back flips. I want to know he can do it all, so doing what I have to do for him will be a piece of cake. If I'm taking piano lessons, I don't want to take lessons from somebody who can play four songs. I want somebody who can sight read Mozart. And if somebody wants to be a great consultant or speaker, they want somebody who is getting $25,000 for a keynote and whose clients are flying first class all over the world because they want his expertise.

Q: When someone comes today to your website—Summit Consulting Group—what they find is that this is no longer a website in the traditional sense. I describe it more as a portal into multiple offerings and content. Perhaps this could be another brand or tag line—the consulting portal?

Alan: There are two things. One is I couldn't do what I do without Chad Barr and his folks at CB Software because of exactly what you said. In fact, sometimes Chad says I generate more content than his people can handle quickly.

The second thing I wanted to say about this portal thing is if you think about it, what I've done is create portals into communities. You know how big I am in the concept of communities, and I do have a trademark—The Architect of Professional Communities®. The reason this is so important is when I suggest a workshop, and I say the workshop is on change management, the workshop is on framing, the workshop is on thriving, whatever it is, I'm not just offering a developmental experience. I'm offering a community experience. And people know there will be some people in that workshop whom they want to be with. They also know that they want that experience under their belt to be able to talk to other people about it. *You create these portals in the communities where people find great value in the total experience and not merely in the learning experience. And that's extraordinarily powerful.*

When you start to rub elbows with these kinds of people in the community, and I mean that metaphorically, it need not always be in person. You're in contact with them, you hear from them, and you can talk to them. Or you can attend a workshop that they might be attending in Sarasota or San Francisco. This is very, very high value. So, these doors I'm opening are literally into rooms of communities of people who—unlike Facebook which has a sort of nasty, drunk aspect about it—are more of a renaissance group, an intellectual group which fulfills your developmental needs beyond your wildest dreams.

Q: Is there any equivalent in the corporate web presence and engagements where, for example, somebody may be a generalist but they also supposedly have a focus on marketing professionals? Will they carve it all in the same space, or at what point will they look to create a separate identity, a separate brand, or a separate website?

Alan: You have to understand that communities overlap, and they embrace each other. So, you can have a wide community where people have read your stuff; you can have an inner community where people have heard you speak; you can have a community within that where people have attended workshops; you can have a community in that for people who are personally coached.

Some communities overlap. Some people have gone to four workshops but not another six. Some people go to three but not the other nine, or whatever it is. You can have workshops that only appeal to certain members of the community: "Six Figures to Seven" as opposed to "Zero to $300,000." So, you want to create this interaction among workshops but also have an inner core of people and an outer core of people. Let people go where they're comfortable.

In terms of the corporate, that's a good question, and you're quite right. You can have the same kind of community aspect with a corporate market. You could be a strategist, but you might have a newsletter for senior marketing professionals. You might have a coaching program for chief information officers as to how they become part of the strategy team and not just the support for it. So, you could take what you do and without sacrificing your primary community of being a strategist, embrace some of these other communities which also might have input to you.

Q: With this in mind, when I asked you a couple years ago about including in my newsletter some retail offerings where most of my distribution list goes to corporate buyers, you advised against it. I think it had this awareness that you need to create some clear boundaries when you cater mostly to the corporate buyer to not overwhelm them with offerings that are retail in nature when they experienced your value as a corporate engagement, not as a retail experience.

Alan: That's exactly right. And don't forget, a corporate engagement could be a $150,000 check. So, if you're selling at the retail level even $10,000 experiences—which would be fairly high—you need 15 people to equal that $150,000, and that really requires much more work and has a lower margin. You don't want to confuse that corporate buyer, but that's also why you don't want to try to take corporate business for $15,000. If you're in the corporate wholesale market place, you want fees commensurate with the nature of that marketplace.

That's why small business consulting is so difficult because you're in limbo there. You have an individual buyer, the owner of a small business—say a $2 million dollar operation—who can't make the large corporate purchase, has no need for the large corporate purchase, and is really a retail buyer who wants a corporate kind of service. You have to be very careful about that marketplace because it's hard to make a sale. Secondly, you could lose your shirt!

Q: In an earlier chapter, we devoted the entire chapter to marketing. In the context of internet marketing, what are the biggest mistakes consultants make that they could cure or should change in regards to internet marketing?

Alan: In no particular order, number one, they should get help. We talked about that on several occasions of having someone who is technologically adept, whose business is this kind of technological creation and implementation, and do it for them at their direction.

Number two, ignore search engine optimization, clicks, and all that kind of nonsense because corporate buyers don't troll the web, and individual buyers who do troll the web will find you because of other things you're doing in your gravity wheel, not because of SEO, appearances on Facebook, or anything else.

Number three, don't overestimate the social media platforms. They don't work on corporate purchases. Just because you can show me an exception—it's 1 in 10,000—and that's no way to try to make a living. They don't work very well either for retail purchases. Most people selling retail on social media platforms are selling services in how to market on social media platforms, or they might be in insurance or real estate. So, you have to focus on more propitious marketing areas.

The fourth mistake is to be swallowed by the internet. You have to strictly, and in a disciplined manner, monitor your time. It's just one tool working for you, and so you can't spend hours and hours on it. The temptation is to do that because you're sitting at home with the screen in front of you, it's easy to do, and you can make an excuse that you're really marketing, but that's not the case.

The fifth is, just because it's the internet, don't be sloppy and unprofessional. You should have a full signature file. People who have only their email address and tell me they don't want people to come to their doorstep, they don't want people stalking them, that's so stupid that I fall off my chair laughing because if somebody wants to kill you, they'll find you! They don't need your signature file! Somebody said, "Could you send me a sample of your press kit?" No signature file. My physical press kit—what am I supposed to do? Slam it into the screen? I have a hard time dealing with that level of ignorance. So, you have to use the internet intelligently and not be sloppy. Stop sending email that's full of punctuation errors. Stop sending email that's full of typos. Stop sending email that's as though you're talking to a friend in the restroom at a football game.

Some guy wanted me to do a webinar. He wanted to pay me for a webinar and sell my book. No signature file. Sloppy writing. I said to him, "I'm suspicious. You look like a scam to me." He wrote back, assured me he wasn't a scam, gave me credentials, and I said, "You better think about your first impression because I was tempted to just delete your email." So, it's a tool that you use, and you have to use a tool professionally and well, or the tool doesn't serve you well. You don't use a pair of pliers to drive a nail into a wall. The nail will be bent, and the pliers won't work any more.

Q: Do you have technology-free time, web-free time, time that you switch everything off?

Alan: Yes, but what I do is walk away from it. I never switch my computer off. It's always on. Yes, I'll turn my back on the computer and tend to something. I'll pay the bills, play a game, read a book, get into a discussion with someone, make some calls, or whatever it is. It's easy to do because my computer is rigged so it can't interrupt me. It can't give me notices. It can't signal me about email because all of those functions are turned off. So, it's easy for me not to use the computer. However, going back to an earlier discussion, in many cases, at least wherever I turn to, I'm still using the internet to some degree. So, I don't tend to make those kinds of discriminations.

This might be of interest to some people. You didn't ask me this question, but I'll answer it. I'm an intellectually curious guy, as you know; nevertheless, what I don't do is go surfing the web just to explore things because that takes forever. If I'm walking in Nantucket, I might go down a path and see what is there. But I don't go out in the morning and say, "I'm going to walk down as many paths as I can." That will take my whole day, and I would rather be at the beach. And the same thing on the internet. I don't just randomly surf.

I virtually will never follow a link. On Alan's Forums if somebody wants to make a point and they have a link that they want me to connect to, I'll seldom ever click on it. If somebody sends me an email and says, "You want to know more about this, click on this link," I won't do it. Now, American Airlines sent me an email today that said, "Please make sure that we have all of the information we need for the new Homeland Security rules. You can go to your account here." That I'll click on because that's in my self-interest. So, I don't go wandering around on the internet, and I find that that saves me a great deal of time.

Q: In other words, choosing what not to do is the key element of how you muster your mental focus and time?

Alan: Yes. I would phrase that slightly differently. I would say that I choose to do nothing other than what I think I really need to do.

Q: Do you still feel that search optimization is a waste of time?

Alan: Yes. I think what happens is people will write me and say, "I use the internet extensively to sell my home-based quilt business to people who need quilts," or "I use the internet extensively to sell to the self-help market where I'm providing diet regimens." Well, they're not listening. What I'm talking about is corporate consulting sales. People keep trying to show me an exception by changing the paradigm.

Social Media and All That Online Jazz

Q: What is your definition of social media?

Alan: I think what we're really talking about are social media platforms. And social media platforms are virtual locations on the web that allow people to interact with each other in a variety of ways. By a variety of ways I mean that you can send messages to each other, talk in real time online, exchange photos, exchange movies, be private with some people, talk to whole groups publicly, broadcast to whole groups, create your own groups, create your own events, and so on. So, depending on the platform, you have a variety of options at your command.

I would also add that these social media platforms are characterized by relatively little restraint. If you go to YouTube, which I regard as the largest social media platform, there are some horrible obscenities and horrible scatological references. In fact, even on Facebook you'll find people using all kinds of profane language at times. Now, you can block them, you can de-friend them or whatever it is you do, but these companies who run these things have very little constraint. Their strategic driving force really is size and growth because it's free to join. The only way they can make money is either by selling ads, selling applications or some kind of service, or building up enough appeal so that they can sell the entire operation to Google, Apple, Microsoft, or some huge organization sometime in the future.

These social media sites aren't even like a bar that you've chosen to go into because of what it's going to be like. There is very little etiquette, very few rules, and so you have to take a lot of the bad with the good. As far as I can see, outside of really low-level recreation, there is not a lot of return on energy there.

Q: Facebook, LinkedIn, and Twitter: What are the distinguishing factors between those platforms as you see it?

Alan: Actually, the one I'm most active on is probably Twitter. I post there every day. I follow no one. Just yesterday, I went over 5,000 followers. I call them readers. I hate the term "followers." My branding strategy isn't to follow anyone and is to post value on Twitter every day. So, I don't post platitudes. I'll only occasionally post some kind of an advisory about a workshop or something that I'm running, and they're things that help people. What I find gets most re-tweeted is when I actually provide dialogue and when I say to people, "If the client says this, you say that." That becomes re-tweeted over the web. So, I post on Twitter every day. It takes me about, oh, 40 seconds.

We've arranged my technology so that what I put on Twitter and I think what I put on LinkedIn or my blog goes onto Facebook. LinkedIn, where I have something like 2.5 million connections or whatever it is, I virtually never use. I find LinkedIn pretty worthless because you're confronted with people who you're told are now connecting with each other, and somebody is visiting Spokane, and somebody is taking a shower, and there are so many people bleating about so much stuff that I just find it pretty useless.

I've never received business from LinkedIn. People come to me and try to get things from me for free, and I find LinkedIn totally worthless. I just maintain myself on there because if somebody wants to join me on LinkedIn, somebody wants to link, I always accept them. I feel if I'm going to talk about these things—just as you're asking me about them now—and comment on them knowledgeably for consultants, then I need to be there and know what is going on. I've changed my mind about some things in life. I could change my mind about this.

Facebook I generally use only insofar as my blog and Twitter postings are reprinted there. I'll occasionally post photos there. My son and daughter are on it. I'll follow what they're doing on occasion, comment on something they're doing on occasion, maybe give them a hard time, but I find Facebook almost void of intellectual interest. On a recreational basis, to me it's not as challenging or fascinating as playing kickball or backgammon. It's just a big bar with everybody screaming. Unfortunately, this old aphorism that there are two dogs sitting next to each other by a keyboard and one dog says to the other, "The good thing about the internet is nobody knows you're a dog," is true. I wouldn't insult dogs, but maybe an amoeba is the metaphor because the level of input is just terribly, terribly alarming. Spending a lot of time on Facebook is almost like verbal acne. You want to take something to get rid of it.

Q: I've heard you say over the years, you never know where the next hit is going to come from. When we think about those social media platforms, are they complementing the notion of we never know where the next hit is going to come from? And with that in mind, is there a way for consultants to leverage them in their business?

Alan: The problem is when I say you never know where the next hit is going to come from, implicit in that statement is that they come from high-probability marketing devices—what I've called "market gravity." For example, you could stand on a street corner at a busy intersection with a sign that says "Will consult. Daily fee $5,000," and I don't know, maybe in six years someone will stop and hire you. But is that a good way to spend your day? Because you never know if somebody might do it. It's like walking down a street and finding a $100 bill—which might happen once in 20 years—but you wouldn't decide that that's how you're going to try to feed your family and go out on the street every day.

On my blog I wrote a comparison of the average time I find people spending on social media platforms. Not blogging, but just on the social media platforms and how that time could be translated into writing articles, doing interviews, networking, speaking at certain events, producing product, doing pro bono work, or whatever it is on the gravity wheel. And I showed that there just is no comparison in the return on that time investment. So, I don't think that social media today—as we're writing this book—constitutes legitimate or high-probability marketing efforts for any consultant selling consulting services to corporations, nonprofits, and large organizations. I don't think that's a wise investment of time. If you want to be on these platforms to look up old pals or sell motorcycle insurance, fine. But that's not what I'm talking about.

Q: You tell us to be provocative all the time. As an example, on Twitter you've elected to follow no one. Tell me a little bit more about the reasoning behind that.

Alan: I'm not trying to poke anybody in the eye, but I'm trying to do this. First of all, it's my brand. It isn't that there is nobody on Twitter worth following, but the fact is that I derive my learning from other sources. So, the probability is if there is a superb person on Twitter who is broadcasting something, who is tweeting, and I really respect this person and I learn from them, they're somewhere else in my frame of reference. I'm not going to get it in 140-character sound bites. For me, that doesn't work.

The second thing is my brand is important, and my brand is that I own the solo consulting niche, that I'm a thought leader—I'm Guy Kawasaki in my field. I think he has 93,000 followers, and he claims to follow 93,000 people. We all know that's impossible, and we all know that somebody else is tweeting for him. He isn't doing all this. I would maintain that he is being disingenuous, and I'm just being honest and open.

The third thing is that you mentioned contrarianism. The whole notion of Twitter etiquette is so bizarre that I just couldn't resist not following anyone. People would say to me, "I've chosen to follow you, and you haven't paid me the return courtesy." I write back to them, but only after I pick myself up off the floor because I've fallen off my chair at this point, "I don't owe you the courtesy of following you because you've chosen to follow me because you want to learn something from me because I post value. I have no obligation to follow you. This isn't a reciprocal relationship." I've never heard of this person. They're not a thought leader. They want to learn from me. Why on earth should I follow them? Why should I go through that conceit? In fact, the people who claim to be following others—who we all know aren't reading their stuff, but they just follow them out of this bizarre Twitter courtesy—are far more hypocritical than I'll ever be.

Q: How do you handle the web attacks on your business, your brain, your personality, and your character when people attack you and try to diminish your repute?

Alan: One of the adverse consequences, as you can expect—as you climb the mountain, as you become a thought leader—is that people who are inferior and choose not to learn and choose not to take on a challenge will try to get their moment in the sun by throwing rocks at people climbing up the hill instead of trying to climb themselves. So, I have a triage about these.

If somebody is critical of me, and they say stupid things like "*Million Dollar Consulting* doesn't have any specifics in the book. Alan Weiss thinks he is a good speaker. He isn't," and things like that, I ignore it because I don't want to shine any light on them. In fact, one really dumb woman who took umbrage of the fact that she approached me to get something for free, and I refused, went crazy and posted this long thing on her blog about me. One of the people on Alan's Forums chose to talk about it and put her site on my blog, on my Forum, and I had a problem with him because the last thing I want to do is to help her get limelight, to help her get attention by throwing rocks at me. That's the first level.

The second level in my triage system is people who are factually wrong and damaging. If somebody were to write, "I read Alan Weiss' *Million Dollar Speaking* book, and one of the chapters in there is taken from *Speak and Grow Rich*," which is simply a lie, a fabrication, I would correct them and tell them that they're wrong. I would ask them to give the specifics, and I don't let that stand. Of course, I learned about these comments on Google Alerts and things like that.

The third level is actionable, and that's when I send my lawyer. Just this morning I found a site called Rapid Share or something. It's one of these crappy sites that takes everybody else's intellectual property and provides it as free downloads. I found two of my books on there being offered as free downloads, and I sent my lawyer after them. He sends a torpedo toward their bow, and usually they see the torpedo coming, and they all panic and stop. They turn the ship. But some of them you have to go farther with. I don't tolerate slander.

You ignore the gnats on the windshield, you correct people who might be legitimately wrong or even if they're maliciously wrong, and then you take action against people who are simply plagiarists, cheating, or thieves. If somebody wants to disagree with me, I don't care as long as they're polite. I welcome commentary on my blog. And as long as people are polite, that's fine.

It's very interesting. When you're in a position of power, you have to be very careful because what you say becomes exaggerated, and people don't apply the same level of scrutiny. They don't apply the same due diligence when a powerful person says something. So, I can virtually make up things and people will accept it. And I try to keep this frame of reference all the time. I remember I once said to a woman who ran our Washington office for a consulting firm I was with, "Every office is a different color. What is this, some kind of modern art?" When I came back two months later, they had painted the entire office one color. I was just being sarcastic.

To give you an example of this, I took a picture of the back of my Bentley, and I had affixed to the rear bumper—just temporarily, I could take it off—an over-sand driving permit for Nantucket. I had bought this separately, and I put it on the back of the Bentley indicating I had permission to drive the Bentley—which is 4-wheel drive—over the ten miles of sand out to the point on Nantucket Island. You could only take jeeps and major 4-wheel drive SUVs out there. I put this on the blog and said, "This is probably the first Bentley ever to be granted an over-sand driving permit in Nantucket." People wrote back and said, "That's quite a distinction; I'm sure you're proud." Finally, I had to tell people it was a gag. So, you have to be careful not just to protect yourself, but you have to be careful that you don't inadvertently cause harm.

Q: Let's go back to another point you mentioned earlier. I read some established, credible authors—in both their books and on the web—give examples of more and more corporate executives spending time online and monitoring the social media and the web, especially the younger generation executives are part of the grid as it is. You seem to obviously feel otherwise. Is it possible that perhaps we haven't figured out an effective way of using social media to talk to those corporate buyers?

Alan: I think you have to separate out several things here. People have a way of treating debate as an on and off switch, and it's really a rheostat. Here is what is happening in this case. There is no question that younger executives and younger managers are much more internet proficient and active on the social media platforms as well as other places. There is no question about that. But let's take a completely different issue.

There is also no question about the fact that even those younger executives are going to make major corporate buying decisions by word-of-mouth, by reference from peers, or by public intellectual property. So, the fact that they're younger and more internet savvy isn't an influence, it's not a vital factor in how people make decisions in the corporate world. We aren't talking about buying pencils here. We aren't talking about buying computer stands. When you're talking about making a $150,000 corporate purchase for consulting services, you need someone to help with a strategy formulation process, or you need someone to help redesign your organization, you're not going to use the social media platforms to find people. You're going to talk to key colleagues.

Now, if you choose to talk to those key colleagues via a personal communication while you're on Facebook with them, LinkedIn with them, or probably emailing them, fine. In the old days, you would pick up a phone or send a hard-copy letter. Today you use much more facilitative electronic means. But the fact is you aren't choosing that resource. You're asking other people about the resource. And you're asking the same people you would have asked anyway; you're just using a different venue

Q: Let me follow on this one further step, and it may sound like a Zen question, but I think it's important, and I mean it seriously. What makes something visible? What makes something visible on the internet?

Alan: What makes something visible interestingly enough is the ability of people to envision it, and so I don't really have to see it. That's why brands are so important, why word-of-mouth is so important. If I can visualize it, it's visible for me. It might not be visible for you, but it's visible for me. So, the more people who can visualize something, who can envision it, the more visible you are.

Now, what makes something visible on the internet is a somewhat different question. What makes something visible on the internet is a graphic representation, and there if you want to be visible, I think you need the consistency of a common logo, a common image, some kind of common presence and brand. And again, that's why if you think about it, my refusing to follow people on Twitter—which is so consistent with my brand—adds to my visibility because people talk about me. I don't care if people are talking about me in a disdainful way. I don't care if they say, "How arrogant." And somebody says, "Yea, who is this guy?" And they say, "Here is his address. Well, I'm going to take a look at him." That's fine. But for the purpose of this book, keep in mind that visibility is a very, very nuanced goal, and visibility on the internet is a very tactical and very specific goal.

Q: If you could wave a magic wand to create a new technology leap, what technology or what capability would you make happen if you had the power to?

Alan: I would create something that combines the iPhone's capability and the iPad's capability that I didn't have to physically carry. What I would do is I would probably try to create the old Dick Tracy wrist radio. There is still too much accouterment. There is still too much stuff you've got to carry around: chargers, cords, and all kinds of stuff. Just like I said earlier, the trouble with printers is they print paper. The trouble right now with technology is that there is too much stuff.

Building Communities—The Lifeblood of Your Business

Q: You have branded yourself as The Architect of Professional Communities. When did that become apparent to you that communities are a big thing?

Alan: It became apparent to me gradually, almost like a rash sneaking up your arm that one day you finally acknowledge. When I launched Balancing Act and other communications of value, people were engaging in interaction with each other, and I would watch people. For example, when I held mentor summits—which is one of the first communities that I really formed at somebody else's suggestion—a woman named Alice Wheaton and I would watch somebody walk along and say, "Have you done this with Alan? Have you done that with Alan?" And they would say, "Well, no." And the first person would say, "You really have to do this." There are people today who are doing that on higher and higher levels, and I began to realize the natural power in people advocating your value on your behalf: consumer evangelism.

Then what I watched in Alan's Forums was people began to answer questions, and my value was simply by dint of having brought them together. When the Forum opened, I had to answer 85 percent of the comments; and today I probably answer 10-15 percent of the comments, and part of that's correcting some people who are inadvertently giving bad advice. It's remarkable how much the community helps each other, but credit still accrues to me having brought the community together.

Q: How do you attract people to the community, and by that I mean get them to join, show up, and participate?

Alan: Let me try to confine this response to something fairly brief. People are attracted to their value, and they're attracted to their own self-interests. So, the more you can cater to people's sense of what's important to them, the more you'll draw people toward the community. There are several devices for doing that that are quite interesting.

I talked about people walking down a hallway and saying, "Have you tried this? Have you done that?" That's extraordinarily effective, and that's why, for example, I encourage people who hold breakfast meetings for prospects to seed the room with clients because there is no more powerful accolade source. That's why I advise people on their websites to have video testimonials from clients. And that's why I provide video testimonials for people in my master mentor program, and so forth. That's a really strong device to get people into communities.

Another is that some people like to be cutting edge, early adaptors, ahead of the curve, and they like to see what is going on. Now, these people can be very fickle, so once you draw them in, you want to make sure that you provide the kind of value they expect, or exceed their expectations so they stay there.

Q: Do you need a critical mass before you start this? If I don't have a lot of people in my database, but I still want to do something to start what you started as a result of the summits, what can I do?

Alan: It depends upon your medium. For example, I started Balancing Act with 40 names of people I was pretty sure would not get upset with me if I sent them a newsletter, so they were pretty safe. I started with 40 names, and today we have over 15,000 subscribers.

If you're using something like Alan's Forums, for example, which is an interactive online community, then you need a critical number of people. Some people have tried this, and they haven't succeeded because they haven't started with enough folks. We first invited maybe 1,000 people who were in my mentor program, or the Society of Advancement of Consulting, or who were in the periphery I talked about—those outer circles who could actually purchase a lifetime membership. We had two groups for free, and people who could purchase, and that constituency was about 1,000 people. We got a few hundred right away—we have over 1,000 people and over 120,000 posts—and it's creating its own momentum. So, that medium required a much larger priming of the pump in order to be successful.

Q: You said people join communities to serve their own self-interest. What has happened with some of your communities is that there has become what you call a water cooler effect. How do you balance that people sometimes need that social part of it, and then sometimes they need to be challenged to get back to the work part of it?

Alan: I don't think there is any problem with a small social aspect to it, but it primarily has to be more than that because there are other ways people can get that social interaction by devices that are more oriented toward that in the community in which you live, in various professional groups you join.

Today, people get it from LinkedIn, Facebook, Plaxo, and things like that. So, a certain amount of that's fine. People kidding each other, joshing with each other, congratulating each other, but the primary emphasis has to be on the self-interest that got them there. Nobody came to my communities primarily for a social exchange. People came to my communities to learn, and specifically to learn in terms of professional services and entrepreneurialism. Anything around that is peripheral to it, and that's fine.

I got a call this morning from a mentoree who deals with a very complex subject in firms—public recognition, crisis management, and things like that. He was asking me how Newport was last week because I was in Newport doing a workshop on self-esteem, and we couldn't speak last week. He called me today and said, "How was Newport?" I said, "Fine. What's on your mind?" I don't engage socially on those kinds of calls, or I would spend another month or year doing it, and that's not why people are calling me. I don't need that kind of icebreaker, and since I don't need it, he doesn't need it.

Q: Some of your communities are virtual, yet so many people in your communities have built personal and business relationships. Can you map out for us how this has happened and how people have taken advantage of going beyond just knowing each other virtually?

Alan: What you're talking about is a single continuum. We love to call things virtual today, but what we mean by that isn't in person. So, it's important to specify that because virtual has taken on this mystical meaning.

Language has two components to it—one is scientific and one is sort of mystical or magical. We tend to assign these magical elements sometimes to language, but virtual is just like war being the least subtle form of communication. Where are we in the continuum?

People who deal with each other who are introduced to each other in a world where they aren't meeting personally—a mastermind group, an internet chat room, a teleconference where people are asking questions, and all these various things I do—often decide that they would like to get together personally because you can't beat personal interaction. So, what do I do? I provide them with the option to do that. Rather than forcing them to find some other way to do that, I provide workshops. I provide mentor summits. I provide "Alan's New York."

I provide all kinds of diverse experiences where people can come together, meet their colleagues in person, and have that opportunity. That way they remain in my overall community, and they're getting even more value by being able to move left and right on that continuum in any way they choose.

If you think about what we were discussing earlier—which is there has to be a core where the gravity is greatest—that's the opportunity for any of us to be at the center of a community. You can't dismiss or underemphasize the fact that if a person is creating this community to draw people, that it isn't just based on a Facebook kind of mindless interaction. There has to be tremendous value there. There has to be intellectual property. There has to be cutting edge thought. There has to be an object of interest. There has to be the opportunity to see, hear, do, and experience things that otherwise wouldn't be available or at least would be much tougher; and certainly, several of these experiences wouldn't be available in the same place.

Q: How does a newcomer to the Forum quickly establish to whom they should listen? Second, as the Forum owner, what is your responsibility to filter some of those ideas so by virtue of lack of participation on your part, that you may agree with the idea if you're merely passive?

Alan: If you engage in any community and you're the newcomer, I think you need to take some time—and that time might be a week or it might be two sessions—where you start to judiciously discriminate among people who are providing a fact and people who are providing opinion. I think it's also always useful to look at people who a year or two ago are where you are now. Besides just looking at the center of the community—who by definition will be a thought leader and an all-star in that particular field—look at people who were where you are now a year or two ago, understand what they're talking about, and say to yourself, "Is this reasonable, pragmatic, and truthful in terms of how I can be helped?"

Stay away from people who just express opinion on everything and don't really demonstrate any evidence of being successful themselves. As I say on my Forum all the time, *there is no faculty*. I'm not interested in people who just tell and don't ask. And I get upset with people—and I've chased some away advertently and inadvertently—who don't want to ask, and who just want to tell people. I don't want people pontificating.

As the new participant, you should always feel free to ask the person who is in the center of the community. People have done that with me and say, "Listen, I've been listening or following so and so, and I'm just not sure about this. What would your recommendation be?" And I'll always say to them, "Between you and me—this is great advice," or "Between you and me—this part is good, and the other part he doesn't know what he is talking about," or "Between you and me—ignore her."

Now, that leads me to the second part of your question. If you have a community that's interactive, you have to engage in it. If it's in writing, as it would be on an online chat room, every once in a while I've had to clobber somebody. Sometimes people have their facts wrong, and they need to be corrected, and sometimes their opinion has no basis in reality.

I'm willing to listen to Peter Drucker's opinions; before he passed away, his opinions were worth a lot to me. I'm not willing to listen to somebody's opinions who hasn't been there and done that. Some people just like to grandstand.

It's your responsibility as the center of the community to be present. As you know, I'm on the Forum every single day. I'm pumping new intellectual property into my blog three, four, five times a week, and I always respond to commentary on my blog either "yea or nay." I'm always trying to be present where there is interactive possibilities; differences of opinion are fine, but distortions of reality are not.

Q: We talked earlier about the benefits to Forum members from the water cooler effect to growing intellectually, creating great business, and personal relationships. Yet one of the rules that we've established for the community and the Forum is no promotion of products and services. What are other various rewards that you feel members can gain from the Forum without their ability to promote their products and services?

Alan: A community is a learning environment, not a selling situation. If you want to come to a community to sell, then you belong on LinkedIn, Facebook, or Twitter where you can openly promote, and they encourage you to do so. You can have pages, groups, and send invitations. Those are designed for that kind of thing. I don't think they're very effective, but they're designed for that.

But when you come to what I call a learning community, you should be prepared to learn, not sell. You should be prepared to listen more than speak. So, the advantages are you'll learn best practices—for free. You'll hear from not only the center of the community but from some people who are tops in their field—for free. You can try out your own thoughts, approaches, and methodology by expressing them intelligently and see how people react—for free.

Even if you're in a part of the community for which you pay—for example, my Friday Wrap, the workshops that I run, and similar experiences—nonetheless, the fees are relatively inexpensive compared to the return. For the Friday Wrap—which can be as little as $500 or as much as $750, but still very reasonable—you'll get 24 hours of programming and hear techniques on a continuing basis that will improve your business. For those who are more advanced, you can join something like my thought leadership conference for $12,000, and you're going to be elbow to elbow with other people at your level. You're going to hear directly, in person, from me and Marshall Goldsmith or David Maister or Meg Wheatley—top people in the country in their fields. It's harder and harder to grow as substantially unless you do something like this.

Q: Many consultants reading this are focused on the wholesale, corporate side of consulting. How would you go about building a community if you were doing the OD work today that you were doing 15, 20, 25 years ago at Merck, HP, and other large companies?

Alan: I'm asked that question all the time. When I was running the west coast office for a consulting firm in San Francisco, I actually created communities. I invited all of our buyers to a conference over the course of two days at which the people who worked for me would make presentations about the work we all knew that they were engaged in, the services that they had purchased from us, problem solving, decision making, and planning skills. We also had guest speakers come in, somebody from the local government, and somebody from the local college.

I had a fellow come in once from the University of Southern California who talked about how to create intelligent career paths. So, we actually created that community, and then I reinforced it by putting out a publication called *Origins* because our company had begun out there. Now, I have to tell you, the people in the corporate office nearly had a fit. We had a corporate PR guy, a Ph.D. in some unrelated field, who was clueless. Instead of seeing this as a benefit, they saw it as a threat; fortunately, the owner of the company thought it was a great idea. So, I was creating those kinds of corporate communities back in 1978-79.

Today, you create corporate communities by looking at your marketplace and saying, "Who makes sense to include?" If chief information officers, chief financial officers, sales directors, front-line supervisors, call center managers, or you name it are key in terms of the products and services you provide, then create communities around them. People don't like to be in communities with subordinates, so you have to stay pretty pure.

I had a colleague, Michel Robert, the fellow with whom I wrote my first book *The Innovation Formula*. He was successful in gathering 20 CEOs at a time to a conference, and he would invite in someone like Henry Kissinger to speak. So, as long as you do it well and there is recognition of your value and talent, you can create these corporate communities without a whole lot of difficulty.

Q: What are the essential steps to convert this interest from a wholesale engagement to a retail engagement?

Alan: I'm not sure you want to. I thought you were going to ask me the other question actually. First, I'm not sure they have the money for it. Secondly, I'm not sure it's even appropriate to think about that.

I would go the other way and say, "What I really have here are retail customers in a wholesale operation. How do I go upscale? How do I get wholesale business out of this?" I would think that management, seeing the people who are working with you outperform people who aren't working with you, would want to engage you on a larger and larger basis.

Q: So this delineation I'm perceiving what you articulate there is—you've got to differentiate between the buyers and the people you engage who aren't the buyers. If you're looking to convert a wholesale engagement into a community outside the company, it's appropriate to do it at the buyer level but not necessarily the subordinate level.

Alan: Yes. There are two ways to convert wholesale to retail. One is you're working with high-level people, and they decide that they would like to work with you individually. So, now you've got a retail customer in that wholesale client. Typically, that's coaching at high levels.

The other way to do it is to take the processes you've used at the whole-sale level and apply them separately to the retail level on a basis that people can afford and where volume makes more sense. Let's just suppose you're engaged in a corporation with teaching these middle managers you talked about better decision making skills. Then you decide that it worked so well, and it doesn't have to be restricted to a corporate setting, that you launch a decision making teleconference series—12 teleconferences, one a month for a year—and you charge $1,000 for an individual to attend that, and it's open to the general public. That's how I would make that conversion.

Q: If a corporate event were $30,000, to replace it with a retail experience you either need to get 100 people paying $300, or 10 people paying $3,000, or perhaps 20 people paying $1,500, just making the numbers up. Can you take us through how you would design an experience in the retail commu-nity that somehow replaces the corporate engagements?

Alan: Let me just push back a bit. I'm not sure I would want to replace it. These aren't mutually exclusive, and so you might choose to replace it, but this could easily be an addition to it, so I don't think it's either/or here. If you wanted to take a discipline that you were applying on the wholesale, corpo-rate level and say, "How can I also apply that on the individual, retail level?" what I would be asking myself is, "How could I do this for the most number of people with the least labor intensity?" So, I would look at my market and say, "Who is most likely to purchase this value on an individual basis, and in what form or forms would it be most attractive?"

If you took a look at senior managers, or entrepreneurs, or people making consumer kinds of sales—let's say car sales people, or insurance sales people, or something like that—you would isolate who those people are and how they would probably purchase. Some of them, for example people sell-ing insurance, are much more likely historically to purchase training than people who sell automobiles. That just happens to be a fact, and I wouldn't try to change that fact; I would go with the flow.

People who are entrepreneurs have a tendency to think they know it all, and so you have to be careful about that marketplace. They're also very, very busy, and they don't use their time well. So, you have to say, "How would I best reach them, and how could I best convince them to make a quick purchase?" I think the best ways to do this are you offer some free value. You prime the pump by offering some free value first, then you get testimonials from people who have used it, and then you hit them repeatedly. The old advertising concept that you have to hit people repeatedly is still very true today. That's how I would organize around that kind of retail market place.

What I would do then—since acquisition is always much more difficult than sustaining things—once I had them into the net once they purchased something or were a part of the community, I would keep providing them with value. I would keep after them to become more and more deeply involved, to go more toward the inner ring, and make sure that they, in turn, became ambassadors for more new people.

Q: What other monetizing opportunities and strategies are available in terms of communities?

Alan: There are two different approaches here. They're not mutually exclusive, but you have to realize they're different. One is that the entry into the community is free, and it's the offers that come up within the community that are monetized. Alan's Forums are free for people in my various communities. Now, don't forget when I say "free," these are people who were in other communities first and paid. So, they paid $3,500 for a mentor program, they paid $400 to be in the Society for Advancement of Consulting; but once you're in my programs, you're in them.

Whatever discounts or free offers you get never expire as part of the value I provide. So, you could have been in the mentor program ten years ago and still take advantage of something that's free for mentorees today, such as newsletters or discounts to my workshops. Once you're in there— let's say you're in Alan's Forums—and you perceive you're in there for free because what you paid me was a long time ago, offers come up for various experiences.

The other approach is that the community itself costs money. If you want to join the workshop or buy the teleconference, those things cost money. The entry fee, so to speak, into that community has to be paid.

Both of those work very well. I think you have to decide how to use them in concert, and what is best for your particular audiences.

Q: At times throughout the years of Alan's Forums' existence, we've seen members stray. The beautiful thing is where other members of the Forum help in the self-discipline of colleagues, but we also had you as the owner or me as the moderator to discipline others, as well as expel a few others. For those who are interested in creating a forum, a community like this, talk about the self-discipline versus disciplining other members.

Alan: I think there are probably three issues here. The first is that just because you can do something better or faster doesn't mean you should do it. So, you want to really heighten, support, and reinforce the learning from within the community; the sort of intrinsic learning that comes out of the community because not only do people learn best that way, but it also lowers your labor intensity. Just because somebody doesn't completely answer a question, or they haven't answered it fast enough, and I think I could add something much better, I tend not to do that unless what I'm adding is really important.

I think the second thing is some people make errors, and they need to be corrected. Some of those errors are things like grammar or punctuation, and I tend to be a purist on that because I want to set the right standard to my communities. But some of the errors are historical fact, or their beliefs about the profession, or they're using a tertiary source, and I'll point that out and challenge them on it if I have to.

The third issue is people who are obnoxious. These are people who have borderline personality disorders. There was one fellow on the Forum who was making points about what he did in the sales process that was superior to everyone else, and I knew he was lying because he joined the mentor program telling me he had no business at all. Then, I have to throw down the gantlet. Either they're going to change or they're going to be gone. Two or three people have changed. In one case happily so, and he has become a very integrated person in the community, and he attends a lot of events, and so forth. But I think in whatever it has been—six years of the Forum—I can think of three people who we tossed off. And frankly, that's lower than I thought it would be.

There are also some people who have left in sort of a huff. And as I've often pointed out, I'm buying stock in huff because so many people leave in it. And good riddance. That's fine. Some of them have left over dopey things. Some of them have left over what they felt were assaults or affronts to their belief systems. There was one guy who had been in the community a long time and decided that anybody who didn't believe in the severity of global warming as postulated by certain European scientists was ignorant. That was his word—"ignorant." He wouldn't back down from that, and a couple of us took him to task rather severely, and so he just retreated. He sulked, and he dropped out of my other communities. And that's fine. I just don't need that in my life. Life is too short.

Q: Talk about the time-shifting concept and how the communities complement or help it.

Alan: The reason that communities are so popular is exactly for that reason. One of the things we've never been able to overcome is communicating well globally. And you don't need Steven Hawking to tell you this. Yet, *per capita*, I probably have more mentorees in Australia than anywhere else in the world, so I have a lot of reasons to communicate there daily, despite having visited 16 times.

But it's a long trip, and you land and it's a different day, different time, different season, and a different friggin universe! You have to acclimate yourself. It's a lovely country with great people.

What the communities allow you to do, and what technology allows you to do within the communities, is to post something or say something and allow the other person to respond at each person's convenience. When I put out an offer for the Friday Wrap, it went out overnight on an automated system. I think the first four or five registrants I had were from Europe because Europe, depending where you live, is six or seven hours ahead of the eastern seaboard in the States, and so they received this before anybody else.

Q: You talk about the concept of reciprocating exponential value or REV, in short. How are communities related to this concept or vice versa?

Alan: That's a community. That's the premise of a community. That's everything we've been talking about. When people join communities, they get value. But by dint of their presence, they gain value from others. Critical mass, attractive people, good ideas, which bring their own inherent and intrinsic value, and they attract still others.

The exact analogy for this is the iPhone app. That's where I got it from. The better the iPhone was, the more people wanted to create apps for it. The more apps that were created, the more people were drawn to the apps, not just the phone. The more that happened, the more Apple improved the phone.

As of today, I think there are 500,000 apps—and I would guess there will be a million by the time this book is published—and more and more people are drawn, and more developers are drawn. The company is drawn to improving the product. That's what reciprocating exponential value is in terms of communities. The people represent those who are writing, creating, and benefiting from the apps. I'm the iPhone manufacturer.

Q: What have you found over the years to be the most rewarding, exciting, or perhaps even intellectually stimulating part of building these communities around you?

Alan: There are several, but the one that comes to mind first is that I'm very impatient. For example, when I plant a flower or a tree, it takes quite a while to appreciate it. I have a tree I saved outside the master bedroom and the indoor pool, and the landscapers were going to cut it down. It grew out of a railroad tie. I said, "No, no leave it. It's an evergreen. I love it." Over the years it grew beautifully, and now it's up to the second floor of our home.

There is another out by our mailbox about 200 yards away, and I see it whenever I come and go through the main gate. I just said to our tree guy earlier today, "Listen, why don't you reduce the bottom branches?" I think they call it "raising the tree." The branches used to hide a hole in the wall, but we've completely replaced the wall with a new one, so we don't need that, and I think the tree will look better without these lower branches. But it took the tree years and years to get to its present, majestic height.

In a community, you can plant something and it grows before your eyes. You don't have to wait three or four years to appreciate it. You don't even have to worry too much about nurturing it. You plant an idea sometimes and—bingo—five people say, "I'll be there." Three people say, "Write about that." Forty people say, "I need to hear more about that." And you know you're on to something. Whether your analogy is a laboratory or a garden patch, it doesn't matter. You're allowed and enabled to immediately drop things into this community and see what chemical reactions ensue, and it's a really fantastic, invigorating, and wonderfully productive environment.

Q: Of the ones that you're aware of who have tried to create communities and have been unsuccessful, what would you recommend that they do differently or could have done differently to increase the odds that their community would have been successful?

Alan: I tell people the same thing all the time with questions like this. What I tell them is, "Look at people who are successful, and decide what they're doing that you aren't doing." Seth Godin says the same thing. Marshall Goldsmith says the same thing.

Most people who are thought leaders say the same thing. Find people who are doing it well, and don't try to become them because you can't, but try to understand what they're doing. So, in terms of a community, what are people doing who are doing it well that's different from what you've done? The probability is there are going to be just three or four areas.

One is I find that people who are unsuccessful don't start with a sufficient critical mass or a sufficient brand. If you don't have critical mass but you have a strong brand, you can do it. If you don't have brand, you can have a large mailing list or critical mass, but they'll be insufficient by themselves.

The second problem is: There is nothing new. You can't just have a discussion where people are chatting about the same things or at the same level. You have to put intellectual property in there that's exciting, challenging, and provocative if it's going to work.

The third is you have to show up. If you're doing workshops, you have to put on workshops periodically throughout the year. Not the same ones necessarily, but you've got to be doing it so people have options. If it's teleconferences, they have to be periodic. If it's a chat room on the internet, you've got to be there every day. If it's a blog, you have to be there several times a week.

You have to show up. Basically, people flock to communities where they find this reciprocating exponential value. Where they find other people—like themselves or who are even doing better than themselves—have gone there, so they have a test. They have a crucible that says this stuff looks like it works. And they want to be around that person who is generating all of this. They might want to be in the inner community, touch and feel, be on a closer basis, and be able to deal one-on-one. Or they might want to be in one of the outer communities where they can just listen and learn and perhaps participate in some things and not others.

Q: You seem to have a crystal ball about things and see into the future the way other people can't. What is coming in the future for communities? What is going to change?

Alan: Chad and I were having dinner in Newport the other night, and we had a sort of interesting experience just trying to park the car. And Chad said to me later, "It seems to me that you don't create stories. Stories come to you." I've been thinking that people don't see the future so much that the future comes to them.

What I see happening is that communities are going to become differentiated. That is, some communities will be very tightly knit around a specific kind of a discipline or pursuit. In the corporate world, that would be something like a purchasing manager community. An accounts payable kind of community. One of the largest associations in the United States is the American Payroll Association.

Then I think you'll have communities that will continue to be so generalized that they're going to suffer dissipation, and they're going to suffer what the insurance people call "churn": constant turnover. That's where Facebook is clearly going. I would think that some combination of Facebook, Twitter, and LinkedIn is going to emerge at some point. But for me—and I think for highly intellectual people and people who themselves generate a lot of value—that's the last place we want to spend time.

Then I think you're going to have communities which actually replace trade associations because my communities constantly grow because there is constantly new value. I'm the master of the domain, to quote a *Seinfeld* episode, in that I decide what is here, I decide on value, and I make judgments. You could make a case for benevolent dictators. Lincoln Steffens said if we had good kings, we would all still be monarchists.

If you take something like the National Speakers Association which purportedly would be a community that caters to professional speakers, you'll find that their numbers, about 3,000 people, haven't changed in 10-12 years except the composition. In other words, their numbers haven't increased. People keep coming, dropping out, coming, and dropping out, which says there isn't enough value to hold them there. It's too egalitarian, not value-laden enough.

Communities are taking the place of trade associations, or you'll see trade associations turning into communities because that's the future for people of specialized interests. When I say specialized interests, it could be something as narrow as accounts payable, or it could be something as generalized as consulting, which is a fairly broad field. But that's what I see happening for sure.

The timing that I was asked about before, the fact that technology enables us on a global basis, makes it even more exciting. The people in these growing economies like India, China, Brazil, and so on aren't these strange people on different time zones or in different places of the world where it's hard to communicate and more.

You're going to find that there is going to be a larger emphasis, larger even than today, on using English. There are some German companies in Germany that demand English be spoken every day. It's the official language of the company, and air traffic controllers all over the world only speak English. That's going to continue to increase. For better or for worse, English is going to be the common language, and it's going to American English. So, you're going to find communities all over the place that interact, overlap, and are going to be of very high value if people are discriminating about what they choose to join, and they'll become fluent in English.

Q: In closing this discussion of communities, what were the greatest challenges that you personally experienced in building and developing communities? In what ways have you changed or been influenced by your communities?

Alan: The biggest challenge is not getting bored. I have a very low threshold of boredom. It's why I rarely do a workshop more than three times, and even when I do that, one will be in London, one will be in Sydney, or wherever. (I'll be in Berlin in January.) My challenge is not getting bored, keeping fit, and keeping excited about new things.

The wonderful aspect for me is that my communities now are so complex in their overlapping and interacting. If you watch one of these virtuosos play an organ, and I've done this several times in person, it's impossible for me to comprehend it as I watch. You have all these stops, you have four keyboards, dozens of foot pedals, and 500 pipes overhead. I don't know how they make such beautiful music with all of those choices in front of them. But I've found with my communities, I'm able to play the pipes. Perhaps you have to build the organ to play it well.

Conclusion

When it comes to technology, leading edge isn't "over the edge." Ask yourself what technology you need to drive your strategy, and do that alone. You can always ratchet it up later if you've been too conservative, but it's very costly to back away from a major investment made because you were imprudent.

Technology isn't something you should do yourself. Find an excellent technical guru or company that will build and evolve your web presence and technology needs. The outstanding ones will also proactively suggest innovations and leading-edge projects for your consideration. Don't waste your time attempting to be your own technologist—unless you're also advising prospects not to hire you and to serve as their own consultants!

Life Balance   12

Thrive

Anyone who has achieved success in life, or expects to, deserves to enjoy it in *support* of, not at the expense of, life priorities. During our lives and careers, we often seem to confuse our priorities, shifting our focus so that we end up with clients whom we know extremely well and families who are *de facto* strangers. Everyone has equal time—about 24 hours a day. When we say we don't have time for something, we really mean that we haven't set that activity as a priority. We need to do better—to blend life, work, and relationships in a way that helps us work smarter *and live better*.

Balance What?

Q: What convinced you to write *Thrive* and then develop a workshop experience following the book?

Alan: I wrote *Thrive* because I had always wanted to do a book on how one should face life not as a victim but as a victor. To face life with a philosophy of abundance and not scarcity.

I was in Birmingham, England a couple of years ago. I had done a keynote, and I was sitting in the back with another outstanding keynoter, Randy Gage, who was going to be on later that day. The two of us were watching the person they brought in from Africa to talk about whatever his subject was. He did this tribal music, talked about tribes, the importance of tribes, and the fact that you have to stick together because everybody is against you. After about seven minutes of this stuff, Randy looked at me and said, "There's another speaker espousing a poverty mentality and victimology." I said, "God you're right."

I can't stand it on a personal level. I can't stand it when people prescribe victimhood as a life direction, and so I wanted to write *Thrive* divorced from professional and business goals. I already had written *Life Balance*. The subtitle is "How to Convert Professional Success Into Personal Happiness." I did that for Wiley. It was the seventh book in my Ultimate Consultant series, so I didn't need to do that again. I wanted to write this book on how you focus on creating a life for yourself where your destiny is largely in your own hands, and love drives out problems. It's okay to be in love with yourself, as well as love others and have others love you, and I think it's even something John espouses in his Gospel.

I talked to my agent about it, and we couldn't get publishers interested to the extent that I could do the book my own way. They were looking at things like *The Secret* and all this kind of fluff that's out there that I really don't believe in. I just said, "The heck with it. At this point in my life, I can certainly self-publish a hardcover book, and that's what I'm going to do."

I hired somebody to manage it, a general manager, Elaine Floyd—and let me give her a plug because she is superb. She got a hold of R.R. Donnelley who prints for McGraw-Hill, Wiley, and all the big publishers. Everything we did was top rate, and I wrote the book the way I wanted to write it, and since then it has been on Amazon. It's electronic, as well, compatible with Kindle, iPad, e-books, and with means yet to be invented.

Q: You also have your book *Life Balance*. Could you help us understand a distinction—the differences between life balance and thriving?

Alan: Life balance is about the professional and personal parts of your life and how you synergize them, how they can be in harmony, and how you don't have a personal life and a professional life—you have a life. How do those blend together? It needn't be 50/50, but it shouldn't be 99/1.

What is true life balance about? In *Thrive* I write about how you take command, and you live a life that's meaningful for yourself that gives you energy. This morning as we're recording this, it's 11:35 eastern, and I've been up since 7:30. I went with my wife to work out at 8:00 this morning and again refrained from killing my trainer. In fact later this week, I have to give him a Christmas present, which just irks me. In any case, I came home, cleaned up, and we have people here cleaning the house and doing the windows. We have three dogs here because my son is back. We have three dogs, two grandchildren, and two of our kids. Our kids fight the same way they did 30 years ago, and of course, my wife takes it out on me.

In the midst of this, I'm writing a book. I took another person into the Total Immersion program who is going to work personally with me. I have plans to do about 12 things today and maybe knock off by 2:00. It's an energizing day, and a day that would put other people, I think, to bed or knock the pins out from under them. I'm doing fabulous, I'm energized, I feel great, and there are all kinds of things I want to do.

My external drive quit, and my computer keeps giving me notices. I got on, ordered a new drive, had it FedEx'd, it will be here tomorrow, and I'll plug it in. When you thrive, you take control of your life, and the little things that inevitably go wrong, ineffably go wrong, you fix. You do something about it, and you get on with it. Things are rather good, and I believe that you create your own perpetual motion machine where the more you do, overcome, create, and improve, the more energy it gives you to do more of that. If you direct that to your personal life, not just your business, you're someone who can help others and thereby help yourself.

Q: In the workshop, one thing that resonated with me was you stated the following four steps as critical in the thriving mindset. You talked about skills acquisition, skill development, resilience, and then thrive. Can you articulate it further?

Alan: I think to thrive you need pragmatics. I don't think you need motivational tapes. I don't think you're going to trot over hot coals (which continue to injure people, by the way). I don't think there's a secret. I don't think there's a prophesy. What I do think is that you thrive by acquiring pragmatic skills and competencies. One of the greatest ones, of course, is language. You acquire them, you apply them, and you're successful at them. That gains you resilience.

When your locus of learning is outside, you realize that if you fail, you can acquire still more learning and overcome the obstacle the next time. If your locus of learning is completely internal—people who don't read books, don't invest in their development, they think they know everything they need to know—when you fail, you're non-resilient and become depressed. You don't have any bounce back because you've shot your bolt. You've done everything you can.

A brief digression, but that phrase—shot your bolt—comes from medieval crossbowmen. These people had to shoot an arrow—a bolt—with a crossbow, and then they had to rewind the crossbow to gain tension again. They were very vulnerable before they could put another bolt in, so for about

60 seconds they were very, very subject to getting themselves killed. Consequently, having shot your bolt is dangerous.

With an internal locus, you shoot your bolt. An external locus you can take more and more ammunition—that's the resilience—and thriving means that you're never as low as your last defeat or bad piece of feedback, and you're never as high as your best piece of feedback or last victory. You have a constant sense of self-esteem and self-worth, and that's what I wanted to do with the workshop. The first one I ran I was very, very happy with, and I'm running another one in Berlin in another month because I wanted to try it in Europe and see what it looked like there. I already have 13 or 14 people in that session, and we'll probably wind up with 18, my goal, which is going to be great.

Q: When you talk about the locus of learning, is that also the distinction that you often talk about between implicit versus explicit knowledge? Are both of them critical for the mindset of thriving?

Alan: They're critical, but they're very different. Implicit and explicit knowledge means the following: Implicit knowledge is knowledge that you have in your head which you can viscerally apply. If somebody asks me, "Who composed 'White Christmas'?" I can tell them it was Irving Berlin. Ironically, he was a Jewish man writing under palm trees in Los Angeles, and he composed the greatest selling music of all time about a Christian holiday. I don't have to look that up on Google. I don't have to check things out. I can use my memory banks to do that. That's implicit knowledge I possess.

Explicit knowledge is knowledge that you gain from someone else to apply. If I asked Chad, "How could I put cartoons up on my blog and do that myself?" he would tell me. Once you tell me and if I master it, it becomes implicit knowledge. If you use my Irving Berlin example and you spread that to others, my implicit knowledge has become explicit.

This has to happen in companies. It's a key part of consulting work. The mass of the company's knowledge—which is explicit—is in manuals and on the intranet. It's talked about. It has to be implicit so I can use it when it's needed. We've all seen people who come to you with the same question over and over. They haven't been able to make explicit information implicit. We all know people who, despite the fact they're good at their job, can't teach others. They can't make their implicit knowledge explicit.

Q: What are some concrete ideas for achieving balance in our personal life and life as a consultant?

Alan: I think that a consultant is best when she or he focuses on intellectual breath and firepower—which enriches personal life and carries over to personal life—as opposed to merely becoming a better and better consultant—which doesn't carry over anywhere. That's a vertical thrust. I think your thrust should be with breadth, and the more breadth you have, ironically, perhaps kind of intuitively, the better the consultant you are.

In any pursuit, in any discipline, in any craft, in any profession, the people I've met who can talk the most about the most things despite their specialty are the people whom I think are best at their specialty. If I meet a great violinist and all that violinist can talk about is the violin, the strings, the structure, and the music but can't talk about how people learn, appreciate music, why some concert halls are better than others, or the role of music in society, he or she is simply not as interesting a person and I don't think as good a violinist.

Q: Let's talk about the role of work in our lives. You've often said that work is the fuel for our lives. Can you explain what you mean by that? How we should view work in this whole balancing act?

Alan: I believe that money is fuel for our lives, and I think wealth is discretionary time, not money; you don't have to keep filling up. You don't have to keep creating fuel. You create as much fuel as you need for your wealth. For some people that discretionary time might be the ability to take a few vacations a year. For others it might be to have their weekends free, and for others a three-day weekend. For me, it's the ability to work no more than 20 hours a week if I possibly can. There are different amounts of wealth given different people's proclivities and predispositions. Money is just fuel for that.

Work to me is one key and perhaps primary feature to *create* money because you can *get* money from investments. You can get money from inheriting it. You can get money from stealing it. There are other ways to get money, and work is the most widespread, legitimate form of creating money which can lead to wealth if you use it correctly.

But work varies. It varies because some people love their jobs, love what they do, and others don't. Some entrepreneurs are extremely happy being their own boss, others hate it. Some people working in organizational life are miserable working for others, but some people love it. The key is that the work you do should engage as many of your talents as it possibly can which will give you gratification in the work and on the job. The fewer of your talents exercised at your work, the unhappier you're going to be. It has nothing to do with the generation of money.

Q: Let's talk about those people you just referred to who really love their work, and many of the people reading this will fall into this category. Many of us are passionate about our work, and we like most of the aspects of what we do. How do we put that aside to pursue other aspects of our lives, and where are the lines of demarcation?

Alan: I don't think you need to, and I don't think you need them. I think if you have processes you use in your work, they're applicable to your life and vice versa. Conflict resolution, setting priorities, sharing credit, accepting blame—those are universal no matter what you're engaged in at the moment.

Further, I think that you need to free yourself. People need to free themselves of the guilt associated with being on a cruise, let's say, and suddenly thinking about work. That's quite all right, just as it's fine at 10:00 on a Tuesday morning to stop doing work and think about a cruise you want to take; we have to free ourselves from these arbitrary lines of demarcation. The original line of demarcation was drawn by the Pope so the Spanish and Portuguese would stop fighting about the new world. I don't think we need that arbiter any more, and you certainly don't need that kind of bifurcation in your own brain.

Q: In your experience working with so many different consultants, if a particular person doesn't really feel as though work is work, and by that I mean a burden, is there any danger of burning out or doing too much? Should we even think about that or worry about that?

Alan: If one considers work as a pleasant experience because that person is using his or her talents extensively and getting a lot of joy out of it, that's wonderful. The only problem would be if that person solely obtained their joys and gratification from that source and only applied their talents there and that didn't occur in other aspects of their life.

For example, I was asked by Boston University to be a guest lecturer one night in their extension program on entrepreneurialism, life balance, and so on. This was a group of about 40 very successful, high-power entrepreneurs who met over the course of the semester. I came in one of their evenings, and we had a very good discussion, except a lawyer in the back raised his hand and said, "I work 80 hours a week on the law. I love the law. I love helping my clients. I love getting them out of scrapes. I love helping them recover things that are due them. I'm very good at the law, and when I'm not with clients, I study the law to get better at it. What's wrong if that's 98.9 percent of my life?" I said, "Do you have a family?" He said, "I have a wife and two young kids." I said, "That's what's wrong with it." You have to use some judgment about what you as a functioning, productive, constructive, and contributing human being owe to those around you.

Q: What challenges have you seen consultants face with regard to trying to plan balance in their life, in other words plan vacations? That's very scary if some work comes up and I've already paid for that cruise that you were talking about. What advice do you have for people?

Alan: There are two aspects of this. One is the stuff you should plan for that's just what you said: vacations, family gatherings, family events, birthdays, anniversaries, and so on. I think you have to plan the next year at least three months before the year starts, and then the family dates become sacrosanct because at that point you probably don't have any engagements. If you did, let's say you promised someone you would go to South Africa or Australia in November, then you work around that. Otherwise, you plan your vacations and family events and then work around *them*. It's as simple as that, and you stop worrying about missing something to make money. You can make money in other ways. In nearly 30 years in this business, I can only recall two occasions when I had to say to a client, "I can't make that, can we change the date?" and the client said, "No, we can't change the date. It's that date. It's a single day conference we wanted you to keynote." For consulting and longer conferences, it's relatively simple to change plans.

The second point is that you can over-plan, and I don't believe very much in planning. I don't believe in business plans at all, and I think that you have to be light on your feet, nimble, agile, and able to make sharp turns. As a solo practitioner, you should be in a speedboat or a sports car, not in a supertanker, so you can skirt around obstacles and accelerate towards opportunities.

Q: I believe you just completed a Million Dollar Consulting® College. I don't know which number this was, but you often speak about how to thrive; and every situation is a new learning. What new learning have you found this time in the Million Dollar Consulting College?

Alan: I don't know what number it was either. I looked on my computer because I keep a separate file for each, and I think it was 16. What I learned from this past consulting college was that I always have scholarships in these colleges. I never announce who it is, but I always have people who are there for free because I believe in paying back. I have these seats in the college, and unless I'm absolutely filled and it ruins the learning dynamic, I offer them. I had two such people in here, and they contributed vitally to the class, just great to the class. I realized that I'm not just doing them a favor, even though my intent was simply to do people a favor; it rebounded to help me, and that's what doing something for others does. They enriched the class, and they made it a much greater dynamic and learning experience. In the future, I have to keep in mind that I have to make sure I choose people, which I've been doing inadvertently, who can also contribute to others, and that's their payment for being there.

The second thing I learned is that as your brand builds, your audience gets more sophisticated. I'm going to do a process visual on this, and I'm going to work on this some more. I've just begun to think about it, but what caught my attention was this group seemed a little more sophisticated than the last group. I had a woman in there who was in a group about two years ago, and she thought it was more sophisticated than her group. They got along better than most other groups. Everyone checked their ego at the door. There were no egos in the room, and I felt that they were very highly participative even though it was a relatively small group of ten people. The course is designed for 15, and I realized that all of these people were accustomed to my work and were coming in with a higher level of knowledge and a higher degree of their own preparation.

The final thing that was reinforced for me in terms of my own learning was when I went around the room, which I don't usually do, and asked, "How did each of you hear of me?" they each heard of me from one of two sources. Either they read one of my books, in this case it was usually *Million Dollar Consulting* or *Getting Started in Consulting*, or they heard me speak somewhere at a very low price or free. For example, I was doing pro bono work at a chapter meeting or something like that, and they heard me speak.

It was one of those two sources, and you can see the power of the accelerant curve and the low barrier of entry up on the top left because these people were all sitting in a $14,500 program.

I just did a program in Key West in early December, and two of the people in that program who didn't come through my auspices, whom I had never met before, have both signed up for Total Immersion. One is a licensed psychiatrist, and the other has a great piece of intellectual property and spends half the year in Australia, so I'm thrilled to have these two new people. The upper left-hand side of the accelerating curve with low barrier to entry is important even for somebody at my stage of the game, and it keeps reinforcing itself right in front of you.

Q: Let's refer back to something you mentioned a minute ago about the person who spends 70 or 80 hours a week in the law. I think it's fair to say that the average American in the last decade is working some 15 or 20 hours a week more than they were 30 years ago. In the '70s and '80s, it wasn't customary to put in 60 or 70 hours a week. Extreme careers have increasingly appeared with the rise of technology-driven start-ups and global 24/7 access. Can you put this phenomenon in perspective for us, and where do you think it's going?

Alan: First, right now American workers have just about the highest productivity performance in the world, far higher than Europeans, Germans, and the Japanese. It's one of the very highest in the world because American workers—despite what you might hear about unions, the American lifestyle, and everything else—are highly conscientious and work very hard.

Secondly, the economic trauma and volatility we've been through has encouraged people to want to keep their jobs, and the easiest way to keep their jobs is to show that they're working hard. That hard work might be physical labor, more ideas, staying late on a case, or whatever it is. It could be service or a product, but those are the conditions that obtain—and that's stimulated longer and longer work hours—both the normal productivity and work ethic in America. The Germans receive 8 or 12 weeks of vacation. You can't run a productive workforce that way, and then the threat of perhaps losing your job despite your competence is a problem.

The third issue is technology that you alluded to. I'm convinced I haven't seen anyone else write about this, and I'm certainly not going to write a technology book on my own. I'm convinced technology has caused subtle discontinuities in society that people are just beginning to realize.

Number one is technology creates more ambiguity, not less. There are more choices, there are more options. There is more uncertainty. You're not even sure if your sources are correct. You have Wikipedia and can't be sure what you're looking at is correct because of the contribution system they have. At one point, they had both Senator Byrd and Ted Kennedy dead while they were still breathing. As far as I'm concerned, as a reference source, that's not very good, and you have this increasing uncertainty and ambiguity caused by technology and everyone's rapid access to it.

The second problem you have is paralysis because of all the choices. I've often talked about the example that I have, I don't know, 250 satellite stations on any car radio, and I only program six of them and usually only listen to three of those. I could hit the BBC when I wanted to, but it's just too much of a pain in the neck. Then you look at cable television, On Demand, or Apple TV and are faced with thousands of choices.

I told you earlier that I worked out this morning. My personal trainer opened a new place, and he got more space by taking over half of a Blockbuster operation. Blockbuster is going out of business because they can't adapt to all this new competition. Technology creates this plethora of choices that tend to paralyze people. They don't know what to do next, what's best for them, and sometimes it's not even worth trying to pursue it, just saying, "I'll take that one."

I talk about this in *Thrive* and *Life Balance,* between working hard and working smart. Too many people are working hard, and worse, too many people are confusing working hard with working smart. Those people who can corral, harness, and lasso technology so that it enables them to work smarter and not harder are going to be the ones who succeed the best.

The final thing is I would predict unless some actions are taken on a federal level in the United States, the big problem in the next decade is going to do with the huge chasm between knowledge and non-knowledge. The education system, ironically, is the best in the world here at the university level; but in the western developed countries, it's among the worst at the primary and secondary levels. Unless we change that, we're going to find people who have access to good schools, or the personal discipline to work harder, or the personal talents to be able to gather, harness, and utilize knowledge better than those who don't have that opportunity. That's going to be worse than a wage gap.

Q: Many of us work with large companies. What are some tips we can offer them? How do you see the workplace in large companies shifting and changing with what you just indicated? What are some keys to help them thrive and lead a better balanced life when many of them communicate globally and work ten hours or more a day?

Alan: I think that what you'll find is that the smart companies, the well-led companies will realize that there's a certain amount of residual talent they need to keep on board which they can't expose to the volatility of the market. They can't expose to downsizing or to competing offers, and you'll see organizations that develop a new brand of loyalty of highly regarded people to create a trusting relationship. Different companies will define that in different ways, but those people with that kind of knowledge, expertise, or contribution will be very highly regarded and will be given excellent opportunities in terms of benefits and pay to stay with the company. The company will identify not only residual help but also transient help, and they'll have no trouble subcontracting, hiring temporary workers, hiring a pair of hands or even a brain which they'll use for a given project and duration.

I also think that organizations will understand that they need to be active and aggressive in creating communities and customer forums. They'll want customers to talk to each other no matter how negatively because if you can control, influence, or even monitor the communications, you'll find what you're really doing wrong. You'll find that you're being accused of being wrong but you're not, and you'll see opportunities that you can do better.

To give you an example, I'm doing a session called "Framed" in Sarasota about how you quickly frame a discussion, frame a client engagement, and frame a marketing meeting. My suspicion is I'll probably do that again—maybe in London or Sydney and the United States again—but I already have 40 people in it.[1] That came out of one of my communities where somebody said, "You keep talking about these framing skills. I listened to a framing CD that you produced from a teleconference. Would you do a session?" I said, "If 12 people sign up, I'll do one." Twelve people in my Forum community immediately signed up. Then I began to market it, and now I have 40 people

---

1.   These were, indeed, also conducted in those cities.

so far. That's going to be, just on its current basis, direct revenue of $50,000 or $60,000 and indirect revenue of another $50,000 or $60,000. By that I mean people who sign up for the mentor program and do other things, so there is an indirect and direct day of about $100,000 still six weeks out. If large companies do that, and you multiply it times $100,000 times the kind of effort they can put into it, you begin to see the power of organizations forming communities, designing things according to their customers, and abandoning things that their customers have no interest in. It's a very powerful new force, and that's really where I see organizations going most profitably.

Q: What about the later stages of one's career? Are we seeing a transition to a different model, different concept about the later stages of a person's career?

Alan: You gave me a softball here that I can't resist. The thing about the Prussian army, especially under Frederick the Great, was that they marched well and had brilliant uniforms. Their field maneuvers were wonderful, and they were a large group of people. They only had one problem. When somebody finally had the guts to fight them, they collapsed. They were a brilliant army for show—sort of like McClellan with the Union army when he was commander in chief under Lincoln before Lincoln sacked him—but the Prussians couldn't fight, and they got whipped.

The retirement age is the same thing. It's a chimera. Airline pilots argue very sensibly that age 60 is a ridiculous time for company policy to put them out on the street because if their health is good, at that stage they've learned more than any other pilots in the skies, and they should be flying the most sophisticated planes. I don't care if my pilot is 70 if he's in good health. If he has 500,000 flight hours, that's the person I want. Who do you think is landing the A380 which blows a Rolls Royce engine? This guy Sullenberger who safely put the US Air jet down in the Hudson—20,000 flight hours—was an expert. You can make a case *prima fascia* that it doesn't make any sense to retire competent people at a given age—because they can get even better.

The second thing is that people are living longer, and the third is that the retirement system in the United States is based on a mathematical artifact. Under Roosevelt in the '30s and '40s, there were 14 people working for every retired person. If you contributed to Social Security, you supported the people who were no longer working, and you put money in the system to support you when you retired. Today, I believe the number is three people working for every retired person, the math simply doesn't work any more, and people have to work longer.

The irony is you see people rioting in Greece or Ireland because the government wants to raise the retirement age. In the UK they want to start having people pay for their own college tuition, and people are rioting against this when they had record-level deficits, are virtually insolvent, and they don't have the resources that the United States has to bail themselves out. What are they thinking? Who is going to take care of them? Are they all going to become German dependents!? It's not going to work that way.

Retirement is going to become simply one of these words that goes by the boards. People are going to want to work. They might not work 40 hours a week. They might work 20. They might work 60. It's going to be up to them. They might go into second or third careers, have dual jobs, job sharing, work remotely, or be entrepreneurial.

I don't know about you, but the people who I've seen throughout my life who hit 65 and retired usually had a very tough time because all the money they had saved and scrimped went to pay for some horrendous health problem, for some relative who was unconscionably irresponsible, or they died early. I'm convinced that you can die of inactivity. You can die of boredom. Your muscles atrophy, and your brain atrophies. You need some charge every day, and I think retirement is going to go the way of vacuum tubes.

Q: If 30 to 40 years ago people went into the workforce knowing they would retire at some point, what is the new mindset if you were to frame this as a new construct? Is it realignment? Is it renewal? What name would you give it?

Alan: Gail Sheehy wrote a book called *Passages* in 1976, years ahead of its time. The fact is we go through different stages and passages of our lives, and those passages are ever changing and shifting because we're living longer and richer lives. In your scenario where people worked just to retire, people looked past the most productive, greatest potential of fun, best years of their lives to reach an age—by actuarial count when this was first implemented—where they would only live about five or six more years. That's part of the early bogus math that when people retired, they should only live five or six more years past 65. Today if you reach 65, the probability is you'll live another 20 or 25 years.

To look past the best years of your life is ridiculous. I think that the realignment is going to be that people will look at their life in stages, and they'll realize that they have things they can do in their 60s and 70s that they couldn't do before. There are things they could do in their 30s and 40s they couldn't do before. I imagine I'll stop scuba diving one of these days. I used to compete in these games that some of our friends would put on long after college ended, and I was always the winner of the sprints because I was a sprinter in school. When I hung up my cleats and retired, I was winning the sprints only by about six inches, and I said, "This is the time to end it."

You take on new things. You take on new pastimes, hobbies, interests, and because life evolves so fast technologically and non-technologically, there are so many new things that we can expose ourselves to. I think people will look at their lives in a different way, and I think that there will still be some people who look at their lives in this arbitrary and rather supercilious decade orientation that you're in your 50s, 60s, or 70s. It's really about your mental spirit, mental health, and the way you relate to others. It's your agility, ability to learn, ability to contribute, and so forth that really matters.

Q: Share with us some of your own personal goals and how you're contemplating and looking ahead at the next decade of your life.

Alan: I'm 66 at the moment and constantly reinvent myself, and I realize that in my late 60s, I'm going to probably reinvent myself drastically because of several of the factors we've been talking about. For example, I threw a huge birthday party in New York for my 65th birthday, and people said, "Only he would throw his own birthday party!" There were people there from Germany, the UK, Canada, Australia, as well as all over the States. I'll continue to write and probably start to change my writing habits because I've written just about all I want to write on consulting (more books on the topic than anyone in history, to be exact). There are one or two more books I might do, and I'm going to redo my proposal book. Other than that, I'm going to go into other areas of writing but continue writing.

I'll probably shift my mentoring to a different kind of dimension. My Master Mentor program has about 30 people in it now, and I want to get 100 people by 2015, which looks eminently doable. I'll probably change my own approach to mentoring rather significantly, start an aggressive coaching program, and I'm having fun playing around with what that will look like. I want to run experiences. It will be an experience in Nantucket. I want to run some workshops on spirituality. I see my life taking on new challenges, going into new areas, learning new things, but also helping people to come along with me so that I'm happy to be on the horse with the lantern saying, "Follow me. I'll take the shots, but follow me and you'll find that we'll reach the other side." That's what I'm looking forward to doing.

Two weeks ago I picked up my fourth Bentley. It's one of the most powerful cars in the world. Certainly, the most powerful Bentley ever produced. I'm looking forward to my next one, so that's what life is about.

Every day is new and different, and every day brings newer and newer ideas. I said to you before I had that idea about something I'm just beginning to toy with. For me, it's a matter of culling down what I want to work on next, and the biggest discipline I've had to learn over the years is the ability to be patient enough to work on one thing at a time because there are just so many things I want to do. I started building models again—I haven't built models for over ten years. I had a new library created, it has great display cases, I just finished a new model, and I'm starting on another one. That's minor stuff for someone else, but when you look at the diversity of my life, my days are just filled with wonderful things.

Q: This is a fascinating discussion. I could sit here and listen all day long.

Alan: The three of you have to come sit in my library. We'll have some Johnny Walker Blue, smoke cigars, and we'll talk.

Q: During the Thrive workshop experience, we talked about the concept that there is nothing wrong with making bad choices occasionally. However, when we make them consistently, there is something dreadfully wrong with it. Why do some people keep making bad choices, and what could you advise so they stop making them?

Alan: I think most people make bad choices because they're not making them for themselves. Most people who make bad choices are using criteria unrelated to themselves and what they need to do. They're making choices based upon what they determine is their obligation to others. They're making choices out of guilt. They're making choices that other people have made out of normative pressure. They're making choices that they believe are the least risky rather than the choices that have the most benefit. For all those reasons, people make bad choices, and on occasion it's therapeutic. But in most cases, it's not therapeutic. It's a question of using the wrong criteria.

I'm an Ayn Randian from way back. Anybody reading this who hasn't read *Atlas Shrugged*, hie thee to a bookstore or to a download and get it.

You have to have a healthy sense of selfishness, a healthy sense of outrage, and take care of yourself. If you take care of yourself, then you can take care of others. That's why people make lousy choices. Some people have bad decision-making systems. Some people don't look at risks. Some people don't clarify their objectives. I won't argue with all that, but I think predominantly it's because people don't make choices based on their own needs.

Q: From reading *Thrive* and attending the workshop, I learned to ask myself, "Is what I'm about to do going to further my outcome?" How do we then sharpen our ability to anticipate the outcome?

Alan: If you're going to make a decision about anything—and I just talked about this in the Million Dollar Consulting College—there are finite possibilities as to what might emerge, especially if you chart a bell curve. Within a standard deviation, there are probably three or four possibilities likely, and even within two standard deviations, there are probably no more than four or five possibilities that are likely to happen. Once you go beyond that, you're talking about mother ships coming down and taking people away into the cosmos.

If you look at those four or five possibilities, you can visualize what each will look like and prepare yourself for them. If you do that, you can prepare yourself adequately for objections that might come up, but most importantly, you can prepare yourself to exploit the success that you'll probably have, magnificently. I don't think people spend a significant or an appropriate amount of time trying to visualize and identify the possible outcomes. They're walking in blind as though they have no idea of what might happen, when in reality, if they put their mind to it, *they do know what might happen.*

Q: Can you give those that struggle with it several tips on how to improve their ability to anticipate, to project a positive outcome?

Alan: Put yourself in the other person's shoes and say, "What are the three or four most likely things he or she will say to me, or he or she will do?" If you're in a buyer's office, and you're following up on a proposal, just as an example, they're going to say, "Let's do it. I'll take option 2." "I have some questions about option 1." "I can't do it right now." "I don't think this responds to what I told you." There are only four or five things they're going to say.

If you're in a social situation, and you want to suggest that people go to your favorite restaurant that night because you think it will really be the best choice, they might say they have their own favorite restaurant. They might say that the restaurant is too expensive. They might say that they don't care for that kind of food, or they have a food allergy. Anticipate all that. Some of those you simply cope with, you give in. I'm not taking people to a seafood place if shellfish gives them a violent reaction. Even though they can order regular fish, they might not want to risk it. I understand that. If they have their own favorite restaurant—this is a matter of taste not principle—I'm not going to argue with them.

I want to know what the range of possibilities are so I can gracefully respond and not overly push something that isn't that important. That's how you visualize, put yourself in the other person's position, and say, "What reasonably might they say?" "How reasonably might they react to this?"

Q: You said that success is about setting your own course and not trying to outdo others. What about your phrase TIAABB—There Is Always A Bigger Boat? Talk a little bit about that syndrome and some people trying to always reach that bigger boat and creating a negative impact on their life and ability to thrive.

Alan: That's fairly simple. If you don't have your own goals, your own measures of what is important to you, successful for you, and important to your family, you'll always be subject to normative, that is, to group pressure. That's why you have billionaires who keep building a yacht that's 50 feet, or even 10 feet, larger than their neighbor's. You have Paul Allen, who helped found Microsoft, building these huge yachts, and the guy from Oracle building these huge yachts; but when push comes to shove, the Sultan of Brunei who has a whole country's wealth behind him will always build a bigger boat than they will. It might not be this year, but it will certainly be next year.

What is the sense of it? You have to be happy in your own skin. You look at some of these big mansions that are built, and I couldn't be comfortable in them. How much do you need? But that's not for the people in there, it's for them to impress others. You have to have a sense of what is important to you and contributing to make your life happy, happy for those in your family, and happy among your loved ones.

Beginning a New Year

Q: Today is the first work day of a new year, and it's a great context to proceed in these inspirations with you and specifically into the next segment of the chapter called "Thrive. Balancing a Life of Abundance." How do you start a new year? What are some of the first things you do in a new year?

Alan: That's a great question. There are probably three primary things I do. One is the fact that I spend a lot of time with the family. My family visits for the holidays, at least during Christmas, and then we go to New York for New Year's. However, this year we stayed here, everyone came to us, and we spent a lot of time with family. My wife actually cooks for three or four consecutive evenings, the press comes to report on such a rarity, and it's a big deal. We have a lot of fun with the family.

Number two is I need to "reconcile" the year. I have a couple of hours of financial things I have to do at year-end, and beginning the new year, and some organizational stuff. I store files on a backup. I create new ones, but these are the files that keep me organized all year. Once I spend an hour or two doing that, I'm set for the next 365 days.

Number three is I take a look at the bigger picture. I get the grunt work out of the way, and then I say, "Okay, what is looking at me in January? What is looking at me in the first quarter? Is there anything I need to change? Are the vacations all set and established? What does my life look like over the next several months?"

That's what I tend to do. I wrote about this recently in one of my articles. Aside from the sort of anal-retentive need we have to keep track of every sunrise and sunset which are going to occur whether we keep track of them or not, the fact is that a new day is a new day. To pretend that January 1st is some symbolically reinvigorating, emotionally regenerating time is kind of ridiculous because you should wake up every morning feeling that way.

Q: How much, for example, of this coming year is planned out? Do you now plan the year differently when you're focused on the retail consumer market versus the time when your focus was on corporate work?

Alan: The process is no different. I plan the year the same way. The content is different, that's all. With more wholesale work, you have to plan more time to be places because the content requires that. With the retail market, since I've really established a very effective remote and technological approach to it, I don't have to spend that much time away from where I am right now, which is sitting in my den with my feet up on the credenza. That doesn't change in terms of process.

The biggest difference is when I first started doing OD work and largely wholesale work, I was traveling 85 percent of the time every week, four days out of five. I got that down to 65 and thought that was good, and got it down to 50 and thought it was good and realized that was still pretty bad. If you look at travel I take for business without my wife—because if my wife's with me and we're enjoying wherever we're going, I don't count that as travel away from home—it's probably between 12 and 15 percent of the time. It can't be less than that because she would throw me out.

Q: How much of your year right now is planned out, and how much do you still leave open-ended for new ideas or new surprising events that will present themselves to you?

Alan: I just swung my chair around here when you said that, and I looked at my calendar. I've got a large calendar specially mounted with all 12 months on it. It's about two feet wide by three feet high, and I use color code; blue is revenue work, red is vacation, and green is marketing work. If you look at the calendar, it's probably 10 percent planned.

What that doesn't count is the fact that every week or month I have several newsletters, several videos, several audios, cartoons, all kinds of things going out like clockwork—sometimes two or three times a week, sometimes two or three times a month. All that's planned into my calendar, but that's all work that comes out of here. A lot of it's already "in the bank." I prepare a lot of it ahead of time. It's not counting the kinds of things that are going out from here on a clockwork basis. The things on my calendar are things where I have to be somewhere or be doing something.

Q: In your mentoring work with consultants, what are some tips and coaching that you offer people to better plan to maximize their opportunities with this idea that January 1st is just another day? We do use this as an important signpost to begin a new year and make some planning. How do you coach people to maximize their opportunity?

Alan: I think you have to look at your life as your life and not some kind of circadian, lunar, or solar system. In other words, some people get to January 22nd and they say, "There are just nine days left in the month. There is no sense starting this now." That's ridiculous. January turns to February on a calendar, but they're just consecutive days.

My advice is to understand what your goals are—work backwards to get them achieved as quickly, efficiently, and as easily as possible—and leave yourself all kinds of discretionary time. Discretionary time is important for two reasons. It lets you enjoy life. It lets you partake of your pastimes and your interests, but it also allows you to be opportunistic.

I think doctors are out of their minds, and they don't make that much money relative to their value. The last time I looked, the average wage of a doctor—not highly paid specialists—is about $125,000 in the United States. I don't mean to be elitist, but $100,000 isn't what it used to be, especially for people who have had all that training, have your life in their hands, and get out of school with $400,000 or $600,000 worth of debt. The problem with doctors, especially general practitioners or what they now call personal care physicians, is that they book back-to-back. They're solidly booked over the course of a week, and they shouldn't do that.

You have to allow yourself time to review things, to explore other things, to allow for emergencies. The same with attorneys who are booking at $250 or $450 an hour; you can't have wall-to-wall, back-to-back meetings like that. Discretionary time isn't only important personally, it's important for you to grow your business. I believe attorneys actually average below $100,000 annually.

Q: As we look at the year ahead, it will be easy for us to become overwhelmed because most of us do exactly what you're talking about. We use January 1st as an arbitrary way of setting the course for the year. In addition to planning some discretionary time in our schedules, how can we develop the habit of celebrating small victories that you refer to in your *Life Balance* book?

Alan: I think you have to do two things. One is you have to appreciate small victories with a strong sense of self worth. You have to say to yourself, "This isn't small. This is significant for me. There will be some that are more significant and have more impact than this, but I did something very important today."

I'll give you an absolutely dumb, stupid, simplistic example that I'm sure a lot of people will say, "Oh, my God. This guy is making all this money with this kind of silly behavior." I have a new desk, and it's tough to get to some of my files where I file my paid bills. They're all the way in the back of a drawer. Long story short, it's just tough to get to them even though they're built to be accessed. When I was changing my files over for the new year, I rearranged the drawer. In the back of the drawer now—which is hard to reach—are the legal and financial stuff I seldom need; in front of the drawer are all the files I need on a regular basis—and now I can reach them simply. I was ecstatic about that. I saved myself a pain in the neck, which I hated doing each time; now it's easy, and I came up with my own solution. Those of you who are reading this, you've already paid your money, so tough! That's my killer example! That's why I saved it for this far into the book.

The second thing I wanted to say is don't just reward victories, reward behaviors. It might not be a significant victory. There might not be a tangible increase from it, but your result was such that you're prouder of your behavior. You stopped eating between meals. You stopped cutting people off. You stopped whatever it was, or you added something to your repertoire. You started asking other people about themselves and learned more about them. Reward the behaviors that are positive as well.

Right now it's about 11:40 eastern U.S. time on January 3rd, and I just opened up the browser I use for my portfolio. The market is up right now 128.96 points, and it's been open two hours. It's going like gangbusters, and I'll tell you two things about this. First is that apparently the business world is thinking that it's the start of a new day, and everybody is entering it with great energy and optimism, and that's the kind of energy and optimism we should have every day.

The second thing is by the time you read this, the economic pessimism will have been largely over, except for the professional victims and pessimists. You'll be able to make of the economy, the technology, and the potential business out there what you will. It's time to master your own fate whether it's January 3rd, August 4th, or October 30th.

Q: In addition to the things that you've just said, when you see a mentoree losing enthusiasm, zeal, or just getting into one of those funks, what have they done or not done to get themselves there?

Alan: First is they don't have the native resilience to help them through setbacks, and if they don't have a high sense of self worth, they're only riding high on a temporary and artificial inflation that they get from their last victory. It's almost like a balloon filled with hot air. The hot air won't last forever. They don't have air worthiness of their own, so it might be that they can't sustain themselves because they don't think that well of themselves.

Secondly, it could be that they've suffered a setback, and while they do have high self worth, they don't have much of a support system. Consequently, they don't know whom to fall back on. They don't know whom to ask for advice, or they ask the wrong people for advice.

Thirdly, they're hanging out with the wrong people. We've had this debate on some social media platforms over the last couple of days where I've said that. I first posted this on Twitter, it went to Facebook, and it's going elsewhere now. I said, "Don't be a big fish in a small pond. You run out of room. You run out of food. You run out of growth."

Somebody said, "I'd rather be a whale in a small pond than a sardine in the ocean." I said to her, "You're really silly because whales in a small pond will starve. They'll die, but fish in a large ocean have all kinds of opportunity to grow." She kept saying to me, "Niche, niche, niche." The whole notion of "specialize or die" has to be replaced by my notion which is generalize and thrive. People need to hang out with others who believe in that kind of optimism, who believe in those kinds of approaches. If they don't have the resilience to stay positive themselves, others can help them get back there.

Q: I see many derail at times—whether it's in regard to their discipline, improvement, physical workout, weight control, or whatever the issues are—and at times I've been there myself. What are some practical ideas in the context of thriving and improving life balance to put ourselves back on track and do so quickly?

Alan: Number one is don't beat yourself up. People are much too hard on themselves. That leads me to number two which is look for success not perfection. For example, if you're trying to make a speech better and you blow a line, don't worry about it. It's not the end of the world. If you're trying to diet better and you eat a piece of chocolate, don't beat yourself up. It's not the end of the world. You can recover from it.

I knew somebody once who introduced me to a new woman he was dating. This guy had been divorced three times. We were at a resort, and he said to my wife and me later that day, "I think I'm going to have to break up with her." We said, "Why?" He said, "We had a fight." We said, "So what?" He said, "When you have a fight, you don't reconcile those things."

No wonder he has been divorced three times. My wife and I said to him, "We fight every day. What is your point?" He said, "You're married all these years. You fight every day?" She said, "Of course we fight every day. But at night we always make sure that we make up, and that's the whole point." You have to look for success not perfection.

Number three is you have to track. You have to monitor. For example, when I get ten pounds too heavy for what I think I should be, I go on a diet. That's my guideline. If I'm four or five pounds up or four or five pounds down, I don't get all excited. If I'm ten pounds over my goal, I go on what is called ASD, which is Alan's Stupid Diet according to my wife because it doesn't work for her. What I do is I weigh myself every morning, and I know where I am every morning, and I watch what I eat that day. Some days I go off it, and even when I'm on it, I always reward myself. I'll have a huge cheeseburger once a week, a steak, fries, or something that's normally not on my diet that helps me with diversity and variety. You have to look at the goal and not the strict steps to get there.

You can't be doctrinaire, but those are the kinds of things that help you control your life. Be very judicious about to whom you listen, if that's not too many prepositions in a row! The fact is that people don't consider the source, and unless the ski instructor is directly in front of you doing what you want to do, you don't have a very good instructor. Consider the source. It has to be someone who has done what you want to do repeatedly and successfully.

I watch people who write one book that doesn't do very well, and suddenly they're experts for everyone else on how to write a book. One guy at the National Speakers Association had every book he submitted rejected, and he wrote a book about THAT and then went out speaking about how to handle these rejections. It's nuts. Look at people who successfully do what you want to do on a consistent basis, and those are the ones to whom you should listen.

A woman at a recent workshop I attended said things that were so simply wrong, unacceptable, and patently erroneous that I didn't know where to begin with it; yet there were people in that room taking notes and avidly listening to every word. If the conference organizers aren't careful about the source, and very few of them are, then the listener has to apply her or his own judgment to evaluate what they're hearing.

Q: Your discipline is second to none. It's just amazing. Your ability to focus. Your ability to create powerful content is both inspiring and aspiring, but I also have to say it's a source of irritation to many of us who can't do that! What are some tips you can give consultants to make a huge difference so a year from now they look back and say, "This has been an amazingly productive year for me"?

Alan: I have a Cartesian philosophy. I think Descartes was right. I irritate, therefore I am! I think what consultants need to do is to basically have four or five key things in mind. **Number one, you can't be afraid to fail.** A fear of failure is daunting, and it's as bad as guilt. In fact, it's a version of guilt. You can't be afraid to fail, so get that out of your mind.

Someone managed one of my self-published books extraordinarily well and spoke at one of my conferences on publishing. I offered her a workshop that I would promote and make an hour's appearance. It would be her workshop, she would get 80 percent, and I would get 20 percent. I would promote her. I would be there for an hour, but the rest would be hers. We had 90 days, and in the first 30 days, three or four people signed up. She just went crazy and wanted it canceled. She was afraid she wouldn't get enough people, and we were only 30 days into it. A lot of people sign up in the next 30 and the final 30 days, so you can't be like that.

Number two is you need to look at either an existing need that you can meet in a powerful way, or create a new need. I wanted to create a new workshop experience and asked, "What is a hot topic?" It's time management, and it's time mastery. *Time Management* and *Time Mastery* are two of the best selling CDs I've ever recorded, and I said, "That's it. What should I call it?" I came up with a tentative working title, and then I thought of the Time of Your Life. What you need to do is take a topic where you think there is need, you believe there is need, and you can create need. Make it sexy, make it edgy, and get it out there.

Number three, there are three things required to create experiences. In some degree, one is a brand, and I have a powerful brand. Let's face it, if I said I was going to read the Yellow Pages in a distinctive way, people would come. Secondly, you need a valuable subject matter that people can relate to their own lives. Finally, you need the environment. When I run the Million Dollar Club in Bora Bora, or I run Thought Leadership in The Breakers in Palm Beach, we have brand. We have very high-level content—the highest level of content you can think of—and we have a great environment that includes your colleagues in the room whom you really want to be with.

When you have those three things, you can't miss. You can get by with two of the three. If you don't have a powerful brand, then have a superb topic and superb location. If you have a brand and topic, but you don't have a location, you could probably get by with it. I've spoken in cinder block basements. If you have brand and environment but a weak topic, you're going to have a problem unless people just love being with you.

If you have only one of those three things, you can't make it at all; and two of three, those two have to be extraordinarily powerful. If you want to create new material, new experiences, new products, or new services, look at those three kinds of things and ask yourself, "How powerfully can I project all three, and if I'm missing on one of those cylinders, how do I get it?"

Q: This is great advice. I'm starting to really like the concept of maybe a tele-seminar from you on how to read the Yellow Pages effectively.

Alan: Could be kind of interesting I think. I might be able to get sponsorship from the people on the pages I read. Who knows?

Q: Performers, and especially stand up comedians, often describe how energizing the stage is for them; they draw tremendous energy from the crowd. Others get energized by this solitary experience of writing as they discover the plot, it evolves for them, and the language and the story flows. What is energizing for you? In what situations do you find yourself energized?

Alan: Let me count the ways. I love to create, and this morning, for example, I worked out. Before I even went to work out, I woke up early and wrote the next segment in the book I'm working on, *Million Dollar Referrals.* I'm more than half way through that, and then I'm going to write *Million Dollar Proposals,* and I'm going to take the current *Proposal* book away from the current publisher. I'm going to tell McGraw-Hill you can either take this book with a big advance, or I'm self-publishing it, and it's going to be your loss. I have that all set in my mind now. That's one of these things I'm looking forward to because I'll finish the *Million Dollar Referrals* book by the end of this month. I love to create.[2]

The second thing is I love to help people, and I love to see people improve as a result of my working with them, and you three are a great

---

2. Both books were written, published, and today among the top-selling consulting books on Amazon.com.

example. We could look at Stuart Cross in the United Kingdom, Phil Symchych in Canada, Libby Wagner in Washington, Rob Nixon in Australia, or Guido Quelle in Germany. You can go around the world and pick out these wonderful examples of high performance and success with whom I've had some measure of contribution, and that's highly energizing.

Third is I love to take risks. I love to take prudent risk and just run something out there, see who wants to sign up and what will happen, and we'll have fun together. All of this, of course, is very synergistic because it all builds the brand. Somebody will say, "Great experience, I went to this," and somebody else will say, "You might have gone to this, but did you go to that?" It just goes wonderfully. Seventy-five percent of my revenues over the past year came from things that didn't exist three years prior, and that keeps me going. It keeps me excited and active. I love that kind of stuff.

The final thing is that despite all that, I still have a great deal of free time, and I use that free time to engage in things that are important to me. Koufax just wandered in here as I said that, and he sat down on one of two dog beds here in my den. I'm working on a model tank in the garage. I have my new car, only three or four weeks old, which I'm having a fabulous time with. My wife and I are making plans to do a whole bunch of things together. The kids just left after being here for almost too long!

All these things are going on in my life, and it's a fascinating life. Who knows, I'm not smart enough to tell you what is around the next corner, but I can tell you whatever is there, I can hop on.

Q: The versatility and the temperament of enjoying and finding energy in many different things is very conducive, very supportive for the life of a fellow consultant.

Alan: Yes, there is nothing worse than a one-trick pony, a one-note song. When you started that question, you talked about something with which I have great affinity and that is performers, comedians, and so on. I must have been told over a thousand times in my life that I should be, or should have been, a stand-up comedian. I hear that all the time, and if you've ever attended anything I do, I use a lot of stand-up humor. Some of it's prepared. I tell a lot of stories, but a lot of it's ad lib, and I happen to like that kind of humor. In essence, what I do is a kind of performing, and when I listen to my son talk about acting, I can relate to a lot of what he is talking about.

The energy that I get isn't only from the live events I do, but the energy I get is from my communities that are active 24/7. I can plug into them any time I choose. It's really a great, great benefit and luxury I have and get energy from that. I could go on the Forum; I could go into one of my subscription bases. I've created this brand new consulting newsletter. These communities keep me energized as well.

Q: In your mentoring work with hundreds of mentorees, how critical is it that people understand what energizes them and where they feel their best?

Alan: It's very critical. The problem is that most people don't look to themselves. They're not very introspective. I'm most impressed by people who I find are natively introspective or at least have learned how to do that. Most people aren't very self-aware.

I talked earlier in these interviews about levels of consciousness and how Margaret Wheatley got me thinking about these things in her book. People have a very low level of consciousness about themselves, and when you're not self-aware, you really can't replicate very easily what you're good at. You're not very sharp. You're not very insightful about what you've done poorly that you could correct, and you're not quite sure how you interact and interrelate with the rest of the world.

Self-awareness is not big on people's plates. Part of it's because of denial. Part of it's narcism. Part of it's because of lack of skill and technique. Part of it's because people are driven externally by stimuli, by media, by the volatility of the world around them so that they're always reacting instead of looking inside and understanding themselves.

Reducing Work and Occam's Razor

Q: What can you tell us about the importance of focusing on output and working backwards to input as this applies to life balance?

Alan: You don't decide what your legacy is on your deathbed. You create a legacy from the time you're productive and functioning in society. My feeling is that you shouldn't consume happiness without creating it any more than you should consume wealth without creating it, or consume money without creating it. Like it or not, the default position is: We're all creating a legacy. We should know what it is, and we should have some feeling as we mature, get older, and have a better perspective about life as to what it is we want to contribute to others and to the world around us. That's what you have to work backwards from.

I hate these bucket lists. I hate these lists where somebody says, "These are the 87 things I want to do in my life. I want to climb Mount Kilimanjaro. I want to go in a submarine. I want to invent anti-gravity toothpaste." Those are just arbitrary and kind of silly inputs really. You just want to do them to say you've done them.

On the other hand, you want to help people adjust to a competitive world better. You want to help people get along with colleagues better. You want to help people make better use of their time. You want to give people more discretionary time. You want to assist others to write well. You want to assist others to communicate better. You can go on and on. That to me constitutes the kind of things you want to work backwards from and try to help create because the more you help others, the more you help yourself.

That's where a vibrant life is, and that's where the creation of income is and the resultant discretionary time. I think rather than arbitrary lists and inputs, you really want to look to the things that you would be most challenged to create, and the things that you would have the most interest and fun in creating—and work backwards from there.

I've been asked a question frequently in my life, which is "How do you make a lot of money?" What I responded is, "Don't try to make a lot of money and learn to love it. Find something you love to do, and that's what you should try to make a lot of money doing."

Q: Why is it so challenging for most to see the simplest solution? What are some ways for people to improve their Occam's razor outlook?[3]

Alan: I think there are two primary reasons for your first question. The first is that people believe that complexity is superior to simplicity. They feel that complex machines are better than simple machines. Archimedes said, "Give me a lever and I can move the world." An automobile is a beautiful thing to see, and I love exotic cars, but the notion of a lever, a screwdriver, or a pair of pliers is rather magnificent. They falsely identify complexity with sophistication and effectiveness.

---

3. William of Occam was a Franciscan friar who posited that the best and most effective route is that which is simplest and most direct.

The second thing is that people don't have the analytic thinking skills to see through to the simple—and I know that's going to sound counterintuitive to a lot of people—but the fact is, acute and assiduous use of critical thinking skills is required to see and utilize simplicity. It's when you don't have these that you get into these convoluted, abstruse, complicated approaches because you don't have the ability to cut your way through to the simple.

To go to the second part of your question, if people want to follow Occam's razor which basically says the easiest course is usually the best, don't start with the alternative. Don't start with your model. Don't start with methodology. Ask yourself what it is you want to achieve. Paint that picture of the future, whether it's 20 minutes from now and a speech you're making, or it's two years from now and a new home you want to move into. Create that vision of the future, work backwards, and say, "What is the easiest, most direct route for me to get there?"

Q: This is fascinating. In the context of this chapter, and I know we explored that in previous chapters, I made the following suggestions or the following statement. When I read Peter Drucker, oftentimes I have to read the same paragraph twice or three times to really comprehend what was said. Yet when I read your material, I get it on the first read. What can we as consultants learn from it and then implement in our own businesses?

Alan: In my case, it's because I'm driven by laziness. If I can write 250 pages instead of 400 pages, that's what I want to do, especially if I'm going to be paid the same way regardless. I want to make this as easy as I can for me. I do probably three things that account for what you just said.

Number one is I have a superb use of language. Think of a huge computer system where you hit a button to get what you want. I can call a word for usage whenever I want it from this huge warehouse, this huge inventory I have.

The second thing is I use examples all the time which bounce things forward, propel things forward, and accelerate things forward. The velocity of my writing is fairly rapid, even though I'm making very key points, because these examples help that instantiation you talked about.

The third thing is I use process visuals—which are a form of example, except it's graphically presented—and people can identify it. A combination of depth and width, language, examples, and process visuals enable you to march very, very quickly.

I'll say again what I've probably said seven times so far in these interviews, but it's very important for people in terms of simplicity: It's important for directness as Occam's razor notion of easiest, and working backwards, and it's what most people I'll safely say don't do. That is, *don't tell people everything you know. Tell them only what they need to know*, whether in your books, in your articles, in your e-mail, or in your responses.

You've seen me do this hundreds, if not thousands of times. I'll say to someone on the Forum or in an e-mail, "Those three paragraphs you just wrote contain one question, and here is the question." People spend too much time making things much more complex and difficult than they need to because they're trying to tell you everything they know instead of what you need to know. They also have a habit, which is for me infuriating, of articulating their cognitive process, and they're helping themselves to understand by stating out loud their cognitive process.

That might be helping them, but it sure as hell isn't helping me. As far as I'm concerned, they should be doing that in private.

Q: Does perfectionism stand in the way of life balance?

Alan: Of course it does. There is no such thing as perfection. God is probably perfect, unless He tries to hit a one-iron. Although some people would argue that—given the mess we're making of this planet—but there is no such thing as perfection for us. I see perfection in a butterfly. I see perfection in a bird building a nest. I see perfection in Mozart's Fifth Symphony, but I think these are touched by God. That's me, but in terms of human, everyday performance, there is no perfection. There is only success or nonsuccess.

When I've worked with organizations as an OD consultant, whenever the topic has been evaluation, I've told them to throw out their evaluation system, 1 to 10, this and that, and just have three criteria: Meets expectations, exceeds expectations, or doesn't meet expectations. Those are the only three possibilities. It's that simple. It's not about perfection. It's about which of these you fall in, and I said if you've got most of your people falling into "exceeds expectations" and you're having a mediocre year, you have a lot of crap on your evaluation forms.

People are obsessed with perfection because they've artificially been exposed to it from super heroes, television shows that always end on a positive note, and people never making mistakes. Life isn't like that.

Q: Deliverables are the enemy of both life balance and Occam's razor. Can you talk about how we become prisoners of deliverables and how our clients start to expect us to address deliverables?

Alan: It's the inability to deal with ambiguity, and people want to latch onto what is distinct, discernible, and definable*, and those are the things you do, not the things you create.* Once you get into the Dante's inferno, the 7th level down of human resources, which is somewhere about a half mile below Satan, you've got people just looking at "What will you deliver? How much will it cost? How many times will you do it? Should we cut the crust off your bread?" That's how they talk.

People have a problem dealing with the ambiguity of results until you remove some of the ambiguity by asking intelligent questions. "What will this look like if we're successful?" "I'm not sure." "Give me an idea. How will it affect your customers? How will it affect your employees? How will it affect your repute? Give me some idea because if you can't give me an idea, then I have no idea why you even feel you were in a bad place now."

"We're in a bad place now because we're only getting three percent response in our customer call center." "In that case, improving that would be important, right?" "That's true. We would like to get a 12 percent response." "Why is that?" "Because that way…" That's the kind of conversation you have.

People fall back on the easy, which is "We can do a three-day workshop." "We want a three-day workshop." "I can provide four." "We'd like eight." This is neither here nor there, and it's never valuable because deliverables are always commodities.

Q: The deliverables are commodities and tactics, and the discussion is one way to get the client to talk about results instead of deliverables?

Alan: Yes. And I'll give you the apotheosis of that transaction. I've had people call me—corporate clients and mentorees—and they'll say, "Alan, I've got this question," and I'll say, "Fine." Half way through the question they'll say, "You know something, I just answered my own question. I know exactly what I should do. I know exactly what you would have said."

I say, "Great. Glad to be of help," and I hang up. I could have said, "Let's walk through it to make sure it's the same thing I would have said," or I could have said, "What a great process. Let's examine what you just did," or

I could have said this and that. No, no, no. Thank you. Have a good day. I haven't uttered a word. I've listened to them for two minutes. They've solved their own problem, and they've gone away again. That's ideal. I didn't tell them anything I didn't need to tell them. In this case, I didn't need to tell them a damn thing.

Q: Have you ever had a corporate client—who had been trained to think in terms of deliverables—after a conceptual agreement conversation say, "Yes, but what are the deliverables?"

Alan: I've never had a senior person say that after such a conversation. After objectives, measure, and value, they've never said that. They have sometimes said, "How often do you plan to be here? How many focus groups might you run?" They had to have said that out of curiosity.

Before the conversation about conceptual agreement, they've often focused on deliverables because that's how they've been educated. Lower-level people almost always talk about that because that's all they're capable of talking about, and that's why I prefer to deal with high-level people. That's why I want to build a trusting relationship, then get conceptual agreement, and then get objectives, measure, and value because it obviates the need to talk about deliverables at all.

Q: We just talked about celebrating the small victories. Can you give us your opinion about the importance of short- and long-term rewards?

Alan: I'm all for rewards. I don't care what term they are. After all, a long-term reward becomes a short-term reward when it gets here, as long as you don't do something stupid and deny yourself something until you accomplish something else.

I was watching a great show with Ray Romano called "Men of a Certain Age." It was a fabulous cable show. It's a piece of poetry. It's brilliant, and at one point he is a frustrated golfer. He is very good. He would love to go on the Pro Seniors tour, and he is hitting these balls with a 9-iron into a garbage can in his office. He owns this big novelty shop, and he says to himself, "If I make ten in a row, then I'll allow myself to do this." Somebody interrupts him after eight in a row, and he misses the ninth and says, "I didn't have to do that tonight anyway."

It's just ridiculous. We deny ourselves as though there is some accountant keeping track. My feeling is we certainly shouldn't reward our bad behavior, but we shouldn't put such demands on ourselves that we deny ourselves things we need to lead a rich life unless we establish some arbitrary input.

Q: You sometimes advocate tithing to yourself. Would you explain what this means and why it's important?

Alan: Yes, I just wrote this again in Twitter and a couple of other places to start the new year, and I'm doing this myself at the moment. It's simply taking a portion of your income, I suggest ten percent, and putting it in some separate account, paying yourself first—beyond whatever paycheck you take, bonus you take, and expense reimbursement. If a client pays you $100,000, take $10,000 and put it in a separate account. It's still there if you need it, but otherwise don't touch this account if you can help it. At the end of the year if you've had a $700,000 year, you'll have $70,000 in there which you can invest, put away for retirement, put a down-payment on a new home, buy a new car, get the roof fixed, contribute to charity, or combinations thereof. You can increase to 15 or 20 percent where you can; if you make $4 million a year, it becomes even higher.

Those are your variables, and I just think people don't tend to pay themselves, or they're the last people they pay. I think it's a great discipline, and it's a good reward that you can see growing as you watch it.

Q: You just reminded us again that it's about success not perfection. How do you measure your life?

Alan: I don't.

Q: You use no measurements?

Alan: What would I measure? I know how old I am. I know how tall I am. I know how much I weigh. What would I measure?

Q: Some will measure their well-being. Their happiness. Some would measure their charitable activities. You speak about these things, but you seem to have a tremendous sense of freedom to be able to do these things and enjoy them in the moment without needing to put any "accountancy of thought" to it. That's why I ask is there another inner measure that you look at?

Alan: The problem with your position is you're running against one of my very prime directives. I have five prime directives. One of them is there is always a bigger boat, and once you start to measure your life, you violate the precept that there is always a bigger boat. I contribute to charity happily, but I don't compare what I do to other people because there is always somebody contributing more. For those who are contributing less, they might be contributing more than I am in terms of what they have left after they give. I just do what I think I can do, what I think is right, and what is appropriate at the time.

Every day I wake up happy. The last thing I want to do is measure my happiness. My goodness, the last thing I want to do is say, "I'm really happy today, but I'm not as happy as I was yesterday." That's going to ruin my whole day. I have the potential to be even happier every day, so I don't really measure my life. I think it's for other people to measure. I think it's for other people to say, "Here is how this guy helped me." "Here is the difference this guy made." "Here is what a pain in the ass he is." That's fine. But I don't measure my life. I just lead my life, and I do my best to enjoy myself and be productive because if I do that well, then I help others enjoy themselves and be productive.

Q: Let me ask you about three similar things, and they may be the same, although I'm curious on how you view these. These three ideas are hope, optimism, and confidence. Are these the same, or are they different?

Alan: I think they're slightly different. I've never thought about this before, but confidence is a condition. Self-confidence is a condition you arrive at through the action of self-esteem. The more you generate, perpetuate, and maintain self-esteem, the more you're a self-confident person, and that's a person who can go through life and survive the ups and the downs.

Hope, on the other hand, is simply the wish that things do tend to be positive. That things do tend to be salutary and that you do well, but it's no more than a wish. That's all that hope is, and people often say, "Hope for the best, and plan for the worst."

Optimism is a mental set, and people can be hopeful or not hopeful. In other words, you can hope your team wins even though you know they don't have a chance, they're vast underdogs. Optimism is sort of a sunny and bright look philosophically at the world around you and how you relate to it. That the things that happen to you will probably be positive, and the things you do will probably be positive, and the world isn't out to get you, and there is a lot to build on.

I would say that if you're self-confident, you're going to be an optimistic person. If you're optimistic, you're not necessarily self-confident, and hope is an independent floating variable out there. I'm optimistic. I'm highly self-confident. I could hope that I win the lottery tomorrow, but that ain't going to happen.

Q: It seems that one of the biggest factors for the sense of optimism and confidence is how much people feel they're in control. Help us understand the link between that sense of control and autonomy to confidence and the sense of dignity and how we need to be mindful of this in our own coaching and consulting.

Alan: It's about control. If you read *Thrive,* you'll see that I talk a great deal in there about autonomy, and autonomy is one of several factors I feel are very important for people. It's the sense that you're in control of your life, and other people and other factors aren't. It's the sense that you have a reasonable idea of what is going to happen tomorrow, even though you can't predict everything. It's the sense that you have a reasonable feeling of influence on what will happen tomorrow, even though you can't influence everything. In addition, that sense of control is augmented and enhanced through use of language, discipline, and proper methodologies that make your life more effective and powerful. All of these skills that you can build, learn, and spread are important to building your sense of control around you.

When people feel they've lost control because they have someone in their inner circle who berates them, a loved one who doesn't support them, they've lost money, they've lost a competitive edge, or they've had a bad setback, they can tend to be very depressed if they're not resilient. *That's why self-worth is so important because it's almost like rebooting your computer. If your self-worth is strong, you can reassert your control fairly quickly.*

Q: Give us final steps to help people reboot their sense of autonomy.

Alan: I think if you have a strong sense of autonomy, it's going to be there, and it's going to be maintained. I think you need to kick-start it, to reboot it by having a support network who can say to you, "Stop feeling sorry for yourself and do this. Remember when you used to do that and how effective it was? Go back to that."

When my doctoral dissertation was rejected and all my class work was done, I said to my wife, "Screw this. I'm not going to go through with this again." She said to me, "How long does it take you to write a book?" I said, "A little over two months. I promise it in four." She said, "How long did it take you to do this dissertation?" I said, "It has been six months." She said, "No, no, no. How long did it take you to write it?" I said, "About six weeks." She said, "Sit down and write it again," and that put me back in my autonomous state.

You have to have people around you, not just to comfort you but to challenge you and say, "Stop being a cry baby and get on with your life." If the autonomy is there, it's easily rekindled. It's like a fire that never goes out. If you haven't established that kind of autonomy, self-worth, and self-belief, you've got a lot more work to do in the best of times. In the worst of times when you're depressed, it's very difficult to establish it.

Q: You had spoken to us at Framed last week about the importance of having general knowledge in order to be a world-class consultant. This discussion offers proof of that because you're discussing things that you've read in history books, you've read in the *Wall Street Journal*, and from other different sources. Could you say a few words about the importance of us balancing the time we spend in pursuing educational events or training events about our businesses with the importance of educating ourselves in other ways?

Alan: When you refer to Framed, you're talking about the workshop I ran in Sarasota last week, the Framed Workshop. One of the things I pointed out in there is if you're going to frame things, you have to have a point of reference and a perspective. If you were born in the '60s, '70s, or '80s, it's hard for you to be as knowledgeable about post-World War II America as someone who was born in the '40s or '50s; yet you still have to deal with some of those people—the senior boomers—in terms of your business interactions. Similarly, you're talking to some people who never saw or used a rotary phone, some who can't believe anyone ever went through life without a phone in their pocket, and so forth.

How do you get these different frames of reference? I call them compensating factors, and part of it's from reading extensively. Reading histories, biographies, science, the *Wall Street Journal*, the *New York Times*, and so forth so you can compensate for not having been there yourself. You can travel to compensate for not knowing about another place. This spectrum of intelligence you have to gather—which you can turn into knowledge and therefore wisdom—is really what enables you to deal with almost any client situation more effectively, and both put yourself in the frame of the client or bring the client into your frame. If you're just going to listen to Jon Stewart to get your news, you're just going to read a paper once a week, or you're never going to leave your hometown, you're in dire, severe likelihood of not being able to relate to an increasing number of people whom you encounter.

The Role of Stress in the Consultant's Life

Q: What is your philosophy about stress? What is good stress and what is bad stress?

Alan: You can't eliminate stress. It's silly to try. It's futile and it's not even a very good idea. The right amount of stress (eustress) gives us an adrenaline flow. It provides us with urgency. A lot of people I've met have very low urgency, and I think that's because there is just insufficient stress in their lives.

Think about it as a bell curve. On the left-hand side of this bell, there is very low stress and very low productivity. These are the people who love to work for the government and the Department of Motor Vehicles. They go to law school, but they get a job as a lawyer in the immigration service (I can't ever imagine anybody spending that kind of money to go through law school and incurring that kind of debt doing such a thing). They do it because they want low stress jobs where they just show up every day, and there is nobody beating them to improve their productivity. They don't have to make entrepreneurial judgments. They don't have to innovate. That's the entitlement mindset, and it's becoming less and less popular because economic volatility threatens entitlement.

On the other end of the spectrum, on the right-hand side of the bell curve, that distribution is of people who have mammoth stress. They're paralyzed with fear, so they have equally low productivity but for a different reason, and that is they're afraid to act. They're afraid they'll get whacked. They unplug their phone. They take their name off the door. They hide under their desk on the theory that if no one can find them, they can't be hurt.

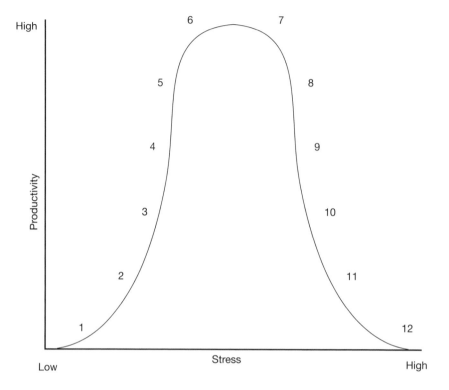

Figure 12.1: The stress bell curve.

In the middle of the bell curve, at the peak, are the people who have pride. They have a moderate amount of stress which they tolerate and manage well. That stress gets them moving, and they'll take prudent risk. They're not afraid of failure. They're not afraid to innovate, to try new things, and these are the people you want working for you.

On the left you have entitlement, on the right fear, and in the middle pride.

If you look at the best sales people in an auto dealership, they're eager to move. They want to find the next person who walks in the door. They have a moderate stress level. You look at some people and they never take their feet off their desk, and they say, "Oh God, another customer walked in." They don't want to be bothered. There are other people who say, "Geez, a customer. What if I blow this?" They're the ones who have the fear.

In any kind of professional occupation, any kind of competitive occupation, these factors obtain. You know the companies that build stress during the day to almost intolerable levels and then put in a gym and encourage employees to work out at night to work it off? That's like putting a hamster in one of these wheels. We all need stress in our lives. We need to deal with the *right levels*, and manage it for ourselves.

Q: In your mentoring with consultants, what do you find are the main stressors, and how do you typically coach mentorees on these?

Alan: There are a few that are consistent. You'll find people stressed about capital. You'll find them stressed about income. If they don't have adequate financial reserves and there is a downturn in their practice for whatever reason—this happens to all of us—they tend to get very stressed and make poorer judgments. They don't take their time. They don't look at the right perspective. They don't make certain investments they should be making.

A second stressor is the client, and the client puts fear into their lives, puts the fear of God into them because they challenge something the consultant is doing, tells them that they're not working fast enough, or says they've changed their mind about something. Because they don't have a good relationship with the client—they haven't built a solid trusting relationship—this becomes adversarial rather than collegial.

A third stressor is when you don't have a good support system. You don't have a spouse, a significant other, a colleague, whomever it is, who can help you when you're down, help you rejoice when you're up, and give you honest feedback about whether something was your fault or not. The underlying cause for almost all of this is poor self-esteem, and a lack of self-esteem will cause stress 11 times out of 10. If you can build a high self-esteem level, you will, by default, vastly decrease inordinate stress in your life.

Q: You've touched on fear and self-esteem as a couple of things that can influence the stress in our lives. How would bias or our point of view or philosophy influence stress as well?

Alan: Perception is reality, right? If our perception is that we're not a peer of the buyer, we're not really as good as we think other people believe, and therefore we're an impostor; or we're not keeping up with technology, social change, or the kind of intellectual firepower that you referred to before—this builds stress. The way people perceive themselves, the way they talk to themselves, and the way they regard themselves, all of that contributes.

As you can see from my comments, the good news is that we can control most of this. You don't need to run to a therapist, but the bad news is that we can control most of this, and we either choose not to or don't have the skills to do so. You hear people say, "I just don't know. My wheels are spinning. I can't get clarity. I don't know where I am. I can't get started on this book. I keep procrastinating." All of that's about fear, and it's about a really poor sense of self-esteem.

Having worked extensively with other consultants since 1996, over 1,000 individuals and over 100 firms, and add to that my executive coaching since 1985, I think I have a pretty good frame of reference. Because of volatile times, and the unknown, and people don't develop intellectual firepower, and because of baggage they carry around that their mother told them 30 years ago, there is a self-esteem crisis among professionals.

Q: You've attained a degree of success that many of us aspire to. Do you still experience stress, and if you do, how do you manage it?

Alan: I do experience stress, and I manage it in a few ways. First of all, things I don't like to do I do first. I no longer have to look forward to them. Number two, my energy level is not depressed for other things I have to do. Number three, having accomplished them I feel better about myself already, and the endorphins are flowing.

Another way I deal with stress is I delegate what I hate doing. I have a gabillion air miles built up, frequent flier points, hotel points, you name it, and I hate, hate, hate trying to use them. Even though I can afford to buy what I want and do what I want, I realize that responsibly I should use these things. What I do is simply go through American Express. I have a private team at American Express, and they use my American Express points and can access my frequent flier points, and I tell them to apply what they can, and that has removed that stressor from my life.

I have this ability to reduce anything I have to do to the barest fundamentals. It's an aspect of framing. I've had a bookkeeper for ten years who comes, picks up my stuff, two weeks later delivers it back to me at my door with all my spreadsheets and balance sheets and stuff I don't recognize for my tax accountant, and we have a harmonious working relationship. I would never touch Quicken in my life. Put a gun to my head, I won't touch Quicken, or is it Quick Books? I don't even know what it is.

That's how you get rid of stress. You deal with everything expeditiously. You delegate everything you can, and I'll tell you one more thing. There are only two things you do with stress. You internalize and then get ill, or you externalize and make someone else ill.

Q: Were you always like this, or did this come with age and experience?

Alan: It depends what you mean by "always." I was a scared little kid, and I was intimidated by the kids in the upper grades. I was pretty successful as a school yard athlete, but there were a lot of kids bigger and tougher, and you could get beaten up very easily. I didn't like to get beaten up, and by the time I got to high school, I was faster and smarter than most people. I had superb grades. I went on to become an exchange student, president of student counsel, and editor of the school newspaper. I also lettered in sprints on the track team. As I said, I was smarter and faster. What kind of inner city white guy can get a letter in track freshman year? I did.

I went to Rutgers University, became editor of the student newspaper, and took great pride in beating Princeton and all these other schools in the New Jersey Collegiate Press Association contest. I won first prize in the state for editorial writing, among other things, and that's when I began to realize that it doesn't matter whether your parents were on the Mayflower or they wound up here in steerage. It doesn't matter how you grew up, and it doesn't matter what your last name is. What matters is (a) building your skills, and (b) being confident about applying them.

Q: One of the best sellers right now is about the Chinese tiger mom. She says that accomplishment comes before self-esteem, and other people are arguing that accomplishment won't come unless you have self-esteem. Where do you stand on that?

Alan: First, I hope that no one is listening to this woman or can even remember her. She is an idiot. You don't deny your children the rights of passage. You don't tell your children they can't watch television because they have to learn to play the violin or the piano. You don't tell your children that they can't go to sleepovers with other kids. Those rights of passage—those interactions with your peers in your adolescence—are as important as being able to read a musical score *and aren't mutually exclusive, unless you have no flexibility or breadth of vision.*

What she is advocating at this point is simply for her own publicity. She has glommed onto this with her book and her appearances. I just read in the *New York Times* about her own marketing, and she is going from speech to speech all dolled up like a donut making these observations about child-rearing, but now all of a sudden she is being more conciliatory because she wants to remain popular and keep earning money. I think that she is full of crap. I doubt anyone will remember her name by the time this book is published.

The fact is that kids need to lead normal lives. If you want to add to your kid's normal life the study of music, literature, painting, or architecture, that's great. I'm all for it. If you want to tell your kids to limit his or her time on the social media platforms—heck, I tell that to consultants. To take this extreme view that the only way to raise a child is to deny them what most other children have and focus them on what is considered to be these elite art forms or pursuits, that's nonsense.

Q: You talked about the fact that some stress is actually good stress. With that in mind, should we manufacture some good stress both for ourselves and possibly for our clients to generate better results?

Alan: Providing you know what manufacturing good stress means—let me give you an example so we're clear. I'm writing another book right now, and I'm closing in on this last chapter, and I know that I had plenty of time until the deadline, but my own personal deadline is that I want to get it concluded in the next week or so for my own reasons.

That's the kind of creative, positive stress I would include in your definition. It's positive because it's a challenge that lends itself to the completion of something. It's realistic, and it's doable. What if, for some reason, I didn't get to it? Let's say my wife said, "Hey, you know we need to attend to this." I wouldn't be crushed by it, and I would get to it later. I still have exigency time because the real deadline isn't for a couple of months. That kind of stress, if that's what you're talking about, is fine. But if the stress that you're building up is because you're afraid to write, it's painful to write, you don't want to go out and make that speech, or you don't want to pick up the phone and call somebody, that's different.

Q: You also indicated that lack of self-esteem will actually cause stress. When one recognizes that the essence is lack of self-esteem for them or for their clients, what can we do to aim for a better cure for that?

Alan: Lack of self-esteem can be remedied in a few ways. One is to build skills. The more skills you build and apply successfully, the more skills you want to acquire; the more skills you acquire, the more you can apply successfully. Your ability to perform well—efficacy if you wish—builds self-esteem.

A second thing you have to do is to examine the baggage you're carrying. You have to examine the false premises and assumptions you're carrying. Some people are able to do that themselves. They sit down and say, "Why is it I think I can't play the piano? Why is it I think that I'm not credible in front of a buyer? Why is it that I think that I can't do this or that?" Some people need help with that, and the first stage of help might be a support system, family, colleagues, mastermind groups, or professional associates. A deeper help with that would be therapy, and there is nothing wrong with therapy. I believe in it a great deal.

The trouble is it takes a pretty good amount of self-esteem to deal with your self-esteem. When I run self-esteem workshops, one of the challenges I put in the promotional material is "Do you have enough self-esteem to attend my self-esteem workshop?" You do have a certain kind of paradox there.

Q: Isn't it natural for us to want to make people happy? With that in mind, what is a healthy balance between wanting to please and self-esteem? When does the desire to please others become pathological?

Alan: I'll tell you the extent to which people want to please others. There was a study done that showed that in almost every single sport, there is a home team advantage. Teams win more at home than on the road, and everybody knows this, and they assume it's because of the support of the crowd—which is psychological. They also assume it's because they know the playing field better—which is a certain sort of mechanical physical advantage.

What the study shows is that it isn't true. The reason people win more at home is that the officials' calls—the referees, the umpires, and so forth—more often than not go with the home team. That's the reason teams win more at home!

They examined why that would be true, and what they found was that the officials were not biased, the officials were not corrupt, but the officials had a subliminal, psychological need to be liked, which is a common human condition. Because they liked to be liked, they tended to make more calls in favor of the home team—the crowd would cheer—rather than against the home team when the crowd would go crazy. They cited the fact that in the National Basketball Association, a visiting player was something like ten times more likely to be called for traveling, which is walking without dribbling the ball, than a home team player. There is no way in that professional level that there is that discrimination—somebody being ten times more likely than another—except if there is some kind of built-in bias to the calls.

Everybody has this passion to be liked. When your passion to be liked is so great that you become super amiable—and by that I mean you subordinate your own objectives to the objectives of others—you may even sacrifice critical needs to meet what are merely others' desires. You're afraid to speak your mind. In fact, when you allow yourself to be damaged in some way financially, physically, or emotionally in order to allow another person to succeed—that's pathological.

I served on the board of a shelter for battered women. What you find is that not only does this transcend economic strata—that wealthy women were as likely to be battered as women from poor homes—but they kept going back to their abusers because of this paucity of self-esteem. They would convince themselves it was their fault, and they really wanted their husbands to love them again.

I think that the key here is a healthy selfishness, sort of an Ayn Randian belief that if you don't help yourself, you can't help others. The first person you have to love is yourself.

Q: The practice you spoke about that you do first thing in the morning what you hate or what presents stress—what is the origin of this practice?

Alan: This is a story I've never told anyone. In the 8th grade, I had very good marks. I was an all-star. We had this science project due, and I hated science projects. My parents didn't give me any help with them. I absolutely hated them, and I kept procrastinating and didn't do it. Even though I was a good student, and I liked the teacher who taught science, the date was coming, and the day before I still hadn't done it because I hated it.

On the day it was due, I went home at lunchtime. I used to walk about three blocks to school. I actually went home at lunchtime and just threw together this miserable thing. It was awful, I turned it into the teacher, and he sort of turned a blind eye. He knew I was a good student, and he gave me a pass, but I was actually down to the very last moment I could do it.

When I was a freshman in high school, again we had a science project. These were the days when you had to take science. I put it off, put it off, and at the very last minute, I put together another terrible exhibit. The science teacher, in front of the whole class, read me the riot act. He said, "Weiss, what is this crap?" He said, "I wouldn't let my five-year-old turn this in. This is garbage." It was around then I said to myself, "Putting things off that I don't like to do makes things worse. What I need to do in the future is get things done early."

The next year there was a science project. I said to my father, who wasn't particularly helpful with these things, "Hey look. I've got this science project, and here is the issue." We looked at something and he said, "Why don't you do this?" Lasers were in their infancy then, and we actually put together the inside of a laser. We used ping-pong balls and things like that to show the inside, and my father helped me get some of the materials. I would never know where to get them from, this was a very rudimentary age, and we were poor. There was a science fair where we had to present these in the gym, and my 10th grade science teacher came over and said, "This isn't the best exhibit here, but it's kind of inventive, and it's not bad." She gave me a "B."

That really demonstrated for me two things. First, you can't put off these lousy things you don't like doing. Second, I had successfully changed my behavior, and it had a positive outcome when I did that. After that I attended to things quickly—if I had a report due or something I had to do in school I didn't like doing. The same thing in college.

Q: Clearly, this was a self-learned behavior. Fascinating story.

Alan: You have to be self-aware. Most people aren't self-aware. Although we're sentient beings, we don't really examine our trials and tribulations. We don't examine failures. We don't examine successes. We're not all that self-aware, and therefore we don't have the capacity to constantly improve. That's one of the problems of being a lone wolf in consulting.

You have to be self-reliant to continue to improve yourself. You have to set those mechanisms in place. If you don't do that, in best case you're going to be stuck doing something good that you've been doing good for ten years, and in worst case, the competition is just going to run right by you.

Q: What are some things that we can do to reduce the stress of walking into a new situation when the crowd isn't going to necessarily be on our side?

Alan: Consider yourself the visiting team every time, and what do you have to do if you're the visiting team? Number one is you have to prepare well. Do the homework on the client. Understand the client as a person, the buyer. Understand the organization. Understand the competition. Understand the environment—try to understand the *milieu* in which you're going to be operating. As a speaker, I've always tried to walk out on the stage before I was due to speak to get the feel of the place.

Number two, control the ball. Visiting teams try to control the ball so that the home team doesn't have excessive use of the offensive weapon. By controlling the ball, I mean control the conversation. Understand how you'll set the agenda. Understand and visualize the kinds of objections you might get, and make sure that you know what your minimum and maximum objectives are.

Finally, if you're in the visiting ballpark, don't get rattled when you hear the crowd noise. When someone does object, don't drop dead on the floor and say, "Oh, my God, I can't." You have to say, "There are three good reasons for that." If somebody says, "Let me question your basic premise," understand that a question is a sign of interest. What you don't want is apathy. What you don't want is silence. If you get rebuttal, if you get objections, if you get questions, those are all signs of interest, and don't get rattled, and you play your game.

Since you always know you're going to be the visiting team, you can take advantage of that. There are some teams that have excellent records on the road, and the New York Giants won the Super Bowl by having a great record on the road. It can be done.

Q: How do we remove ambiguity and focus on specifics as you so easily do?

Alan: Reduce the ambiguity by asking yourself, "What is it that really concerns me? What evidence, what behavior really concerns me?" Don't allow yourself to talk in terms of generality. Instead of saying, "Wow, I have a real communications problem with her," what you say is, "She isn't listening because she keeps interrupting. I have to ask her to be more patient before speaking."

You also can't generalize from a specific. If one person says something, good or bad, you don't say, "Oh, woe is me," or "Wow, I'm great!" That just creates more ambiguity. That you have to test, and if you don't have empirical evidence, and you don't have observed behavior, you have to test to see whether you're accurate or not.

Another thing I would recommend is don't accept the ambiguity of others. Don't accept others telling you that there is a morale problem, there is a breakdown in spirit, or that somebody isn't a team player. No one knows what the heck that means. I suggest that you always look for specificity, and you don't allow yourself to wallow in this kind of ambiguity.

Just a quick example from a consulting standpoint. Any number of executives have said, "We want to go from good to great" based on Jim Collins' clever title of his book. A lot of consultants say, "Fine. I can put something together for you." My response is, "Tell me something: I don't know what the hell that means. How would you know that you had achieved greatness? How do you know you're not great now? Why do you think you're good now? What would that mean to you?"

"I don't know, we can always improve."

"What would indicate that you're improving? There must be something you're not doing now that tells you that you must do it better. What is that?" That's how you move from the ambiguous to the specific.

Happiness and Spirituality

Q: You say that thriving isn't about being first, it's about being happy. How do you mean that?

Alan: What I mean is life is short, and no matter what your pursuit is, no matter what happens to you, no matter what you choose to do, you're a lot better if you're happy. It's not about being first, it's not about being best, and it's not about being biggest because those are impossible to attain even if they really meant something. You've heard me say there is always a bigger boat.

This psychologist at Harvard, Dan Gilbert, has done fascinating work on synthetic happiness, and he says the people who say, "Getting fired was the best thing that ever happened to me," aren't rationalizing so much as creating their own happiness. His research shows that those people are generally happier, more productive, and more positive than people who are only happy at what you might call traditional happiness events like a birth, anniversary, or a birthday. It's a pretty fascinating dynamic to think about.

Q: You wrote in *Thrive* that there is nothing as central to thriving as love and intimacy. Can you help us understand this perspective?

Alan: I don't think that humans are meant to be isolated animals. I think that humans need companionship because if you're sentient—which means you're self-aware—that means you're also aware of what is going on around you. I think that people have an innate need to share that with someone. It's lonely to even undergo your victories alone, never mind your defeats. I believe that intimacy, love, and someone who can support you very closely are important. Whether people find that in modern society in a traditional marriage, a nontraditional marriage, or simply a partnership—whether it's a same sex marriage or a same sex relationship or not—people need intimacy. They need someone to love them, and they need to love someone else because that will get you through the day no matter what the trials and tribulations.

People have written books about why bad things happen to good people. Life isn't fair. There is nobody with a green eyeshade and sleeve protectors sitting up there making sure that life balances for all of us. Life is unjust at times, and consequently, you need to get through that, and you need to rejoice in the victories. You need to rejoice when things go right, and too many people suffer through the troughs and then just shut their eyes at the heights and hope that it isn't too scary. That's a lonely way to go through life.

Q: No one has mentored more consultants than you have, and you've probably run into a fair number of people who left some other situation to go into consulting because they thought it would make them happy. Can you tell us what the key elements of happiness are, and when people don't find it, what are they missing?

Alan: That's a heck of a good question. I'm not sure that the key elements of happiness are consistent for every one. If I had to pick out some commonalities, I would say it's the following.

One would be a sense of autonomy—you control your own fate to the degree it's possible. You can't achieve immortality. You can't guarantee that you'll be insulated from disease. The degree to which you can control your own fate day in and day out, however, is probably important.

I think a second element of happiness is the development and exercising of talents that provide gratification. Some of those talents are what you might call business and professionally related. Some of those talents are recreational or entertainment directed. Whatever they are, if they're present in sufficient quantity and quality, I think the use of one's own talents is a component of happiness.

I also think recognition—positive feedback from others—is important. The sense that one is valued. The sense that one is helping others, is relied upon by others, and is appreciated by others is a source of happiness. That's why I think that it's very tough to be happy if you're lonely. Robinson Crusoe wasn't terribly happy being a castaway on that island, and then he found Friday, and he was somewhat happier. If you think of the movie where Tom Hanks was a modern day Robinson Crusoe, when the FedEx plane crashed in the ocean, he actually had as a partner—a Wilson volleyball.

We all need that kind of companionship, and I think it's a part of being happy. When that companion is able to recognize you or multiple people can recognize you, it's a part of being happy. I think it's a successful integration into society, an acceptance that you're a valued member of society, and you can extrapolate that in a lot of different ways. It would include being seen as a successful member and contributor to your family, your business, your community, your social activities, and so forth.

Q: You don't always call it optimism, but a consistent message that you give us in your blogs, newsletters, and presentations is related to keeping an optimistic attitude even in the face of setbacks and adversity. What role does this optimism have in happiness for consultants?

Alan: It's key because what you believe is how you act. The way you talk to yourself informs your behavior. If you get up in the morning and say, "Here is another fabulous day. I wonder what I'll make of it, but I plan to do something terrific," then that's going to inform your behaviors for that day. That means if something comes up that's adverse, you'll deal with it adequately. If something comes up that's wonderful, you'll deal with it so that you can exploit it. You'll have that kind of momentum. If you wake up in the morning and say to yourself, "God, another day. I wonder what is going to fall on my head today," you're going to look at any minor triviality that's negative as a horrendous setback, and even if it's positive, you'll look at it with suspicion.

People's attitudes, I'm absolutely convinced, will determine how they act. People's attitudes, in turn, are influenced by what one's basic beliefs are. Optimism is reliant on the belief that you're okay, other people are okay, it's a wonderful world and you can contribute to it, and you're going to provide value and it's okay.

It's not wrong to be happy and to consume happiness as long as you're also generating happiness. Too many people have a belief system that says they're not worthy, they don't deserve it, and life is treacherous. Theodore Dreiser, the fabulous writer, said once that this is "a dirty, stinking, treacherous, rotten world, and 99 out of 100 men are bastards." He was a great writer, but I wouldn't want to hang out with him.

Q: Some people are just naturally sunnier than others are, so optimism comes more easily to them. Can we learn optimism? Are there things we can do?

Alan: Yes, and before I talk about learning optimism, let me point out that there is a perkiness wall. There is an optimistic limitation. There should be a governor because there are some people you could smack in the face and they'll say, "How lucky I am!" There is a perkiness quotient beyond which your teeth start to rot, but in terms of normal optimism and normal happiness, you can learn optimism.

Martin Seligman, the psychologist, has written a book called *Learned Optimism*, which is probably the best book he has written. He is a good writer, a good guy, and *Learned Optimism* is a fabulous book. It's all about self-talk, and it's exactly the point that I was making a few minutes ago. His contention is the way you talk to yourself will inform how you behave. If you think you're lucky, you're going to be tentative. If you think you're talented and deserve what you get, you're going to be forceful and assertive. I'm probably doing violence to what he is writing about, but essentially that's what it is.

Anybody can learn optimism, but what does that depend upon? It depends upon with whom you're hanging out. It depends upon your ability to take in additional information, diverse viewpoints, and not just isolate yourself to the world you're currently living in.

I've created a "Framing" Workshop, and one of the points I make is we all have to compensate for what we're lacking to be able to frame issues better. We're lacking certain travel to certain countries. We're lacking certain historical precedent. I wasn't alive when Lincoln was shot. My son is amazed I was alive when Kennedy was shot. I happen to know geography, and some people don't. You have to compensate for what you're missing to have a good sense of how to frame issues. Similarly, you have to have that kind of comprehensive reference base so that you know what you're missing, how to get it, how to be optimistic, and how to be positive.

Q: Your communities provide these opportunities for optimism, correct?

Alan: I've always asked people who are challenged about something, "Has anyone ever done it anywhere who is remotely similar to you?" If the answer is, "No. No one in my position, at my age, in my location has ever done anything remotely like this," then my response is, "Then this is truly break-through, and you have to prepare yourself for that. It requires certain skills and talents, and you have to understand that maybe the odds are against you, and you might fail, but you're failing a good cause."

If somebody says, "Yes, other people like me have done that under similar circumstances," then I tell them, "Stop whining and get it done."

Q: Talking about learning optimism, what are the relationships among general learning growth, reinvention, and living a happy life?

Alan: It depends what floats your boat. For me, change, improvement, innovation, creativity, reinvention—all those things make me happy. A lot of people are threatened by them. I think the real issue here isn't that some people are happy and unhappy, even though that's true, but is the fact that some people attain happiness with much more modest goals and accomplishments than others. I think you're happiness quotient if it's satisfied, if it's sated in a very modest manner, prevents much further growth.

You could make a case to me that if somebody is driving the same bus route for 40 years, you want their happiness quotient to be simply doing things on time, being courteous to riders, making sure the bus is safe, driving correctly in traffic, and so forth. We need people like that, and nothing against bus drivers, but you can't have a country of bus drivers. You have to have people who are motivated and made happy by trying to put somebody on the moon.

Q: Could you give us a distinction between religion and spirituality, and what does spirituality mean to you?

Alan: I'm a practicing Catholic. I'm a Eucharistic Minister in the Catholic Church, I converted about seven years ago, and before that I wasn't in any organized religion. I think that religion connotes for most people an organized approach to the belief in a deity and accompanying values, whether it be an afterlife, redemption, salvation, or whatever those beliefs are.

One of the issues about Christianity in the Catholic Church that appealed to me that transcends into the spiritual is that forgiveness and toleration are key to the belief system. You might say that hasn't always been the case in actuality, and I won't argue that, but the doctrine, the theology is about forgiveness and toleration. That appeals to me a great deal because what has always occurred to me is that none of us is perfect, and we ought to stop trying to be perfect—which is why you've heard me talk about success not perfection for 25 years. How do we succeed, and how do we do it in the right manner? That's why we also talk about ethics in this book.

Spirituality for me is not an organized set of beliefs or religion. Spirituality goes back to one of my favorite examples that I use so often—we're sitting here on a hunk of rock traveling at 85,000 miles an hour around an exploding star. Please don't tell me that you don't have faith. We could be extinguished any day. The dinosaurs were, and they ruled for 200 million years. When they were exterminated when that meteor hit the Yucatan, the Tyrannosaurus Rex—one of the most fearsome creatures ever to roam the earth—was still evolving. Goodness knows what it would look like today.

Humankind has been here from between 100,000 and 200,000 years, depending on the scientific source. You can use different estimates for that, it's all over the place, and every time I put it on my blog, somebody gives me hell for it. Humankind is generally believed to be in that area, you can pick your number, but it's very brief compared to 200 million years for the dinosaurs!

Here we are sitting in this universe that we can't begin to understand. Nobody knows what happens if you go straight up. Nobody knows what happens if you just keep going. Nobody knows what infinity is—whether it's Einstein or Stephen Hawking—no one knows. Spirituality, therefore, to me is an inner ember that glows and says I'm a member of this universe. I'm a member of this planet. I'm a member of this species, this group of human beings. I intend to try to play a vital role and to have faith, and in this case, the faith may or may not be in a God, but I'm going to have faith in myself and in my life so that I can make the best of it.

I think that inner ember I talk about, this feeling that it's not just you, is that you're part of nature. I think if you have spirituality, animal abuse will be very important to you. It would be very painful for you. I think if you have spirituality, the wanton destruction of forests or poisoning of the atmosphere and water will make you very unhappy; as will the way we treat the less fortunate—be they people who are homeless, poor, have mental problems, or who are in prison. Dostoevsky had a brilliant line. He said if you want to judge the degree of a civilization's sophistication, if you want to judge the merits of a civilization, enter its prisons.

For me, spirituality is a matter of being within the world around you, cognizant of it, and willing to play a role in that world that's contributing, sensitive, and positive. Can that transfer to a religious system where you're going to a certain edifice once a week and doing certain rites? It can. Can it transfer to a religious system where you believe in a God, a deity, an afterlife, but you tend not to attend that particular house of worship? It can. Can it extend to someone who doesn't believe in God at all but believes they're a spiritual person? Of course it can. These things can be interrelated or not related, and spirituality to me is extraordinarily important in any case.

I find myself now gazing out the window in my den at about four or five feet of snow, looking at the birds who are flocking to the bird feeders and what is left in them. I have to refill them, wondering how the birds are doing, knowing they know there is food there each day, and they don't feel the need to thank me, and they probably don't even associate it with me. I do something for them, and they do something for me unknowingly which is they provide me with a good feeling. I can watch them. They're entertaining. They're pretty.

There is this symbiotic relationship that occurs in nature that for me is what spirituality is all about. It also helps you through the imponderables. Why do dogs live a short life? It doesn't seem right. Why do wonderful people come down with diseases? It doesn't seem right. Why are there floods, why is there revolt, and why is there evil? It doesn't seem right. You have to have the inner resources to deal with this in a life the meaning of which is often obscure to the "naked eye."

Q: Just to clarify one point, it doesn't sound to me that one needs to believe in God in order to be spiritual.

Alan: In my definition, no. You can ask a priest, rabbi, or minister—which almost sounds like the opening to a bad joke—any mom or dad, or anyone else, but I think spirituality and religion overlap and can be very tightly integrated or can be quite separate. I think they're both in the eyes, the actions, and the beliefs of the individual. I certainly would think if you're religious, you're spiritual. I'm sure somebody, somewhere will cite me an exception and write me a letter, but if you're spiritual, I don't think it means you're also religious. I think there are a lot of people who are neither religious nor spiritual.

Q: Do you think there is a place for spirituality in corporate life?

Alan: You see it every day. You see people exercising their beliefs. I talked before about the belief in the value that you provide, not in making money. The happiness is in providing value. Unlike what a lot of people would have you believe in the media—and unlike some writers who feel that management is evil, and it's up to people to fight management, and all this kind of nonsense—most organizations, not all, but the great preponderance of organizations are trying to do good and contribute to society.

Drucker said that an organization isn't like an animal or a plant that simply lives to perpetuate the species. An organization lives to contribute to the environment around it, and most organizations do. They provide employment. They provide goods and services which people need. Sometimes they're vital like drugs, and sometimes they're simply a bagatelle. Sometimes they're simply a video box or a game player, but nonetheless, people's lives are improved from them. There are very few organizations, outside the Batman movies, that are hell-bent to create evil and suffering. Some of them have done it, and some of them have done it accidentally, but the great preponderance of organizations are spiritual in that they believe in what they're doing. They're providing insurance, security, and a better life for people.

When I worked with Merck for over 12 years as a consultant, they won America's Most Admired Company five years in a row.[4] I'm not saying that was due to me, but they weren't attracting people who were coming to Merck to get rich because you didn't get rich there as you might in investment banking or real estate sales. They were attracting people who believed in what Merck was doing: Bringing the greatest in scientific research against

---

4.   *Fortune Magazine's* annual poll of executives.

the greatest public health needs. Is that spirituality in the work place? I would make a case that it is.

Q: I feel that spiritual experiences are probably hard to come by. I want to increase my own spirituality, and others I believe want to increase that experience as well. What can one do in order to improve or increase their spiritual being and experience?

Alan: I don't agree with you. I don't agree that it's very difficult to have spiritual experiences because, to answer the rest of your question, all you have to do is watch a tree that's barren in the winter sprout and bloom buds in the spring and then have 400,000 leaves come forth as spring turns into summer. Explain that to me.

It's more than chlorophyll. It's more than some kind of automated response system. It's miraculous. Watch a caterpillar become a butterfly. Watch a goose, this ungainly creature, come down for a soft landing in a pond as though landing on an aircraft carrier. Watch the fact that people can drive on a highway at an average of 70 or 75 miles an hour, 12 or 15 feet from each other, and there isn't carnage resulting every day. In fact, it's so rare that when there is a deadly auto accident, it's reported as a headline.

Think about the fact that people create music, create film, create live experiences, and every day of the year you can access these either in person, in print, on the internet, on television, or in a wide variety of ways. If you take this broader look, this 85,000 miles-per-hour hunk of rock look, you'll realize that the things happening around you can create a tremendous spirituality about you.

The problem is that too many people are blind to it. They just walk down the street with their head down worrying about getting to work at 9:00, the meeting they have at 10:30, will they eat too much for lunch at 12:00, will they be able to get through commuter traffic at 5:00, and hope they have a decent dinner at 7:00 and the kids don't have too much homework and bother them at 9:00. If that's the day you're living, you're not going to be very spiritual.

Q: A couple of months ago I had dinner with you, your son Jason, and your wife Maria. During that discussion we explored a topic that was very profound, and part of the topic on spirituality was divinity. We talked about the concept of divinity as pertained to people like Beethoven, Mozart,

Picasso, and da Vinci. Tell the reader your take on divinity and how you feel it may touch people like you, us, and others.

Alan: My personal belief system is that there is a deity. I do believe in God. I don't think the universe is an accident of some kind of scientific development that we don't understand. I think that there is some kind of motive force behind it, and I ascribe that to God. I don't believe in the anthropomorphic God who sits on our shoulder and whispers in our ear every day, and that's why the whole aspect of toleration and forgiveness is so important. I think men and woman have free will.

I also believe it's a far greater act of faith to believe there are purely scientific or accidental reasons for us being here, in an infinite universe we can't explain, than to believe in a supreme creator. That's just me.

Consider the compositions of Beethoven who was deaf, and take a look at the work of da Vinci. This is what I mean when I talk about "framing" because it's hard to do this simply through other media. If you go to St. Peter's in Rome and look at the Pieta—forget the religious aspects of it—it's Mary holding the dying Christ. If you look at this piece of work, it's transfiguring, and how a human being created that is beyond me. The same would apply to Michelangelo's David or the work of Rodin.

Most of the work that's immortal—the art, the songs, the music, and so forth—have religious origins. That's because they were commissioned by people who wanted to pay homage to God, and they were the only people who could afford to have this done, but that's a story for another time. If you look at these great works that are eternal in terms of their appeal and impact, I don't think they're simply the works of people who got lucky. I think they're the works of people who've been gifted.

You can take contemporary examples. Frank Sinatra led a sort of dastardly life, but here is somebody who worked with the greatest composers and arrangers in history and produced the greatest popular song interpretations ever recorded in this country. It was just an amazing gift that he had, and despite everything else about him—a very imperfect man by any standards—this is what he was able to create. I heard Michael Bublé the other day sing a classic Gershwin song, and he has a great voice, but it paled in comparison to the canonical Sinatra—whose phrasing, breath control, and interpretation are works of art.

Whether it's a scientist who is able to create the formula for getting a rocket ship to a certain point of escape velocity; somebody who can put paint on canvas or notes on a page; a person who can walk on stage and create something that an audience is spellbound by; no matter what the endeavor, people who can do that consistently and well, I think, are beyond simply disciplined or lucky. I think they've been gifted and also have been able to find their *métier*. They've been able to find the right expression of their talent, and it's rather rare or we wouldn't talk about it so particularly.

You can name the top 10 or 12 classical composers. You can name the top dozen or so great painters, sculptors, and so forth. Your lists might differ somewhat because of personal preferences, but the same names are going to be reappearing and reappearing. Because of that, I think there is a divine nature to life.

Q: You talked earlier that you've gone through a religious conversion. What was the trigger that impacted that instrumental decision in your life to say, "I'm converting to accept Christianity"?

Alan: I found that something was missing in my life. I was very successful, but I knew that there was a void. Something was missing. My wife has been a practicing Catholic all her life. Our kids were raised Catholic and baptized, which was our agreement, and I thought was a very smart thing to do. I think every child should be raised with some form of religion (I regret that I wasn't), and then they can make up their own minds as they gain adolescence or adulthood. I think it's easier to have it and decide you don't need it than not to have it and try to decide you do need it.

I felt this void in my life, and I finally admitted to myself that I had been praying all my life. My contention is that everyone prays. It's not an accident that people say, "Oh, my God," "God bless you," or "God willing." Even proclaimed atheists say these things, and please don't tell me it's mere convention. They don't need to do so. I found that everybody prays, and it's not just a random act. No one writes a letter, signs the letter, puts it in an envelope, seals the envelope, puts a stamp on it, and leaves it on their desk. They post it. They send it through the mail expecting it will go somewhere. I don't think anyone idly prays either. When people are *in extremis*—and this is where you get the phrase "there are no atheists in foxholes"—they pray. Whether they've believed in God or not, whether they've been critical or not, they pray.

People pray sometimes for mundane and trivial reasons. You see players make the sign of the cross in basketball before they shoot a free throw, which is somewhat ludicrous but also somewhat instructive. You see football players who make a great play point to the skies. You see people who accept an Oscar, an Emmy, or another award first thanking God. I'm not defending this or being critical of it. All I'm saying is that people are praying on a regular basis; therefore, they're praying to some divinity with the hope of being heard. Once I admitted that to myself, I then realized that I should stop kidding around and hedging my bets. You can't have it both ways. I don't think it makes sense to simply call upon God *in extremis* or even to have a book published but not acknowledge God in your life.

Since I've been exposed to the Catholic Church through my wife, I like the rigor of it. I like the open and honest sort of confession that you make in terms of the priest and liturgy that says openly and candidly, "The mystery of faith," and there it is. There are no equivocations about it. Faith is a mystery. Jesus Christ's death and resurrection is a mystery, and the church accepts that. It's a mystery and we don't understand, but here is what happened, and here is why we should pay some attention to it millennia later.

I also believe that billions of people who believe in Christianity haven't been "taken" by sharpsters and frauds. Among those billions are people who are very bright, very intelligent, and made intelligent choices. Two millennia ago something happened, and look at all of the writing and ritual that has come down through the ages. How many things last for 2,000 years on a fairly consistent basis without change? The fact that this has been manifested all this time isn't testimony to me that people are afraid, that they're cowed, or they follow some blind tradition as a lot people would have us believe. I think it's a testimony to the fact that something spectacular happened and has created this longevity of belief.

For me, the Catholic Church made sense, and for me, "in for a dime in for a dollar." I became a Eucharistic Minister, which means you help provide the host and the holy wine during the services when you're called upon. It became an important part of my life about seven years ago. I haven't missed one church service one week, no matter where I am in the world.

In Bora Bora, for example, we took two friends of ours on a boat ride and went to a Catholic church on an island where, instead of bells, they used a conch shell. No matter where you are in the world, it's interesting how the local traditions influence the service, but the same things happen at the same time. It's wonderful for me as a Catholic to know that no matter where you go—I've been in Spanish, French, Italian, and all kinds of different language services—you pretty much know what is happening because the same thing happens at about the same time. That has been rewarding for me, and I'm happy I did it.

Q: What direct experience can you comment on in terms of the sensory, the physical experience in association with the Holy Spirit? How do you experience the Holy Spirit? What language will you use to describe the experience?

Alan: To me it's a question of receiving advice as to what the right thing to do is. It's sort of a centering. It's this help which you could ascribe to your experience, your frame of reference, and to your history. I feel that every once in a while there is the advice, the notice, the prompting, the hunting as if you were sort of a German Shepherd—here, look out that window. Take this trip. Don't go back. You heed it.

Q: The experience is one of guidance, direction, and a sense of inner knowing or a compass of what is right? It's not necessarily in a sensory physical dimension?

Alan: It's never physical. It's always this input, this intent, this advice, this feeling of what is right. I think that's how I arrived at that decision then.

Q: When you encounter somebody in your mentor program who lacks a spiritual foundation, what symptoms do you see? How do you know?

Alan: They're very superficial. They never look below the surface. They only deal with what is immediately in front of them, so they're not good at etiology. They're not very good at looking for causes. They're always dealing with effects. They often feel that they've been treated unfairly. They often feel that they've gotten bad breaks. They don't feel that they're in control of their fate or their destiny at all, and they're not very convivial people. Consequently, they're very uninteresting to me.

I think that anyone with a strong sense of humor has a spirituality about them because you tend to look at the ironies and the paradoxes of life. You can look at Jerry Seinfeld and might say, "I don't think that's a spiritual person." I think he really is. I think Lenny Bruce was. He was arrested 16 times for a vulgarity that is common on Facebook today. I think true, witty comics—not people who just stand on stage and use obscenity—are spiritual people because you have to see the intricate fibers of the pattern of life.

Q: Would you say that most of the successful consultants that you've known would qualify as spiritual people?

Alan: Yes, because they have a much more profound view and understanding of the world around them, and most importantly, they have much more of a curiosity about the world around them. Spiritual people are intellectually curious. They're not afraid of ambiguity. Spirituality doesn't have right and left turns, and B following A, and so forth. Consequently, they're much more curious than people who aren't spiritual, and that curiosity leads them to much greater learning and the ability to use that learning.

Q: You've been in a field of individual and organizational change for more than three decades. How has this perspective, when we're talking about spirituality, influenced or shaped your work?

Alan: I used to view organizations without sufficient depth and breadth. I think that as you start to look at the interplay of systems, people, processes, structures, and so forth, you get this multi-dimensional view. You realize that it's like an airline pilot who has to think three-dimensionally. We tend to look at an airplane going up or down, right or left, but it's also doing something else as it does those things. I've piloted a few planes, and I appreciate that experience. By the way, that's part of framing. There is this three-dimensional aspect of flying, and the same thing in organizations.

It's multi-dimensional, and you have to understand that as one thing moves, three other things are moving in varying directions, and you have to accommodate that. I think if you have a spiritual center, you don't get upset when things aren't going exactly the way you thought. You understand more that somebody is opposing something, not because they're trying to be obstreperous. Not because they're trying to throw you under a bus. They're opposing it because their self-interests aren't being met, and you have to arrange a way for their self-interests to be met as well if you really need these people to come along.

You understand the delicacy and differences between things like commitment and compliance, the difference between cause and effect, the difference between strategy and planning, the difference between input and output, and so forth. These very subtle distinctions can create profoundly different outcomes.

I compare it to shooting an artillery piece. If that artillery piece is one degree off where you want the shell to land, you're going to kill friendly forces. If you shoot a rocket someplace, and it's a tenth of a degree off when you shoot it, it's going to land in another universe. Spirituality, in terms of any kind of work but especially consulting work, tends to keep you on target.

Q: There is a saying in Hebrew that means "know before whom you're standing." Is that possible notion influencing your actions, your behavior, and your thoughts about performing good deeds in this world?

Alan: I don't think so. I don't think that I'm concerned each day about a reckoning. I'm not concerned that St. Peter is going to meet me with a list of transgressions and tell me that he isn't giving me the keys to the kingdom. That doesn't worry me. I think that as long as you do the best you can, you ask for forgiveness, and you try to help others, you're fulfilling your role.

I do think, in a very pragmatic way, that what you said has some real meaning in consulting. I meet countless people who don't understand whom they're standing in front of. You'll meet people who don't correctly take into account the nature of the buyer, their colleague, the competitor, or whomever it is, and they simply make assumptions based on their own frame of reference. This goes back to everything we've been talking about. You have to have the right frame of reference.

I'll have people who come up to me and say something like, "Travel is great. I went to Canada. I went to Montreal, and I'm going to tell you how important that travel is." Okay, fair enough, and my wife would say to me to be patient and listen. If you're ignorant to the fact I've been to 59 countries, and I used to run a Canadian operation because you don't even bother to say, "Have you ever been to Canada?"—then you don't know whom you're standing in front of. That applies to all kinds of folks.

I just wrote on my blog yesterday "Adventures in the publishing trade," and one of my long-time editors at Wiley—who has published a lot of my consulting books—told my agent that she wasn't interested in my book on speaking because it wasn't my background. I'm in the Speaking Hall of Fame! I have speaking credits that are beyond most. I'm one of two people in history with the highest accolade of the National Speakers Association and the Institute of Management Consultants. There are only two of us in history to receive such honors, and I said to her, "You've never, ever read my bio. You've never looked at my website in all the years we've been working together." She stopped talking to me and stopped corresponding with me. That's the degree to which people don't know whom they're standing in front of, and it limits your ability to influence. It limits your ability to be successful yourself and make intelligent choices.

Q: What goes through your mind, spirit, and emotion when you feel in the moment, and you are connected spiritually?

Alan: The advantage here is that I feel that way most of the time. I said before it was the one thing missing in my life. I feel that way most of the time, and there are times I'm upset with American Express, I've stubbed my toe, or Buddy Beagle has had an accident in the pool room, but by and large that's how I feel. I realize how fortunate I am, how appreciative I should be, and I have sympathy for people who can't get there or haven't gotten there.

I remember one of the early trips I made to St. Peter's when my wife and I were touring Italy long before I converted. This must be 20 years ago. We were walking through St. Peter's and no matter what your belief system is, St. Peter's is an amazing place. There is a profusion of side altars there, each one with magnificent artwork, benches where you can pray, and candles. There must be dozens of these spread around the periphery of St. Peter's, and as I was walking along the side of this great cathedral, I came upon a small chapel that was empty except for one nun who must have been in her 70s. She was hunched over with a rosary, praying in front of the altar. I forget what saint it was, but the nun looked totally at peace. As I walked by I remember saying to myself, "How fortunate she must be." It's possible for all of us no matter what our occupations, our avocations, or our intents. It's a question of whether you seize it or not.

Conclusion

One of the worst mistakes any of us can make is to "compartmentalize" our lives. We don't have a personal life and a business life. We simply have a life. Time is the great equalizer, since we all have the same number of hours a day. How we spend them and how we view them holds the key to our thriving, not merely surviving.

If you feel the world is out to get you, it probably will. But if you believe that existence is largely what you make of it, you'll probably make out just fine. If you manage to help someone else along the way, that's money in the bank and the recipe for a successful life.

13 | The Consultant's Tool Kit

Every consultant needs intellectual firepower. You need to be well read and have command of the language. You need very sharp analytic skills, crisp observational skills, and clear listening skills. You also need the ability to communicate very, very well. You need to be able to subordinate your ego, and be flexible enough to deal with a variety of different personality types successfully by adjusting to them and not insisting they adjust to you.

There is a set of behaviors and a set of skills that a consultant should have in a kit. As you go through life, you might find a better tool to replace an older one or a new tool you hadn't thought about using that you put in there. Basically, you need to be able to read with comprehension, to write with expression, to speak with influence, and to listen with discernment. These are the general skills that will allow you to put more specialized tools in your toolkit.

What Are the Critical Elements of a Consultant's Toolkit?

Q: Why a toolkit?

Alan: In your toolkit you need the kinds of skills and content that are appropriate for your specialty and client. To give you a specific example, let's just say for argument's sake that you're dealing with strategy, and those are the kinds of clients you're consulting with on a strategic basis. You're helping them formulate strategy, implement strategy, examine strategy, come up with new strategies, and so on. In that case, your toolkit should include a few strategy models that would be appropriate to use depending upon circumstances.

It should include the reference base where you're familiar with great strategists and strategies that have failed and been successful. For example, if you haven't read Peter Drucker, who virtually invented strategy at GM, then you're deficient. You also need the skills to facilitate a group of very high-level, very opinionated, successful people who aren't going to buy things just on the basis of your say so but who want to be shown. You'll also need the skills to avoid conflict when the senior vice president of R&D points to the senior vice president of sales and says, "It's not a problem of commercializing the product. It's a problem of the sales force being too ignorant to sell it."

Q: When it comes to understanding change, what would be a comparable reference to Drucker in the change management field?

Alan: Change is so fungible! I don't mean that as an oxymoron or even as a redundancy. Change is so flexible, and there are so many things involved in it that it's hard to cite just one reference. For example, the key aspect to think about with change is who is going to exemplify the change? Change leaders and change agents are always within the organization. I've never felt that an external force such as a consultant could be a change agent.

Having said that, you'll find some people who are really superb talking about change from different points of view. William Bridges has written a great deal, primarily in small booklets, about how to create organizational change, how to monitor change, guide change, and be successful at change. He does very good work. Edgar Schein wrote a magnificent book called *Process Consultation* which is about applying processes to create change in organizational settings. Change is such a generic term, it's really difficult to say here is the key and here is the source.

If you talk about leadership—to go back to Drucker on strategy—I would say you probably want to look at John Gardner as one of the great writers on leadership. Warren Bennis wrote *The Unconscious Conspiracy: Why Leaders Can't Lead,* and almost everything else he wrote was derivative, but that book was an essential *tour de force* on leadership. If you were looking at hygiene theory or motivation in the workplace, you're talking about McClellan, Hertzberg, McGregor—that group of people who specialized in those issues.

Q: As you think about the most successful consultants in your community, what do they have in common in terms of pursuing new tools for their toolkit?

Alan: Probably an intellectual curiosity, a thirst for learning, an emphasis on wanting to be more successful than they are. That success doesn't have to be financial success. It might mean expanding their practice to embrace other disciplines or creating more discretionary time for themselves by working smarter, but they have an insatiable thirst to improve themselves through learning. They're lifelong learners.

They're also not afraid to fail. They're fearless about trying new things, taking some bumps, and learning from that. They can subordinate their ego. They aren't constantly trying to tell me, "Oh, I've already done that. Yes, I've done that. Thank you, but I've already…" It's that kind of honesty and candor that I think represents those people the best, and fortunately in the community, there are a lot of them.

Q: Tell us how you decide which workshops to offer?

Alan: I just spoke about this. I was on a panel in Atlanta yesterday morning, a Million Dollar Mindset panel, and one of the questions we were asked—there were about 300 people in the room—was about tribes. I said that I don't use the word "tribes." I use the word "community," and the reason is the cognate of tribes is tribalism, and tribalism is narrow and exclusionary.

I believe in communities which are ever broadening and embracing, and within these communities, when people come up with an idea, you can see a chain reaction. The chain reaction is about whether other people respond to it well. It hasn't been marketed, it hasn't been tried, it hasn't even been explained in many cases, but if people say, "I would really go to something like that," and you see you have a critical mass developing—that's what I tend to follow.

For example, if I find that somewhere between 12 and 20 people say, "If you did this, I would go to it," barring poor scheduling or whatever, I'll then start to market it. I'll say the first 12 or 15 people who sign up will get a preference. They'll have dinner with me, or whatever it is, but I'll give them some kind of *quid pro quo*. That way I get my 12 or 15 people, and then we get another 12 or 15 people who have been watching this, and then I start to market it publicly. In the case of let's say the Framed Workshop, we had 45 people in Sarasota from that technique. In the case of Best Practices which I began a couple of years ago—and I've now done four or five times, which is more than I like to do it—the very first event drew 133 people to Rhode Island at $1,000 a person.

Where communities engender, what they spawn are these ideas that people take hold of and become evangelists for. That's why forming your own community is so important, and that's why these generic communities—Facebook, LinkedIn, and so on—serve certain social purposes, but they don't serve *this purpose* well at all. Forming your own communities is what helps you in this regard.

Q: Aside from Best Practices which you offered so many times, what are some others that you consider your most successful or that you've had feedback about that people really appreciated?

Alan: I broke up a lot of the discipline that you're talking about today. For example, I had a program called The Strategist, and I ran that in Rhode Island, Sydney, and London—and the total was probably about 120 people among the three sites. Then I broke out another one called The Coach, and I've done that several times. I usually like to do things in the U.S., London, and Sydney if I can. I did something called Self-Esteem which people are still asking me to do again.

Framing Skills

Q: What is your definition of framing?

Alan: It's creating a focus on the critical issues that need to be addressed with a client, and the client might or might not realize that these were the critical issues. It's isolating these issues and removing the superfluous, irrelevant, and noncritical.

I think it was probably a couple years ago when I started just accidentally to say to somebody, "Look, here is how you frame this." The word just seemed to take hold. It had resonance. I love to be succinct and brief, and in one word it did create what I wanted it to create.

If you think of the difference between a lot of photographs or artwork that you see, it's really a question of what is framed and how it's framed. The product still has to be of high quality, but the framing can really make a huge difference. I just loved the metaphor, and I kept using it.

Q: Why do so many people confuse problem solving with decision making?

Alan: I think there are two basic reasons. In my experience, the first is that they tend to use the phrases interchangeably, and no one has ever corrected them. Just as you'll hear people say "imply" when they mean "infer." These are two different words. Imply is the speaker, infer is the listener. They mean two entirely antipodal things, and they can have a vast difference in meaning if you're reading this. However, people tend to confuse them because they're sloppy, and no one has ever corrected them. It's intellectual slop.

The second problem is that people don't understand the process behind problem solving or decision making. Consequently, they don't really understand they are two different things.

Q: Is one of the values we as consultants must bring to the buyer to help fix or update their erroneous thought patterns?

Alan: Let me put it this way since I don't start with the premise that anyone is damaged. I'll listen, I'll make a determination about whether the buyer is using the right terminology, the right approach, has connected the right dots, and if so, I can accelerate what I want to do. If not, then I have to go back and make some adjustments.

Q: As I listen to these incisive distinctions you make and how you speak to the power of specificity, precision, and language, what occurs to me is that you have a form of delight, of excitement in your ability to create these powerful distinctions. That is in part what continues to propel you to new, clearer, more powerful articulations. There is a whole love affair that you have with language that really drives your success. Am I describing this correctly in terms of your interior experience?

Alan: I think you are. I want to add one thing to it though. The language is a means to an end, and the end—what I really love—is watching people grow and learn. That to me is extraordinarily exciting. When I was up on the dais yesterday, there was a moderator and five panelists, and I was very funny. I was very humorous. There was clearly a distinction amongst us, and I was different from the others.

The reason I enjoy that isn't for my ego. I did this for free. The reason I enjoy this is people will pay more attention to me, they'll tend to learn more, and they'll tend to join my community, enrich my community, and enrich the people in my community. You need to stand out in a crowd if you really want to help others. You know this oxygen mask principle I talk about all the time. You can't help others unless you're helping yourself by continually improving what you're able to do and investing in yourself. Then you can help others because you can really stand out in a crowd.

I would say that the most distinctive things presented yesterday— which were also the most pragmatic in that brief 90 minutes that we all had on stage—were presented by me. That's what I love to do. I love to challenge people and get them thinking, and even though that might just involve two out of ten, that's okay with me.

Q: This was a free engagement. Is that something that you do as part of your marketing gravity?

Alan: I do *pro bono* work for organizations that represent professions which have been good to me. That's one way I pay back. In this case it was the National Speakers Association Eastern Conference in Atlanta. When NSA or the IMC—the Institute of Management Consultants—ask me, if my calendar permits and it makes sense, I'll do it.

I'll give you an example. As usual, when I was done I had a car waiting outside with the engine running, and the door open, so I could make a plane back and have dinner with my wife at a reasonable hour. As I'm running out of the room, a woman grabs me and says, "I want you to do an interview with me on Twitter." I said, "Walk with me while you're talking." She tells me that it will be her 100th interview. She does these special interviews that are live-time on Twitter, and she would be honored to have me as her 100th guest. She put this book out that has been very well received and gave me her card. I said, "I'll tell you what. If you're serious, send me an email."

I got an email this morning first thing from her saying, "I'm following up. I want to do this." I said, "I'm having a hard time understanding this. Call me later in the day." She called me. She explained the details. I had looked up her book on the internet, and her book is in a very good position on Amazon. She is serious about what she talks about.

I liked her attitude, so I agreed to do this for her. I said to her, "Your audience isn't like mine, but I'm happy to do this as a favor to you." She says, "What about your standing offer?" I have a standing offer, which I made from the stage, that I have 2,000 followers on Facebook, and I have 5,000 on Twitter, and I have 60 million connections on LinkedIn, and if anybody can show me how to get 50 cents from all of them, I'll split it.

She said, "I think I'm prepared to do that." She talked about that. We arrived at a deal where she would use her proprietary lists from her book, her Twitter work, her blog, and everything else to promote a very high-value thing that I would provide at a very low price which we would split, and we would do this as a test with a goal of making $10,000. I'm involved in this, and you never know. I've always said I'm not smart enough to say where the next hit is going to come from, but she was very professional, she approached me, we're working on this joint venture now, and who knows. I think when you do good, good will follow.

Q: Do you look at those combinations of words and think about pros and cons almost in a debate fashion, or what is it that goes through you to really articulate the pros and cons of each one?

Alan: There is an interesting dichotomy here. There is a duality of what you just asked me. On the one hand, I very quickly think of what the most effective phrase I want to use is, and even if the phrase I'm faced with is an effective one, I want to think of a more effective one. If you think about it, what I'm doing is reframing the conversation in my benefit, and this is why framing is so important. By using my phrase, my word, my indicators, I'm reframing this so that now everyone is oriented toward me.

The second aspect of what you're saying is this. If you had said to me, "Alan, just for the sake of argument, prove to me why tribe is better than community as a word," I would have said to you something as follows: "Tribes have a certain cohesion to them. They have a culture. They have an admission process. They protect themselves against commonly recognized enemies. Communities can allow too many people in. They're too porous. They don't have one set of cultural rules. The laws may vary based on favoritism. Tribes have a clear..." I can go on and on like that. I don't happen to believe that, but I can probably beat 99 people out of 100 at that argument either way.

Q: Give us some practical ideas for the consultants out there: What can we do to improve both sides of the debate quickly and effectively?

Alan: One is you have to have a massive vocabulary. How do you develop that? You develop it by reading, writing, having intelligent friends, doing very difficult crossword puzzles and acrostics, and so forth and so on. You can develop them by picking three different words each day and adding them to your vocabulary. You can do it by copying every word you don't understand in your normal reading and making sure you look it up and keep that word handy.

The second thing is you have to have a very broad frame of reference. I can give you a metaphor using a toothache, a battleship, or interstellar travel. You have to have a reference that's created by massive reading on a variety of different topics and a creative mind which is why I read so much fiction and science fiction. You have a wide frame of reference from travel, from lack of ego, from allowing things in, from experimenting, not being afraid to fail, and engaging in different pursuits. I don't have any problem when somebody says, "I'm not going to eat shellfish because I have an allergy." But if somebody says, "I'm not going to eat shellfish. I just don't like the look of it," I have a real problem with that. I happen to love uni, which is a very special kind of Japanese food and could be eaten as either sushi or sashimi, but it has a very peculiar texture and a very lovely taste. It's the mark of a true sushi eater if you can eat uni, which is sea urchin. A lot of people won't try it just by looking at it, and that irritates me.

I don't think that's what life is about, and you have to be willing to try things to increase the span of your knowledge base, to increase your perspective. The greater your perspective, ironically, the wider and broader your perspective, the more universal it is, the more you can focus on any single issue or thing and understand what it constitutes in the enormity of things.

Q: Looking at your journey over the past 20-some years of where you started to where you are today, with the knowledge that you have today, and the amazing success you have created early in your career and throughout your career, for the consultants to use it as a learning experience, what have you taken into your toolkit and added or dropped over the years that consultants should be aware of at different junctions of that journey?

Alan: I'm not sure I can answer that question with any specificity. I'm always looking for process models. I'm always looking for things I can apply across a broad spectrum of content because that to me is the most efficacious thing to do. It's the least delimiting. It's the most diverse. Occasionally, I've had to learn content because I need to be conversant in things. I know what a loan defalcation is if I'm in a bank. But it's the processes I look for, and the ones that you generally see are the ones that I pull out of the toolkit most often, just as you would only use a certain kind of Allen wrench, no pun intended, only in a situation when you need an Allen wrench. There are others I've dropped out of the toolkit because they've become obsolete. I have better ways to do things. They're no longer relevant, or they don't provide me with the leverage that I need to really stand out in a crowd.

I'm constantly examining what is in there because if you never take anything out, it gets too heavy, and you can't carry it anymore. The mental equivalent to that is you can't recall to the front of your mind quickly enough what you need.

Q: You talked about improving processes, greatly improving and focusing on your vocabulary, and integrated learning among other ideas. I'm looking for additional pragmatic ideas or advice from you on what consultants can do to significantly improve their framing skills.

Alan: I think you have to master the kinds of analytic skills that we've pointed out that I've been talking about. You have to understand that they're relatively limited, and you can master them. You need to read about them, learn about them, and apply them.

I was fortunate enough to work in a company for many years that specialized in some of these. I've developed my own. Very seldom do you use these processes in their totality, but the great benefit, the great pay back, the ROI is you use them "on the run." That's why you quickly see me frame things, or quickly say that's cause not effect, or quickly say it's this not that because I know how to use these mentally very, very quickly.

Q: During your Framed Workshop, you posed some case studies. What was fascinating to me is to recognize that probably all of the participants that took the hot seat with you have put on their filters, their expertise, and they framed it completely the wrong way. Doesn't that just demonstrate the danger that we bring our biases, our filters, and we're possibly applying the wrong frame?

Alan: Yes. However, let me suggest something to you. If you go back through this conversation today, the more perspective, more experience, and more vocabulary you have, chances are the better your filters are going to be. We all have biases. We all operate through the acculturation, education, heredity, and DNA coursing through our lives and veins. The fact is that the broader frame of reference we create, the less likely it is we'll be looking through too narrow a filter or wrong colored filter, and I think that's important. I think that's the antidote to what you're talking about.

I had something on Alan's Forums yesterday. I put up a case study, and to me it was a no-brainer, it was a very simple thing. There was a misunderstanding. Do you tell your wife and kids you can't have dinner that night, or do you tell the client sorry, you have to go home and have dinner with your family? The fact is that you have dinner with your family all the time. It's not clear whose misunderstanding this was, and this client is putting food on the table for you, so you stay with the client. I don't think there are two ways to look at that except, of course, there were on the Forum, and that's because people didn't frame it correctly. They looked at too narrow a spectrum, and they didn't look at the totality of the thing which tells you in an instant that you can have dinner with your family any time.

Q: In the workshop you also explained the horizontal and vertical focus in discussions with prospects. You said we shouldn't get vertical too soon. What does this mean?

Alan: I think what I was talking about is that you shouldn't delve down too deeply at first on an issue. Sort of like my beagle starts eating from his food bowl and goes crazy trying to get to the bottom right away. What you should do is look laterally and see how many things, how many kindred elements also fit into this issue. That will enable you to create the correct frame. If you simply dig deeper into one thing you latch onto immediately, you get it in your teeth and won't let it go. Your ability to frame is severely compromised because you're not looking at the entire landscape.

Q: As you pointed out in the workshop, we'll often miss an opportunity. If we go in with a particular frame of "I want to make this about what I do instead of about what the client needs," then we miss those opportunities. You spoke in Framed about assertive and also, I think, aggressive framing. What do you mean assertive and aggressive framing?

Alan: You take something that you're excellent at, something you want to market, something you want to influence someone else about, persuade someone else to do, and you say something like this: "There are five reasons why you should work only with a solo practitioner. Number one, you're not dealing with a whole raft of people coming in to learn your business and charging you for it. Number two, you're not supporting the overhead of 16 offices

across the country. Number three, you'll have immediate response in this."
You can apply that to any pursuit or any kind of argument, but the fact is
you're creating a frame for the client, you're painting the client into a frame.

I'll give you another example of that. A client says to you, "We've never
hired consultants here." Rather than say something that's very, very ambiguous and dangerous like, "Maybe this will be the first time. I'm sure you had
good reasons for that. Could you tell me why that is?" you say instead, "You
would be surprised at how many of my best clients told me that at our very
first meeting." Now you have painted this person into a frame, into a picture
where your best clients exist. That's what I mean by aggressive framing.

Q: Do you do "there are five reasons for" as a form of a riddle with yourself
to say that and then you find out what the five reasons are?

Alan: Partially that because I enjoy the challenge, but it's more than that.
I found that psychologically when you tell people there is a number, they
tend to listen more closely. They tend to accord you much more respect as
an expert, as someone who has thought this through, and they're temporarily stopped until they've listened to your total number. They're not going to
argue with you until they hear your numbers out. It's a very effective discussion device.

Q: What are some other tools I can use to develop this practice of assertive
and aggressive framing?

Alan: I would advise you or anyone take the three or four most important
aspects of your value and create an aggressive frame around them as to why
people really can't live without them. Then I would also take the two or three
objections that you face that give you the most trouble, and I would create a
frame around those to deal with those aggressively.

For example, if somebody says, "We have no money," that's when most
consultants immediately pack their bags. My response to that is, "Look, I'm
not even talking about money right now. I'm talking about value, and there
is always money for the right kind of investment. Your lights are on. You
have security people here. You're paying salaries, and so forth and so on. It's
not a question there is no money as a resource; the question is priority, and
what I want to show you is your priority is best invested over here."

Q: In what ways have you used framing skills in your nonprofessional role as
a family man, spouse, and father to make your life richer?

Alan: I use them all the time. They're not necessarily designed for one thing or another. I remember when my son called me because he didn't get the part in a play at school and he was distraught. I quickly said to him, "You're feeling angry. You're feeling hurt. You're feeling this. You're feeling that." He said, "That's right." I said, "You have several options in front of you. You can refuse to perform in a subordinate role. You can protest to the dean. You can tell your friends not to support the play and so forth. I understand that, but the only thing that matters right now is what you really do about it.

"Your feelings are justified. I would feel the same way. The options you have in front of you are clear. Now the question is one of character. What do you do about this?" In the course of 60 seconds, I turned that conversation from my son feeling sorry for himself to my son feeling he had his fate in his hands and could do something about it that was constructive. I think whether you're dealing with family, friends, colleagues, or whatever, these are extraordinarily important tools to have.

Q: In this example the framing skill was number one, making a distinction between feelings and behavioral response; number two, delineating options of behavioral response.

Alan: Yes, and acknowledging exactly where my son was because when you don't do these things, with the best of intention you tend to commiserate, the conversation goes on forever, and it doesn't get any better. It's just commiseration. What you have to do is resolve these issues. Personal issues, business issues—they need some resolution if they are bothering you, and this was clearly bothering my son, so it needed to be resolved. When you're resolving something that's bothering you, the more quickly you can do that, the better off you are.

Q: Your acknowledgment in this example was your ability to name what he was feeling?

Alan: Right, but if you think about it, my acknowledgment was really the framing of where he was.

Q: Just like you said, there are five reasons for this, 13 reasons for that. You also recommend that we always anticipate the buyer's objections, and I realize we had a whole chapter discussing objections. In the reference of framing, how do you recommend consultants develop the practice of improving their ability to think light on their feet? Especially if they come up with their five reasons for this, and by the time they mention number three, they can't think of number four and five. Give us some tips there.

Alan: Give yourself a break. Cut yourself some slack. Just be in the moment. Stop thinking so much about the sale. Stop worrying so much about saying the wrong thing. Don't feel that there is some perfect interaction that has to occur here. You have to be willing to be in the moment.

The interesting combination of all of the things we've been talking about is that you have this arsenal of weapons; if that's too strong, let's just say a huge toolkit. I like to think in terms of an arsenal of weapons at your disposal, and in the moment you decide when and if to use which one. You decide the right degree, the right choice, and the right force, but you can only do that by staying in the moment and understanding what is in front of you. That's why if you walk in with some kind of script in your mind, you're probably going to have a lot of trouble.

Q: You were explaining an insight recently in terms of forest fires. Explain that again, and I'm curious if there isn't an analogous situation to organizational and corporate life?

Alan: I'm saying that scientists who study forest fires determined that when they're allowed to burn out, and you don't try to extinguish them or control them, in the burned out areas there are certain insects and animals that reappear that haven't been there before because they only thrive in recovering areas. They don't thrive when there is lush growth, thick canopies in the trees, and so on. The plants and trees that come back are stronger than ever, and then the animals return.

We see the same thing here in the winter where I am. When we have a harsh winter, things return with a vengeance. My neighbor is about a quarter mile away, but he was concerned that when the electric company came through to trim the trees to keep them away from the wires, there wouldn't be enough privacy between our homes. I told him, "Don't worry. In the spring you won't be able to see me, and I won't see you," and sure enough that's what happened.

Organizations are the same way. If you purge an organization, that is you don't merely downsize it but get rid of dead wood, you have some trauma. You get rid of organizational aspects of it that aren't working so well.

It comes back more strongly because the resultant energy and resources that are there are directed into more productive and profitable things.

I think we're seeing this as a result of the recession that we went through in the last couple of years. This recovery that's underway is equivalent to the tree limbs that were weak being knocked down by the ice storms here. Some financial weakness was purged out of the system, both people and companies that were overextended have been cleansed, and while I know that's painful, I think the resultant structure will be stronger than ever.

Q: You're drawing a parallel also between evolutionary biology and organizational life?

Alan: Yes, it's pretty clear that organisms adapt not just through generations, but they adapt while they're alive, and you might not see a physical change, but you certainly see a behavioral change. I just learned this watching my dogs. They know exactly which drawer to go into to get the dog treats, and if I change the drawer, they'll adapt to that. They arrange their habits so they follow me at certain occasions when they think they'll get a ride in the truck or get a treat, and other occasions they ignore me because they know where I'm going isn't going to help them at all. Those are the two dogs who live here. You bring in a strange dog, he wouldn't know that, but he would learn it in the next several days.

There is a certain Darwinism about the way organizations work. There is a great quote, by Flannery O'Connor, that says, "Societies are brought forward by inequality and people who are the best, not by a forced equality and an attempt that all will be the same." That holds true for individuals, groups, and organizations.

Q: Following from what you just explained, what differentiates consultants who have superior observational skills from those who don't?

Alan: There is a great bromide that says something like, "Are you going to believe me or your lying eyes?" Basically it happens when somebody is giving you some kind of crazy story and somebody says, "That's not borne out in evidence; it's not borne out in the environment. Are you going to believe me or your lying eyes?" Consultants who have the acuity to appreciate what is around them are going to be the best. Let me say here that women are far better at this than men. They're better behaviorally because they tend to have more empathy for what is around them, see more, and engage in what Helen

Fischer in her book *The First Sex* calls a "web-like thinking." There is also the fact that physiologically, women have more cones and rods in their eyes and can actually see colors and distinctions better than men can. Consequently, those consultants, irrespective of gender, who can look around with awareness are those who are going to be best.

Walter Lippmann had a fabulous line. He said, "We can't look back in nostalgia, and we can't look forward in fear. What we can do is look around in awareness." I think that's a very pithy way to say that consultants have to be aware of their surroundings and their client's surroundings and take that into consideration in their analysis.

Q: Apart from asking the women around you what is it they see that you don't, what are some of the other observational strategies that you use?

Alan: First of all, don't overlook that first one. For example, my dog, Koufax, the German Shepherd, is a sight dog. German Shepherds are large dogs. He goes out in the yard, lifts his head up, and looks around. Buddy Beagle, his companion, my other dog, is a scent dog. He immediately puts his head on the ground and starts picking up tracks, scents, odors. Between them they cover the waterfront. Koufax is looking, Buddy is sniffing. They both have very good hearing, and my lesson here is don't say, "Aside from asking a woman." I think the important thing is that we ask others who can compensate for some of the things that we're not good at and that we lack.

Having said that, it's always best to get another reading on a situation because you're colored by your own biases, experiences, and so forth. I think what you need to do is not to be so involved in trying to anticipate what comes next. I think what you have to do is not to try to superimpose these templates you might have in your head and say, "Okay, this is an S4-3 situation. I'm going to involve this kind of a model." That's why I say never lead with your methodology because people who do that try to stuff the situation they see into one of their preexisting boxes. The definition of a blivet is a five pound bag into which you try to put ten pounds of crap. You have to constantly digest and analyze what you see around you, and to do that you need a healthy intellectual curiosity.

While I'm talking to you, I'm looking at the screensavers that come up on my very large computer screen—my cinema screen—and I'm watching pictures of the house in the summer, travels we took on the Queen Mary II, and so forth. I look out my window slightly to my right and I see some squirrels scurrying around trying to get up onto the bird feeder. A plane is now passing overhead silently which is going to land at the nearby airport, and I realize that I wouldn't be able to see that plane in another couple of months because the trees will fill in. These are all the things that go through my mind while I'm talking to you, and you never know where you can pull your next example from or what you can learn from.

Q: I think what we're asking further to this is why is it that you see things that other people don't? How would you frame this insight of you being able to see what others don't?

Alan: I think there are three key elements for me. Number one is you have to have the experiential base that tells you what to look for and how to look. Someone who depends on the forest for their clothing, their nourishment, or their safety will develop a keen sense of what is edible and not, how to identify it, what trails are safest and why, what has passed this way before. In my case, my experiential base tells me how I can do things the most quickly, the most efficaciously, and make the highest impact because I know what to look for. Just as someone might say that plant is edible and the next one isn't, I can say this course of action will work and that one won't.

The second is what is the degree to which you depend upon this for your livelihood? In the case of that person in the forest, it's absolutely essential. In my case, it's absolutely essential because that's what puts me above the crowd. Those people who are most successful in the forest will best be able to defend themselves, develop a technology, explore more, and improve their lives. In my case, as a solo practitioner I can stand out more, create intellectual property, and constantly be ahead of the curve.

The third thing is what is your Meta learning? In other words, how have you learned to learn? I maintain that that's all college should do is teach people how to learn. What is your nature of learning? Some people survive in the forest better than others because they pick up things quickly, they're not afraid to try things. If they get sick from something, they know they shouldn't do that again, and so forth. In my case, I can put an analogy together about cleansing an economy, cleansing a company, or whatever it is very, very quickly because I've learned to use words, examples, metonymy, analogy, metaphor, and so forth very, very quickly.

Q: Give us a detailed brief about improving our observational skills.

Alan: I ran something called Alan's New York, and the folks who were in this experience were in my suite at The Palace Hotel, and I said, "Let's go over to this window." We were looking out on Rockefeller Center, Saks Fifth Avenue, NBC headquarters, and so forth. That's what we were looking at from the 44th floor, directly overlooking St. Patrick's Cathedral. I said to them, "Tell me what you see." People described what they saw in different ways, and then I described what I saw which was somewhat different.

If you put yourself in that kind of a situation, look at a tree and say, "What do I see besides a tree?" Watch some ants moving over the lawn and say, "What am I seeing there besides ants moving over the lawn?" I tend to see things on various levels because I insist that I do that because it's fun and it's learning.

I watch some of these conversations on Alan's Forums that I don't interfere with while I'm observing them because there's some principle that says once you start to inject yourself, you forever changed it. I just try to observe them, but the discussions are interesting on several levels. The content is one, the process is a second, and a real-time learning that's going on is a third. The way people use examples or don't use examples, see a narrow field or see a broad field, and so on. What you do is simply take time out during your normal day, and you focus on things and ask yourself what are you really seeing?

Q: You've talked about observation which of course involves seeing. Could you talk about another of the senses and that's hearing? What mistakes do you see consultants making because their listening skills aren't good enough?

Alan: They don't hear. I don't mean that flippantly. They think they hear what the client, the prospect, or someone in the company is saying, but they don't. They're hearing either what they want to hear or they simply are hearing noise, and they don't use interpretive skills. If you watch people who constantly cut other people's sentences off, which isn't all that unusual, if they do that habitually it's because they're constantly assuming what the other person is going to say which means they are projecting. They're putting them into a certain box that says in this situation when you start a sentence like that, here is how it's going to end. When people do this to me, after one or two times because it infuriates me, I say, "Look, you need to let me finish sentences because maybe you're much smarter than I am, but I don't think you're so smart that you know what I'm going to say every time." The fact is they usually don't know what I'm going to say.

The second problem is that they have restricted hearing, and that's while they're talking to me, they don't listen to anything else. I often find that I can hear phones ringing that are going unanswered. I hear an alarm going off that nobody cares about. I hear some people who are gossiping at a level where they can be heard and don't seem to care or don't seem to realize it. There is a lot you can hear both directly in the conversation and in the ambient atmosphere that's very important.

Q: Like observational skills, it comes down to paying attention?

Alan: Yes, it comes down to paying attention, and you should be sophisticated enough that you can pay attention to the person who is talking while concurrently paying attention to the environment around you.

Q: What can consultants do to improve their listening skills?

Alan: Quite a few things. I'll just give you an example of a few; otherwise, I would be giving a program here, but the first is don't cut other people off. Don't be so eager to contribute. For people who have a chronic problem with this when I coach them, here is the exact mechanism I give them. I tell them, "When another person stops talking, before you say anything, just say to yourself, 'One thousand one, one thousand two' because that brief two seconds is not going to make anyone uncomfortable. That will ensure you that they haven't just stopped for breath because nobody takes two seconds to breathe, and you want to make sure they're truly stopped."

The second thing is separate out where you want the conversation to go versus your ego needs. If somebody says, "I've been to Venice and stayed at the Danielle," you don't have to chime in and say, "I've been to Venice, but the Cipriani is much better." You say, "Really, how did you like it? What did you think of St. Mark's Square?" You need to subordinate ego if you really want to listen to the other person.

I think a third thing is that if you want to build your listening skills, test understanding. Test your own understanding. What happens is you stop speaking and I say to you, "Linda, here is my impression of what you just said and what you meant. Tell me if I'm accurate." Then you use different words. You say, "I think what you said was this." Then you're either going to say one of three or four things. You're going to say, "Alan, that's exactly what I meant" or "Alan, you said it better than I did" or "Alan, you're slightly off base" or "Alan, you haven't been listening." When you test your own understanding like that without your ego involved, you can tell yourself how well you've been listening and how much you have to change it in the future.

Q: Is it ever okay to interrupt a client or a prospective client who is running amuck with the conversation?

Alan: Yes, you should, and you should develop these techniques. What you should say is, "Linda, excuse me a minute. I hate to interrupt you, but I think you just said a couple of things so important I don't want to miss them. I think you said there were three keys to this project. Is this right?" Then you repeat them.

A second thing you could say is, "Linda, excuse me. I hate to interrupt you. I'm sorry and this is my fault, but I'm not sure whether you said the priority is this or the priority is that. Could you just help me with this?" Notice I'm taking the onus on myself. I'm excusing myself. I'm accepting the blame, but I'm redirecting the conversation.

Q: It's a beautiful day in Shaker Heights, OH. I'm looking outside my window, the sun is shining, yet the snow is on the ground. There is not much activity other than just looking at a very beautiful, photo-like scenery in front of me. I heard a branch of a tree just fall down somehow. Your ability to look at that photo and then translate to a business case study or another learning has manifested itself through your blog and your writing amazingly well. What crosses your mind as I just described this picture? Come up with a quick business analogy to that.

Alan: Yes, here is what came across immediately when you said that. There is a beauty outside your window in the contrast. It's a sunny day, but there is snow on the ground, and it's exactly that kind of contrast that creates interest. In a business environment, what you want to do for your prospects, clients, employees, and so on is create contrast that they don't normally see together but represents something that's gratifying, productive, beautiful, or whatever it is that they can say, "Wow, that's unusual." That's the kind of thing that struck me when you said that.

Q: That's amazing. I also recall very clearly the amazing experiences we shared together at Alan's New York in your suite overlooking the beautiful scenery in New York, and each one interpreted completely differently, and your spin on that was completely different. As a matter of fact, one of the things I recall very clearly from that conversation is you commented on how taxis or cabs in New York had a law that they couldn't enter the intersection. Can you articulate it quickly for us?

Alan: One of the things I talked about was here we are in this huge seemingly chaotic city, but there was this masterful order at work, there were right angles everywhere. All the blocks were right angles, and as you looked at the rooftop gardens, the recreational spaces, the ice rinks, and things like that, what you found was everything was symmetrical. They were all rectangles, squares, or something like that, and there was this almost natural order that came about.

When you looked at the taxis who know they'll get a rather serious fine if they blocked an intersection, you saw all these yellow cabs around. They looked like ants marching all over the place but with some kind of predestination, and as they whipped in and out of traffic, sort of tried to outdo each other and cut each other off—nonetheless, they all stopped like soldiers and didn't block these intersections. There was even order among that chaos, and the lesson there is that people do respond to rewards and punishments, and they do it without having to be enforced every day, just knowing that it will be enforced and it might be them.

Q: Give us the top three things of what are the best practices for improving as a consultant when it comes to facilitation.

Alan: I think the first would be that you bring your own intellectual property. You bring your own intellectual capital. Rather than just move the deck chairs around—it's your turn, it's your turn, let me record that on the easel— I think the additional thing is that you provide your own intellectual capital. You could say, "Listen, I understand what you just contributed, but there is no evidence anywhere in the world of that ever being the case. In fact, there was a company in Hong Kong that failed trying to do just that and another one in Chicago."

Number two would be that you resolve conflict productively and constructively. You'll find whenever you facilitate, there will be various interests in the room, and the interest should be reconciled. The interest should be productively recombined so that there is a consensus outcome.

That leads me to the third thing which is you have to create the rules of engagement. For example, I tell people, apropos the second issue, that a consensus is something you can live with, not something you'll die for. When I come out with a statement like that, people tend to laugh but they keep it in mind, and it gives them proportion. When they start arguing about something or trying to sort of restlessly agree on something, they're reminded "You don't have to die for this cause, but can you live with it?" I do that throughout the program. Those are three things that I think are very important in facilitating to get things done quickly and with a minimum of hostility.

Q: Same concept if we now talk about analytical skills. For consultants to improve their analytical skills capability, how many points should you come up with, give us those points, and what can they do then?

Alan: For a consultant to improve analytical ability, in no special order, first of all they need the intellectual firepower to do that. They need a substantial amount of reading, experience, and interaction so that they have the tools to be good analytically.

The second thing they need is to know how to apply those tools and when. We already talked about framing and problem solving and the difference between that and decision making. They need to know which tool to apply and how to apply it.

The third thing is how to tell if they're right. They need some kind of metric or calibration because they might apply the same analytic tool over and over, but if it's not doing the job it's supposed to do, it's not solving the problem, it's not helping make a decision, it's not uncovering risks, it's not setting priorities, or whatever it is, then even though they can use it well, it's not a very good tool.

I think that if you want to develop analytic skills, you have to challenge yourself. You can't jump to conclusions. You can't jump to cause. You can't project it. You have to be willing to take a little bit more time, a little bit more risk, and ensure you have all of the information and that you're applying techniques that you can then validate.

The final point is that if you want to be highly analytical, you need to be able to define the situations you're observing. I'll give you one example of that, and you've heard me say this before. Situations are either structured or unstructured. I was taught this by Victor Vroom who was sort of a pioneer in situational leadership theory with whom I worked for many years. What Vroom said was, "A situation is structured if you know what information you're missing and how to get it. I might not have everything I need, but I know what's missing and know where it resides. It's unstructured if you don't know what's missing, and therefore you don't know how to get it." In this case, I don't know what I don't know.

As a consultant, I've always said the second case—unstructured—is always more valuable, and you can charge more because it's more difficult. In terms of analytic skills, which is our subject here for the moment, it's much harder to be analytic in an unstructured situation because you don't have all the information you need. You have to be aware of those kinds of overriding factors as well.

Q: We were in a situation with a mutual client that we were working with at your home in Rhode Island. The four of us were sitting in your kitchen, and I felt the client the first ten minutes of the conversation was going on a tangent in 50 different directions. Your ability to quickly listen and then frame it for me saved the moment; I felt unable to frame the situation.

Alan: Remember the time you spoke to someone and in two hours you arrived at where they needed to go, and I arrived there in about seven minutes? On a different occasion, you said, "We both reached the same place. I just took an hour and 15 minutes longer than you did." If you start to multiply that by weeks, you have some problems there.

I'm always trying to move as fast as I can while safeguarding quality. I drive exotic cars. I love fast cars. I like to drive as fast as I can while being safe. You can't just go tearing off if the road isn't good; if there are other people on the road; if you don't know the road; if your car isn't in good repair; if there are going to be police officers around, and so forth and so on.

The same thing applies in business. You want to go as fast as you can because speed has an intrinsic value. If I can help you fast, you're better off than if I helped you slow. But you can't do that at the cost of not analyzing and not recognizing things accurately.

Q: At the risk of coming up with a new cognitive theory, what I think you're unearthing there is that many people learning from you struggle with the velocity of this process because we find that there is one part of our brain that's engaged in the conversation—in the facilitative and directing of the conversation—and then many people feel they need to step back from that to connect the dots to then be able to come with a clear framing. You seem to be able to do this on the fly in the moment, and I think that's one of the arts, one of the things that people continually are mesmerized by in watching you do. Help articulate the process that will build this in-the-moment ability to internalize. What is it and how can we emulate this process?

Alan: I'll tell you two things, one of which I think you'll agree with and the second of which you might not even want to put in the book. Here is the first. I had a car full of people, we were in my Bentley coming home from dinner, and I took a turn. The speed limit was 25 mph on the turn, and the turn is actually engineered probably for 85 mph—that's the margin of safety you have—and I took the turn at over 100 mph. People in the car were screaming, but the car never wavered. The car went around it easily because the car is engineered to do that. Why can I do that? Because I'm in control of the car, and when you're in control of things, you set your own speed.

I can control where I am. People say, "Gee, you're an introvert. How come you're such a successful speaker on the stage?" It's because when you're on the stage and speaking, you control everything around you. People don't realize that. You're completely in control if you're good. When you control, you set your own speed, and I'm usually in control, and I set the speed full throttle in everything I do. I'm against the firewall unless I have to apply the brakes because something is happening, but the speed itself doesn't frighten me.

The second thing I'm going to tell very briefly, otherwise we'll be on this forever. Starting in the '70s I developed a theory of familiarity. My theory of familiarity—I was playing around with this in my 20s—was that the more familiar you are with something, the better you are at it, and the more quickly you're better at it. If you go out on the stage before anyone is there and get a feel for the room, when you go out there and are introduced, you have a familiarity with the place, and that aspect no longer is daunting. There is no tension or stress from that aspect. If you know the people who are going to be sitting in front of you—they're not a stranger group—you're even more familiar. If it's a speech you've given before, you're even more familiar.

As I began to extrapolate this, I realized that you can actually create almost a false familiarity. You can create familiarity that gives you the comfort to operate at maximum capacity and maximum speed. I resolved that that was going to be by maximizing experiences, maximizing challenges, not being afraid to fail, maximizing language, reading extensively, and so forth, and it turns out I was right. At least I was right for me. Even if I'm thrust in a new situation with other people—it's new to all of us—I'll find enough familiarity to make me much more comfortable, more successful, and allow me to go much faster. That's how I can travel at this speed.

Q: How do you develop such pragmatic examples?

Alan: I'm basically lazy. That is, I don't like to spend a whole lot of time doing things I don't have to spend a whole lot of time doing. If you're going to sit down and read a 600-page novel, you're going to read a 600-page novel, but some people read faster than others. Some people speed-read, but I think the real key should be speed comprehension because I find that people who speed-read don't understand very much, but that's me.

I don't like to spend more time doing something than I would otherwise normally have to spend or that my maximum capacity allows me to spend. An example is an "accelerator" of a conversation. Examples are like getting on a bus. You don't have to walk for 20 blocks, but what you have to be careful about is that the bus is going to the right destination, it's an express not a local, and it's not so crowded that you can't be comfortable. There is an example of an example, but the fact is that examples are wonderful ways to get people to immediately see what you mean.

If you try to tell someone what a spiral staircase is with your hands clasped behind your back, the best people are going to say, "It's a set of stairs that revolves around itself and around an imaginary central pivot continually forming a 360-degree turn until it reaches its destination." Something like that is about as articulately as I can do it under those circumstances. What most people will do is stick their index finger in the air and say, "It goes like this," and they'll make a corkscrew motion. In two seconds you can explain what otherwise takes you 30 seconds, and it's much clearer. That's why examples are important. They move things along rapidly.

Q: What you describe as laziness I see as the habit of instantiative thinking. I don't know if there is such a word or I just made it up, but if there isn't, then probably you ought to have the copyright on this word instantiative thinking. I think what we're asking here is how would you advise us to build this practice?

Alan: Let's clarify that instantiate means to make the intangible tangible. To make something concrete that's otherwise conceptual. The way you instantiate this practice is that when you speak to others, when you write, in your normal activities you build in examples instead of taking the long way around the block to get next door. Consequently, the more you use them, the better you'll get at them, and the better you get at them, the more you'll use them.

The reason is that it's so efficacious and enhances communication so much that other people will react to you better. When you use examples at meetings, suddenly people will listen to you more than others. If you watch people at a meeting, you'll see that the speaker more often than not will direct his or her eyes to just one or maybe two others but not the whole six or eight sitting there because these are the most influential people or the ones they most want to impress. You'll see this continually.

I was on a panel recently, and somebody sent me a picture, and the eyes of all the other panelists are on me. This is a phenomenon I've been used to forever. I find that I'll be in a room and people will be looking at me more than others because they really find it's important to impress me. The way you fulfill that quest and the way you can bring people on board is to use the kinds of examples that make you a center of interest, that make you a point of interest, and that will help you command a room.

Q: Are you comfortable when all eyes are on you?

Alan: Of course I am.

Q: Have you always been comfortable in that place?

Alan: No. When I was in kindergarten, the teacher couldn't figure out a place for me in the Christmas play, so I was made the announcer and had to wear a tie. Think about this. Think of the prescience that this kindergarten teacher had—I had to wear a tie, and I hated it. I cried, and cried, and I hated it. All the parents came, and I still cried, and I still hated it. I despised doing that.

Then I got to high school and became the president of the student council and would address the entire school once or twice a month when we would have these big assemblies. Suddenly, those kinds of skills led me to be an exchange student in my junior year. Four of us had to compete by answering a question in front of the 17-person teacher's committee. I just knew walking into that room that I was going to beat the hell out of the other three. These were substantial guys. No, it wasn't always that way, but it was that way from an early time.

Q: What is your advice for consultants who would say they don't feel comfortable to have all eyes focused on them?

Alan: Knock it off.

Q: You're a master at metaphors and analogies. You advise us to use them in our speaking and writings. How can we get better at this?

Alan: I think the best way is to study the metaphors, the metonymy, the litotes, and all of these verbal structures that most impress you. Then ask yourself, "How did the author or the speaker come up with this, and why does it impress me so much?" Then you'll realize with that deconstruction how best to build them into your speech. For example, when somebody says, "Sandy Koufax really wasn't a bad pitcher at all," what they're really saying is he was one of the great pitchers of all time, but they're saying it with an opposite effect. You say, "Wow, that was very impressive the way you said that," and you say, "How can I build that into my repertoire?" You say to a client, "The strategy work that we just completed together isn't exactly the worst thing that ever happened here." That's how you start to use this stuff.

Q: You're also a master of using humor. Would you consider this a tool for a consultant's toolkit?

Alan: Absolutely, for 45 reasons, but let me just give you a couple. A lot of people were tweeting as a result of this panel discussion I did in Atlanta, and whenever my name is mentioned, these tweets come up on Twitter somehow. I don't know how it works but they do. They're called "mentions" or something, and a couple of people said, "Alan Weiss ought to be a standup comedian. He didn't follow his true calling." Of course, I was told this only 7 million times. I was the only one up there using humor extensively while making my points.

The reason that it's so important is that humor reduces tension. It releases endorphins, and just like depression, tension masks talent. Your throat gets constricted, your attention wanders, and your mental acuity is not where it should be because you're so nervous. When you use humor not only do you rest yourself, relax yourself, and give yourself permission to succeed, but you're reducing the stress level of the learner. I've been in the learning business since 1972, and unequivocally, people learn better and faster when they're having a good time. There is just no debate about that.

I think every consultant should try to build humor into what they do and have a sense of humor.

I've found people with the best senses of humor also have the highest intellect. When I interviewed people for clients, one of the things I always checked for was humor because that was one of the indicators of intellect to me along with vocabulary.

There are three kinds of humor, generally. One consists of stories, one consists of jokes, and one consists of ad-lib or spontaneous humor. Stories are great because they combine a kind of example and a humorous vein. If they're sarcastic, they should always be self-disparaging. You shouldn't use somebody else as your bad example. A story that's humorous is very, very powerful.

Jokes are not. Jokes are contrived. They've probably been heard before. They have a set up, a punch line, and they're generally artificially inserted, so I would stay away from jokes.

The third, ad-lib humor, is the funniest humor of all. It's the riskiest because it hasn't been tested. You have an idea how people in this moment at that time will accept it, and of course I tend to gravitate towards that. It's very, very funny business, but you have to be very careful. You have to be bold. You have to be absolutely confident that if it fails, you can recover.

Q: Give us some tips for that because in a high-risk or high-stakes situation, a consultant may stay away from ad-lib humor when that's exactly what he or she needs to incorporate.

Alan: I would say the following. First of all, if you say something you think is funny, smile. That gives a subliminal if not direct hint to the listener that what you're about to say you think is funny so they won't take it the wrong way. They might not agree with you, but at least they won't take it the wrong way. In other words, they won't take it as sarcasm or irony or something like that. You want to laugh about it.

The second thing is that you want to try to quickly put together what the likelihood is that it will be received in good humor or whether it will be received as a threat. You have to have a critical mass of people who would accept it and see it as a perfectly tolerable and acceptable comment.

You also have to have an escape plan. You have to be prepared to do something if it doesn't work. You'll hear veteran comics who have lines prepared, and they'll say something like, "I've got something educational to tell you." They'll say something, and it bombs, and they say, "I didn't say it was funny. I just said it was educational." They'll have their "out." But it can be dangerous. I'm out there on the edge sometimes, and I don't have an escape plan. I'm going through the ice if it fails, but I'll have to just crawl back out again.

I have quite a few, but one of my favorites was the first time I ever did a keynote for Toyota which went on to become nearly a $200,000 client. This was my first keynote, they invited me out, and it was Phoenix in July. Everybody was just moaning and groaning. It was 114 degrees in the shade, and they were doing this when they were getting organized for the year. The vice president who was running the show came up and said, "I've heard all of this stuff, and here is why it makes sense for us to meet here, and get over it."

I was introduced, I went up there, and I scratched the beginning of my talk and said, "Listen, I know why you're here in July. I know the reason." It was dead silent. I said, "The surface of the sun was already booked." And the place just went wild, and after that I could do no wrong. One of the advantages of ad-lib humor is that if you do it well, the result from that is extraordinarily positive.

I was introduced once at Merck in Canada by a senior vice president. It was an after dinner award ceremony, and he said to these people, "Alan Weiss is our speaker after dinner. He is a consultant. He has a great reputation. But you know what a consultant is. It's somebody who knows 40 different ways to make love and doesn't know any women. Ladies and gentlemen, Alan Weiss." The place roared, and as I walked up to the mike, everybody shut up to see what I would say. I said to them, "I guess the first thing I should do is introduce myself to the women in the audience." That went on tape, it became a classic event in Merck's history, and it's still on this old tape that I have.

I was the keynoter at the National Speakers Association annual convention, each day has a keynoter to open that day, and the two who preceded me showed pictures of their kids and their grandchildren, and you were seeing this all over the place. The speakers were basically lemmings, they follow each other, very derivative.

I'm sitting backstage, amidst all the electronic equipment, all the crew, it's a big deal production, and I had this brilliant idea. I took out of my wallet two little pictures of my kids, and as I walked up the ramp, I put them in my jacket pocket.

I was introduced and started by saying, "It has obviously become *de rigueur* here in the Speakers Association to show pictures of your children and your grandchildren. My wife has said to me that what good will this ever do us because I don't use PowerPoint, I don't use Blackberries, I don't do any of this, and nobody will ever see it. Well, I brought you the pictures."

I took out these two pictures which were two inches high each, and I held them up before 1,500 people. The place just went wild. My wife told me that the director told one of the cameras actually to focus in on the photos, and now you see me holding up these two-inch photos close view on the camera, and my wife said the place just went nuts. Once I did that, every single thing I said was golden. What did I do? I poked fun at the ritual. I poked fun at myself for just having these two little pictures and no electronic means, but I poked fun at everybody else by saying, "Come on, let's all be more original than that." These are the kinds of things I habitually do.

I got up in front of a financial planning group in New York. I had walked in during the presentation of the prior speaker who was one of their people. There must have been 50 people in the room, and they were all on PDAs, Blackberries, iPhones, and all kinds of stuff, just roaring away on these keyboards. I was introduced and said, "Okay, listen carefully. You'll have these PDAs in your hands forever, and you're going to have me for the next 59 minutes. Make a choice." Everybody smiled and put down the instruments. Could I have really ticked off a whole lot of people doing that? Yes, but to me if you want to stand out, you have to be willing to be out there exposed.

Q: Let's explore that a little bit. In the example with Merck, the guy who introduced you kind of opened the door with a little bit of edgy humor, and then you just walked through it with your comment. How do we know where the lines of good taste are?

Alan: Those lines are constantly moving, and when he opens the door like that as you said, and you have a bunch of drunken people in front of you, you have more latitude for action. You have to use your judgment about the environment you're in because there are differing rules for differing environments. I wouldn't go out on a keynote in front of a health organization and say, "Let me tell you how I was introduced at Merck" because that becomes a story inappropriate for the surroundings.

You have to judge where you are and what conditions make sense if you're going to use ad-lib humor. That comes with experience and a certain degree of risk taking, and if you're conservative, you're just not going to do that. But for me, I would rather take a large risk for large reward than minimized risk for minimal reward. That's just who I am.

Q: Do you hear of any consultants using ad-lib humor that violates sort of conventional wisdom of you don't say sexist, racist, and ethnic jokes?

Alan: All the time.

Q: You're still hearing them?

Alan: Yes. All the time. Some of them are deliberately outrageous. I saw one speech where the guy walked into the audience and said to this woman, "What's your name?" She says, "Sue." He said, "Sue, in my religion that's a verb." I looked around and half the audience thought it was extremely funny, and half the audience were outraged. But you still see this kind of stuff.

Q: Are there any hard and fast rules about what to stay away from?

Alan: You stay away from sex, drugs, and rock and roll. I mean that figuratively, but you generally stay away from religion, sexual innuendo, and obscenity. I knew a comic in New England, Dave Fitzgerald. He passed away seven to eight years ago, and when I went to his wake, it was one of these Irish wakes. The line was two blocks long. He was just a wonderful guy. He used to play these comedy clubs, which I could never do. People would come in drunk, they were throwing footballs in the comedy club, and the two people who preceded him were obscene. They thought the way to make people laugh was through racist and profane phrases, but Dave was clean. Dave could galvanize the room with these funny, clean, humorous stories.

One time he did a National Speakers Association chapter, and he used one profanity there, and it was a strong profanity. It wasn't hell or damn, and he used it at a specific time. There was a little bit of a vibration in the room, then everybody laughed, and he moved on and finished. Later on in the day, Dave pulled me aside and said, "How did I do with the S-word?" I said, "I thought you got away with it." He said, "Right up to the time I said it, I was debating it as I was speaking in my head, but I thought I would give it a shot." I said, "This is a freebie, so what could happen?" He said, "That was exactly my thinking."

Q: We have all run into people who have a sense of humor. They're very good at responding to humor, but the ability to create humor seems a little bit rarer. What advice can you give consultants for improving their humor creation abilities?

Alan: Watch Jerry Seinfeld. He is the greatest observational humorist I've ever seen, and just as I can find examples by looking out the window, Seinfeld can create comedy. This is why maybe if my trajectory were two degrees to the left, I would have been a comedian or a comic writer. Seinfeld does jokes about a boy with a disease in a bubble, about a puffy shirt, about marble rye bread. He does jokes about the people who need a scooter to get around. He does jokes on stereotypes. He talks about people who are low talkers and high talkers. He talks about people who look different in different lighting.

I've seen Seinfeld in person two or three times, and I watched every one of his situation comedies the first time, and they're as funny in reruns. Julia Louis-Dreyfus was a pretty good performer before she got on that show, and she still is. The other two, Kramer and George, never really did anything after that, and the reason is Seinfeld wrote with Larry David who does the cable show "Curb Your Enthusiasm." Seinfeld and Larry David are two great observational humorists, and they find humor in normal surroundings.

There is one segment of the show where George and Seinfeld are pitching a show to NBC, and the NBC executive says, "What is the show about?" George says, "It's about nothing." And the guy says, "How can we have a show about nothing?"

"It's easy. We do this every day."

Of course, it's a double entendre because that's what Seinfeld's show is about—nothing—there is no plot line. The executive says, "I need an example. I need some substance." George says, "Okay, what did you do after you got up this morning?" He says, "I brushed my teeth. I had breakfast. Got dressed. Got in the car. Came to work." George says, "Anything else happen?" The guy says, "Nothing. Normal morning."

George says, "There's your show." And the guy says, "That's no show." Of course, the humor is that's *exactly* what Seinfeld was doing.

If you watch a show like that where they can take just a mundane incident and turn it into this egregious humor, then you learn how to find humor in any environment. Seinfeld's humor was clean, and it poked fun at everything. He was non-biased in who he would poke fun at, non-prejudicial, and it was just an extraordinary undertaking. Today Seinfeld is worth, I don't know, $60 gabillion? The residuals alone probably run to $80 million a year, and he deserves it.

Q: I've heard you say it many times that humor is actually a sign of intelligence, yet so many smart people don't use it or are just simply not funny. First of all, why is it that some of the intelligent consultants out there are simply not funny? Other than possibly watching Seinfeld, what other practical ideas can you give us to become funnier and more effective?

Alan: First of all, don't confuse intelligence with education, cleverness, or smarts. I think the people you're referring to might be educated, academic, smart, clever, and well versed in their methodology, but that doesn't in my book necessarily make them intelligent. I went through college, undergraduate school at Rutgers, with a lot of people who got an education but were no more intelligent when they got out than when they went in.

If you want to develop more habits to develop your own humor, ask yourself what makes you laugh. Ask yourself what makes somebody else laugh, and deconstruct it. I'm always telling people to work backwards. Deconstruct things and find out what makes others laugh, and then see what you can do that is compatible with your personality and with who you are. Very few people can tell jokes well, and you probably shouldn't do that in any case. Everybody can tell stories, and excellent speech coaches, like Patricia Fripp, do this all the time. They teach people how to tell stories, and a lot of stories become funny if you use the right meter, the right cadence, the right order, and you embellish them just a bit.

Chad said to me once, "Stories seem to come to you." That's because I'm always looking around, and I'm evaluating everything as a potential story. Simple as that.

The Process Visual

Q: What is a process visual, and how did you coin that word?

Alan: A process visual for me is a graphic representation of some interaction in a diagnostic capability so that people more easily can focus on what it is they're trying to accomplish. They began formally around 1999. We were in the second or third Odd Couple—this program I used to do with Patricia

Fripp which is about marketing for speakers—and I had been asked for the umpteenth time about how to get people to come to you. Anticipating this, literally during a 15-minute break, I put this circle on the board, and I listed the components that would draw people to you. I came up with about 12 or 14 at the time, and they were things like networking, speaking, products, and so forth. I had the internet as just one entry, not broken out, and I took a look at this and said, "Sort of coming toward this big body, this planet or the sun, I'm going to call it market gravity."

I presented this, and a guy in the front named Steve Cohen, who was there for the second year, says to me, "This is really a great advancement over the way you've explained this in the past. Why don't you do a book of these because you seem to draw things on occasion sometimes with premeditation but sometimes on the spur of the moment." I immediately said to him, "Oh God, nobody would buy a book like this." He said, "You really ought to think about it." He would stay after me and drop me a note every few months.

I said, "I need a name for these. What am I really talking about? I'm talking about a visual that describes a process. Since I'm a process consultant, I deal so much with processes, it's helpful to try to depict these." I wanted an original name, at least one I hadn't heard, so I called them process visuals. I created this book called *The Great Big Book of Process Visuals or Give Me a Double Axis Chart and I Can Rule the World.* In the introduction I acknowledge Steve Cohen for getting me to do this. It became so popular—it's self published, sells for $75, and has a CD in the back—that I created another one a couple years ago called *The Son of Process Visuals, The Second Great Big Book of Process Visuals,* and they've become extremely popular. That's the origin, and I use them all the time. In the Million Dollar Consulting® College, I actually have a segment of about 45 minutes or so where people create some that uniquely depict the processes in their own businesses.

Q: Should we expect perhaps the mother of all process visuals in the future?

Alan: I hope not.

Q: I also heard the saying that a picture is worth a thousand words. What do you see are the key advantages of using a process visual?

Alan: They speed things along so that people say, "Oh, I see where we are now." I would also maintain that they're useful because you can use them in the diagnostics, or you're with a prospect and say, "Where do you fit in here?" You have circles, triangles, and double axis charts, and it doesn't matter, "Where do you fit, what percentage, or to what degree?" And the client and the client's people are trying to decide where they fit.

You can use it diagnostically, and you can also use it prescriptively. When you're in a project when people expect you to be prescriptive, at that point you're saying, "You see what's on this chart? Here is where you are. We have to move over here. There are three ways to do that." They're universally applicable and so catholic in use that for me, trying not to use them is like trying to describe things with my hands tied behind my back.

Q: In relationship to framing, it sounds to me what you're describing—the process visual—helps frame the situation. Can you talk more about the whole conceptual process of leveraging the process visual to accelerate, speed, and articulate the framing process?

Alan: It's very simple. If you think about it, when you try to explain something to someone strictly using words—and I'm a master of words—you still have to use a great many words. When people see a picture of something, they not only tend to understand it much faster, but they can point to things that you commonly see. In other words, it's no longer what is in your head in—your cognitive process—and in their head—their cognitive process—which will be two different things every time.

If I told you to think of a square right now, you're thinking of the same geometric form I am, but it's either larger or smaller than mine, and a different color with a different background. Try to have someone appreciate a Shakespearean play reading the playwright's words as opposed to seeing it acted out, and you're able then to compare notes because you're watching the same thing. You still have certain filters, but nonetheless, you have a much greater commonality.

Q: Are process visual and process model one in the same? I think the phrase you said was if you're going to do strategy with your clients, you need to have a few process models in your hand.

Alan: A process model means that you've prepared a sequence of events that's going to result in a certain outcome. If the outcome is a strategic document, the resolution of conflict, or greater market share, you should have these tools available. These tools can be small or large, but you should have a model that allows you to start working in a disciplined and methodical manner.

For example, my model for resolving conflict is to decide early whether it's about alternatives or objectives. I can do that through observation and listening, through questioning, through several different methods, but nonetheless, that's the first step in my model. If I wanted to make that into a process visual, I would put those elements on an easel and let people see it in relationship to each other. They overlap but they're two different things.

Q: Pursuing the process model, when you design a two-day workshop like Framed or any other very successful workshop, how do you work the design of the process?

Alan: I actually ran something called the Workshop Workshop where I taught people how to create workshops, and I look at things in 90-minute segments. My day is from 9:00 to 4:00, and there is an hour for lunch from 12:00 to 1:00. You go from 9:00 to 10:30, and 10:30 to 12:00, and then 1:00 to 2:30, and 2:30 to 4:00. You take 20 minutes of breaks out of each of those, and it's even a little less.

The first thing I do is say, "What is the end result I want to create? That is, what should the participants be able to do better when they get out of here? There has to be that kind of outcome-based activity here. What do I want them to do better, and what are the major components that will enable them to do that?" Then I back that into my 90-minute segments, and that tells me how long this has to be. If I can do that in 90 minutes, I'll do that. If I can do it in a half day, I'll do it. That's why some of my programs are one day or one-and-one-half days because I realize I need more time to do it. I work backwards. You look at the Million Dollar Consulting College which is four-and-one-half days long, and it's soup to nuts on consulting. It's the largest thing I've ever done, and it has been around for 16 or 17 sessions now. You can bet your bottom dollar that I can't get that into less than four-and-one-half days or I would have, but most people would be doing that in two weeks.

That's how I arrange my workshops, my clarion call is success not perfection, and I'll deviate from that as things come up. I'll move faster, insert an exercise, or I'll follow a question that somebody raised because I realize it's really valuable. About the sixth or seventh Million Dollar Consulting College, somebody brought up something and I said, "You have to unbundle." They said, "What does that mean?" I said, "Look, let's do a little exercise," and I did this unbundling exercise for 40 minutes, and people just loved it and went crazy.

I said, "I'm no fool" and moved something else, changed some other things, and from then on that was a 45-minute segment which is half of a 90-minute module on unbundling. If you look at it though, you have the capacity to do these things whenever you like, it's an organic process, and I keep learning and improving it.

Q: Give us one more example of you articulating for yourself the outcome of an event or a workshop and how you design the process to deliver that result.

Alan: Let me tell you two things. If you take something like Best Practices in Consulting which was a one-and-one-half day workshop, I said, "Okay, coming out of this, people should have a grounding in what consulting is about, how it's different from coaching, know who the major thinkers are in consulting, know what the major steps are in consulting, and so forth." There was some pre-reading, and I think I had people read *The Capitalist Philosophers* by Andrea Gabor. I also realized I would need materials for that, whereas in Framed I didn't need any materials. As I worked back through and picked my major components, I realized that when I talked about strategy or coaching, I needed to talk about it in overview, to show where it fit, who tended to buy it, and how you tended to be prepared for it but not in detail. Consequently, after that when people said, "Boy, I was really thirsty for more with this," I created out of that the Strategist, the Coach, or whatever, which were simply components of the larger picture, but which I could deal with in much more depth in a workshop of its own.

The other thing I'll add to that is something you didn't ask me, but as you go through this, you have to understand that adults basically learn in approximately this manner. There is a discussion of something, then there is the conveyance of the method, there is this practice with the method, and there is feedback on how well your practice went. Then there is application to your own life, and to actual work. If you just help people understand how to speak Latin and you send them into a Greek-speaking world, they're going to lose the Latin and go back to Greek.

You need that process, and it's so simple it's unbelievable. It's basically what, why, how, example. Here is what it is we're talking about. Here is why it's important to you—that's the motivational aspect. Here is how you can do it—these are the techniques and methodologies. Then here is an example of how it's done—now you go do it, I'll give you feedback, and then tell me how you apply it to your work. That's what the Million Dollar Consulting College is based on and much of what I do is based on. It's that simple, and we shouldn't try to make things overly complex.

Q: Getting back to process visuals, is there a distinction between how you use these in a one-on-one situation to how you engage a group with process visuals?

Alan: There can be. It's not necessary but you can. For example, I might with an individual simply draw it on a pad and not be more formal than that. With a group, I have the option of thinking about whether I want to prepare something in advance or not simply for legibility's sake. However, the more these things seem spontaneous, the more powerful they are. With a group, which you can't do with an individual, the most powerful thing is to have a diagnostic up there and ask people where they think they are. Point to different people in the room who are peers, who are extensively working together, who are supposed to be in support of each other and have very different ideas about where they are or where they're going. If three people think the driving force is market, two people think the driving force is product, and three people think the driving force is income and profit, you have a real problem.

I've used those to great benefit because when I say to the buyer, "Don't you think your people need to be singing out of the same hymn book here?" there is no arguing with that statement. In fact, the buyer is usually standing up screaming, "What are you talking about market served? You know we're a product company." The CFO is standing up saying, "Are you nuts? This is all about margin." I love those arguments that take place because they have to look to me to resolve them.

Q: This spontaneous one-on-one is what you may call the napkin moment? You're in the middle of a conversation, there is a napkin on the table, you take it out, and you draw something on it as though it appears for the first time, and the buyer is stunned.

Alan: Yes. I had a guy down here last week from Canada for a Total Immersion date. He has a company that's about $2.5 million, and he is building it toward about $7 million. He has employees and said, "I want to show you my card deck." I thought he was going to do a card trick. Instead, he showed me a copy of the PowerPoint slides he used with a prospect. He said, "What do you think?" I said, "Never do that." He said, "Okay, if I don't use the PowerPoint slides, what if I just use these visuals?" I turned them over too. I said, "Never do that because once you do that, you're in a sales pitch. You can use the same type of visuals you have as if you just thought of them as the situation presents itself. Instead of using a deck of 40 of these, you might only use five or six at the right point, at the right time, maybe different for different prospects, but that will be far more effective because now you're having a conversation and not making a sales pitch."

That's the real beauty of this, and it's why my process visuals aren't really meant to be sequential, take place in a certain order, and why I don't simply use PowerPoint. In the Million Dollar Consulting College, I use about 80 PowerPoint slides which are necessary for the kind of learning, but I don't really call them process visuals in and of themselves. There is a process visual inserted here or there, but I'm drawing on the easel all the time as well.

Q: In the example of the person you just met with, why do some consultants use process visuals with great agility and fluency and others don't?

Alan: I think it's because when you have the comfort, confidence, self-esteem, and the intellectual capacity to be able just to stay in the moment, have a conversation, and be so comfortable with who you are and what you do that you can bring these up naturally, you do that. When those factors don't all exist to a significant degree, then you tend to choreograph more, you tend to script more, and you tend to be more afraid of the spontaneity of a conversation.

You see this with speakers all the time. The poorest speakers I know are those who memorize their speeches. Who five minutes in are always telling the same joke, twelve minutes in are crying at the same spot, and most of them if you ask them a question, they have to go back to the beginning again. It's that kind of orchestration that takes place when one is really uncertain. It's the difference between listening to the Boston Philharmonic playing Bach's "Goldberg Variations" and listening to Louis Armstrong on a recording improvise in a jazz group. They're both music, but one is much more unexpected by the crowd and causes them to join in, dance, and be excited. The other is more like a theatrical performance where you've already read the script, you know what is coming, and you only get upset if they go off script. They're very different approaches.

Q: It strikes me the distinction you're making here is one of those golden keys that we keep asking you about. It's a distinction between the scripted orchestration to the spontaneous, in-the-moment orchestration. We can't get enough insight about what is it that allows you the freedom to create that unscripted, in-the-moment orchestration?

Alan: I'm reading the biography of Louis Armstrong. I just finished one of Sinatra, and I'm about to start one on Humphrey Bogart in addition to my other reading. This one about Armstrong I wouldn't have read, but my wife gave it to me as a Christmas present, and it was a good Christmas present because it wasn't something I would have purchased.

A lot of people feel that Armstrong even predates Sinatra as defining American popular music because he doesn't sing on the beat, and he was almost on a counter beat many times. As I read this biography about his music, and it's written by Terry Teachout the very famous *Wall Street Journal* arts critic, the fascinating thing is that Armstrong was amazingly improvisational. He would hit 18 high Cs in a row. He would do things with the trumpet, before he split his lip very badly, that were unheard of to that day, yet the trumpet had been around forever. They called it a coronet before that. This's why, just by way of brief digression, I tell people that they need to read voraciously. Here is a biography about a jazz musician, but I can bring this into my work, understand what was happening, and apply it to myself and to others.

The fact is, I'm improvisational. If I were a musician, and of course I'm not, I would be an improv musician. That doesn't mean I can't sit and play a set piece. So could Armstrong, and he could play it well. The fact is that he made his stardom, his mark, by being this great jazz improviser. Jazz itself is an improvisational art form, and I tend to think of what I do in consulting as an improvisational art form. I lay the groundwork, I talk about value-based fees, I talk about finding the economic buyer, I just started my new book on writing proposals, and so forth. I can codify all of that, and just like there are musical notes and then chords, the fact is that I've been light on my feet and improvisational because I've been in the moment. I understand the crowd. I understand the tenor of the times. I understand the zeitgeist, and I think that's what people don't understand and don't have the capacity to understand which is why they rely so much on scripted stuff.

Q: What do you understand to be the distinction—what cognitively happens differently—when a person is scripted, to when the person is in the moment, engaged in the way you're describing?

Alan: There are quite a few things going on, but essentially take a look at this. There is this great philosophic debate that says, "What came first, words or thought?" A lot of people just say right away, "Of course, thought," and they don't even think about it. Of course thought, you have to have thought to know what you want to say. However, it's an interesting proposition because you can make a case that you can't think if you don't have words. How do you think of anything without words? Some primitive Homo Sapien, some Neanderthal, some Cro-Magnon, or whoever is sitting there saying to himself, "I need to get food," but he knows what food is.

When you start to think like that, you realize that it's not important so much to make the distinction because it's a philosophical pursuit. It's important to act combining these things, and what I'm saying to you is you have to act on the combination of emotion and cognition. I tell people all the time that logic makes you think and emotion makes you act, and I do that to simplify it but on a much more sophisticated basis. If I were doing a program—sort of Inside Alan, Alan 601, or something like that—I would move away from the stuff I've created that people can buy into easily and use effectively. I would point out the fact that if you really want to achieve this level, then you need to be able to use cognitive and emotional ability simultaneously thinking about, understanding, and feeling what is happening in the room and what is happening in your environment. That is, if you watch musicians who are improvising, they adapt to what is going on with the audience, volume, pitch, and everything else. If you think about consulting, it's Machiavelli's comment: You suit your manner to the times.

Q: Is this how you meant zeitgeist, or did you mean it in the broader sense? Beyond reading the room and the people you're with?

Alan: I mean both. There is a certain environment in which you directly find yourself, but there is also a greater ethos. In other words, right now the ethos is volatility, globalization, technology, instant gratification, and so forth. You have to be aware of those things. Just as an example, you're not going to go into an organization anymore the way you might have in the '50s and say, "If you implement this, in five years you'll be seeing the results." Today, nobody even believes in a five-year plan if they're sane. It's both the immediacy and the greater universe you find yourself in.

Q: I notice that the movie "The King's Speech" created tremendous buzz and is striking a chord. What can we learn from this about the spirit of these times?

Alan: "The King's Speech" is deceptive because the movie was well written and beautifully acted. It was lyrical the way it was acted. But the fact is it's not a very important movie, and not many people will admit that. If you're at a cocktail party and say, "It wasn't that great a movie for this reason," you're going to get clobbered. I enjoyed the movie tremendously, and I advise people to see it, but here is the key. You have these royals who are there by accident of heredity, who can spend any amount of money they want, having to grit their teeth to be sort of low class and plebeian enough to accept the help of someone who, when they find out doesn't have sterling credentials, they want to drop him again. They're not paying attention to how good of a job he is doing; they're paying attention to whether he is credentialed or not. He heroically overcomes that, but the royals don't. He helps them overcome that.

I point out that probably the greatest thing out of Britain ever may be Churchill's rallying the nation during World War II. I've never seen anything so magnificent, and that's far more important than anything the royals did. My goodness, Louis Mountbatten, who everybody loved but had a tragic death at terrorists' hands—they didn't know what to do with him. He was a naval officer, they promoted him up the ranks, he almost ruined an entire flotilla of destroyers once by ordering the wrong turns, and he winds up as viceroy to India.

I don't think we learned too much from "The King's Speech." I think what we might learn is people love the underdog. They love to overcome adversity. They love to think of themselves as the sort of the person who has the inner caped crusader, and what they need, however, are the tools to do that. There is no magic wand or magic potion. There is no waking up in the morning with the muse sitting on your shoulder.

The good news is in this kind of a society, you can rise to great heights, but you have to master things. They're the worst kind of hard work. Mental hard work. Emotional hard work. This issue about self-esteem is huge. People just don't believe in themselves, and if you don't believe in yourself, you can forget everything else because it's not going to happen.

Q: What do you mean when you speak of the *zeitgeist* of the moment?

Alan: I'm not going to try for a universal field theory which has eluded the likes of Einstein and Hawking, but I'll tell you this: If you consider issues such as framing, analytic skills, perspective, cognitive and emotional processes, process visuals, and so forth, the fact is I could deal with the world better than most people because I can process more information than most people and use it well. I have this higher level of consciousness, to quote Margaret Wheatley, because I have so many tools.

Part of those tools are passive and part are assertive. The assertive part is language, but the passive part is that I understand history, I understand geography, and I can talk to anybody about almost anything. I can't talk to an expert in prehistoric times with the same knowledge base they can, but I can certainly conduct a conversation with them, I can be informative, and I can be an engaging partner in that conversation. The fact is, I have this three-dimensional perspective which allows me to create instant context, and when I create instant context, I can measure my responses. I don't usually under-respond or over-respond because context tells me what the appropriate response is to be effective. That's the kind of Alan 601 I was talking about earlier that's very difficult to teach, and you can only do it with certain kinds of people who are very open and have certain attributes themselves.

Q: You talked about the word instantiation. Would you explain what that means and how it relates to process visuals?

Alan: I came across "instantiate" years and years ago. Instantiation is the ability of taking something that's theoretical and conceptual and translating it into the concrete.

Let's say that you need to reach conceptual agreement with a buyer, and you say, "Here is how you do that. You ask these questions. What would you like to see as a result of this? That will create your objectives." Now you're instantiating this conceptual agreement with a buyer. That's why it's important.

Q: Are there ever times when a process visual will confuse things?

Alan: Sure, if you're not doing it right. Yes, I've done that.

Q: The metaphor bombs, people don't get it, and you end up worse off than you were before?

Alan: I'll give you the analogy. We have all probably heard someone who is asked a question say, "That's a good question. Let me give you an example," and thereafter follows either 20 seconds of embarrassed silence or an example that makes no sense. That's what happens when you try to create an example without thinking for a nanosecond about what you've been asked, but you just reflexively say, "Let me give you an example." That generally ruins the entire direction of where you intended to go.

The same thing here. If you don't use the right process visual, or you attempt to create one on the spot that's inaccurate, you have a problem because people will argue with it. What I find is people arguing the wrong thing. In other words, I've heard people who have been in my workshops say, "Shouldn't the first quadrant in a double axis chart be in the upper right, not the upper left?" Someone will say, "No, it's the upper left, not the upper right." I don't care as long as you understand the concept! However, if I put the quadrant up there and the categories or factors I'm using are confusing, people are going to argue that rather than try to understand where they fit. That's the danger, and that's what you really have to avoid.

Conflict and Change Management

Q: What is the reason for conflict in organizations and between individuals?

Alan: Conflict exists primarily in my experience because of disagreements about one of two things. People either disagree on a destination, an outcome, a route, a result, or they agree on the destination, but they disagree on the route to get there. You and I might agree that we should expand in Europe, but you want to do it by an alliance with local companies, and I want to do it by establishing independently owned offices. On the other hand, you might still want to expand in Europe, and I might feel that now is the time to put money aside, reduce debt, and not expand. We don't even agree on the objective. That's about 95 percent of it.

The other five percent is miscellaneous. Some of it's the chemistry that you hear talked about all the time where people just aren't getting along, there isn't a good fit, and egos are at war. While that happens even among very senior people, it's not the primary cause of conflict by a long shot.

Q: If the people don't agree on the destination, what can a consultant do to help them focus on getting that taken care of before they start talking about anything else?

Alan: I believe the first thing you do is find out who owns the decision, who owns the plan. You ask are we equal owners of this, or is this owned by marketing, sales, R&D, manufacturing, or is it the CEO's project? Who owns this because they're the final decider? They're the final arbiter of what that destination should be. If it's a shared ownership and we disagree on the destination, then what we need to do is look at the greater picture; in other words, why are we looking at expansion? We want to increase profitability, and you have to move it up a decision chain.

As you go up a decision chain by asking why, you broaden the decision. As you go down the chain, you ask how, which narrows the decision. Consequently, you want to see if you can arrive at some compromise on what constitutes the best destination for the both of you. If you can't do that, then you have to go to somebody who will serve as an alternate. Even though it might be a joint ownership between you and me, we both report to the chief operating officer, and we have to go to him.

Q: Have you run into situations when the CEO says, "I can't really tell you who owns this, but we all have to agree on it, and people just don't agree on it"? Kind of passing the buck about who makes the decision question.

Alan: Have I run into it? Yes.

Q: How did you resolve that?

Alan: I tell them to cut the crap. That's ridiculous. It's a ridiculous statement. You do hear it, and I'll simply say, "Listen. I'm not walking out of here. You might think you can send this issue out of here, but unless you have three strong men outside, you're not going to send me out of here. This stops on your desk. What is it you want to do? What represents the greatest benefit to you, and let's get our ducks lined up."

These leaders, and occasionally you find them who insist on this bizarre consensus leadership, are basically afraid to make a decision. You can't allow that to happen because ironically you want to talk about not agreeing on destinations. In leadership there is often something called a lack of goal congruence which means the people down below in the organization don't agree with the leadership's destination. The leadership wants to take the company here, but the employees don't want to go there. When you're that kind of consensus leader, if you turn a decision over to people who don't share your beliefs and goals, you'll never get anywhere. You'll never be successful.

Q: Were you usually brought into an organization for some other reason and uncovered the conflict, or did somebody call you and say, "Alan, we need your help. We have a conflict"?

Alan: Both. I was called in at times because there was conflict that had to be resolved by a dispassionate outsider, but at other times I was working on a project and found it hung up because there was conflict. I was at a major organization on Wall Street in New York, and reporting to the CEO were two peers—senior vice presidents, a man and a woman—who hated each other. They took separate entrances into the building so they wouldn't find themselves in the same elevator. Consequently, their staffs hated each other, their silos hated each other. It just went down the ranks. One of the most stereotypical turf battles you'll ever see.

Their conflict wasn't so much a personality conflict; it was a conflict over power because they each had a different alternative in mind to how the company moved forward. One favored an alternative that was best for his unit, and the other favored an alternative better for her unit. Once again, while people said, "Oh, they just don't get along, it's personality," it really wasn't. It was the fact that they had different alternatives, and that exacerbated all the other problems.

Q: Can you walk us through some of the methodologies that you've found very successful in helping clients address conflict?

Alan: The first thing you do is you recognize it. You recognize the elephant in the room and say, "Here is the conflict." The immediate second thing you do is you find cause. First, you identify it. Secondly, you find the cause of it, and I just gave you three or four different causes, two of which are primary. The third thing you do is you resolve it, you correct it. You don't live with the effects. That is, you don't take adaptive action. You don't put band-aids on it, you take corrective action. You get it off the radar screen.

In the large organization in New York I was talking about, I said to the CEO, "We have a really good situation because we have a commonality here." He said, "What's that?" I said, "You. Both of these people report to you, and you're letting them conduct themselves like two warring parties. He said, "What do you suggest?"

I said, "What I suggest is this," because he would get the two of them together in his office, they would give each other lip service, walk out, and start hunkering down again. I told him that he had to have a company-wide meeting with all of the senior people, 100-200 people, and he would introduce the meeting. Then he would have them on the stage together announcing the new initiative, the part each one was going to play, and how they would collaborate. That's exactly what we did.

Q: Did they quit fighting after that?

Alan: Yes, they didn't like each other any better, but they committed publicly to what they were going to do so it would be apparent to everybody. I talked before about secret polling, and the opposite of that is when you make people accountable publicly. It's very hard for them to withdraw. A technique I used to use in strategy sessions was I would open with secret polling. Where do you think we are? What quadrant? But as we started to get well into the strategy, maybe the second, third, or fourth session, whatever it was, we would have critical issues, and I would say, "Okay, who is accountable?" I would put the name down, the accountability, the date something was due, and I would then publish and disseminate that. That's pretty embarrassing when you don't meet your accountability, and it's easy for the CEO to see who isn't carrying the water.

The same thing here, when you stand up on a stage and say, "This is my accountability toward this, and this is her accountability toward this." If it's not done, it's pretty clear what happened, and there was actually a movement on both their parts to make sure they couldn't be blamed for holding up this project. The CEO said to me, "Oh my God, this worked so well." The fact is, he could have done it himself, but this is what I get paid for.

Q: Have you ever addressed a conflict situation by just putting the two people in a room with each other and you?

Alan: Yes. When Bill Gates was actively running Microsoft, he said at one point, "There is nothing magic about motivation. You just put a couple of people in a room, and throw in raw red meat." That's called the IT approach to the management theory. I've gotten in a room with two people and said to them, "You're embarrassing yourselves. You're embarrassing your organization. Let's work out what this is about, and let's create a win-win situation." I would say I was successful in that about seven times out of ten.

Q: The reason it wasn't successful the other three?

Alan: People are just so ego driven, so hateful, so insecure, they have such low self-esteem that they feel any compromise is a personal rejection, a personal underpinning of their status, and they won't stand for it. You see some sick individuals.

There are only a few business books over the years that have really made sense and proven themselves to be true. One was *The Peter Principle,* and it maintains that the cream rises until it sours, and since you don't have very good succession planning systems in organizations and you don't have very good evaluation systems, by and large you get people continually promoted by being conservative, staying off the radar screen, and never taking risk. They don't threaten anyone until they reach a level where their incompetence is so egregiously apparent that now you have to live with this issue.

I found a lot of senior people who were simply inept, incompetent because of this rule, and some of them you have to say to the CEO, "I can do no more. Your choice is to live with this huge pain in the neck, or get rid of him."

Q: You talked about the difference between objectives and alternatives. How do you introduce these into the conflict resolution process?

Alan: As I said before, you just say, "Look, an objective is a destination, an alternative is a route. Which are we arguing over here? Do you agree we should go to Europe or not? It's that simple." The reason I use these very simple concepts and very simple process visuals that we talked about is that anybody can understand them in three seconds.

Q: Is there a process visual you use to help people understand objectives and alternatives?

Alan: Yes. It's embarrassingly simple. I draw a square and say, "Destination" and draw five arrows to it and put "Alternatives" and say, "Are we arguing about the square or the arrows?" Then I hand out crayons.

Q: We also talked about conflicts over priorities, and you mentioned that there are three things to consider. Seriousness, urgency, and growth. How would you represent this in a process visual?

Alan: I just draw a graph. I draw a chart. Across the top are those three categories, and that's the horizontal on top; down the left I draw an entry for each item they have. If they have four issues, I put four entries. If they have twelve issues, I put the twelve entries. Then we go across from left to right and I say, "Let's rate these either high, medium, low, 1 to 10, or whatever you like, and let's see what we have." At the end when we're through with these five, six, or ten, we take a look. If anything says "high, high, high" or "10, 10, 10" those are the ones that are going to be the highest priority.

Q: Any other best practices you can share with us for helping our clients handle conflict?

Alan: Don't take it personally. Understand that it's a normal part of life, that a certain degree of conflict is very healthy; that is, you want people to feel comfortable debating and arguing about things if it synthesizes a greater outcome, a greater resolution. Conflict in and of itself is not unhealthy.

The failure to effectively resolve it is what is unhealthy. I remember there was an airliner in bad trouble, a jumbo jet, it was a two-person crew, but there was a third pilot up there who was a check pilot. Something went terribly wrong with the controls, and the pilot was trying to keep the plane level by using different thrusts on left and right engines, which is extraordinarily difficult even for a veteran pilot. The three of them were talking about what to do next, what made sense, and occasionally they would disagree with each other.

When some psychologists took a look at the transcripts later—all this was on the voice records—and the plane had landed successfully, they came to the conclusion that these three men with tremendous expertise were better off debating openly and arguing about what to do than they would have been if the captain of the plane, who was of course actually in charge, simply was dictatorial and gave them both orders on what to do. The ability to raise issues and argue about them among intelligent, positive, constructive people is an asset. The debit is not knowing what to do about that.

Q: When we're facilitating a group, a team building, strategy session, or something like that, when people tend not to be very communicative and gloss over conflict, what can we as consultants and facilitators do to encourage robust debate?

Alan: I like to use metaphors. People will say, "We need to address the elephant in the room," and everybody knows what that means. I use a phrase that I learned at Hewlett-Packard. They said, "We have to put the dead rat on the table." I just love that phrase. Under the table you know there is this dead rodent that's starting to smell, so put it on the table, and let's acknowledge it. You have to be honest with people, and honesty is always better.

I remember when I was a client service guy at a consulting firm, I was at Honeywell and a client I met with there always argued with me, gave me a hard time, wanted exceptions and deals, and it was just such a pain in the neck. I finally said to him, "Ron, every time I come here I feel like I'm fencing with you, and it's really getting tedious. Why is that?" He said, "You feel that way?" I said, "Yes, here is what we say to each other, and you know I'm here to be of service to you. You're here to use our services as best you can." After that we had a great, candid relationship. You surface things and then deal with them as intelligent adults.

Q: Our job is to put the dead rat on the table if they're not willing to?

Alan: Our job is to tell people "You should be an intelligent adult, so start acting like it."

Q: How do I deal with conflict when I'm impatient and upset myself?

Alan: When you allow emotions to enter any kind of conflict in a large way, it's almost like these shields that were dropped on the Enterprise on "Star Trek." Other weapons couldn't penetrate, and after a while the shields might get damaged, but once they were down, nothing could get through. The same thing happens here. Once you start with the emotionalism, these defensive shields drop, and you can't get through. You should never belittle the other party, and you should never take a superior position unless you're their mentor, their coach, their boss, or somebody they look up to anyway, and you know they're expecting some tough love.

If it's a family member, a peer at work, or a colleague in a club or something, what you should say is, "Listen, John. Obviously, this is very important to you, and I don't think I'm on the right wavelength here. Why don't you explain to me why this issue is so important so I can understand it better." Take the onus on yourself, and if you do that, the other person will speak honestly, and you'll be able to reconcile it more quickly.

You might still think it's a minor matter, but the case here is the other person doesn't, and you'll be able to get it behind you and move on. You can't really afford to make light of something because you're only looking at it through your own lens, and for somebody else it might be awfully important.

Q: You also indicated that some conflict may actually be positive, constructive. With that in mind, identify for us the difference between what I would refer to as needed and constructive conflict versus a destructive one.

Alan: Constructive conflict is conducted by people who want to improve something, not because of their own vested interest, not because it benefits them at the expense of someone else, but they really believe that things should be improved. Consequently, they're arguing for a better future: of money saved, of results maximized, of less stress, of more health, of more beauty, of finer aesthetics, or whatever it is. That's healthy conflict, and people who deal with conflict in a healthy manner are also those who know how to compromise, reach consensus, and give in when they have to.

Unhealthy conflict in my view is when people dig in their heels and want to prevail for the sake of prevailing. They do have a vested interest. They want to defeat someone else. They want someone else to lose. They want to win at someone else's expense, and it's all about ego and their private agenda. That's unhealthy conflict. That's the kind of thing that as a consultant you want to be able to identify, and as a human being you want to try not to engage in.

Q: Help me understand further the difference between influencing and a conflict because to me the discussion could attempt to influence them, but then the client may say, "I realize it. I understand what you're saying. There are other issues that are happening. I just can't do it. I know how important it is. I know it's to my best benefit, but I can't move it further any faster than I'm doing it right now."

Alan: What I'm really hearing is a priority issue, not a conflict issue. The client is saying, "I have priorities that are above this." What you're saying to me is, "Yes," but this is the highest priority that you can see. You're not in your client's business, and that's why I think it's really a case of influence. I think what you have to do is convince the client that simply delaying this to deal with other issues they have is going to create even more problems than they think they're resolving right now. You have to raise the priority of doing this.

There are also times where the client does have legitimate competing interests. They've lost two exceptional people, their technology has gone down, the bank is calling a loan they didn't expect, or there is a personal illness. When these things happen, they legitimately do perhaps have higher priorities, in which case you have to go with the flow, and you have to allow the client the luxury of defining what his or her own priorities are.

That's why you should always get paid in advance. That's why you should always insist on payment terms that are met irrespective of the work progress so that your financial flow is safeguarded when the client does have significant and realistic other priorities. I had three contracts out just before 9/11, all of them were nonrefundable, and I had collected the money for all of them. Then after 9/11, I contacted all three clients and said, "Listen, I'm going to make an exception, and if you want this money back, I'll give it back and we'll cancel what we have going." All three clients said to me, "No, no. We gave you the money, keep the money. We'll use your services in a different way or later on, but we need a couple months here to take a deep breath." They were all New York clients. That's what happens. There was a far greater priority than that particular project at the moment, but we got together at a later date. You have to be flexible.

Q: From your experience, what would you say are the warning signs that a conflict is absolutely getting out of hand? What do you then do to prevent it from getting out of hand?

Alan: There are a lot of warning signs. One is that people stop talking. They cease communications. You see this in married couples. It's the silent treatment. One just shuts up, and all communication stops. That's a horrible, horrible sign of conflict.

A second is just the opposite with people screaming at each other. There is an emotional reaction, not a rational reaction, they're screaming, and the screaming gets to the point where it can be invective. It can be profanity. It can be things that are hard to take back, hard to retract. The judge says to the jury, "That objection is sustained, disregard the previous comment." You can't un-ring a bell, and the reason lawyers do that is the jury can't disregard the previous comment, and the lawyer wants them to hear it. Some things can't be retracted.

Another sign that a conflict has gotten out of hand is that performance dips, and the conflict has become the prevailing absorber and usurper of talent and energy, and everything is going into the conflict and not into the company. All of these are signs that your conflict is getting out of hand. I remember being in a consulting firm where we would spend easily 80 percent of each day just talking and arguing about the politics of the firm, and about 20 percent of our talent leaked out to the client. It can get that bad.

Q: When do you think the conflict passes the point of possible no return?

Alan: The conditions I just indicated are when you have to take strong action. You're better off taking action either to prevent it or to deal with it in a healthy manner before it gets to that point. I've seen people transferred, fired, or whatever to remediate the conflict because you just can't leave the person there any more. Unfortunately, sometimes they are promoted, but you have to physically separate people.

There was a situation in a subsidiary of Merck at one point where Merck had purchased this company, and they brought in a consultant who had worked with Merck who I knew for a long time as president of the subsidiary. The son of the founder of the subsidiary, who Merck had bought this from for billions of dollars, was the executive vice president, and his son was awful. He was hell on wheels, and he got into conflict with everybody. He would humiliate people. He would argue with people. He would dress them down publicly, and every time they brought in a coach, he would give lip service and say, "Right. Yes, I have to change my ways," and walk out of the office and start all over again. He didn't care because his father's instructions were "You have to take care of my son. I'm going to sell you the company, and you have to take care of my son," and the new president felt responsible for that.

When he brought me in and I realized in 24 hours that I wasn't going to make a difference either, I said to the president of the subsidiary, "You've got to fire this guy." He said, "I can't fire him. We're going to take care of him because of his father." I said, "Okay, but I'm going to tell you something. Do you think that the Merck senior executives would put up with this kind of behavior?" He said, "No, probably not." I said, "What do you think the Merck board would do?" He said, "They would be horrified." I said, "I've got news for you. Everybody thinks this is you." He stopped what he was doing, and he looked up at me and said, "What?" I said, "Everybody believes that you're the one behind this because otherwise you would never condone this kind of nasty, ugly behavior. He must have your permission and encouragement to act this way on your behalf." Two weeks later he was gone.

Q: You found his own self-interest and used it as leverage?

Alan: That's right, and it took all of 2½ minutes. That's exactly right. This guy wanted a future with the company, and if what I was saying was half true, it wasn't the executive vice president who was going to be fired first; he was going to be first.

Q: You spoke about influencing skills. What are the keys to influence? What are the essential influencing skills?

Alan: The best work on this is Roberto Cialdini who wrote a book called *Influence.* I think it's really a superb book. From my point of view, the key influencing techniques would be, first, demonstrate that something is in someone's enlightened self-interest. I say enlightened self-interest because sometimes cheating and stealing might be in someone else's self-interest, so—moral, ethical self-interest.

Number two is understanding the difference between musts and wants and being willing to compromise on wants while safeguarding your musts. That's a healthy way to influence others and to compare, contrast, and compromise.

Number three is to create a sense of urgency. You can create a sense of urgency out of scarcity. This opportunity isn't going to last. We have a window of opportunity closing.

Then there is normative pressure which is to create the understanding that a lot of good people are doing this, and for those who want acceptance, guarantees, and assurances, that's a very effective technique. You're part of the in-crowd. You're part of the mainstream. A lot of people like to be there.

The final thing I would mention is framing. I always try to frame people into the picture I want to paint. If you want to influence them, you let them know that they're within a framework of people that they would like to be in. Leading edge, early adapters, thought leaders, ahead of the curve, state of the art, whatever it is, that's where they want to be, and they'll be more prone to listen and more prone to take your suggestions if you can do that.

Q: Some people say that influencing is about moving other people with your ideas in such a way that they believe that these ideas are theirs. How do you feel about that?

Alan: That sounds rather manipulative. I think you can influence people to follow their own ideas that they've been reluctant to do for one reason or another. A lot of times you would like people to do things they're already considering, but they're afraid to, they see too many adverse consequences, they see other priorities. I don't think it's a question of them following just your idea. I don't think it's that manipulative. Certainly, it can be. Some people have defined leadership as getting things done through others, meeting your objectives through other people. My feeling has always been that if people can identify their own well-being within your objectives, they're going to be much more committed to doing what you feel needs to be done.

Q: Why do people have struggles with making decisions, and how do we help people who are afraid or struggling with making decisions?

Alan: Let me start psychologically. I used to run a behavioral consulting firm, and people whose behavioral predispositions are in such a state that their assertiveness level and attention to detail are equally high have a great deal of conflict when making decisions. If I'm a very assertive person, I'm going to get things done—do it, do it, do it—but I also happen to have a rapt attention on detail which means I don't want to move unless every "t" is crossed and "i" is dotted. As you can imagine, I'm going to be very indecisive. I'm going to vacillate a lot.

Other things that cause indecisiveness in my experience are fear of being wrong; fear of failure, that slap to your ego—and if you look at the best entrepreneurs, they have no fear of failure. If you look at the best sales people, they have no fear of failure; otherwise, the first couple of rejections will kill them. A lot of people fear failure, and they won't make decisions.

Others are afraid of people. They're afraid, even though they might be their superior, let alone peer, of what others may think. They're afraid others might not rally to the cause, and they would rather have a consensus decision. They would rather have other people actually making the decisions so that they don't have to. Politicians are often in this mold. We have a governor in Rhode Island right now who I think fills that bill.

Some people have trouble making decisions because they don't like to be the bad person. They don't like to make tough decisions—which means taking away a benefit, firing someone, causing harder work—because they just want to be popular. They don't want to be seen as enforcing tough rules on people.

The final thing I would mention, in a little bit different dimension, is that some people don't make decisions because they don't have a decision-making process. They literally don't know how to make a decision, and they wander, they weave, they run around the block, and they squirm. The problem is that if they had the right tools, they would make the decision, but they have no idea how to make it.

Q: If you were responsible to redesign the curriculum of early school, would you make conflict resolution and decision-making processes part of fifth or sixth grade to equip youngsters with these basic fundamental tools?

Alan: Yes, and I would also include priority setting, problem solving, and planning. I would include a dozen key processes that will stand them in good stead for all their lives through college, into the work force, and through relationships. Absolutely. I think that schools especially in modern times need to spend 35 percent of the time on content and 65 percent of the time on process because a lot of the content either obsolesces or it's easily looked up. Learning how to learn, which is a process, is something most kids are never taught.

Q: We'll need to reeducate or develop a whole new cadre of teachers that would actually be able to communicate these kinds of skills because likely the future teachers in the classrooms would need this training or development themselves.

Alan: I can't speak for other countries, but I'll tell you in the United States we have the greatest university system in the world, and people flock here to go to it. We have probably one of the worst primary and secondary education systems in the industrialized world, and the reason is we train our teachers entirely incorrectly. We put them through teacher's colleges, teacher's training courses, and we certify them as teachers rather than developing a broad-based skill set of the kind of processes they need and that they need to impart to others.

We have them taught by professors of education who are all but hopeless. It's like putting wings on a turtle. The turtle will never use those wings. It's physiologically impossible. Their entire teaching system, certification system, what they do in the school system, and the unions that they belong to are antithetical to the kind of education that we have to provide our kids. What is happening in the United States to kids in public primary and secondary schools, with rare exception, is criminally negligent.

Q: How do you deal with angry people, and how would you coach youngsters to deal with anger?

Alan: The first thing to understand is that most of the time anger is self-anger that's redirected. When somebody is exceedingly mad at you, a lot of times we find this for no reason we can discern, right? That is, it's not the case where you just spilled coffee on their lap, insulted them in public, broken their leg, or stole their watch. When somebody is exceedingly angry with you in the normal course of human interaction, it's usually self-anger that they're redirecting. They're preserving their own identity by not letting this anger chip away at the mortar and brick of their own existence, and they have to redirect this.

What you need to do is say, "You seem very angry. Why is that?" You have to listen. That's what a therapist does. First you identify, "You seem very angry." "I'm not angry." "Then why are you shouting?" "Well, I'm angry." "I can see that. Why are you angry?" "I'm angry about this." "Right. You're angry about that, but why are you angry? I understand you don't like that, but why are you so angry, and why are you so angry with me?" "Because you're the one who decided to do this." "Right, but you were in the meeting, and you had a chance to say what you wanted to say." "Right, but when the second meeting occurred, that's when you made the decision." "Yes, but you weren't at the second meeting." "I had a good reason not to be there." "You might have. I'm not blaming you, but I can't read your mind, and of the people who were at the meeting, five out of six decided we should do this. Tell me. What would it take to make you happy right now?"

If you watch an employee in a Ritz-Carlton or a Four Seasons Hotel— and virtually never in an airline—if an angry customer walks up to them, they'll say, "I'm terribly sorry. What will it take to make you feel better?"

Q: What was this skill you just demonstrated to us in this dialogue?

Alan: All I did was defuse the anger.

Q: You listened carefully, you reframed the questions with empathy, and you looked to create a different outcome and make the other person happy?

Alan: Don't make this too complex. If you look at fire, it requires three things. It requires heat, it requires oxygen, and it requires some kind of incendiary source—fuel. It requires heat, oxygen, and fuel, and if you take any one of those three things away, I believe the fire goes out.

Similarly, you don't feed anger. You don't give anger oxygen. If you give a fire more oxygen, you get a larger fire, so I want to remove the oxygen. I want to remove the fuel. I want to remove whatever I can, remove the heat, and I'm not going to get angry back. The worst thing you can do is get angry back. Now the emotional shield is dropped, and there is no communication. "So is your old man." "So are you." "Yes, you too." Nothing is happening.

You want to say, "Why are you so angry?" If you keep your voice level and you show what appears to be a sincere interest, you'll defuse the anger. People don't keep stomping, yelling, and jumping up and down when the other party isn't feeding fuel to the fire.

Q: Five managers in your 360 assessment told you that your buyer has a temper issue. How do you handle it? What is your next move?

Alan: My first move is to say to them, "What do you mean by that, and what is your evidence?" A temper issue is a subjective description. I want to know exactly what they observed so I know what they're talking about; and if all five say to me, "When we give him news he isn't expecting, he starts to scream and yell," then I understand what they're talking about. If they say to me, "He gets very upset when we don't meet our plan that we guaranteed we would make," I'm not quite sure that's as bad a temper issue.

I want to know what the observed behavior is, and it's not just some kind of euphemism they're using for something else. If I find out that it's consistent, it's evident in the environment, and it's observed behavior, then I'm going to present it to my client and talk to him about it.

Q: Let's take the first example, the description of the behavior you articulated. How would you frame a conversation like this with your buyer?

Alan: I would say to the buyer, "Listen, I have some feedback for you from the 360 work I've been doing," and I'll talk about a couple different things. Then I'll say, "One of the issues that came up was the fact that the feedback cites you as losing your temper in these kinds of instances. Let me just give you an example. You were at a sales meeting, and you asked for questions. You solicited questions, and one of the salespeople asked you about the compensation system for next year. Instead of responding, you began screaming that you're tired of hearing questions about the compensation system. Is that what you recall happened?" That's my first question.

Q: The first step is simply sharing the evidence and giving the other person an opportunity to recall whether that was their experience as well?

Alan: That's right. You want to verify whether the information you got is accurate and whether the other party will agree that it happened because if the other party agrees that it happened, you have a much easier time taking the next steps. If the other party doesn't agree that's what happened, then I want to say, "Fine. In your view, in your memory, what do you think happened?" That's the discussion I want to have.

Q: Again, the guidance is you drive it to an observed behavior conversation rather than projected judgments and views that aren't based in any real observation?

Alan: Everything is about observed behavior and evidence in the environment because otherwise what you have are people who project. People who transfer. People who jump to conclusions and try to get into one's psyche. All you can really deal with is what actually occurred, what people saw and heard, but not what people surmised.

Q: Is this also the principle you apply in a situation when somebody blames you for something that happened to them? How do you recommend addressing and responding to blame whether proven or not?

Alan: Those are two different things. I would say, "You seem to feel that I was the cause of this. Is that right, and why do you feel that way?" If they are obviously right and I was the cause, it was my fault, and I was wrong, I'll apologize. If I was the cause and did this but it was necessary and they're acting irrationally, then I'll talk about why it was necessary, and I'll ask them why they're reacting in such an overly exaggerated manner. If it wasn't my fault and they're just describing this to me, I would ask them why they feel this is my fault.

Q: Let me take you to a different behavior and ask how do you best respond to someone that exhibits self-pity and sullenness?

Alan: Those are two different things. If somebody is feeling sorry for themselves, I ask them why. They might be feeling sorry for themselves with some good reason. A pet might have died, somebody is ill, they got some dreadful bad news, and you have to let people talk about that. You say, "Gee, that must have been awful," and you listen to what they have to say.

Some people feel sorry for themselves, though, because they didn't get a promotion, they didn't score as high as they would like on some test, or they weren't recognized as much as someone else, and you have to tell them basically to knock that off. Point out the good things that are happening in their lives, give them some proportion. I find that people who feel sorry for themselves without a really good reason don't have proportion. They don't take the time to understand how fortunate they are or what is going well. Sometimes people lead such narrow lives they aren't able to do that, but they need a better sense of proportion and why they're so basically well off.

When people are sullen, though, that's different, and again you have to find the cause. If we describe being sullen here for the sake of our discussion as sort of being unhappy, not contributing, sort of an absorber of energy while not providing energy, not participating, you have to ask that person and say, "You seem to be really low. What is going on?" You always have to attack causes of these things. You can deal with the effects in terms of a band-aid, but if you really want to change behavior, you have to find the cause of it.

Everyone feels pain. Not everyone has to suffer.

Q: Some people demonstrate sullenness because they found that that's the way to get people to give them attention. Is that your experience too?

Alan: People use all different kinds of attention-getting devices, and the key is not to enable them. If somebody is sullen and you keep trying to cater to what they want, you'll just enable that behavior. After a legitimate attempt or two, you need to say to them, "Okay, listen. If you can't change your behavior, then don't come here any more because I'm not going to continue to intervene with you."

Somebody on the phone the other day in the Mentor program kept asking me questions that were just to get his head sort of patted. One question he asked was, "How much should I practice this speech I'm going to make?" I said, "I'm not answering these questions any more. You're asking me questions that you know the answer to. You want some kind of arbitrary criterion that I give you so you can say you met, and we're not doing that. Do you have any more questions?" You just can't engage in that, and we enable too many people by thinking that we're providing them with help by really responding to behavioral disorders, to inappropriate behavior that we shouldn't be responding to. The worst are the passive aggressives, absolutely the worst beyond all.

Q: Say more about the passive aggressives and how you handle passive aggressives.

Alan: I find that passive aggressive is the worst borderline personality disorder in the world. I think they've taken them out of the Merck Medical Book of dysfunctions; nonetheless, passive aggressives are people who give off one vibe while trying to create another.

Your kid will be at a dance recital and they'll say, "Your child was very good in that recital. I guess they weren't selected for one of the leading roles." It's this damning with faint praise. The way you deal with passive aggressives—because they can absolutely suck the energy out of you—is say, "Molly, that was very hurtful. Why would you say that to me?" Just hit them right between the eyes.

She will say, "I didn't mean this to be hurtful. I meant your girl was very good."

"Then why did you have to mention the fact about not getting the leading role? As a matter of fact, she didn't try out for those roles, so how could she have gotten them?" or "Those roles only go to seniors, and she isn't a senior." You have to go right after someone like that. These are behaviors from people with deep, deep insecurities who want to try to drag people down to their own perceived level of inferiority, and they'll try to do so consistently.

Q: How different is this strategy to the way you'll address and deal with bullies?

Alan: A bully operates from a tremendous sense of insecurity, and bullies try to drag you down to their perceived level of inferiority as well. The research shows that the preponderance of people as adults who have bullying behavior were abused as children in one way or another. Not all of them, but a lot of them. The way you deal with a bully who is bigger than you are in the school yard is to run away.

In adult life, in offices, and in businesses, the way you deal with a bully is by saying, "Screaming at me, calling me names, and making threats will not change my behavior. All it shows is that you don't have a good reason for wanting to do this, other than volume." If you confront a bully, the bully will have to back down in the workplace; and once that happens, the likelihood is he or she won't bother you again because the tactic didn't work. When you give in to a bully, when you say, "Oh, God, he is going to shout and scream at this. Let's give him what he wants," or "She is going to make a federal case of this. Let's give her the chairman's job because that's what she wants," you just encourage more of that behavior. Bullies have tremendous insecurity complexes. That's why they act that way.

Conclusion

Your goal is to improve the client's condition within a reasonable time frame in such a way that the client can sustain the improvement. Sometimes that means "putting the dead rat on the table" yourself or encouraging the clients to do so. Sometimes that will cause conflict. Conflict over the best interests of the organization is common, healthy, and desirable. Never try to eliminate it. Resolve it so that positive results ensue.

You have to rise above the fray—to have a strong sense of self-worth and a good sense of who you are. You have to be able to discern what is really impeding your happiness and well-being as opposed to what is just a minor upset in the environment.

Best Practices and Lessons Learned

14

Consulting—advice giving, counseling, guidance—has been around since people began living and working together. Although the title of "the oldest profession" has been misplaced to another line of work, some claim that consulting done badly is of the same ilk. When we walk away from a client, that client's condition should be better than it was before we arrived, or we've failed. And the improvement should be more than momentary. It's that simple.

Consulting, as we know it, can trace its origins to MIT, Booz Allen Hamilton, Frederick Taylor, and others. Through the decades, stellar practitioners have honed their skills through trial, error, and experimentation to help us arrive at our present state. Although no one knows for sure how much revenue is derived from total management consulting, estimates put the figure at close to $400 billion. The continued development and application of best practices explains the huge gains.

What Is a Best Practice?

Q: What is a "best practice"?

Alan: That's a really good question because people use the term all the time, and they don't bother to define it. A best practice is something that provides extraordinary results most of the time for most people, and it's transferrable. It can't be a best practice if it's not transferrable. In other words, if you read some of these executives' biographies, they'll tell you about why they were so successful leading company X, Y, or Z, but the fact is a lot of that isn't transferrable. It's because they met someone, they happened to have a unique situation take place. A best practice has to be transferrable.

Most people make the mistake of assuming best practices are external, but a great many best practices are internal and people overlook them. It's like going out to mine for gold when you have gold ore on the floor of your home, but you don't bother look down.

Q: If you say it's one person's best practice, is it possible that one person's best practice isn't a best practice for someone else?

Alan: It's possible and, again, it's an interesting distinction you're making, but here is my quarrel with it. The connotation, maybe not the denotation, of best practices is that they have to be largely transferrable. Consequently, when *In Search of Excellence* was first written—probably the seminal book in terms of best practices that organizations should follow to be successful, leading to everything else has followed through *Good to Great*—the popularity of the book was the fact that executives and leaders could read it and emulate some of what they found in there. Maybe not everything and maybe what worked for me didn't work for you and vice versa, but we could emulate something.

If you say to me, "Alan, what is your favorite technique for this?" and I say, "Chad, my most effective technique is doing that," if no one else can do that, it's not really a best practice. It's just one of Alan's strengths.

I tell you that I can write a page in a book in five minutes. I doubt very many people could do that no matter how much they practiced because it combines my ability to touch-type, my knowledge of a particular field, and my command of language. While you can find other people who might be able to do that or come close, you can't really say, "Folks, here is the best practice for writing a book." I think it has to be more generalizable and acceptable more universally.

Q: How do we then create best practices, and why are those best practices so critical for the success of us and others?

Alan: Let me point something out here so that the tail isn't wagging the dog. I don't know that you want to create best practices. I think you want to identify best practices, and the reason I think that's a difference with a distinction is this: If you set about creating best practices, you really are starting from scratch and saying, "What can I create that everybody can use well?" and so forth and so on, and that's a long, hard climb. However, if you sit back and say, "What is it that people are doing that I find are translatable, transferable, conveyable, or purveyable? What is it that I'm doing that I can teach others and they can do as well or nearly as well?" That's quite different. Identifying what already works and putting it into a form and format that others can use is far less labor intensive and far more efficient than trying to create best practices from scratch.

A quick example—this is a book on consulting. I can walk into an organization that has several different sites, and they can say to me, "Here are two great challenges we have." I can say, "Fine. Let me walk around your own place first." I visit their different sites, and I come back and say, "Here are four common measures, four common results, whatever, that are important in these areas. Some of these sites do it better than others, so why don't we raise everybody up first of all to the top site in your own company? Then I'm going to look outside and see if your competitors have higher standards, and if so, then we'll raise you up to their standards." The beauty of all this is that those standards can be met because somebody is meeting them in a fairly large-scale way.

Q: One of the key distinguishing factors, as you pointed out, is they have to be transferrable and identifiable.

Alan: Yes, you have to be able to tell people how to do it. Not just what it is but how you get there. If you say to somebody, "Here is the best practice. You should place something on your blog twice a day, every day," or "Here is the best practice. You should be in contact with your entire client base once a quarter." The immediate question that comes to mind is "How do you do that?" Somebody says, "Here is how you create a newsletter to keep in touch with your client base that you can create in 30 minutes by using four different categories, two paragraphs in each, and putting it on this database." Now you're talking points. "What" is a concept that I can embrace, but what is transferrable is the "how."

Q: As we're focusing or doing a better job in identifying them, what should we think about to distinguish between a best practice to a common practice?

Alan: Best practices raise people's ability to perform. If you give me best practices and I'm already meeting or exceeding them, they're hardly best practices, and that goes back to what you were saying earlier. It might be your best practice, but I don't care. This individualized best practice doesn't matter. What matters is a more catholic, universal best practice where most people, even if not everyone, can raise their game. That's the criterion for me.

Q: Could they become stagnant eventually?

Alan: Best practices become common. High technology and technological breakthroughs, as they get smaller, cheaper, and more copyable are no longer the breakthrough they were. You find Apple creating more and more iPhones iPads. The same thing with best practices. Once people adapt to them or adopt them and use them well, they're no longer a best practice. It's a common practice, and now you have to find a new best practice. That's what lifts all the boats up in a rising tide.

Q: As the best practice becomes common practice, don't I need to change my mindset to keep evolving them and creating new ones?

Alan: No. You need to identify more because new ones will emerge. You have to look at this not as groups but individuals. You have millions of people, hundreds of thousands of people, tens of thousands of people. It depends what your cohort is, but even in my community there are tens of thousands of people, and if you include my readership, it's hundreds of thousands or maybe millions of people.

You have to understand what your universe is, but within that universe you have all of these individuals who are constantly trying new and better things. They'll create things either through a deliberate innovate process that we talked about earlier in the book or through spontaneity, serendipity, or accident. Sometimes it's better to be lucky than good, and what you have to identify is who is doing what and how it's happening. This is no tangential point, it's a pretty important fact, and this is why we all have to stay abreast of developments in our profession.

In consulting, coaching, facilitating, speaking, professional services, architecture, law, dentistry, I don't care what you choose, we have to stay abreast of what is going on. We're reading trade journals, being coached or mentored, we're in a professional community, in a mastermind group, and we're reading and listening and viewing developmental stuff from authorities and thought leaders on a regular basis. Unless we're doing that, we're not going to be adept at identifying and utilizing what the current best practices are.

Q: I want to tell you this is pretty profound because my mindset was I'm developing best practices. What I understand now is I need to keep focusing on developing myself, innovating, and creating while then identifying best practices.

Alan: If you think it's profound, I'm flattered, but the fact is this is the very key point. First of all, you don't want to create too much work for yourself. I'm a productive guy, I can't imagine sitting here and saying, "I'm going to create three best practices today." I do keep abreast of what everybody is doing, and one of the benefits of all of these communities I create, monitor, facilitate, run, and so forth is people are always giving me ideas. I soon learn what is working better than others, whether I initiated it or someone else did. It doesn't matter.

The next point you have to understand is that life doesn't have a finish line. Life is a continual race, and you're constantly looking to run fast, to run slow, to rest up, to take a shortcut, to sprint, to jog, whatever it is, but you have to constantly be moving or somebody is going to pass you by.

Do you occasionally invent a best practice for yourself? Of course you do, and it works for you. Do you occasionally invent best practices that work for yourself and will work for others? Yes. Then you spread those, but you even have to be able to identify that you've done that. The third condition is that other people are identifying these things that you want to adapt for yourself and exploit with others.

Q: What do we need to do to better identify powerful best practices, and how do we then avoid the status quo trap?

Alan: You avoid the status quo trap by constantly staying in motion because just because I'm doing something well, I'm not comfortable that I can't do it still better. This doesn't mean I get up every day and say, "How can I learn to type faster, or how can I write 85 books?"

It does mean that my mind is open. It's like these people who say, "I don't eat shellfish." "Are you allergic to shellfish?" "No." "Why don't you eat it?" "I just never wanted to try it." Just get away from me! If you've eaten lobster and tell me you don't like it, if that's possible, I'll accept that. You're allowed to have your own taste buds, or you might be a vegan or whatever it is, and that's fine. But for goodness sakes, don't tell me you aren't going to try something just because you don't feel like trying it. You have to have an open mind.

The answer to your first question is that I think we were talking about my looking in the yard here, watching the squirrels, and realizing there are squirrel feeders as well as bird feeders. You have to look at life with a slightly different mindset, with a slightly different perspective, with a slightly different view. Every day I have is very productive in variations of tones and hues, scents, and observations. If you're going to get up every day and just go through the paces, then you might as well get a job driving a bus or working in a factory because you're losing all the advantage of being a solo practitioner.

Q: Let's go back to this concept of the transferrable nature of best practices. You're a guy who likes high-end cars, yet we know that if you were to take one of the systems out of your Bentley and try to put it in a Ferrari, not only would it not work, it would break the car. Is there anything like that in consulting that works for one kind of consultant that won't work for another?

Alan: First of all, let's tackle your analogy here. The fact is that manufacturing really stepped into high gear when they began making interchangeable parts. For example, in the Civil War it was very important when they were able to produce revolvers and rifles with interchangeable parts in the North. Now instead of each Enfield rifle being created from scratch by a veteran craftsperson, they were created with bolts, stocks, and barrels and simply fitted together. In the field if something went wrong, you didn't have to throw the gun out; you just got a new breech, a new barrel, or whatever.

That raised the tide for all kinds of quality, all kinds of purchasing, and brought prices down. There is a level—and it's a pretty high level—at which this kind of transference is possible. For example, going back to your autos, what you learn in creating engines for a high-end Cadillac sedan can also be used in the Cadillac SUV and vice versa. What we learned in safety for the Bentley can also be used in safety for the Ferrari. As a matter of fact, the Bentley wood makers and leather makers who are in Crewe, England who assemble the car—are also used by Lamborghini because of their expertise. Those things are eminently transferable.

What you talked about in your analogy there was like a body transplant, and what you can't do is take an entire body of work and transfer it. The whole point about best practices is you don't take an entity—an entire thing—and transfer it; you take the aspects that will work for you. Now, I'll concede you this: As you get more sophisticated and better at what you do, the ability to transfer best practices becomes somewhat more limited. It's not by any means impossible but more limited because you're already operating so well in so many areas. The less veteran you are in a profession, the more best practices is like a fire hose. The more sophisticated you become and successful in the profession, the more you become the thought leader, the best practices become more like a fine stream in certain places. I think that's the proper analogy.

Q: What do you say to lawyers and others who say, "That best practice just won't work for me"?

Alan: These are the people who refuse to eat shellfish.

Q: You just get away from them?

Alan: Yes. I'll take a minute to explain this. Lawyers have, by and large with rare exception, a very limited education. Extraordinarily narrow. They've gone to undergraduate school and focused on pre-law, commonly political science which is what I took—but I had the benefit of a liberal arts education which was mandatory back then at Rutgers. Today there is no such mandatory liberal arts education, and they won't take science, languages, or things that aren't directly related to their pursuit.

Then they get into three years of law school which is incredibly narrow. Only in the last few years have the MBA courses, for example, included the personal side of the equation and not just finances. Even today they don't do it sufficiency, and the lawyers have this very narrow education, and they're graduated with this huge debt.

They enter into law either in a corporate office where they work 80 hours a week, or they claim 200 hours a week for the purpose of their billing trying to become partner in three years before they get thrown out, or they go into a private practice where they'll starve if they don't do house closings and simple wills. They don't take on a broad-based education, and they can't understand how to run their business. When you boil everything I said away, what you're left with is lawyers are lousy business people, and they wouldn't know a best practice in business if it stepped up and hit them in the head. Their inclination would be to sue it.

Q: How do you communicate to people who are interested in adapting or adopting your consulting model? What I would call non-negotiable best practices such as only talk to the economic buyer, don't talk to the gate-keeper, that sort of thing.

Alan: That's what I try to talk about in most of my books. Just yesterday I got the first editions of *The Consulting Bible*, which has recently been released. This is the most comprehensive book I've ever written on consulting. It's somewhat more comprehensive even than *Million Dollar Consulting* because I talk more about methodology and not just marketing in *The Consulting Bible*. It's full of best practices all along the line, and the fact is that—*Million Dollar Consulting, The Consulting Bible, Getting Started in Consulting,* and *The Million Dollar Consulting Toolkit*—if you look at those kinds of books and apply them to consultants who are relatively new, they're going to get a lot of best practices out of there they can transfer over because of the phenomenon I talked about earlier.

If you look at consultants who are veterans, more sophisticated, and more successful, then my books such as *How to Establish A Unique Brand in the Consulting Profession,* and *Million Dollar Proposals*—these become then the best practices for them because this is not the hose any more, it's the more pinpoint stream focusing on specific needs that they might have. That's how it works with any profession, and if you put enough best practices out there, my feeling is that the people who want to learn from me are adults, and they're going to pick and choose those things most appropriate to their current developmental needs.

Q: I've been working with you for approximately six years now, and during that time I've been in many meetings where I've almost heard the ping in the back of your head go off. As you look back on those six years and even before that, how many of the process visuals that you're using almost as gospel now in your *Bible* and in your other works came from your interactions with the Million Dollar Club, the Hall of Fame, or the general community?

Alan: All of them.

Q: You describe yourself frequently as an introvert, but you're saying that this interaction stimulates your best thinking.

Alan: I'm not an introvert. There you have it. Here and now. Of course I'm not an introvert. If you deal with me for seven seconds, how on Earth can you think I'm an introvert? It just shows what I can get away with if I talk with confidence, volume, and I want to make a point.

I put up a chart at the beginning of the Self-Esteem program, and I had quadrants, lines, and arrows. I said, "Get together in groups of five," and I sat people at round tables. I said, "I'm going to give you 15 minutes. Given these variables, I want you to name each quadrant." People were killing themselves, just killing themselves, and at the end of 15 minutes I said, "What have you got?" They came up with everything under the sun, and I told them, "This chart is complete crap! I made it up in the elevator this morning. The variables don't make sense. Nothing makes sense. The relationships don't make sense, but because I put it up here and told you that they made sense, you're trying to come up with names, but not one person told me that this was crap."

It's pretty easy to stand out in a crowd if you have the behavior, the confidence, the wherewithal to do it, and sometimes you tell little falsehoods because you want to help people to learn.

Q: Introvert or extrovert, it sounds as though interacting in groups to identify our own best practices and those of others would be time well spent.

Alan: Yes. I think of a dysfunctional introversion when you're shy, you're timid, you're reticent, and you're really afraid to speak up even to participate—that's a real developmental problem. Average introversion where you tend not to take the lead, where you let others speak first, and where a little prompting is needed to help you but then you interact—that's okay. There is nothing wrong with being an introvert. It's fine. In fact, introversion and extroversion are not opposite sides of the same coin nor are they value statements, value judgments. None of that really matters. What matters is situationally how do you perform?

Q: What is charisma? What makes for charismatic people?

Alan: Charisma is in the eye of the beholder, but if you want to try to attach some kind of commonality to it, charisma is an infectious excitement and passion. People want to follow someone who excites them. This is why as an organization when you're hiring people, you should hire for content or process skills perhaps, but the primary thing is to hire for enthusiasm. You can teach process, you can teach content, but you can't teach enthusiasm.

There is this passion, this zeal that someone imparts to others and views in others which people want to follow. What characterizes it or constitutes the charismatic need of others? Someone who provides that for them. You can have someone like El Cid who they propped up in the saddle after he was dead, and people still followed him to victory when they sent the horse in the right direction. You can have Jonestown and people in the jungles of South America where they drank poisoned Kool-Aid and died. Charisma isn't necessarily a positive, but it's something where people feel bound to follow you.

There is an analogy in leadership. You can be a leader through different means. In other words, you can have hierarchical power. That is, what is described on your business cards. You're the vice president, and the director reports to you. You can have the power to punish. You can have the power to reward. Usually those come hand-in-hand, but not always. People follow you because they can be punished and rewarded. You can have the power of expertise, and the power of expertise means people follow you because you have information, insight, knowledge, even wisdom about how to proceed, and they want to follow you.

The fifth is what I call referent leadership, and referent leadership means I want to refer to you because you're so powerful, you're so inspirational, and you're so much the person I would love to be that I'm going to follow you. Referent leadership to me is the same as charisma, and people want to follow you because they believe in you, they trust you, and they feel that your destination is their destination. If you want to see charisma at any given time, just look in on the stage at one of these fire and brimstone preachers, and you'll see the audience filled with folks who are enrapt by every word and every interpretation.

Q: When we look at Phil Jackson and Michael Jordan at his prime, we see two different kinds of mastery. Phil Jackson was able to transfer skills as a coach. Michael Jordan was the person to say, "Give me the ball" when it's 20 seconds to go, and it's a critical time. What is the distinction in the Jordan charisma versus the Jackson charisma?

Alan: I'm going to push back on that because my opinion is that Phil Jackson doesn't have charisma. My opinion of Phil Jackson is that he as a coach probably had more star players to work with than any other single coach. Part of his great record in the game is the fact that either through luck, circumstance, trades, or whatever, he was able to coach some of the greatest players ever.

As an analogy, during the great years of the Boston Celtics, Red

Auerbach coached that team, then Casey Jones, and then Phil Russell, but frankly, my dog could have coached it because those players were so good they were going to win no matter what. If you look at the Celtics today, you have three All-Star players on there who are absolutely selfless. It's the talk of the league. Unlike the Miami Heat and other teams at this writing, these three stars on the Celtics are just selfless, as opposed to some who are just prima donnas.

That leads me to the second point about Phil Jackson which is the skill he does have is he is able to manage these huge egos, and I don't know that he is transferring skills. I think what he is doing is he is able to organize and synthesize the varied skills, talents, and egos on these teams into some kind of cohesive whole. Where there have been other coaches with star ball players who haven't been able to win because of the egos and everything else, Jackson has been able to do that. That's the tribute I would pay to him, not so much that he is transferring anything.

In the case of Michael Jordan, Björn Borg, Sandy Koufax, Tiger Woods at one point, and you could go on and on, what you're looking at there is a combination of physical, physiological, emotional, cognitive, and mechanical skills that come together in this almost witch's alchemy to create performance at a level that few people will ever reach, and that's why those skills aren't transferrable. If you want to talk about transferrable skills and best practices, you should be talking about Tiger Woods's swing coach or Björn Borg's serve coach. Those folks are the ones who can raise anybody's game, but when you bring a ball player or an athlete in with the other attributes I just mentioned, you bring it into an entirely different cosmos.

Q: You're making a clear distinction there between the person who is able to take that practice to the ultimate level of performance, and the coach who is able to transfer and convey that practice to other people.

Alan: That's right. I tell people all the time, "I can't control and can hardly influence your discipline and your talent." We're talking in these sports analogies you raised about physical ability. That's less important in professional services, and that doesn't become so much of a factor, but if you look at that, that's not a factor you can control either. You can provide the best training professionals, you can provide training rooms, you can try to enforce training time, but basically that's an individual pursuit, and it goes back to discipline.

I think perhaps the point that emerges from all this is the degree to which best practices improves someone's position—so that they're simply better than they were, they become outstanding, or they become state of the art—has to do with what they bring to the equation in terms of their own talent, discipline, cognitive ability, emotional presence, and, I would contend, even spiritual beliefs. I don't mean religious beliefs, I mean spirituality.

Q: What advice do you give when someone asks, "How do I build my charisma?"

Alan: You can't. That's just silly. First of all, no one has ever asked me that question, ever. Secondly, the way I would answer it would be the way I answered you, it's just silly. Charisma isn't something that you create. Charisma is bestowed upon you by others. Gandhi didn't set out to say, "I'm going to build a charismatic following." What he set out to do was to say, "I think the road here is nonviolent protest."

Q: Let me reframe the question. What practices can help a person develop their presence?

Alan: That's different. If you want to develop presence—the demeanor that creates attention—what is presence? Presence is the ability to command a room. It's the ability to influence outcomes. It's the ability to get people to follow you. It's the ability to get things done through others. If we agree on all that as presence, how do you create a presence?

Number one, you look the part. You dress well, and you dress as a successful person in your clothing, your accessories, your grooming, and so on. I just watched a video of a woman yesterday on stage, and she is a very good speaker, she was dressed well, she was on stage before 1,000 people, and she had bare legs. First of all, right away on the video it didn't look right, but I told her she knows she needs to get coaching here. It's just not appropriate for what she is trying to convey. It could be something like that.

Secondly and more importantly, you create presence by having intellectual firepower. You have to be able to speak on a wide variety of topics; not expertly, but at least conversantly, conversationally. You need to have strong language skills. You need to be able to use metaphor, metonymy, analogy, and examples.

You also need a sense of humor, and that's helpful for two reasons. First, it defuses tense situations, and secondly, it helps people to learn. It helps people to accept you, especially if you use self-effacing humor.

You can't be afraid of failure. You have to be willing to take blame and share credit, but you can't be afraid of people not liking you. You can't be afraid of being rejected. You can't be afraid of something failing.

If you take a look at those behaviors, traits, and attributes, that's someone who has real presence—it's someone I want to listen to. They're well read, they're intelligent, they use excellent language, they make me laugh, and they're confident yet not arrogant.

Q: For the sake of the distinctions you're making with us in this chapter, can you clarify the distinction and the definition you have for behavior versus skill?

Alan: A skill is something that you can learn through training, application, from a book in many cases, or learn through interaction with others, such as on-the-job training.

Behaviors are often predispositions, and that means they revolve around comfort zones. Behaviors can't be learned in a training situation. Behaviors are coached. I can train you to ask the right questions to close the sale, and I can teach you ten questions to ask, but the behavior you need is to be assertive, to interrupt the other party when you have to, to clarify before the other party tries to move on, not to accept "no" for an answer, and so forth. Those behaviors need to be coached and practiced; training improvement is almost infinite. In other words, as long as you have the inclination, you can learn more and more forever, but behavior changes are finite.

If your predisposition—and this is reliant on the DNA coursing through your veins, your nurturing, your acculturation, your education, and so forth—is to be low assertive, I can make you high assertive sufficiently to run a one-hour meeting, and I can coach you on how to do that. However, if you take a job that requires you to be highly assertive for 40 hours a week, the chances are you'll not be successful, and no amount of coaching is going to change that because the investment you have to make in terms of energy and stress to make that degree of change for that long is almost disabling.

Q: I believe the distinction you made here is critical because it demonstrates why it's so critical to participate in live events, live engagements. These behaviors that you're pointing to are much better, more powerfully transferred in the live engagement with you in your events. It's not something that you can just acquire easily by listening to an audio or a video communication.

Alan: Training can help me to do things that require no other people. I can be trained to create a PowerPoint presentation on my computer. There is no one else here except Buddy Beagle sleeping next to me. However, behaviors are by definition interactive, with some exception. If somebody bites their nails and they shouldn't, that's a behavior you need to break, and I'm not quibbling with that.

What we're talking about is the ability to persuade others, deal with others, and work in interactive environments, and you're absolutely right. You have to go out and do that because that's the only way you'll get feedback. That's the only way you know if they're effective or not. There is a key distinction, and what happens is too many organizations try to improve behavioral shortcomings through training. That's never going to work.

Q: The additional reason why we placed best practices at the closing of the book is because we wanted to use the opportunity to review some of the material we covered in this amazing journey and recapture some of the best practices in a few of the important areas. What are the key best practices that you teach—and you shared with us to an extent in this journey—in specifically helping consultants influence their prospects and clients?

Alan: In terms of influencing prospects, the best thing you can do is (a) Make sure your prospect is indeed a buyer because otherwise you're going to be wasting your time trying to influence anyone; (b) Make sure that you develop a trusting relationship with that buyer so the buyer is willing to share with you; (c) Once you have a trusting relationship, get conceptual agreement around business outcomes which are objectives, measures of success which are metrics, and the impact on the organization which is the value of the project; then (d) Create a proposal based on that conceptual agreement that (e) Gives the client options so that the client can choose among the best ways to deal with you. That's for prospective buyers.

For an existing client, the best way to influence the client is to remain in contact on a regular basis presenting both the good and the bad. In other words, too many consultants wait to talk to the buyer until something has gone wrong, in which case the only direct feedback the client is getting from you is bad. You should be telling the buyer, "Here is what is happening good. Here is what is happening well. Here is where we're meeting our deadlines. Here is where we're ahead of deadlines. Here is an unexpected pleasant surprise." Then when you have to say, "Uh oh. We didn't get the support of

R&D," that's one piece of bad news among six pieces of good news. I think you should stay in regular contact, provide good news whenever you can and as much as you can, and then you should help the buyer to understand how to exploit the successes that are occurring and what makes sense to do from there.

That's pretty much common sense, but if you want best practices, that's what you ought to be doing. I think because consultants are often afraid to try to close a sale or make waves while they're in there because they're always constantly afraid of whether they're going to be accepted and paid, they think too narrowly.

Q: We covered this quite extensively in this book, and I'm now focusing on brand and building a brand. Summarize for us what are the key practices that we discussed with you on this journey about building your brand as a consulting solopreneur.

Alan: The ultimate brand is your name, and you should always be moving toward making your name a brand as a solo. In other words, "Get me Aviv Shahar." Secondly, you can have multiple brands that don't involve your name but involve other aspects of what you do under one umbrella, which is fine. Finally, you always keep in mind that a brand is a representation of uniform quality, so whatever you choose to put under that brand has to be of uniform quality in terms of not only the results it produces but also the things that people can identify with. The words, the models, the approaches, and so forth. Those would be the key elements in establishing and perpetuating brands.

Q: What are some of the best practices that you use—and you already pointed to earlier in your work as a mentor and as a coach—that you would highlight for those of us that work with clients in the capacity of coaches, CEO coaches, and so on?

Alan: I'll talk about mentoring because it's different from coaching as we established prior. In terms of my mentoring, number one is you have to educate people very quickly, right at the outset, as to how you're going to work together so there are no false expectations, there are no unreasonable demands, and that your time is preserved.

That leads me to best practices number two which is you have to be very, very careful about preserving your time. Basically, you want to make sure that you keep things brief, that you're frank and honest, and you practice what I call tough love in these cases so that you're not afraid to confront people with what the actual issues are.

Number three, you need resources that you can direct people to so that you don't keep reinventing the wheel. The more of these varied resources you have, the better off you are, and you can direct people to—in my case, Alan's Forums—where they'll get answers from colleagues. I can direct them to my website and blog where there are thousands of free things to download— text, audio, and video. I can direct them to my books. I can direct them to my workshops. There are all kinds of things I can do so that they can learn on their own, and I don't have to answer every question every time.

The final thing I would mention here—I could probably name 30 of these things—is to keep aware of the distinction that you talked about earlier between skills and behaviors. I can coach people through behavioral change, I can teach them things to change their skills, but I should never get those confused and neither should you.

Q: On a recent question to you on the Forum, you replied in terms of how to best reply to a CEO. You said, "I'm sorry John, but the terms you laid out aren't in your best interest, nor are they in mine. I haven't worked with a meter running in years, and my best clients find my project fees create outstanding ROI. I'm happy to talk about that, including your benefit and mutually agreeable payment terms, but I'm afraid an hourly rate is out of the question. Sophisticated consultants aren't working that way any longer since our billing creates an ethical conflict." When you wrote that on the Forum reply, did you have that somewhere and copied and pasted, or do you reproduce this every time at the point because it's so much a part of your DNA, so much a part of your living best practices?

Alan: Yes, that's right. It's the latter. I respond to each one situationally like that, and the words might change from time to time, but the intent will always be the same. That's the uniformity, but it keeps me fresh, and I think that's a good practice for anyone. Don't forget, I provided that response in probably 30 seconds, touch typing on my keyboard. If you can't do that and it's going to take you seven minutes to make that response, you might say seven minutes isn't very long, but it's an eternity if you multiply that during the course of a year.

Q: What were the best practices that you communicated in this quote?

Alan: That value-based billing is always superior for both the client and the consultant. You don't let a client, a buyer, or a prospective buyer under any circumstances tell you, force you, or push you toward an hourly or time-based approach. You simply can't consider that.

Q: I'm going to hit you with five words or five concepts. What I'm looking for is quick, rapid firepower of best practices. Word number one: creating intellectual property.

Alan: To be a thought leader, you need intellectual property, and the best practice is that you need to create this and formalize it on a regular basis. The way you create great intellectual property is to create a lot of it, and then decide which is being accepted the best and which is making the best impact.

Q: Improving one's discipline.

Alan: You need to work backwards from your goals, understand what your personal and professional goals are, and work backwards in bite-sized chunks and then schedule them. The problem with this is that people either don't take the discipline to do what I just said or they allow their objectives and activities to be subordinated to others which is no way to ever succeed in life.

Q: Attracting talent and improving your own.

Alan: If you want to attract talent, become an object of interest. If you're a corporation, become an entity of interest. If you want to improve your own talent, find out for yourself what other people are doing that you want to do that they're doing better and understand what skills or behaviors you need to change.

Q: Become and act fearless.

Alan: Find out what causes fear. If it's your ego, check it into a coat closet. It doesn't matter. If it's fear of failing, ask yourself, "What will failing really do to me here? Am I going to get thrown out of my home? Is my spouse going to leave me? Will they have to put me in a hospital?" In all probability, 99.9 percent of the time, no. Find the cause of the fear, deal with it, and move on.

Q: Finally, best practices to effective, powerful marketing.

Alan: My feeling is that you need to draw people to you, and the best practices for drawing people to you of all the ones that I talk about are publishing, speaking, and peer-to-peer referral. Those are the ones that are most powerful and most likely to get you short-term, medium-term, and long-term business. In my book *Million Dollar Referrals*, I point out that every time you make a sale, you really make two sales. One is the immediate money you're paid. The second is the referral business down the road. Too many consultants ignore one of the two sales they're making and don't get all of the benefit that they should be getting from the difficult job that finally concludes when they bring a new client on board.

Q: Just two more Alan. Setting strategy for our own businesses.

Alan: The best practices for yourself is don't confuse it with planning; that is, take a true strategic view. Paint a picture of what you want to be in the future, and then work backwards with the discipline I talked about earlier as to how to get there. Understand there are only two business models in consulting: One is a solo practitioner, where you're taking all the money out every year and living a good life, but you're not going to sell something in 30 years except perhaps some of your intellectual property. The other is building a company with infrastructure, employees, and so on where you take out less money but hope to sell the company itself in 30 years or so. Don't be stuck in the middle of those two. Pick which one you want to pursue.

Q: Life balance.

Alan: We have one life, and we don't have a business life and a personal life. We have one life. We have 24 hours every day. We get to choose how to live it. Nobody else does. We get to choose how to live it by and large. Nietzsche said, "A day has 100 pockets if you know what to put into them." You have to start understanding what it is you have to put in them.

Q: You're leaving in a few hours to another trip, is that correct?

Alan: Yes. We're heading to London for some business and pleasure and then on to France for pleasure.

Q: I'm curious to ask after all these years of travel, are you still looking forward to it?

Alan: Yes. I look forward to it because I arranged it. In other words, I'm doing the Million Dollar Consulting College in London, and I'm also doing a day for another client over there, and I love London. I've been to London two dozen times, I love the city, and we belong to clubs there. The Million Dollar Consulting College is now being done in its third continent, and all that's wonderful.

Then we're going to take the Eurostar over to Calais where it goes nonstop, and a car will pick us up and take us to Normandy. We've always wanted to visit Normandy, and we'll spend a few days. My wife is with me, and we're going to have a great, great time in London which we know and in Normandy where we've never been. I look forward to that kind of travel. I don't look forward to going through security checkpoints, standing in lines, and so on, but such is life.

Q: Since this is a chapter about best practices, what are your best practices around travel, and how do you organize yourself to deliver work away from home in terms of best practices?

Alan: Those are two very different questions, so my best practices for travel are these. I either take only carry-on luggage for shorter trips—I can go away for several days with just carry-on luggage—or I FedEx my heavy luggage. For example, on this trip the luggage is already at the hotel Baglioni in London, verified by FedEx and the hotel, so we don't schlep our bags, which is a technical consulting term, through airports, and so forth and so on.

The second thing is that it helps to spend extra money to be comfortable. Limos pick us up and take us to the airport, they take us to the hotel, we're guided around, and either American Express in the States and overseas or the hotel concierges make all of the local arrangements I need. If we're seeing a play, if we need a restaurant, whatever it is, a third party takes care of it for me just based on my instructions.

We tend to travel so that it's comfortable for us, and we cut nothing close. For example, when we go to Florida where we have to connect to get there, we never have connections that are less than 90 minutes, even if that means waiting for three hours. We'll go to an airport lounge—we belong to all of them—we'll go get a good meal someplace, which you can now in most airports, or we'll do *something*. We're never scrambling. That's very stressful. We always travel first class, and we always try to make ourselves comfortable. That's important about traveling—to maximize your comfort and use third parties.

In terms of work, I travel with my laptop, my iPad, and my iPhone. I can do anything there that I can do at home because I use Drop Box—which is a great application which replicates whatever you have on one platform with the others. If I wrote a part of a chapter in a book today, when I got to Logan Airport in Boston, it would be on my laptop, my iPad, and my iPhone. If I wanted to finish it on the flight, I could do that. When I got to London, I open things up, and then back here on my main computer, whatever I did would be replicated back here—so it's very easy to work when you travel. The only thing I do is I alert people who might be calling me that I'm not going to be easy to call because of time changes but that email is fine. I just find all that ridiculously simple. There is no problem.

Q: In terms of your delivery and planned engagements as you travel, what are some key practices there?

Alan: Always allow yourself at least a day to acclimate. For example, we're getting there tomorrow morning, Friday morning, I'm not doing anything until Saturday, we have Sunday off, and then I start again on Monday. Always allow yourself a day to acclimate. Always allow yourself time to enjoy yourself because there are always other things to do. London is intriguing. It has great museums, fabulous culture, and wonderful things to do. Even if you know the city well—if you don't know the city well, it's a brand new experience for you—be experimental, be exploring.

I knew somebody who traveled the world and only ate Italian food. It was just nuts. Wherever they were—Denmark, Belgium, Australia, Singapore—all they ate was pasta, and that's just nuts. You have to be more explorative than that, and you have to be willing to learn, grow, and gain from the local culture and local circumstances to which you're exposed.

Those are the kinds of things I think are important to conduct business. Ask for help. Somebody can always find something you need. There is always somebody if your room isn't ready—they can set you up in the hotel's club, or they can find a lounge with Wi-Fi. Somebody can always do something to ease your day, and don't be a martyr. Ask for help, and find out the best way to get it done.

Q: When you talk about be experimental and explore, is that something you do just as a point, or do you do some reading before you go to a new place to study more about history or culture? What is your way of exploring and preparing to explore?

Alan: I do two things. One is I like to ask people who have been there, and those are the best references rather than just reading something because you know the other person, you trust them, and you know their taste. We have a restaurant in London we're going to try that was given to us by the owner of a boutique where Marie shops, who we've known forever, and she picks great restaurants. She has found a new one in London because she goes over there to buy clothes in London and Paris. I'll ask people who have been there and done that.

One of the reasons I'm taking the Million Dollar Club to Stresa on Lake Maggiore in Italy is that there are all these places I can visit, and we wanted to be in Europe this time around. Somebody who has been to Aminta, the resort we're going to, just raved about it, and I sent out some more feelers to people and found out it's just spectacular. Same thing with Bora Bora where we were last November.

The other thing I do is I investigate a country's background. For example, if I'm going to Chile, Venezuela, Monaco, or wherever it is, if it's the first time, I'll print out a page from an encyclopedia. It's the kind of page that says what the currency is, what the major industries are, a brief history of the country, and so forth, and you can read it in five or ten minutes and have some groundwork. You have some context. It's important to know that the annual income is $12,000 or $36,000 or $4,000. It's important to know that there were three revolutions. It's important to know that they operate on the Napoleonic Code or the English Common Law system. I find those things interesting, and it helps give me context when I get there.

Q: Many close down their shop while on vacation or find it to be a great chore to perform work tasks, as has been reported to us on the Forum and other channels. Your mindset is completely different. Can you talk about that a little bit?

Alan: I have no problem in the middle of the day at home kicking back and having a drink, a cigar, going to the pool, playing with the dogs, or driving the car. It doesn't matter to me. Similarly, I have no problem whatsoever getting on a business call or checking my email while I'm traveling even on vacation. I just don't see those as mutually exclusive. It's not like I pay, it's not like I invest four hours a day on my email when I'm traveling, but to check it in the morning and the evening just to see what is going on to me is just reasonable.

I'll tell you what isn't reasonable. I remember when we were in this beautiful resort and a woman's husband comes down to the pool sometime after lunch, and I said to her, "What took him so long to meet you here?" She said, "Oh golf." I said, "He played golf this morning? It's kind of hot." She said, "No, no, no. He watched a golf tournament on TV." That to me is just dumb. For goodness sakes.

In any case, I think that your willingness to take a phone call, to respond to email, even to write a book you're working on, or post something on your blog, why wouldn't you do that? I find travel wonderful for creation. I have a twice-a-month column here in the local newspaper in Rhode Island, and I'll write my next one "Dateline London" and the one after that "Dateline Normandy." I did one from Bora Bora, and the editor loves it when I write from abroad. I can compare things at home and abroad, post on my blog, and put up some photos.

For me it's no problem whatsoever. I've never understood people who say, "When I'm with a client, I can't do anything else." "I'm on vacation. I can't think of anything else." That tells me that's a very narrow mind, somebody with no flexibility, and people with no flexibility have problems in any case.

Q: I have to admit that being on so many of those trips with you, when you select those amazing places, it also helps create memories of a lifetime. I don't mean that not selecting such amazing places won't create memories of a lifetime, but you pick and choose those places with great attention and great care. Can you talk a little about when you're going to a new place or an existing place like London, how do you decide to go to those amazing places? You've been there before, and you love going there versus exploring new things?

Alan: In this case we're seeing a new play that we've never seen before. I'm staying in a hotel I've been in before because I'm running the Consulting College, and I wanted a place for which I've had some reference, but my wife has never been to this hotel. It's a very cool place. It's across from Kensington Park, and the house car is a Maserati. What else could you want? We'll go to a restaurant or two that we like. We'll go back to Scott's, probably the best restaurant in London, but we'll try new restaurants too.

Then we'll both go to Normandy where we've never been. We've taken the Eurostar train before, which is great. Then when we come back from London, we'll stay in a new hotel. We'll come back for one day before we fly home, and we'll stay in a hotel where they have a cigar bar. I've gone to the cigar bar, but we never stayed in the hotel. We'll add that to our frame of reference. No matter where I am, I like to try to combine the new and the old. In a new city everything is new, but I'm a believer both in tradition—going back to some of the same places—and trying things new as well. They're not mutually exclusive.

Q: The next territory is OD (organization development). Share some top best practices that you used in your OD work.

Alan: Organization development is a very broad field, and it's tough to come out with a succinct list of best practices, but I would say the following to try to answer your question. The first is that you should look at processes, procedures, systems, physical environment, structure, and people's performance. You need to look at all of the factors involved. Some of you can recall a case study I use in the Million Dollar Consulting College where very few people get the right answer. It's a real example because the answer is structural not interpersonal, and you have to look at all elements.

The second thing I would say is never to assume anyone is damaged. Too many people get into OD and they think the buyer—the very person who is smart enough to hire them—is also stupid enough to have caused the problem. Don't assume your buyer or anyone else is damaged. You might want to assume people have different self-interests, but that's not the same as being damaged or deficient.

The third thing is always think of the easiest resolution. Don't implement 27-step models, don't go back through history to look at the six great thinkers in the area, and don't convince yourself that only every aspect of your methodology can save the day. Ask yourself, "If that's the end result, what is the quickest, easiest way to get there? Occam's razor will almost always prevail.

Q: Not too long ago you conducted a workshop that you called the Workshop Workshop. Many of us offer workshops as part of our methodology.

Could you walk us through some of the best practices that you've uncovered in your own work?

Alan: I deconstruct workshops into 90-minute segments. My workshops tend to go from 9:00 to 4:00. There is a breakfast, and a lunch in between. It's 9:00 to 12:00 and 1:00 to 4:00. I find that after 4:00, people's attention really starts to flag, and so does mine for that matter. The 5:00 p.m. closing time I find a completely arbitrary and useless line of demarcation, and I've decided they're going to be 6 hours, 9:00 to 12:00 and 1:00 to 4:00 minus two 15-minute breaks, which takes another half an hour out of the day, and I'm pretty religious about that. In other words, I don't let people take a break for 30 minutes. I start on time, I end on time, and the breaks are on time.

That gives you roughly four 90-minute segments, two in the morning and two in the afternoon. You could say that's really eight 45-minute segments, or it's two 90, or however you want to break it up. I just work with four 90-minute segments, and I ask myself, "What is it I'm trying to get across? How can I put that into some kind of learning design where people understand it, they can practice it, they can get feedback, and they can apply it? How can I do that within 90 minutes ideally, allowing enough time for the group given the size of the group?"

Then I look at the number of ideas and points I want to make, and that tells me how many of those modules I need. Again following the path of least resistance here, I want to have as few modules as possible. If I can do something in 1½ days, I would rather do that than do it in 2½ days. The Million Dollar Consulting College is 4½ days, and I guarantee you that that's the smallest amount of time I can get it into. Other people would be doing it in two weeks, but I can't get it less than 4½ days given its design. Its design is for a maximum of 15 people, though.

That's how I tend to create a workshop, and then I worry about things like handouts, audio/visual, and so forth. A lot of my sessions don't have any visuals at all other than me and an easel and pad. Some of them I use PowerPoint. Again, it depends on the content I'm providing and what the best learning method is going to be.

Q: You start with the objectives and then decide how many modules it will take to address each of the objectives you have?

Alan: Yes, and my feeling is that the basic course of action you take, the basic sequence is with adults you discuss something during which they can question, confront, challenge, and so on. You discuss whatever it is you want to have people think about—and basically that's a "what, why, how, example" format. Here is *what* it is we're talking about. Here is *why* it's important. Here is *how* it's done. Here is an *example*. That's my rigor.

Then after you've discussed it in that what, why, how, example format, you let people practice it. They can practice it on a case study, interacting with each other, using preparatory work you've asked them to provide, or whatever it is, and then they get feedback on that practice so they can hone their skills. This worked well, this didn't. What happens when you're faced with this? I had a challenge using it here.

Finally, you want them to apply it in the real world, and the transition from the classroom—which is very sterile in the workshop—to the real world is application. If I'm doing it, I tend to create accountability partners so people can talk post-workshop about how they're doing and keep things going. When I do this in-house, I usually try to insist that the superiors of the people in the program meet with me at some point so that I can apprise them on how best to help their subordinates who have been to the program use what they have and have it reinforced.

Q: What is your observation when workshops fail, what went wrong?

Alan: There is a limited amount of things that can go wrong, in no special order. One is that the content wasn't good. That is, it wasn't new, wasn't valuable, or it wasn't relevant, and the content turns people off. A second thing is that the delivery wasn't good. The content is valuable, but it's a droning, uninteresting delivery. Think, unfortunately, of your average college professor. A lot of course material can be fascinating. Some of it's deadly dull, but some of it can be very fascinating, but if the professor is dull, that's a problem. The delivery is an issue.

A third thing is the environment. The content could be good, the delivery could be good, but the environment could be distracting, it could be off-putting, it could be simply uncomfortable, and that will also affect learning. The final thing is preoccupation, distraction. That could be caused by a colleague in the class who gets out of hand, who never shuts up, or thinks he is a member of the faculty. It could be caused by something happening in the organization that supersedes what is going on in that class. For example, there is a rumor of a divestiture. It could be caused by an individual's personal situation. There is something going on in one's personal life that's causing them not to be able to pay maximum attention. Those are the kinds of things that can cause a workshop to fail.

Q: Many consultants spend a great deal of time putting together a workbook or elaborate handouts for the participants. What is your view on that?

Alan: They generally are pretty stupid, and I'll tell you why. Some of these workbooks have things by people who pose as experts in adult learning. You'll see something like this: The workbook will say, "Whenever I build a new building, to protect myself I should make sure I purchase adequate_____" and there is a blank. After you talk to the instructor, you're supposed to fill in "insurance." I would fill in "finding a new program." What happens is a lot of this stuff is just so basic, elementary, or downright embarrassing that it's dumb.

Some handouts make sense. For example, handouts that are copies of any PowerPoint that you use, any slides that you use—assuming your slides are good—are useful because participants like to write on them. When I use these copies—as I do in the Consulting College—the visual is at the top, and at the bottom there is space for notes. People like to augment the visual with their own notes about what I've described. I don't generally like to just put lists of things up there I can talk about or put in a handout, and the visuals in particular, the graphics and imagery, they want to note. I think those kinds of handouts make sense.

Actually, less is more because the last thing you want are people to take massive handouts, put them on a shelf, and let them gather dust. What you want ideally is something they can put on their telephone, on their desk, in their briefcase, their Filofax, or insert electronically in a PDA which they can use every day as a point of reference. Usually, the easier it is to use, the more application it will get.

Q: We have seen some interest on the Forum of people getting into keynote delivery. What is your advice for best practices on delivering a great keynote?

Alan: Keynotes are generally about 45 minutes to an hour. Occasionally, they're 90 minutes. A keynote technically is the opening general session, plenary session speech of a conference. It's supposed to ring the "key note" for everything which follows. A lot of people will say, "I was a keynoter, I closed the conference." That was a plenary session, but you weren't really the keynoter. Or, "I'm the fourth general session keynoter of the day." No, not really, you're the fourth general session speaker. The keynoter was the first person. Having that technicality out of the way, as opposed to a concurrent session—a plenary session occurs when everyone is present.

They're usually 45 minutes, maybe 90 minutes, more likely an hour or so, and here are best practices. Number one, in the first 90 seconds, people are going to decide the degree to which to listen to you, so your first 90 seconds has to be captivating. That means, make sure the person who presents you is succinct. It's not their day, not their show, not their speech. Give them a paragraph to read that takes about 30 seconds, no more, and insist that they read it verbatim. "Oh, I've done this for a long time." "Read it verbatim." "I lost it." "Here is another copy. I always have one with me."

Secondly, you walk on—and in the first 90 seconds—you want to captivate them with an illustration, a demonstration, a story, an anecdote, some example, with something that says to people, "It's important to keep listening."

Then you want to make a limited number of points. This isn't unlike a sort of miniature workshop in that if you have an hour—let's just say you have six points you want to make—at maximum you would have ten minutes a point, but you have the front material and end material, so you probably have more like seven minutes a point. You have to be careful about distributing your time. The great keynotes, if you listen to outstanding keynoters, what you listen to is a story and a point. A story and a point. Occasionally, a second story but the stories are always germane, relevant, and illustrate the point so that you don't have to spend another 4,000 words trying to make the point.

The last thing you say—the last 90 seconds—is what people will remember the most. In the last 90 seconds you want to summarize what you've done, issue a call to action, and sometimes even tell a story if the story serves that purpose to give people motivation to take what they've learned and use it. You can't get a lot of skills transfer, but you can get people excited, you can provoke them, you can make them think and want to try things differently. The more relevant stories and relevant humor—not jokes—you use, the better people will learn because it relaxes people, and it will relax the speaker as well.

Q: Patricia Fripp teaches the people in her classes to just start talking. "I wish you could have been there. Let's start with a history lesson." What is your feeling about that, or do you think we should greet the audience?

Alan: Oh no. I don't think you should greet the audience. I hate it when a comic walks on stage and says, "How are you folks tonight?" It's trite. It's ridiculous. They're trying to calm their own nerves and get an artificial cheer. To me it's not a professional thing to do, and the same applies to a speaker. You don't come out and say, "Good morning. It's nice to be with you. I want to thank Ms. Jones for inviting me." Get to the point.

It's much more dramatic if you walk out, take a breath so the people are watching you, and let three seconds elapse. It's not going to be the end of the world, and then say, "I think it was around 2003 when I boarded a plane that was colder inside than it was outside." People are going to listen to your next words. Starting with a story is a great idea, and if you're going to use humor, it should be self-disparaging humor—not at someone else's expense—and it should be original. That is, it should be a personalized story, not some joke or anecdote about throwing sand dollars into the ocean, the electric parade at Disneyland, or the lighthouse that a ship is approaching that everybody has heard 4,000 times.

Q: When should we take questions?

Alan: I suggest that you take questions throughout the speech. That is, if there aren't 1,000 people in front of you. You take questions as you go because it shows you're involved, and the chances are other people have that same question, and it will give you some calibration on where the audience is. I would always stop and take questions about five or ten minutes before the ending. That way you can answer questions and then summarize.

What you want to say is, "Let me pause here for questions," and you see what questions there are. Always have material ready in case there are no questions, you handle the questions, and you keep an eye on your watch. When you see you have about three minutes left you say, "If there are more questions, I'm sorry I have to stop here to honor your time, but I would be happy to talk to you once I'm off stage, talk to you one-on-one, but let me take the final three minutes to summarize." You always want to leave people with your summary, never on Q&A.

Q: Assuming the audience is a little smaller, say 50 to 100 people, in taking questions throughout, should I invite them to do this when I start, invite this at the end of segments, or how should I do that?

Alan: Once you open, after your first 90 seconds and you're going into your first point say, "By the way folks, if any of you want to ask questions, I'm going to allot some time near the end, but don't be bashful about asking me now. Just put your hand up. We have some people with hand mikes, and they'll come over to you and give you one, or there is a microphone in the aisle which you can move up to. When I see you standing at a mike, that will be my trigger that you want to ask a question, and I'll take you as promptly as I can, given where I am in the presentation."

If you're asked a question and they don't use a mike, repeat it so that everybody can hear it, and give yourself some time to think about it. The basic steps in taking questions are repeat it, respond to it, and then review. I repeat the question, I respond to it, and then I say, "Did I answer your question?"

Q: What fascinates me about you over the years is that you've never been puzzled and unable to answer any question—whether it's from me or anyone in the community—that you're faced with. On the other hand, during the Thought Leadership dinner with Marshall Goldsmith, I asked him a question and he was humble enough to say, "Chad, I'm not qualified to answer this." Here is an example where maybe that is a tip for me if I'm asked such a question just to say, "I'm unqualified." I want to be better than that, and you gave me some tips about being well-read—obviously the *Wall Street Journal*. Anything else that as a consultant I need to do to walk into those unprepared moments where I'm going to be asked a question that I need to answer eloquently and possibly not have thorough knowledge to answer?

Alan: This is another issue of process and content here. In terms of a process—of you being asked questions where you don't know what is coming—you have to stay calm. You can't look at these as if a pitcher were firing 100 mph fastballs down the middle, and you have to make contact. Look at it as a game of volleyball where you have the ball in play over the net, and you want to just tap it back to the other side. I'm not talking about professional volleyball where they go for these kill shots; I'm just talking about a recreational game. The process here is to remain calm, think about the question, and give it your best response.

That leads me to the content side. You said Marshall said, "I'm not qualified." You say I answer all the questions. There are two kinds of content here. That is, one is factually-based content where you say to me, "Alan, how many companies have you consulted with? What has been your most popular kind of consulting? What is your favorite kind of intervention?" All of those are factually based.

Then there is opinion reaction, and that's where I really love to be. The value of opinions of course is that if they're well founded, you use examples, and they're justified or validated or supported by the credibility of the person giving them, then they become fascinating replies, and people think about them. Drucker was famous for this. Drucker would be talking about some factual thing about the Federal Reserve, or how the key for management consultants was that it was finally taken away from regulators in the 1920s, or something, and then suddenly he would be telling you something which was strictly his opinion. You've gone from land to sea, or from air to land, or whatever, and you hardly realized it, but it's okay, and it's this interesting blend that he used to do when he wrote. If you have an opinion that people don't agree with, that's fine. It's the basis of discussion, controversy, and debate. If someone has another opinion, you certainly can't fight it to the end of your life because they're opinions.

On the other hand, if it's content based—if it's factual based and you have the facts and the other person doesn't—then you're obligated to say to them, "Look, here are the facts. You're arguing the facts with your opinion," from whence comes that favorite phrase, "Are you going to believe me or your lying eyes?" That's how I look at these kinds of interactions, and to me a question is always a fascinating exploration. It's never a challenge, never a threat. If somebody said to me, "What are the key elements in producing fission or fusion or something?" I would say, "Hey, beats the heck out of me. I think you need a lot of heat."

Q: What have you identified as the best practices to raising fees?

Alan: Don't be afraid. Understand what your true value is, and change your mindset so that you honestly believe and understand that people believe they get what they pay for. If you do that and you understand that your obligation is to provide people value—and that people in this world are compensated better for the more value they provide—you should have no trouble raising fees. I would also say to people you have to watch out whom you hang out with. There are too many people who are professional victims, who are afraid, and who practice what the psychologists call "projection" which is—if I can't charge fees like this, then neither can you. Run from those people. Get them out of your life.

Q: At times when we work with our clients, we deal with high egos. What are some of the best practices to manage egos of clients while at the same time wanting to be candid and frank with them?

Alan: Leverage them. If somebody has a strong ego, which isn't a federal crime the last time I looked, leverage that ego—so that they provide the clout you need for the project, they find the money you need for the project, they take the leading spokesperson or champion role you need for the project, and so that people understand that my own self-interests are going to be advanced by playing more of a role here. That's okay. That's the buyer, and people like that.

If you find that people's egos are running amuck—they take command of meetings, they don't listen to others, and they want their name on every chair in the place—then you have to talk to them. That's an exception, and that's a borderline personality disorder.

Q: What would you say are some best practices for choosing trusted providers? What are some best practices to select those people and engage them in order to help you propel your business forward?

Alan: Probably a few simple criteria. One is, as we were talking about before, you want a peer-to-peer reference. You want a reference, a referral, an assurance from somebody whom you respect who has used them in the past. Secondly, you want to make sure that they have their credentials. Do they have a body of work? Do they have intellectual property? Are they thought leaders in their field? Are they clearly able to do what you want to do on a consistent basis? If what you want to do is write books and you found somebody who has never written a book who is going to coach you—that's not good. If you find somebody who has written just one book and now they're coaching others on how to write books—that's not good. If you find somebody who has written ten books and they can coach you in writing a book—that's good. Make sure that they're able to and have demonstrated they can do what it is you want to do.

Finally, make sure that the chemistry is right. This isn't about finding a friend, it isn't about being bosom buddies, but make sure that the other person's philosophy, their speed, and their orientation to business is consistent with yours. In other words, leave room for you to grow and change, but basically you should have a similar value set that you're out to improve the client's condition, and so forth. If you find the other person is simply mercenary, all they want to do is make money, the client be damned, that's a different set of circumstances.

Q: Identify a few of the best practices of these professions, and then articulate what or how these can be translated into the consulting, mentoring, and coaching field. The first profession is a *landscape designer or architect*. What are some of his or her best practices, and how are these translatable to consulting?

Alan: Ideally, their best practices are to look holistically at what they're doing. They don't just design a portion of the yard or a piece of the house. They look overall at the environment, the fabric, the color, and the plants. For consultants, the ability to look at things holistically and not just narrowly, through a narrow lens, to look through a telescope not a microscope, is important.

Q: *A cab driver in the city?*

Alan: Great cab drivers know where they're going. London cab drivers know where they're going. They've practiced it, they know all the landmarks, they know the best routes, and they know how to keep their cab clean and their clients comfortable. For consultants, you have to know where you're going. You have to know how to get there quickly, how to take the proper detour when you hit traffic, which would be obstacles, and how to keep things neat and clean for your client.

Q: *A nurse?*

Alan: Nurses have to deal with conflicting demands. They have to deal with a doctor's orders. They have to deal with things going wrong with patients. They have to deal with demanding patients. They have to deal with regulatory matters. They have to deal with safety in procedures in terms of administering meds, and so on. Consultants too have to deal with a lot of conflicting demands. They'll have different clients making different demands on them. They'll have demands from their family and loved ones. You have to deal with those demands in a context where, just like the nurse, first do no harm and make sure the patient is improved. First do no harm and make sure you're improving the client's condition.

Q: *A detective in the police department?*

Alan: Detectives are great framers. Detectives ask, "Did you hear this? Did you do that? When did this occur? How often was that?" They're highly assertive when they have to be. They won't take no for an answer, and they're very adept, the good ones, at finding inconsistencies. The same thing for a consultant. You have to watch for cognitive dissonance. You know the great Sherlock Holmes story where the dog didn't bark, and here you have to be aware and sensitive to the fact that it wasn't the dog barking but a dog that didn't bark. In other words, it wasn't a customer complaining but a customer who didn't complain. You have to be that kind of keen framer and investigative person who validates what they hear and see and finds inconsistencies.

Q: *A great chef?* What can we learn from his best practices?

Alan: Great chefs take ingredients that no one else would dream of to make fantastic meals, and they combine the senses. The sensory appreciation of culinary art is olfactory, visual, and tasting. Consultants need to combine different ingredients as they see fit, not just the same ingredients all the time. There is no sense making a pot roast when somebody wants *coq au vin*. You have to design your ingredients for the kind of results that you want to create.

Q: *A 747 commercial pilot?*

Alan: Pilots need to stay calm in emergencies, and they also need to stay vigilant. Marshall McLuhan once said, "The price of eternal vigilance is indifference." If you put it in today's framework, the security people at airports who look at that screen all day long might stop seeing things altogether. How long can you do that? An airline pilot in terms of an emergency has to stay calm, go through the manual, or go through the rules. On the other hand, when nothing is happening, and there is no emergency, that pilot still has to be vigilant. He just can't sit back and let the autopilot work; he can't afford to doze. It's this interesting combination for a consultant to be ready to handle the unexpected. The client says, "We have to end the project, or we're going to sell the division. There is a new person who has come on board." On the other hand, if the project is going along just fine, don't put it on autopilot. Make sure you're asking for referrals. Make sure you're checking for people doing the real work and not just giving lip service, and so forth.

Q: Talking about 747s, what are your best practices in building model planes?

Alan: Success not perfection. There are people who build model planes, and my specialty happens to be armor—it happens to be tanks. There are people who build these things to 1/1000 of reality, and they'll move something by a 1/16th of an inch. They'll do great investigative work into original sources, photos, and everything else.

My feeling is that this is recreation, that I don't build models because I'm trying to recreate reality. I'm building models because I'm trying to enjoy myself. Consequently, when I had my big electric train set up here, the trains would derail all the time, and every session I had with them something derailed, something crashed, something failed, a light wouldn't go on, but this is how a real railroad is, too. In consulting you're not going to have a perfect day ever. You're not going to have a perfect client ever. You yourself aren't going to be perfect ever. Get used to it, enjoy yourself.

Q: What about *a city mayor*? What makes an effective city mayor, and what can we learn as consultants?

Alan: A mayor has to do two things really well if you talk about best practices. One is run for the office, and second is serve in the office, and they're quite different skills and quite different behaviors. As a candidate, you have to kiss the babies, keep everybody happy, go to cookouts, and debate on the trail. As mayor, you have to make some tough decisions, cut budgets, and get support from other kinds of people to make things work. The same with a consultant. With a consultant it's the marketing and then the implementation. You have to have a certain set of skills and behaviors on the marketing side and then a different set of skills and behavior on the delivery side. That's why so many people who deliver well are lousy marketers and wind up working for someone else or subcontracting because they can't market. Just like a mayor, you need those two very different sets of skills if you're going to be completely successful.

Q: *A rock star musician.*

Alan: Rock star musicians need to do a couple things well. First of all, they need to know music well. It's always surprising to me as I watch "American Idol" and things like this, that these people really know music. If you listen to the judges, they really know music. The second thing is you have to be able to improvise. You just don't sing the notes, you sing some other things too, or you play some other things too. I think it's a combination of knowing the fundamentals of the talent but also having the talent to do things that others don't.

The same for a consultant. You have to know the fundamentals of consulting, but then you have to be willing to improvise as needed. You have to have the confidence and the skills to make beautiful music even when you're departing from the written score.

Q: *The President of this country?*

Alan: The President's best practices are to create as much as possible a unity, a bipartisanship, a commitment rather than a compliance among people to follow a certain path. That's how John Kennedy got us on the moon in nine years even after he passed on. That's how Lincoln reconciled the country. It's how Roosevelt got us through the Great Depression and the war. It's how Churchill got the UK through a terrible time in the war.

You need that kind of unifying ability, and I think outstanding consultants can create consensus among clients even when you have different self-interests represented and some honest opinion that's not completely consistent with the direction of the project. I think that kind of leadership and tough love is needed in both cases.

Q: What would you say are the best of the best identified best practices of Alan Weiss?

Alan: Intellectual firepower, highly developed sense of humor, and a total lack of fear of failing.

Q: Before leaving best practices, I would like to ask you as a parent, what are some best practices you recommend for parents?

Alan: I think you have to instill values in your kids. The most important thing you can do these days is to help them develop a set of values that creates ethical behavior, that shows them what the proper way to interact with others is. I think you have to be forgiving, tolerant, and set the right example.

You have to understand that kids often learn by failing, and you can't put too much pressure on them simply to be the best and succeed. You have to put pressure on them though to be disciplined, to try, and if you do your best and try your best and you're prepared, then it's not about winning anymore. I think you reward the behavior and not necessarily the victory.

Q: What advice have you given your children about choosing a spouse?

Alan: I haven't. It's not my place to do that, and I would think that watching this long-term marriage that my wife and I are in gives them enough examples of what that's about.

Q: Someone once said that the two most influential or important choices people make in life are choosing a spouse and choosing a career path. Do you agree generally with this frame of mind?

Alan: I think the most important choice you make in life is what your value system is—or what you believe in. Today, relationships aren't based on marriage so much any more. People live together. Even marriages undergo divorce far too easily. It's not the sanctified and sacred thing it used to be. No matter what your belief system is. No matter what your religion is or isn't, marriage doesn't hold the same place in our society that it once did, nor do partnerships, nor do relationships. They're too disposable these days.

Careers can change. It's very unusual for someone to embark on a career and stay in it, and that's why so many people wind up in consulting or professional services; they began somewhere else as I did. I think the key choice you make is what your value system is. What do you believe in? What do you believe about yourself? Where do you believe you fit in the world? That's why I think spirituality is so important. I think that's the ember that helps you decide that.

Q: As we finish this last chapter, we would like to focus on some specific tactics we can use to implement the ideas we've discussed for these many hours. We would like to take some time to discuss your list of 11 things that you introduced to the grad school several years ago. Basically, you told us that when you face a client situation, it's one of these 11 things. We would like to go through each one and ask how you discovered that this was one of the 11 things, what you did to address it, and what we can do when we face it. The first of the 11 you said was probably this: Leadership is inept in that key people aren't serving as avatars of the behavior they're seeking in others.

Alan: That's fascinating. The issue here is that people and organizations don't believe what they read or hear, they only believe what they see. You can hang all the wall plaques you want, you can make all the attempts at motivational speeches that you please, but people at the end of the day believe what they see. They believe what they're looking at. Consequently, I think part of your question is how I resolve these things. What I've done is I've found both the formal and informal avatars, and I've advised them on how to act if they want to get people to act consistent with their goals. It's as simple as that.

Q: What type of buyer were you working with when this first occurred to you that this was one of the 11 things?

Alan: I don't know when they first occurred. These 11 things emerged as palimpsests; they emerged from beneath the page and suddenly took form at one time or another. I wasn't up on a mountain getting the tablets, but they emerged for me as time went on.

I think that what I saw pretty early in my career was the fact that there was cognitive dissonance. A buyer would tell me that he or she wanted one thing, but they were acting in a way completely contrary to how they wanted people to act. It's the famous story of the leader who is cheating on expenses and can't understand why the employees are cheating on expenses.

Q: Let's drill down a little bit. What was the conceptual agreement discussion like when you were with some of these clients?

Alan: Conceptual agreement being objectives, measures, and value: The objectives would be for the employees to take a certain kind of stance or have a certain kind of behavior. Let's just say, for example, you expect your telemarketers or your call service employees to make the customers who call feel appreciated, resolve their problems on one call, and even stimulate them to reorder. For an objective like that, we all see American Express and others send out questionnaires to people situationally and say, "Did our representative make you feel trusted? Make you feel like you were worthy? That you're an important customer?" and so on. The metric would be "Were they solved in one call? How do people respond in the surveys? What is their repeat business?" The value of course was more business, at less cost of acquisition and also less failure work which means that the problem had to be jumped up to the next level of management.

The key here is that I would have to tell the people who are managing these people that you yourself couldn't refuse to take calls. When somebody said, "Excuse me John, a client, a customer is on the line," you can't say, "I don't want to deal with it now, I'm busy." Similarly, you can't say that you're going to measure people in terms of number of calls per hour because if you're measuring people in terms of number of calls per hour, then you're acting in a contrary manner as the cognitive dissonance. What you expect them to do is take time to make them feel comfortable. Those are the kinds of things—just common sense—that emerge when you look at these kinds of dynamics.

Q: Your methodology was to do some surveying in focus groups, or something like that, so that you could come to these conclusions?

Alan: Yes, it was very simple. First, you would observe what people were doing on the phone. I used to have a setup in one company where I would actually listen on the phone in a separate room, and people wouldn't know I was listening. They had some kind of electronic gizmo where if they had 40 people on the floor, I could actually plug into any of the 40 and listen unobserved. Nobody would know I was on the line and hear how things went very spontaneously, as opposed to sitting there with them. Of course, just observing somebody alters their behavior. This way they didn't know they were being observed.

Q: What sort of value are clients willing to pay for when we address issue number one?

Alan: As I mentioned, they pay for settling a problem the first time without doing the failure work of it having to go up several levels of management. They'll pay for the fact that they might get new business, additional business out of what began as a complaint call.

Everyone has experienced this by now, and if you haven't, I'll clue you in. If you have a complaint with a company, the person on the phone can't handle it, and you keep asking for a supervisor, you'll eventually get someone who will handle you. It might not be your ideal solution, but it will be remedial. That is, they'll provide you with something, and we all know that.

What I tell my clients from time immemorial is since you and I both know that's going to happen, settle it at the front line. Give these people the power, the empowerment, to settle this at the front line because by the time it gets to you, even if you offer them less than the person at the front line, what will happen is the company's expense will still be greater because of what was involved in getting to you. Hence you have the example everyone talks about where Ritz Carlton employees right down to the front line are empowered to take care of customer complaints by spending company money. Even though they might spend more than the customer would otherwise demand—the customer might have been happy with a drink, but the employee bought the customer a dinner—it still doesn't matter. It's still cheaper to do it that way.

Q: It sounds as though, at least with number one, the client isn't going to say, "Alan, come in and help me be a better avatar of the behavior that I want others to have." They might call you in and say, "Fix my call center" which wouldn't seem related at all.

Alan: That's why you have to go back and change the behavior of the person leading it. People usually don't recognize that it's their behavior that is the key to determine change. I think you started drilling down too far here. The point is that if you want to create change in an organization, the easiest, fastest way to do that is to have the most visible and respected leaders change their behavior. That's how simple it is.

Q: It sounds as though the point is these aren't going to smack us between the eyes. We're going to have to be aware of them and look for them because the client won't lead with them.

Alan: The client won't lead with them, but a good, seasoned consultant can identify these 11 things on my list pretty readily. That's why I got out of OD consulting because in 90 seconds I could say, "It's number seven, number three, and number one. That will be $250,000," except I wasn't going to get away with that.

Q: What is the difference between finding the avatars and developing the avatars, and which is your preferable approach?

Alan: They're both important, and I think the sequence you just mentioned was the correct sequence. In other words, first you have to identify who it is who is going to influence others' behavior. Sometimes it's obvious. You know there is a vice president who heads the division, there is a general manager who heads the profit center, but sometimes it's not obvious. Sometimes there is a key salesperson who is simply one of the sales crew but is so respected that people follow his or her lead. That's the first thing. The second thing is you make a judgment, and you build a relationship wherein you change their behavior—which usually isn't too difficult—to be consistent with the way they want others to act.

Q: Team building is sought when in actuality the organization has committees and needs committees not teams. Why?

Alan: I never understood what team building was about. These retreats where you're supposed to go out and you come back two days later and you have been "built." I don't get that, and when I started to look around organizations, one thing became just apparently clear to me.

I try to make things visual all the time. They're easier for me and others to understand. I would draw this picture of what a team is—a team by definition and according to a lot of books has to have a common goal, they're rewarded or punished collectively, they all meet their goal or they don't, they're often self directed, they often determine how they're going to distribute their own bonus money for example, and they determine pretty much how they operate. It's a very empowering thing, and they do this in a consensus basis even though there might be a team leader.

What I found is that was seldom the case in organizations. There were usually committees, and committees are people who come together and share resources, ideas, and information to the extent they're comfortable doing it without jeopardizing their own perceptions, their own positions. Ninety percent of the clients I've dealt with who think they have teams actually have committees. It's like saying to me you want to help my car go faster by cleaning the windshield. Cleaning the windshield will not help my car go faster. Organizations that try to use team building on committees might as well be engaged in that kind of futile act. It just doesn't work.

Q: When the buyer identified objectives, did they call you and say, "Alan, we want you to do a team building project," and you discovered they didn't want it, or how did this come about?

Alan: That's what would happen, but they weren't objectives. The buyer would give me an arbitrary alternative, and the buyer would say, "We would like to have some team building work done," and of course I would say, "Why?" The client would come out with a variety of objectives. "We have too much duplication of effort, we have too many turf battles that we have to resolve, and we think we should have a more seamless client interface." All of those are legitimate objectives, but then when you look at why those things are or aren't happening, what you find is it's because the client is expecting teamwork from people who have no motivation to act like a team.

Q: At that point, how do you redefine the objectives with the buyer?

Alan: I don't. What I say to the client is, "These objectives are lofty, worthy, noble, and all that kind of stuff, but let's look at what we have here. Your arbitrary, alternative team building session isn't going to work because there is only one of a few remedies here. Number one is you don't need a team for this. You should have a committee. You should have people with varied interests coming together in a healthy sense of confrontation. If that's the case, then let's work on that dynamic. On the other hand, maybe you do need a team, and in that case you have to form one, and you have to change the reward system, the communication system, the accountabilities, and so forth. In the third situation, you might already have a team, you need a team, and it's appropriate, but what you have to do here is help the team clarify what it's supposed to be doing and make it better and more expert at what it's supposed to be doing."

Q: Walk us through some methodologies we could use if we face this sort of thing.

Alan: The first thing you do is to ask, "Why do you want this?" You don't accept an arbitrary alternative like team building. The second thing is you look at the structure. Are these people involved in a pursuit where they're mutually rewarded, mutually punished, self directed, and so on?

What is most common is you have a vice president of strategy, vice president of marketing, vice president of R&D, and vice president of sales. That's not a team even though you might call it that! It's a committee of people coming together, you recognize this, and then you ask yourself, "What is actually needed here to meet the client objectives?" Normally, you don't need a team to meet the client objectives. It's an arbitrary construct that people try to put together.

Q: Did you do some interviews with senior teams to get their perceptions, or how do you come to these conclusions? What do you do?

Alan: You can usually do it just by observing what is going on and asking a few people a few things. I'm driven by laziness. I like to keep things as simple as possible and not get into complex methodologies. Normally, I could actually ask the buyer what the buyer wanted, determine what was needed, sit down and watch this group at work—this nameless group for the moment—determine what it really was, determine what was really needed, and then start to make some adjustments.

Q: You rely very heavily on your own observations and not necessarily what people tell you?

Alan: You can never rely on that. There is this old phrase "Are you going to believe me or your lying eyes?" I'm going to believe my lying eyes, and even if I trust the client implicitly, my obligation as a consultant is to validate and verify what the client tells me. The client might be honest-to-God wrong, might have been told the wrong things, might be trying to fool herself or himself into thinking something else, or might have a different interpretation. Who knows what? All these things are possible.

I like to watch people at work. I'll interact with them. I'll interview them. I'll run focus groups. I might do other things, but I like to watch what is actually happening because behavior to me—observed behavior and evidence in the environment—is the absolute platinum standard.

Q: What happens if you go to a group, you shadow the people, you attend the meeting, or whatever it is, and you figure out that the buyer really hasn't identified the objectives or really doesn't have his finger on the pulse of the problem? What then?

Alan: I don't know what that means because if I'm doing that, if I'm engaged in that work, we would have already had the objectives clarified. At that point I'm implementing. That means I've established objectives, measures, and value with the client, and I felt that the client's objectives are valid. The client might feel that there is a certain cause or a certain issue that needs to be resolved, and I find it's something else, but that has nothing to do with the objectives that are achieved.

Q: This is not about information gathering? This is after you already have a proposal...

Alan: I don't do information gathering. I don't do "needs analyses." Somebody writes to me that they want free help and says, "What can I read, what can I do to get an excellent client discovery?" I said, "I have no idea what the phrase means. You're new to the profession. I've been doing this for 30 years. I don't know what you're talking about."

Q: Okay, issue three. There are silos headed by powerful people defending turf.

Alan: A classic problem which is as obvious as a ham sandwich, and what you find is this is after the objectives have been set. It doesn't matter what the objectives for the project are, it doesn't matter what the goals are, but you're in there working and what you find is there are two or three or six silos that are staunchly defended by people who see each other not as even potential committee participants but as rivals. They're rivals for their boss's position. They're rivals for the bonus pot. They're rivals for popularity. When you see that, you have to knock down the silos. You have to create alternative routes of communication so everybody isn't going up, over, and down.

Q: What are some of those alternatives?

Alan: You have to engage people to talk laterally so that they don't have to go through their management structure, and you prove to your buyer that that saves all kinds of money, which it always does. Just picture if you and I can do something directly on this right now, we're going to get it done. If you tell me you have to go through Chad, and he has to go through Aviv, and then over to me, and these two are in different parts of the building, in different countries, or one is traveling, your expense multiplies exponentially.

The more you can get people to talk to each other at the lowest levels possible, the more you're saving money. That's what I prove to the buyer, and that's incentive for disassembling the silos, or as I call it—poking holes in their sides. When you do that, all the grain runs out.

Q: I can picture someone thinking, "Alan, you haven't worked with my client. The people at the top of these silos are so powerful, and there is no knocking them out or poking holes in the silos. How can I attack this?"

Alan: If that's your feeling, then get in another line of business! I'm not even interested in helping you. If you feel that things are hopeless, you really don't belong in this business. If you feel that people are so powerful that you can't approach them, you don't belong here. If you feel so intimidated because somebody is making a lot of money, they're loud, they have a large office, they have a lot of responsibilities, or whatever it is, you have to get over that. There is no silo that can't be punctured. There is no silo that can't be broken apart or in which you can't poke holes. The key is to know how to do it.

Q: How do you engage the buyer in using his or her power to do this?

Alan: I just told you. You show them the cost efficiencies. You show them that it's much more effective, it's quicker, it costs less, and so on for the people at lower levels to communicate laterally than to go up, over, and down each time they need to talk or each time they need information from each other.

Q: Always coming back to the objectives and pointing out how a particular change of behavior will support them?

Alan: If you want the buyer to help you, if you want the buyer's clout, what you have to prove to the buyer is it's in his or her self-interest to do something: Lower cost, more efficiency, and greater speed I would think are always in the buyer's self-interest.

Q: That sounds as though it could apply to any of these 11 things.

Alan: It does. That's why it's so easy to identify these things and get them done. When you're asking me about objectives, the objectives for all these 11 things don't really matter. The objectives for all these projects don't matter because these are 11 things I encounter after I'm engaged in the work, and once I'm engaged in the work, you can deal with them very quickly.

The issue for me is that even though I can deal with them extraordinarily quickly, I still had to slow down because the client would require a week examining this, two weeks to get people together, or something over here. It just got laborious and boring.

Q: The fourth thing. Problem solving is prized over innovation and "black belt 9 delta" nonsense takes over people's minds like a bad science fiction movie from the '50s.

Alan: Yes, there has been an overwhelming focus on problem solving, and lean, and quality, and all this because—my opinion is—the senior managers didn't want to think about these issues real hard, and they purchased programs that they thought would take care of it.

My favorite example is being with a company in North Carolina that manufactured a certain kind of equipment. I accompanied the president of the division with his entourage around the plant looking at—I don't know what they were—these Kaizen charts, these stupid pie charts and bars above each machine. The operators and the supervisors are explaining them, and I looked over my left shoulder and there is a machine behind us leaking oil on the plant floor. I tapped the shoulder of one of the people in the entourage and said, "Hey, you got a leak over there." He said, "Yes, not now. After we finish the inspection." That's the kind of nuttiness that goes on!

The fact is that problem solving is important, but when you have secretaries, and I've seen this, rearranging their desks under some Kaizen principle attempting to be more efficient, the lunatics are running the asylum. Decision making of course is a pursuit quite different from problem solving, and when you start to use them interchangeably, everything gets lost. The case with this point is if you can simply help people understand the difference between problem solving, decision making, planning, and innovation—all of which have different starting points—you can boost productivity immediately.

Q: It sounds as though some of these things that are very tactical in nature would appeal to those consultants who allow their processes to drive their businesses. Have you found that to be true?

Alan: Nobody should be in love with their methodology. Nobody should walk in saying, "Good, I can use all seven steps." Our goal is to improve the client's condition, and our goal is to improve the client's condition as rapidly as possible. That's why I have value-based fees and not hourly fees which are contrary to a quick fix.

My feeling is, the point of these 11 is that I can do it in a jet-assisted, turbo-charged manner if there were no constraints, and people didn't mind me just doing this in half a day. Any consultant should look to shorten his or her stay with the client by expeditiously improving their condition and not worrying about using all the methodology in their toolkit.

Q: We're going to point number five out of the 11 points. You said in point number five "The organization is bureaucratic in that it focuses on means and not ends."

Alan: Yes, my definition of bureaucracy is an organization that treasures means over ends, and even though you're getting a certain result, they in effect tell you, "I'm sorry you didn't complete the form." I'll give a splendid example of this, and I can actually name names here.

Eight or ten years ago whenever it was I was working with Andersen, their consulting operation—not Accenture which broke off as their own consulting firm—assigned me to one practice. It was the outplacement practice, I believe, and they asked me to help them move toward value-based pricing, and this particular unit was very amenable to doing that, so they picked a good unit. They were motivated to do it, they were a great bunch of people, and we converted their thinking, philosophy, and practices to value-based fees.

Sure enough, one of the pilot teams went out and they sold about a $425,000 piece of business. They got back and the internal accounting people told them that they couldn't process the credit because they had to break it out into time spent on each of 12 different categories, or whatever it was, because the rest of the company was doing hourly billing.

The head of the practice came to me and said, "What am I going to do now? We sold this business, but we can't bill it, and we can't start." I said, "It's very simple. Whom do you report to?" He said, "I report to this general partner." I said, "Write him a note and tell him that the accounting people aren't accepting this, and he has two alternatives. He can either tell the accounting people to make bigger boxes and take in the $425,000, or he can tell you to reduce the sale to $90,000 which will allow them to put it in the proper boxes." And 24 hours later they had a $425,000 sale, and accounting managed somehow to expand their boxes. For accounting, there was a question of means over ends—and you find that in organizations all the time—and that's what creates this dumb bureaucracy which gums up the works, and in this case delayed a sale by a day and could have delayed it by a month.

It's one of the reasons I can't stand human resources. They act like traffic cops, and with some rare beautiful exceptions, instead of expediting things, they're always slowing things up—and that's the triumph of means over ends. Don't forget when people don't have power, they make up power. Artificial power is the essence of bureaucracy. Psychologically, people can't live in organizations feeling they're powerless.

When I worked with a consulting firm, the president and I traveled to Japan, and we were in Narita airport in a long, long line. Just a terrible, ugly, inefficient long line. We finally get up to the Japanese immigration officer, who speaks very little English which I would expect—you don't have much multilingualism in the U.S. immigration—and he takes my form, grumbles a little bit, and stamps it. He takes the president's form—he is just behind me—and the president has filled out his form in red ink. The guy says to him in half English and half Japanese, just red in the face, that this form can't be filled out in red ink, it has to be blue ink. It isn't that he is scanning it or anything—it's just the regulation—and my boss put up a big fuss. A supervisor came over and backed up the guy, my boss had to fill out a new card, they wouldn't let him do it there, and he had to go back to the end of the line.

I've seen that, and so have you, countless times. It's the triumph of means over ends, and one of the reasons I've been so effective is I focus strictly on ends in my own life and in my client's lives. Too many consultants, let alone their clients, are consumed with means.

Q: You just said that artificial power is one manifestation of bureaucracy. When I look at my client's organizations or my own organization, how do I know that I'm looking at a bureaucracy or possibly a complex situation that has gone through complex processes?

Alan: It's very simple. Just ask yourself and ask your client, "Are the actions you're seeing in front of you expediting the product, service, and relationship with the customer or are they slowing it up?" That's the answer. If they tell you, "It's slowing it up, but it's ensuring us of quality. It's ensuring us of validation of payment. It's ensuring us of this and that," it's bureaucracy.

What does the bank tell you all the time? I'll walk into the bank and some teller I've never seen before because she was just hired wants to see my identification. All the other tellers there know me, I've got seven figures invested in this bank, and she will always say the same thing, "It's for your protection." No it isn't. It's for their protection.

When you're calling a help line, you're making a purchase, or you're calling with a complaint, you'll hear all the time "This call may be recorded for quality purposes." *They're not recording it for quality purposes because the quality never improves.* They're recording it to protect themselves, and that just adds to the bureaucracy. When you have all these phone menus and you have to go through seven numbers before you get to a human or whatever it is, that's the essence of bureaucracy because it makes our lives as consumers tougher. It's not helping us at all.

Q: What are some of the tips we can help implement and execute to reduce bureaucracy when we see it?

Alan: Look at the results you want to achieve, work backwards, and ask yourself, "What is the quickest way to get there?" One of the questions I'm always asking in a proposal with a client is, "What is it you want to achieve?" The client says, "These are my objectives," and we talk about that. Then when I'm devising the methodology, I'm backing up from the objective and saying, "What are the fastest ways I can get the client to that new level of performance?" I'm not saying, "Let me start with the different things I can do and see where I can build them in" because my value and fee are not based on the different things I can do, but rather on how quickly I can move the client to the newly desired condition. That's what you have to look at to avoid bureaucracy. What is the end result? How do we get there?

Q: So let me test one more assumption here. You said that the organization focuses on means and not ends. Is it possible that part of the reason for bureaucracy is the end is not clear enough for the organization to focus on?

Alan: Rarely. The major reasons for bureaucracy are one, people aren't empowered—and so they create artificial power. Two, the company is overly conservative, scared—and feels it needs to protect itself. Three, there is a misplaced emphasis on what is really a value—and the company thinks it's how it does things rather than what the customer receives.

I collect stamps, and I'm an advanced U.S. collector, but I also have a collection from Thailand, and it's hard to find Thailand specialists from whom to get stamps. U.S. stamps, even on an advanced level, can be obtained from auctions and so on, but Thai stamps are harder in the United States. I find this company that specializes in Thai stamps and I said to them, "If I send you a want list, can you fill the want list, we'll agree on a certain charge per month, every month you can send me the stamps, and I'll pay you the bill." They said, "It would be easier if you went on our website and ordered." I said, "It's not easier. I've been to your website, and I have to put in each stamp I want, try to locate it, and many of them you don't have. It's very time consuming. I don't want to spend 30 minutes or an hour trying to pick out stamps. If I can send you the want list electronically, which will take me 60 seconds, you can then fill it and have my business." They said, "That's not how we like to do things." That's the stereotypical, prototypical, archetypical, perfect example of a small business that's bureaucratic.

What I've found in my career is that size isn't the issue. That is, there are large firms which can be very results oriented and innovative, and there are small firms which can be highly bureaucratic. This stamp company, which is probably a mom and pop operation—and I'm that rare collector who can spend anything on these stamps even in a recession—couldn't recognize the value they were staring in the face but had to do things their way. That's why small businesses fail, and that's why large businesses have poor margins.

Q: What have you seen among those in your mentoring program—what are consultants doing to make it hard to do business with them?

Alan: Consultants are their own worst enemy. I'll just rattle off a few obstacles that we discussed at other points during these interviews, but one is the fact that consultants feel that they have to employ their methodology and all of their methodology. A second is they're afraid. They're afraid to move boldly. A third is that they focus on perfection and not success, and the fact is every project is imperfect—but the real issue is that the client's condition improved to the extent the client expected it or even better, and consultants spend way too much time on things.

I'll give you a couple of quick examples just from my Forum. Every day I'm on Alan's Forums (AlansForums.com) three or four times, and I find conversational threads that are bewildering. I find people spending, God knows, hours worried about their data backup. Some of them have backups that in case of a tornado on top of a flood on top of a nuclear war, the thing will be circulating out around Alpha Centauri. My goodness, make a backup on the floor on a hard drive, and get on with your life.

There are other people who use things like frequent contact, constant annoyance, or whatever these convoluted software programs are to follow up with clients. I run a $3 million business working 20 hours a week, and these people aren't doing what I'm doing, and they have all this stuff to follow up on client projects! One year I had 36 client projects, and these were OD clients, not coaching, not mentoring. I kept the entire information source and follow up within I think it was 36 cubic inches, which is approximately the space between my ears. I would like to think that if you lost the files of valuable clients, *they would eventually call you!!*

Finally, you find people who have virtual assistants and help running their offices, and I just don't get that, especially in this technological age. I didn't use help like that before the computers, but why do you need virtual assistants and part-timers every day to help you run your life? I swear to you, consultants are spending more time trying to organize themselves than they are improving the client's condition. That's why I'm running a program, The Time of Your Life. People need to take control of their lives again.

Q: Point number six you said, "There is excessive staff interference instead of support typically from human resources, finance, IT, and/or legal."

Alan: These support positions are supposed to be expeditors. The reason to have any support position is that it should expedite, that is, avoid duplication, spread best practices, provide on time/just-in-time support where needed—but that has been transmogrified. Legal steps in with a legal opinion on why you can't do something because lawyers are archly conservative. The accountants step in with an opinion as to why the billing practices are wrong because they're paid to be archly conservative. Human resources steps in saying that nine policies are violated because they're paid to be archly stupid.

What happens is you have all of these support positions trying to justify their own existence and wind up getting in the way, and you don't have any kind of expedited relationship with your client. What you have is a delayed relationship with your client. You can usually sweep out these people. That is, marginalize them. Get them off the main dance floor. Put them against the wall hoping somebody will ask them to dance, but get them out of the way so that the business can proceed in a streamlined manner.

Q: How do we help management reduce that interference mindset and allow then the support staff to focus on proper support?

Alan: You always have to go back to the same thing. You always have to go back to the capitalist self-interest, and what you say is, "Look: You're spending more money on these processes than you need to because all these people are involved. You're delaying your response to the client because all these people are involved. You're not able to do this. You're not able to do that. Your cost of acquisition is too great. You're not solving problems the first time because all of these people are involved." You get them the hell out of the way. That's why you only want to deal with buyers. A lot of buyers will think because they have a vice president of human resources and a 27-person human resources staff, it must be important, but the mere existence of something doesn't make it important.

John Muir was the great naturalist. Muir Woods, a gorgeous place, is named after him outside of San Francisco. Somebody was complaining to him about poison ivy and the fact that poison ivy has no positive effect at all. It can't be made into medicine. It's not a food for anything. It's just a terrible sort of detriment to mankind, and they said, "Why is it made?" John Muir said to them, "Perhaps you've never considered it might have been made for itself." As far as I know, God didn't create human resources, and they weren't made for themselves. I don't know why they were made, but if they're going to do anything, you better get them set straight so they help you out. The same applies for any support position.

Q: On point seven you said, "There are too many meetings that are too long and overwhelmingly focus on sharing information, the worst possible reason to have a meeting. The organization's talent and energy are squandered internally instead of applied externally."

Alan: Yes, I can hardly improve on what you just read. I've always told people I can walk through any organization in a single day, remove 20 percent of the management, cut meetings by 90 percent, and no one will ever know the difference except on the bottom line. Organizations tend to have too many people, but they also have way too many meetings, and meetings shouldn't be an exchange of information. You can read things to exchange information. Meetings should only be about decisions that have to be made and only those decisions that require a variety of people to be involved in the decision making. When you restrict them to that, you do wonders.

I can't tell you how many senior people's lives I've changed by asking them the following questions. "How much time are you spending in meetings?" "Way too much." "How much?" "Sixty percent of my week." "Uh huh. Why do you go to this meeting here?" "Well, my name is on the distribution list." "Right, but why do you go?" "They expect me." "Yes, but why do you go?" After I do that 12 times, they finally say, "There really is no reason for me to be there." I say, "Okay, cross that one off. Why do you go to this meeting?" I can reduce their meetings to maybe one or two a week. Meetings are notorious for being held for the wrong reasons, for people attending because they're afraid not to attend, or for believing they're actually important and they're not. They're tremendous time drags.

Q: What is the key benchmark to a must-have meeting and the proper structure to make sure it's as effective as possible?

Alan: A meeting should have the following criteria. A meeting should have a results agenda, not an item agenda. As a result of this meeting, the following things will be accomplished. The following things will be changed. The following things will be improved. That's number one.

Number two is a meeting has a finite timeframe that somebody keeps track of, and for my money no meeting should ever be longer than 60 minutes. Some people you might have read about actually have meetings with no chairs in the rooms so people have to stand, making them want to get out of there as soon as possible. I don't go that far, but an hour is all you need for a meeting, and shorter is fine.

Number three, somebody has to run the meeting who knows what the hell they're doing. That might be the leader, or it might be someone the leader designates who is simply an expert facilitator. Number four, meetings have rules of engagement. That is, there are no accusations, there is no personal stuff going on, people shut off their phones, they shut off their iPads, they don't allow their staff to interrupt them, they focus on the issue at hand, and they debate things on the merits. Somebody enforces those rules of engagement. If you do that, you can run a meeting in 20 minutes.

As a result of the meeting, you've decided, for example, that customers who have a legitimate complaint about a certain product will receive two weeks of free service, or instead of closing the Florida office, it's going to be combined with the Atlanta office, or the company lobby will be opening an hour earlier with a security guard posted because some people want to come in to work early, and we should allow that. Whatever it is, grand or small, it's a result. That's how you get to it.

Q: Point number eight you said the following. "The customer's perceptions of the organization's products, services, and relationships are different from the organization's perception."

Alan: Yes, in a lot of my books I have a strategic profile, and what it says is, "Your products, your services, and your relationships are either competitive, distinct, or breakthrough." I have my clients fill it out, and for that matter I have people in my mentor program fill it out, in my Million Dollar Consulting College fill it out, and I say to them, "What do your customers think of you?" Inevitably they fill it out in terms of how they think of themselves, and it's very useful to compare notes because people often have a distorted view of themselves. They think their service is better than it is, or they might think it's worse than it really is.

The only people who matter are the customers. It doesn't matter what you think. The only thing that matters are the customers because they're the ones who are going to give you money or not. I've found that there is often a disparate belief between the customer and the company as to how they're perceived that needs to be reconciled, and that's easy when you start asking the customer.

Q: Are you suggesting somehow that the customer takes an equivalent of the strategic profile to rank myself?

Alan: No, I suggest that the consultant go talk to customers, and ask them how they perceive the company in whatever factors you're looking at. You give them some criteria for doing that so there is a consistent metric in the feedback. That's what you do, then you compare it to how the company feels, and you see what is disparate and make adjustments.

If the company feels it's superb in service and the clients feel that they're just competitive, you have to ask yourself, "What do we have to do to become better than we are to move from competitive to distinct or break-through?" Conversely, you might find that you really are spending more on service than you need to. You think that you're distinct; and the customer thinks you're breakthrough because you have overestimated the competition. These things are very useful to find out.

Q: Issue number nine is the following. "The reward and feedback systems are not aligned with strategy. They're not encouraging the appropriate behaviors and/or are discouraging the appropriate behaviors." How do you discover this, and how do you address this issue?

Alan: When you look at a company's strategy—if that's part of the project—you want to understand what the goals are, and again you work backwards and say, "Fine, what kind of performance will get them there?" And then you look at things like rewards, communications, and so forth, and ask if they're pushing in the right direction or the wrong direction. It's no different from saying, "Where is our port of call, how is the wind blowing, and how do we adjust our sails to get there?" Sometimes you can go straight in, sometimes you have to tack, and that's what you want to look at.

I'll just give you a quick example similar to one I gave you earlier. There was a case—this was some years ago—but United Airlines was telling its reservations agents that they wanted to stand out from the competition—most notably American—by careful customer care and actually helping people choose the least expensive routes, choose the most ancillary benefits such as hotel stays, rental cars, and so on, yet they were measuring these people and rewarding them on numbers of calls per hour! You can't have it both ways.

Q: You suggested in an earlier call that we advise clients to shift their work plan from task-based, task-driven, to a value-based work plan. Is that aligned with this same idea of then being able to reward people for the value they create rather than for the way they spend their time?

Alan: I think you need to reward people for the contribution they make towards your goals. In this case we're talking about strategy in particular, and I think you reward people for that. I remember one case where I said, "This department as a whole is underperforming, yet 85 percent of the people in the department have an evaluation that exceeds expectations." I said to the buyer, "How the heck do you reconcile that?" He said, "I don't know. I've never thought of it that way. Why don't you go find out?"

I went to the department head, I sat down with the evaluations, and the very first one I picked up I said, "Okay look: Charlie here received 'exceeds expectations.'" I said, "Yet he didn't provide any more business than the others did; in fact, he is very average. His clients haven't renewed at a rate above average. How did he get an 'exceeds expectations'?" The guy smiled and said, "Oh, you don't get it. Charlie comes in at 6:45 every morning, gets the coffee on for everyone else and has donuts for people. He is invaluable." That's the kind of nonsense you find.

Q: Number ten issue is strategy and planning are mistaken for each other. Can you share a concrete example of you encountering that issue and how you address it?

Alan: It's just chronic, and it's really worst at high levels because at low levels you would expect them to be tactical and worried about implementation and execution. The higher you go, you would expect more of a strategic framework. I remember sitting at the board of a very large nonprofit—50,000 members in Washington—and they said, "We're not really making much progress as a board. Can you take a look?"

What would happen is, first of all, the board was too big. They had 50 people, and I told them they should probably have 14, but they wanted to represent every interest within the group. The board would sit around and start to say things like, "How should we plan to expand overseas to include the same kinds of professionals overseas? Can we become an international outfit?" That's a strategic issue, and then the next comment would be, "The problem is that I don't know that we have the capacity to service people internationally. I don't know that our call center can handle that, and I don't even know if our technology is compatible." Somebody else would say, "It's not only that but where would the funding come from? There is a problem with that," and suddenly they're worried about the sandwiches in the cafeteria. You see that chronically with boards, and it's not even a ping pong game because the ball stays too much on the tactical side.

Q: A very senior executive told me last week, "I would like you to come and help us in our strategic planning." I had to hold my response because you just shared with us that strategic planning really is an oxymoron. What is the appropriate response? What is the appropriate reply to a senior executive asking you to lead and help design strategic planning?

Alan: I have to admit this is the place where I get a lot of push-back when people are irritated with me because they just love to talk about strategic planning. They think I'm pulling a nicety here, that I'm splitting hairs, but what I tell them is strategy is top down. The senior people set the direction—they establish the framework for the organization within which decisions are made which will set the nature and direction of the business. That's strategy.

Planning is bottom up, and in typical planning you ask your sales force, "If you did this amount this year, what are you going to do next year?" The sales force is always highly conservative because their bonus is based on beating their estimate. That goes up to the sales managers, and they cut it back still more because they're concerned about their bonus, and they're afraid the sales people are too liberal. That goes through the sales vice president who cuts it back one more time just for good measure. Now you go to the marketing department, the R&D department, commercialization of product, and all of that, and once you have seven or eight departments reporting up, once it gets to the senior executives, their hands are tied. You have a 2.5 percent growth rate because everybody is being archly conservative to protect their money!

Strategy is just the opposite. It paints a picture of the future that you then work backwards to try to achieve. Strategic planning as a phrase makes no sense, and I think it's more than just semantics. I think that you have to be clear on what strategy is, and you have to be clear on what planning is.

Q: That's a great clarification. The last and eleventh issue you framed is career development and succession planning are not wedded. What are some key tips to senior executives about the distinction between these two?

Alan: Stop trying to build a bridge across the river by building from both sides at once using different engineering firms, one of whom is using the metric system and the other is using feet and inches. It's just a recipe for disaster, and what happens goes back to my earlier conversation. Succession planning is usually lodged with the executives. It's a strategic issue. But career development is lodged—guess where? In human resources, and it's like asking a cheetah to try to keep up with a mastodon. It just doesn't work. The mastodon is going to get lost in the mire. What happens of course is the cheetah is still with us, and the mastodons are extinct.

The senior people have to understand that these are gears that have to mesh. It's a bridge where the roadway has to meet in the middle within centimeters of exactitude of alignment being true. You have to take the responsibility for overseeing both career development and succession planning. Career development should feed succession planning. Here is the difference: Not everyone is a viable candidate for succession planning, but everyone is a viable candidate for career development because everybody should receive constant development that helps them do their job better and helps them fit better with the company. These gears have to mesh, and it's up to senior management to make sure that they do.

Q: What are some key principles or best practices that you've consulted senior executives about effective succession planning?

Alan: You have to do it frequently. In other words, you have to at least quarterly have a discussion about succession, and you have to understand the following: There are some people you have who are now available and ready to take the jobs of their boss or a boss. It doesn't have to be a direct line of succession. There are some people who can do it with development. They might need skills acquisition. They might need to serve on an international assignment, whatever it is, but they can get there with development. There are other people who aren't going to get there. They've reached their level of competence, and it's unreasonable to expect them to go farther. This means that you should expect if you have too many people in the first category that are ready now, you're going to lose some, and that's okay.

General Electric is famous for losing top executives because they had such deep bench strength. Larry Bossidy, when he finds out he isn't going to be CEO of GE—Jack Welch gets the job—goes over to Allied Signal and has a fabulous career there. You can name 12 people who did that at GE.

Secondly, with the people who need development, that's where you have to coordinate with whomever is going to do that development, whether it's human resources, the line functions, or whomever. Make sure that the development is consistent with the jobs you want them to eventually be in line for.

Thirdly, you're going to have holes. You're going to have jobs in the future where you don't have good candidates today, or the candidates you have will fill different jobs, and that means you have to recruit them. You have to have a relationship with search firms, or you have to have an active recruiting process or both. Holistically, that's how you have to look at this, and you have to take a personal interest in this.

I remember the old Chase Manhattan Bank used to have something called Rockefeller's Room where they actually had photos of people who were in the succession planning system and the departments in which they would probably rise to. This might be an apocryphal story, but presumably I was shown the door once. I don't know what was behind it, but I was shown the door, and only three people had keys to this room—that's how secretive it was—and I don't know if that's necessarily good. I think people who are of high potential should be apprised of the fact that their superiors feel they're high potential because it keeps their eyes on the ball, and it keeps them motivated to stay with the company, but that's a different discussion.

Q: Do you believe every executive needs to identify their preferred successor in case they are hit by a bus, abducted by aliens, or can that be a premature selection? What is your guidance on that?

Alan: Everyone in a key position should identify more than one possible successor, even if that successor isn't in their direct chain of command. One of the reasons for that, apart from alien abduction, is that you aren't going anywhere yourself unless the company is completely comfortable that in moving you, they aren't ruining that job, and that there is the assurance somebody competent can take over. One of the biggest hindrances I've seen for people's careers is that there is no one to take over for them.

Q: One of the most successful executives I worked with in Hewlett-Packard, in a series of positions, always hired himself out of a job because he trained and nurtured somebody. This actually was the way he progressed. I think you commented in some other discussion that this is one of the practices that leaders need to bring to the table. They train the people to take their position and move on.

Alan: If you want to identify a strong leader, look at the leader's subordinates. Strong leaders have strong subordinates. You want to see a weak leader—weak leaders have weak subordinates. It's almost an infallible and immutable point.

Q: Winston Churchill said, "Now this isn't the end. It isn't even the beginning of the end. But it is, perhaps, the end of the beginning." We have been on this journey together for quite a few months which has been personally—and I believe I speak on behalf of all of us here—exciting and exhilarating. I've been with you for a decade, and I constantly learn, and this journey of working on this book together has been a remarkable learning experience for me.

What surprised you in this particular journey?

Alan: That's a very good question. I chose you three because I thought that you had a history and a tendency to really ask insightful questions. I also thought you were diverse enough to bring different viewpoints and collaborative enough to work together well. That's not an easy thing to do with three people. This has worked very, very smoothly. I don't know what has gone on behind the scenes, but from my end it has been easy, and of course I'm selfish, and that's all I care about.

I think the surprise to me was that you were able to explore with me the interstitial aspects of this. In other words, there is a connectivity, there is an underpinning, and there are relationships between things that meld both our personal and professional lives that serve as both cause and effect. I think we explored in all of these recordings—and what will be on all of these pages—some of the important things that people might not consciously review or think about but are nonetheless extraordinarily important to provide value to others and therefore to be a success in life. I think it came forth rather easily, and at this point I'm eager to see what it looks like both on the printed page and in audio form.

Q: Whether it's surprise of learning, maybe the other part of my question would be what have you personally learned that you didn't know before this particular journey?

Alan: I think there are a few things. One of the most pleasing aspects is that this entire book has been extemporaneous. In other words, you've never, ever shown me one question in advance. All that we knew about were really the chapter headings, and once we had those, I didn't pay any more attention to them. I just sit here looking at the backyard with my feet up on the credenza with a bottle of water. That's how I've done every single call. I'm not looking at any notes, the screen, or anything, and I have no idea what you're going to ask me next. The ability that I have to bring together various aspects of my life and various attributes in my work to me is very fulfilling, and what I've learned is that you need to allow yourself to succeed.

I gave a speech yesterday for an hour at a consultant's meeting, and there were three speakers. The one after me had a slide set up for the 60 minutes, and the one after that had handouts. I was the first speaker, and really all I had was the title of what I was talking about and one or two ideas. I didn't even make notes this time, and I think that I'm much more effective when I do that. I've always known that, but it's constantly reinforced. I think that the lesson for all of us, and maybe the lesson in my own help to other people at this point, is that you have to free yourself up to succeed. The more you're restricted to form, the more you're restricted to rote, the less effective you are.

People ask me all the time about discipline, and the interesting thing is there is this great discipline in freedom. There is great discipline in having the confidence in yourself to not be tied down to a script, to an approach, or to the preparation. While to a certain extent that's a high-wire act, it's an exhilarating, exhilarating experience.

Q: For the people who are going to read and listen to this book—whether they're primarily consultants, entrepreneurs, service providers, whoever it is—when they discover this treasure, how are you hoping they'll use it?

Alan: I hope the treasure isn't sort of the curse of the mummy! You find it, you open it, and suddenly everybody's hair falls out! I hope that what they'll do is they'll use the one percent solution. Improve by one percent a day, and in 70 days you're twice as good. I would hope that each individual would choose for himself or herself what makes the most sense, what has the most nuggets, what represents the greatest improvement for them, and they'll try to use it, and practice it until they get good at it, and then they'll choose another thing and do it.

At a lot of these events where I speak, people will approach me to sign books, and these are books they've had from me for ages, and because they know I'm there, they bring them to be signed. Some of these books have Post-It notes on every third page, every other page has yellow highlighting, some of the pages are dog-eared, and they show me this as an example of how valuable my stuff is. I start to think unless they've done that over years, how much of that can you take and use? You need to focus on one thing at a time, and when you're focused on one thing at a time, you get good at it. Then you can focus on another thing, and the more you do that, the better you get at that, and the faster you can do it. You have to take one bite at a time, and the question is, "What is the right bite for you?"

Q: When we started doing this book, you told us how many books you had written, but I think you've done several more since then and maybe since we last talked. What is your total now?

Alan: Wait, let me just see what time it is here. *The Consulting Bible* just came out which is 41, *Million Dollar Referrals* would be 42, *Million Dollar Consulting Proposals* would be 43, and my book with Chad, *Million Dollar Web Presence* would be 44. Forty-four books which are either in the works to be published or for which we have signed contracts. Forty-four would be the number right now—and that doesn't count editions of books like *Million Dollar Consulting* is in its fourth edition. It does include different languages, so if a book comes out in a different language, I do count it as another book.

Q: Okay, so this is your 45th book that will be coming out?

Alan: Unless I do something in between, yes.

Q: What is different about this book? In your writing of it with us and your exploring the different topics that we looked at, what was different?

Alan: This is a far wider-ranging book than anything I've done. The book that just came out this last month, *The Consulting Bible*, is probably even more comprehensive than *Million Dollar Consulting*. I talked a little bit about the history of consulting, the future of consulting, methodology, and so forth, while *Million Dollar Consulting* is primarily a marketing book. This book is far wider-ranging because it talks about personal opinion, about personal experiences, about a variety of things including one's personal and professional life, and it really spans a lot of things that have happened over the entire course of my career.

For one thing, it's much more comprehensive. For another, as I've mentioned, it's totally unscripted, and even when I'm sitting down, I don't use notes when I write a book. I write from my head to the screen, but I have a table of contents, a chapter heading, and four or five sub points. When I write directly onto the screen, the way I normally do it, I know what the sub points are, I know what the ones that follow are, and I know what the ones that precede it are. Here I don't do that. I just respond to your questions in real time, and this book is a very extemporaneous kind of book. I don't know what will emerge after the editing, but I imagine it will remain that way.

Q: I think when we get the final edition of this finished, it will be two written volumes and approximately 40 hours of audio. You mentioned just a minute ago that people should look for a one percent solution and decide which bite they want to take of this elephant. Can you give us some advice about how to prioritize? Does it make a difference if I'm a beginner? If I'm seasoned? How do I approach this?

Alan: If you're a beginner, I think you need to realize that this is a marketing business, and I would look to how I get myself established, how I get my name out there, and how I attract clients. The analogy would be when I was fired in 1985, and I found myself suddenly without a job with very little severance. Nobody could say I was born on third and think I hit a triple, and there I am standing with 400,000 consultants around me wondering how to stand out in a crowd. I think the marketing, establishing who you are, and attracting clients would be the proper thing for a newer person.

For a person who has had some success, some moderate success—maybe partially through their career—I would say that building a brand, perhaps looking at global presence, looking at remote work, and establishing more breakthrough products and services might be the thing to do. Then for the veteran—the person who is farther along in his or her career or has had a great degree of success, high six figures, seven figures—I would suggest that life balance, legacy, licensing, remote work, and so forth would probably be the things to be looking at. That's just my assessment, that can vary, but that might be a way to break it down.

Q: It seems as though we have so much content here, people can re-read it when they're at different points in their careers and then go back to the other priority.

Alan: Yes, and I think that the book and the audio can be used as a sequential experience, and they could also be used as a reference work where people look up particular topics that make sense to them.

Q: Some of your mentorees are very successful. You have mentorees that bring in north of half-a-million dollars and some that generate more than several million dollars a year. How do these people engage you? How do they use your mentoring?

Alan: I have quite a few mentorees who are making well into seven figures. Almost all of them have boutique firms, they have employees or subcontractors or whatever, but there are a lot more than when I began this program, and I'm happy to report that.

The way they tend to use me is very situationally. They'll call me for a five-minute chat on something specific once a month or twice a month, or they'll say, "We need to get together for a day. What is the best way to do that?" We'll spend five hours on something intense, and then we might not talk again for a few months. Some of them attend very specialized workshops—for example, the Thought Leadership Workshop—and they pick and choose the experiences they want. Some of them stay very involved in the community because they find that the more they give, the more they get. Others stay out of the community, they stay on the periphery and simply maintain a relationship with me because they have their own world that they're engaged in.

There is a variety of different ways people use me, but the commonality would be that there is momentum. There is continuity. Frequency isn't as important as momentum and for some people, two months later I can pick up a conversation that left off 60 days prior without a problem.

Q: Can you give some concrete examples to the kind of questions that these very successful mentorees typically ask you?

Alan: On a tactical basis, the questions are, "I've never faced a situation like this before, and I'm smart enough to know I need to sort this out before I go in. Let's talk through this." "I'm looking for newer and fresher marketing ideas because I've already been there and done that, and I think the markets are changing."

On the strategic side, they'll say things like, "How do I appeal to a newer and broader, higher level, different, marketplace?" "How do I go from wholesale to retail or retail to wholesale or embrace both of them?" "What would be the ideal structure for my company two years from now if I keep heading in this direction?" Those are the kinds of discussions that we have, and while they vary from person to person—we're no longer talking about who the economic buyer is, and we're no longer talking about how to write a proposal.

Q: When consultants get to a spot of having too much business or more business than they can handle, what is your typical advice?

Alan: That's an interesting issue because it's like the Loch Ness Monster. People love to talk about it, but it doesn't really exist. Somebody made it up, and I'll find the toys under the bed someday and the camera that was used. You can't have too much business.

What you can have is *inappropriate* business. What you can have is business you're managing poorly. If we're talking about quality business, appropriate for you, you don't have too much business. You might have business you should have let go of long ago because it's no longer interesting, it's no longer profitable, it's no longer right for you, or it's no longer appropriate you do it. That's an issue. You might have business that you're not handling correctly. You're spending too much time, it's too labor intensive, or you're letting the client dictate terms. That's an issue. Please don't tell me that if you're talking about high-quality, high-revenue, low-labor-intensive business which is the ideal business I talk about, you can't have too much of it.

One year—and this is about nine or ten years ago when I was still doing a lot of OD work—I had 36 clients in one year, and that was before technology is where it is today. Having too much business is ridiculous, and when people say to me, "Alan, if I do this, what if I get so much business that everybody wants me to start next week?" I say, "Call me then, and we'll handle it."

Q: Will Smith likes to say that he is driven by fear of fear, which means he is prone to attack any hint of fear in himself by doing it. He will go directly to do whatever where there is a hint of fear, and it strikes me that your approach on consulting has been quite similar. Do you recommend that we as consultants take this attitude?

Alan: There is a big difference between me and Will Smith, obviously, but in this case, here is the issue: There are some things you should fear. Fear is not a bad thing. Fearing what you shouldn't fear is a bad thing. For example, fearing that the buyer might reject me isn't valid. I shouldn't fear that. Fearing that I'll make a mistake isn't valid. I should stop fearing that. Fearing the approbation of strangers or even friends isn't valid. I should stop fearing that.

However, if I'm hiking on a trail and a rattlesnake appears in front of me ready to lunge, I should be fearful, and I should take appropriate action. If I come across a bear rifling through my food supply, I should become very fearful. Fight or flight is a legitimate response if it's appropriately employed. It isn't fear that's the problem. You can't tell me that Will Smith overcomes his fear of rattlesnakes by jumping on one when he encounters one. He runs for his damn life! And that's what you should do. That's a time for flight. It's the false fears, it's the ego fears that we need to eliminate from our lives.

Q: That's a powerful distinction.

Alan: Yes. If you see somebody at 80 or 90 mph tailgating you and you don't fear that, you're out of your mind.

Q: How do you look at endings in general, and especially remarkable or exhilarating ones? What is your mindset?

Alan: I don't look at endings. Why look at endings? It's just another start. It's just another beginning. A day might end, but there is another day tomorrow. A movie ends, but you're going to see another movie. When you start to get all kinds of weepy over endings, the problem is your life suddenly stops for a minute.

The reason that people say "God bless you" is that it was thought that when people sneezed, their heart momentarily stopped, and they needed a blessing just in case. Of course it's a fallacy, but it's one that became believed, people feared it, and the same thing with endings. We make these big deals over something ending. Of course it's sad to see some things go. It's sad to see some relationships go, some experiences go, some accomplishments go, but there is always a new beginning.

That's why I was talking yesterday at a speech that retirement is a completely fallacious concept. It doesn't make any sense, and I'm not talking one's motivation, I'm just saying that pragmatically it makes no sense. There is no such thing as "retirement." It's an artificial construct, and we have to stop putting things in our lives that cause us sadness because they end.

We should appreciate what has happened, especially if it's not likely to be repeated. I had a 65th birthday party which I thought was fabulous, and that's not going to be repeated. That was an event, it was great and I'm happy, and now I'm happy today. I don't think we should look at endings. I certainly don't focus on them. I'll tell you this. I sat in a play the other day which I wish ended a lot faster, so I'll grant you that.

Q: Regarding the fear concept you just talked about, when a consultant faces fear, short of getting over it—and I realize I'm talking in generality here—what are some ideas to overcome a fear or multiple fears?

Alan: You have to isolate the fear. Someone once said—it might have been Sigmund Freud, I don't really know, but it wasn't I—that psychotherapy is nothing more than taking small fear and turning it into stark raving hysteria. That's what therapists do. I think the underlying cause for that statement is that when you isolate a fear, you come to grips with it face-to-face, and when you say things like, "There is a communications issue, there is a technology issue, there is an interpersonal issue," you're not facing the fear, you're hiding the fear, and you're camouflaging the fear.

You have to come face-to-face with the fear itself. I'm afraid of snakes. I'm afraid of spiders. I'm afraid of a long-term commitment. I'm afraid of using technology. I'm afraid of being rejected. Once you come to grips with the specific fear, only then can you help somebody deal with it because now you know what you're dealing with. Now you know what the proper resolution or coping techniques are. If you don't know what the fear is, you have no idea what to suggest.

Q: A typical fear I hear about is business-wise, I don't have enough business in the pipeline, revenues aren't coming in, I almost feel debilitated to move forward.

Alan: Right. The real fear here isn't having sufficient money to pay the bills, would you agree?

Q: Yes.

Alan: That's what you isolate as the fear, and once you're aware of it, recognize it, and isolate it, that causes a certain amount of comfort, a certain exhalation. You say, "Okay, you're right, I don't have enough money." Now you say, "Let's look at that. Before we look at bringing in new business, some kind of desperate attempt here, some kind of magic cure as an anodyne, why don't we take a look at this? Do you have credit cards where you have credit left on them? Do you have equity in your home? Do you have retirement savings? Do you have this? Do you have that?" With most people, you can show them that they have time, they have space, and they have assets that either are liquid or can be made liquid to see them through.

You can also say to them, "Look, there are alternatives. You can get a job and go back into the workforce. You can go back to where you came from. You can do this. You can do that." Once you start to talk about these techniques and people can choose among them, now you're saying to them, "Okay, don't be afraid of this thing simply because it's there. Take a look at the alternatives to deal with it, and this should lower your fear. You'll still be concerned, you'll still be very aware of it, but it won't be this stark raving fear that you don't know how to deal with."

Q: With this message of renewal and optimism, I would like to ask you about the next ten years. Rather than ask you what you'll do in the next ten years, I would like to ask how do you approach thinking about your next ten years?

Alan: With not too much detail. I know that I want to continue to write, to continue to help others in a coaching framework, and to continue to take advantage of developments and technology to do brand new things. A pragmatic and mundane example would be to create some apps that I want to do or whatever apps turn into. I want to engage in being able to do a workshop in Rhode Island that's simulcast all over the world to people sitting in classrooms in Mumbai, Beijing, or Vancouver. I want to remain a vibrant force for as long as I can in as many areas as I can.

I want to pursue my hobbies and interests. I want to pursue fine wine, good food, building models, playing with dogs, and so forth. I've always said to anyone who wanted to listen or asked me the question of all the activities I'm involved in—I'll continue them as long as I'm at the top of my game, and I know acutely what the top of my game is. The rather frightening thing is that I'm actually getting a lot better in some of these things where I didn't think I could, but once I'm no longer at the top of my game in some of these issues, I'll simply move out and focus on the other ones or bring in something new. I'm not interested in tap dancing on a stage if I can't dance any longer.

Those are the kinds of things I see in the future, without any particular order or any particular detail. I'm not smart enough to tell you what is around the corner necessarily, but I do subscribe to what Steve Jobs talks about. That is, I'm ready to jump on the next big thing.

Q: Let me just turn the table around for a moment and just see before we wrap up this final chapter. Are there any questions that you would like to ask us at this point?

Alan: I would ask you one question. Given what your expectations were when I approached you with this project and now nearing the end of at least the writing stage of the project, what were you farthest off base about? What do you think the biggest revelation was that you didn't anticipate, or what preconception did you have that turned out to be completely something else?

Linda: I would say the biggest surprise for me was that I've read nearly everything you've written, I've attended nearly every workshop you've given in the last five years, and listened to nearly every CD. I thought I knew your material inside and out and therefore was a good candidate to help in the construction of this book, and I anticipated that I would know 80 percent of your answers. I would say that was way off. For example, when we talked about getting to the economic buyer, I knew what you were going to say in those answers, but my percentages were way off. I was surprised in every phone call that you said something that I hadn't anticipated at all.

Aviv: I would say that the weave, the range, the scope, and particularly the in-the-moment live integration of the questions, and the recent experience and how it all is integrated throughout rather than in separate buckets. That for me is the essence of this experience.

Chad: There are a lot of similarities in probably what I was going to say here.

I've been so close working with you on so many different levels, and many times in live workshops you give an answer and hear the "whoa" in the audience which is a very special moment because typically it's a very profound moment for all of us. Over the years I've had many of those, and I wasn't as vocal during our conversations, but I have to admit that in every conversation, there was at least one, possibly multiple moments that personally for me was the "whoa" moment. It's just starting because I was so engaged in the moment of learning with you but also thinking of the next question. The next phase for me is as we start to really take the time to read the book and listen to it as intended for the participants, I'm looking forward to rediscover a lot of those amazing nuggets that will help me in every aspect of my life and business.

Conclusion

It takes time, insight, repetition, and volition to really understand what you're dealing with in consulting or in life. Forget about looking to the stars for the moment. We don't always know what is around us or beneath us. As you read this book, I urge you to look at every day as something new—to find something novel and unique. Look around you in awareness. Don't look forward so much in anticipation, although that's good to do, and don't look backwards in nostalgia, although that could be good to do too.

Look around in awareness because what you find around you might be simply stunning. That's the story of my life.

Index